Mutuality

MUTUALITY

Anthropology's Changing Terms of Engagement

Edited by

Roger Sanjek

PENN

UNIVERSITY OF PENNSYLVANIA PRESS

PHILADELPHIA

Published by
University of Pennsylvania Press
Philadelphia, Pennsylvania 19104-4112
www.upenn.edu/pennpress

Printed in the United States of America on acid-free paper
10 9 8 7 6 5 4 3 2 1

A Cataloging-in-Publication record is available from the Library of Congress
ISBN 978-0-8122-4656-8

Contents

Introduction

Deep Grooves

Anthropology and Mutuality

Roger Sanjek

We can begin this volume's collective examination of mutuality by asking: Why do we do anthropology at all? What values underpin anthropologists' commitments to lengthy academic training, to fieldwork, to writing and publication, and to communication with various audiences? Why do we do what we do?

Anthropology, I propose in response, has two contending value systems that motivate our work. One I will term the *academic-career complex*, and the other I call *mutuality*, which is the collective focus of this book.

The academic-career values that motivate us as professionals include the satisfactions of discovering and deepening an expansive anthropological worldview; our advancement along career paths to initial employment, work and research opportunities, and promotion; and approval and esteem from colleagues. These last may be evidenced in requests to speak and in invitations to participate in meeting panels, conferences, and essay volumes; in publication acceptances, peer citations, and favorable book reviews; and in professional honors and prizes. As we are thus "disciplined" by the discipline, these values and rewards define us as individuals within a professional world, aspects of which we become aware of only after we enter it.

For many anthropologists, however, there are, in addition, other values, brought from the wider social worlds in which we have grown up and in which we live as persons, actors, and citizens, which include the value we place upon mutually positive relations with the people we study, work with, write about and for, and communicate with more broadly as anthropologists. These values too may bring welcomed, even career-long satisfactions and may complement or even outweigh professional goals and achievements. The essays in this book explore how these values of mutuality and the efforts they inspire operate in the relationships between anthropologists and the communities and wider social orders within which they work and live.

Sometimes the two value sets pull an anthropologist in opposite directions—either inwardly, toward the world of other professional anthropologists, or outwardly, toward the larger social worlds that produce and reproduce us. At still other times, the two value sets may be compatible, even "in synch," motivating anthropologists both to pursue professional academic goals and, at the same time, to adhere to and advance values of the people and communities they study, work with, live in, and may originate from (see Ames 1986; Jacobs-Huey 2002; Lippert 2007; Sanjek 1987).

The contributors to this book have constructed anthropological careers incorporating mutuality in many ways. Here they provide examples from past, longer-term, and recent work in which mutuality has been paramount. Some from the start have defined their research and professional objectives by issues, concerns, and values originating in their own communities; others have done so later in their careers. Still others have discovered avenues to mutuality through fieldwork and community-based projects, consultations, and advocacy. Many have emphasized mutuality in publications involving and reaching nonanthropological collaborators and audiences. Several also have done so via various old and new media, in museums and public programs, and in health-care settings.

Mutuality is not something new or recent in anthropology, but neither is it intrinsic to it. Many anthropologists past and present, like the coauthors of this volume, have valued and practiced mutuality in their choices of where and what to study, how they conduct fieldwork, and with what audiences and publics, and in what forms, they share and disseminate anthropological findings and knowledge. The voices in this book are not unique, and experiences and perspectives similar to theirs could be and have been related by many colleagues (see, for example, Aiyappan 1944, 1965; Bennett and Whiteford 2013; Blakey 1998; Bond 1988, 1990; Chavez 1992; Checker 2009, 2011; Cohen 1976; Deloria 1944; Drake 1980; Fiske 2011, 2012; Harris 1958; Hopper 2003; Howell 2010; Kiste 1976; Koff 2004; Lamphere 2004a, 2004b; Leacock 1969; Mafeje 1971, 1975, 1978; Medicine 2001; Mullings 1997; Nader 1976;

Obbo 1980; Rylko-Bauer, Singer, and van Willigen 2006; Sacks 1988; Spradley 1976; Stull and Broadway 2004; Zavella 2011; Zentella 1997).

When mutuality is aimed for and achieved, more than individual career goals or interpersonal relationships may be enhanced. Just as greater mutuality between archaeologists and "descendant communities" has been a salutary result of the 1990 Native American Graves and Repatriation Act (Killion 2007; Thomas 2000; Townsend 2004), so also will growing awareness and practice of mutuality in social-cultural anthropology boost our "brand" among the greater public and among our current and future students. Moreover, the much discussed "crisis of representation," to which postmodernists have alerted us, may in significant part recede as values mutually shared by anthropologists and those we study, learn from, work with, and write for displace the inwardly focused concerns of academia and its arbiters.

Plan of the Book

Mutuality: Anthropology's Changing Terms of Engagement results from an invitation to contribute chapters that I sent to sixteen colleagues whose work within the deep grooves of fieldwork and collaboration I admired.[1] Ten were able to attend a session at the American Anthropological Association annual meeting in Montreal in 2011 to present and discuss early versions of their chapters. The volume is organized into four sections, *Orientations*, *Roots*, *Journeys*, and *Publics*, which are followed by a concluding chapter.

Orientations

The first section, "Orientations," establishes the broad terrain and themes of *Mutuality*. Garrick Bailey, in "Anthropology and the American Indian" (Chapter 1), traces the relationship between Native Americans and anthropologists from the late nineteenth century to the present, a tale of declining mutuality. He includes reflections on his own role, working on behalf of the Osage and other Indian peoples, in recent struggles over museum exhibit representations. In "The American Anthropological Association *RACE: Are We So Different?* Project" (Chapter 2), Yolanda T. Moses tells the story of the leading professional association's largest public program ever, which has brought up-to-date anthropological thinking about what "race" is and is not to nationwide audiences in museums and science centers and to users of its *RACE* website. These two chapters address major impediments to mutuality in anthropology's past and present—its objectification of indigenous (and other studied) peoples and rejection of their "native point of view" and the historical development of "scientific racism" to classify and rank culturally generated segments of the human population, with tragic consequences and costs. These two chapters also describe what anthropologists are doing to rectify these impediments and increase mutuality, work in which the authors have been directly involved.

The next two chapters address mutuality in ethnographic fieldwork and collaboration. In "Mutuality and the Field at Home" (Chapter 3) Sylvia Rodríguez recounts her career transition from early "extractive research" abroad to collaborative fieldwork and public anthropology in her New Mexico home community of Taos. Then in "'If You Want to Go Fast, Go Alone. If You Want to Go Far, Go Together': Yup'ik Elders Working Together with One Mind" (Chapter 4), Ann Fienup-Riordan explains how her collaboration with Yup'ik elders in Alaska has evolved, using recent work on weather and the environment to illustrate what she has learned over four decades.

Roots

The second section, "Roots," concerns the values and experiences that anthropologists bring to their work from their family and community backgrounds, which may include histories of migration, travel, mass incarceration, political movements, and conflict. "The Invisibility of Diasporic Capital and Multiply Migrant Creativity" (Chapter 5), by Parminder Bhachu, explores the past and present Punjabi craft caste global diaspora, of which her family is a part, and conveys the impact that familial experiences and stories play in the topics she has chosen to study and write about. She illustrates the importance of mutuality in both her anthropological tracing of historical trajectories and in connecting contemporary generations with the histories and sensibilities that produce them. Deana L. Weibel, in "A Savage at the Wedding and the Skeletons in My Closet: My Great-Grandfather, 'Igorotte Villages,' and the Ethnological Expositions of the 1900s" (Chapter 6), interrogates her ancestor's display of Bontoc Igorot men, women, and children at U.S. world's fairs a century ago—a form of countermutuality that also involved several professional anthropologists of the day. She then describes her ongoing collaborations with Filipina Igorot anthropologist Patricia Afable and with the now globalized Igorot descendant community.

Lane Ryo Hirabayashi, in "Thinking About and Experiencing Mutuality: Notes on a Son's Formation" (Chapter 7), reflects upon his community-based research in the 1970s with his father, anthropologist and ethnic studies activist James Hirabayashi. He specifies the values and methods he learned then and continued to use in later work, including book projects about Japanese Americans and Japanese migrants that involved both Hirabayashis and other Nikkei scholars. Rogaia Mustafa Abusharaf, in "Cartographies of Mutuality: Lessons from Darfur" (Chapter 8), describes how she was inspired by her socially conscious father and family members while she was growing up in Khartoum. She focuses on how incidents and memories from that time, and also mutualities from her student days, have affected her research among Sudanese migrants abroad and at home and, more recently, in her multisited fieldwork on the Darfur crisis.

Journeys

In "Journeys," the third section, the contributors address mutuality in their various career pathways, which include working in an applied research organization, a museum, independent practice, a nursing home, a statewide health-care reform project, and a medical school, as well as in academic departments. "On the Fault Lines of the Discipline: Personal Practice and the Canon" (Chapter 9), by Robert R. Alvarez, considers several facets of mutuality: among colleagues, in conducting fieldwork and contract research, with the people we study, and between each anthropologist and his or her professional heritage and identity. In "Listening With Passion: A Journey Through Engagement and Exchange" (Chapter 10), Alaka Wali links her emerging appreciations of mutuality and aesthetics in, first, research in Harlem and, later, field projects and collections work in Chicago and Peru for the Field Museum of Natural History.

Susan Lobo, in "Why? And How? An Essay on Doing Anthropology and Life" (Chapter 11), describes strategies and accomplishments during Lobo's career as a practicing anthropologist, including her long-term collaboration at Intertribal Friendship House in Oakland, California. She closes with wise observations about writing across a range of formats and for various audiences. "Embedded in Time, Work, Family, and Age: A Reverie About Mutuality" (Chapter 12), by Renée R. Shield, situates her research and work career within the fabric of the mutualities and negotiations one weaves as family member, ethnographer, colleague, citizen, and life-course navigator. Her personal and anthropological experiences reinforce for her Martin Luther King, Jr.'s observation: "We are caught in an inescapable network of mutuality."

Publics

"Publics," the final section, focuses on mutuality in relation to anthropology's many nonacademic publics—the people we learn from and about, collaborate with, live among, communicate with, and seek to affect as audiences for our writings and collaborative efforts. These publics range in scale from the macro, even national, level (as in the AAA *RACE* project discussed by Moses) to the micro, often deeply interpersonal, level of fieldwork partners and subjects. These publics include museum goers, fellow community members, general readers, and policy makers, among others, and they also embrace, as the chapters in this section attest, persons who may be disabled, racialized, economically vulnerable, and locally and internationally displaced.

In "Dancing in the Chair: A Collaborative Effort of Developing and Implementing Wheelchair Taijiquan" (Chapter 13), Zibin Guo tells the heartening story of the adaptation of a traditional Chinese healing art for wheelchair users and its subsequent introduction nationwide in China, as well as promising applications in the United States. Brett Williams, in "Fragments of a Limited Mutuality" (Chapter 14), reminds us of the contingent, uneven, and frustrating course mutuality can take as the community ethnographers and friends she portrays struggle at the short end of an unequal income distribution while resources, invisibly and deviously, flow daily from poor to rich.

Lanita Jacobs, in "On 'Making Good' in a Study of African American Children with Acquired and Traumatic Brain Injuries" (Chapter 15), relates how empathy, love, and grief arose in her relationship with a young boy whose hospitalization she followed as ethnographer for two years preceding his death from a brain tumor. She identifies the obligation she bears to "make good" in writing for audiences of which she and her subject's family are a part. "On Ethnographic Love" (Chapter 16), by Catherine Besteman, offers a close reading of recent anthropological thinking related to mutuality, including that of critics and resistors. She then considers models for mutuality that she embraced in fieldwork in postapartheid Cape Town, South Africa, and that she later employed and extended in bridge building between Somali Bantu refugees and white Americans in Maine.

Conclusion

My *Mutuality* coauthors have vitalized and expanded the concept of mutuality along many dimensions. In the Conclusion, "Mutuality and Anthropology: Terms and Modes of Engagement," I reflect on how my own appreciation of mutuality developed within the deep grooves of an anthropological career—as outsider and insider, fieldworker and citizen—over five decades. I ask how the kinds of writing we do, from theory-driven journal articles and books for academic peers to modes accessible to diverse readerships, including policy and public opinion audiences, impede or enhance mutuality. I consider, as well, past and present anthropological engagement with mutuality in old and new media, museums and public programs, and health-care settings.

The volume closes with brief exploration of how anthropology's two value systems might be brought more fully into mutual balance.

PART I

ORIENTATIONS

Chapter 1

Anthropology and the American Indian

Garrick Bailey

American anthropology is rooted in the study of American Indians. It was American Indian specialists, more than any group of researchers, who established the intellectual foundations of American anthropology. The reason for this early focus was simple: there was much basic research to be done, and Indian communities were nearby. In an anthology of papers published between 1888 and 1920 in the *American Anthropologist* (*AA*), the American Anthropological Association's flagship journal, some 63 percent, nearly two-thirds, were clearly concerned with American Indians (De Laguna 1960). In a second volume, for 1921–1945, papers on the American Indian dropped to 46 percent (Stocking 1976). After World War II and the increased global involvement of the United States, greater funding for the study of more distant populations was made available, and attention to Native Americans diminished further. In the third *AA* anthology, covering 1946–1970, only 18 percent of the papers concerned American Indians (Liberty 1978c, 4; Murphy 1976).

Native Americans Versus Anthropologists

To promote his new book, *Custer Died for Your Sins*, in 1969, Vine Deloria, Jr., published portions of chapters 1 and 4 as "Anthropologists and Other Friends" in *Playboy* magazine. The strategy worked, as both the article and book received a great deal of national attention. However, his criticism caught anthropologists by surprise, because they had long considered themselves to be the strongest and most active supporters of Indian rights. Anthropologists, particularly cultural anthropologists, had done far more than merely research and write about traditional Indian culture. Many anthropologists had been involved in various Indian rights organizations, including the Lake Mohank Conference, which began in the late nineteenth century, and later, the Association on American Indian Affairs. Concern over Indian issues had led to the emergence in the 1940s of what was to become "applied anthropology." In the 1950s, Sol Tax, arguing that applied anthropologists were accomplishing little other than academically defining the problems, decided on a more activist approach, which he called "action anthropology." Securing funding from a private foundation, in 1961, Tax sponsored the American Indian Chicago Conference, a meeting of five hundred Indians from all parts of the country, at his home institution, the University of Chicago. After a week of discussions, the conference produced a forty-nine-page document, "The Declaration of Indian Purpose."

Prior to 1961, however, one of Tax's students, a part-Cherokee anthropologist, Robert K. Thomas, had already started the Summer Workshop on American Indian Affairs in Colorado. This workshop brought together Indian college students to discuss Indian issues. In the same summer as Tax's 1961 meeting, students from the workshop organized the National Indian Youth Council (NIYC), the first of the national Indian activist organizations. By 1969, Indian activist organizations such as the American Indian Movement, Indians of All Tribes, and others had developed throughout the United States. More militant and aggressive, these organizations eclipsed the NIYC as the public face of the Indian movement, occupying first Alcatraz Island and later the Bureau of Indian Affairs (BIA) offices in Washington, and Wounded Knee, on the Pine Ridge Reservation.

Influenced by Deloria's writings, American Indian activists publically voiced a strong antianthropologist bias. To many American Indians, all anthropologists are alike, and although their strongest objection to anthropological research was the treatment of human remains by physical anthropologists and archaeologists, it was cultural anthropologists, because of their closer personal contact with Indian peoples, who experienced most of the personal abuse.

The Origins of American Anthropology

Why, by the late 1960s, had the relationship between anthropologists and American Indians become contentious? At first, the answer seemed simple. In

1879, the Bureau of American Ethnology was established at the Smithsonian, and the systematic anthropological study of American Indians began. In that same year, the Carlisle Indian Industrial School opened, and an official policy of forced assimilation—the destruction of traditional cultures and social identities—was initiated. American Indian cultures and identities were going to be extinguished, and anthropologists were going to become the custodians of the intellectual and tangible properties of the Indian past. Thus the Office of Indian Affairs (renamed the Bureau of Indian Affairs in 1947) took control of the Indian present and future, and anthropology assumed dominion over the Indian past. The Indian activist movement of the 1960s and 1970s was concerned not just with regaining control over the Indian present and future but with the past as well.

As I examined the question, however, I realized that the answer was not quite that simple. In 1851, Lewis Henry Morgan published *League of the Ho-de-no-sau-nee or Iroquois*, which is considered the first major ethnography of an American Indian society. He dedicated this book to Ely Parker, a Seneca, stating that the study was "the fruit of our joint researches." What is little recognized today is that during the nineteenth and early twentieth centuries, educated Indian intellectuals were deeply involved in the formative stages of the emerging discipline of anthropology. These early Indian collaborators included George Hunt (Kwakiutl), Francis La Flesche (Omaha), James Murie (Pawnee), J. N. B. Hewitt (Tuscarora), William Jones (Sac and Fox), and Arthur C. Parker (Seneca), to name only some (see Liberty 1978a). Many authored or coauthored anthropological books and articles or were in some other way publically acknowledged for their work. They were not anonymous "informants." The majority were employed part-time by museums or other institutions to conduct independent field studies. Some were employed as full-time anthropologists: La Flesche and Hewitt by the Smithsonian and Parker by the New York State Library and Museum. In 1904, William Jones became the first American Indian, and only the twelfth individual in the United States, to receive a PhD in anthropology. However, this close collaborative relationship soon changed.

This process of change in the status of Indian intellectuals in anthropology is well illustrated in the career of Francis La Flesche. I first became acquainted with La Flesche's work as a graduate student in the 1960s (see Bailey 1973). His works proved to be an invaluable source of information, but on the whole, I found La Flesche's Osage publications confusing and ignored most of their information on cosmology and ritual. In the 1970s, I continued my research on contemporary Osage social and cultural institutions (Bailey 1978, 2001), but toward the end of that decade, I turned to studying the Navajo, which occupied the better part of ten years (Bailey and Bailey 1986). In the late 1980s, I returned to the Osage and undertook a rereading and analysis of La Flesche's more than two thousand pages of Osage publications; in the early 1990s, I studied his notes and other writings at the National Anthropological Archives (Bailey 1995, 2010). As a result, I came to see the nature of the continuity that linked the contemporary Osages with their ancestors. Continuity was not to be found in formal institutions but rather in ideas, concepts, and beliefs that were alive and well in the collective minds of members of the contemporary Osage community. This knowledge was transmitted not just in words but also through the formal structuring of the physical behavior of individuals and through the use of a variety of material symbols. I came to realize that the key to understanding the culture history of the Osages was a more complete understanding of Osage traditional religion—in other words, in La Flesche's studies (Bailey 1995, 4–9).

Born in 1857 and educated at a mission school on the Omaha Reservation, La Flesche participated in Omaha religious activities as a boy and even joined their last bison hunt. The younger brother of the well-known Indian activist Susette La Flesche, he accompanied her on her lecture tour of eastern cities in 1879–1880. In Washington, he met James Dorsey, Alice Fletcher, and other members of the emerging anthropological community. After a failed marriage, he secured a job in 1881 as a copyist for the Indian Service in Washington and continued his education, studying linguistics with Dorsey and law at National University (now George Washington University), from which he received his LLB and LLM degrees; he also worked with Alice Fletcher on her research. In 1885, he published the first of his academic papers. Later, he coauthored *The Omaha Tribe* with Fletcher (Fletcher and La Flesche 1911), and in 1910, he left the Indian Service to take a position as an ethnologist with the Smithsonian Institution's Bureau of American Ethnology to study the closely related Osage (Alexander 1933; Liberty 1978b).

La Flesche was an activist whose objective was to change white America's misconceptions of the Indian. In *The Middle Five*, an autobiographical account of his boyhood, he stated that "the object of this book is to reveal the true nature and character of the Indian boy. . . . it may help [them] be judged, as are other boys, by what they say and what they do" (La Flesche 1900, xv). Later, in a published lecture given in Philadelphia in 1903, he stated, "The real character of peoples is never fully known until there has been obtained some knowledge of their religious ideas and their conception of the Unseen Power that animates all life." He further stated that the reason white Americans did not understand American Indians was whites' belief "that they alone possess the knowledge of a God" and that Indian religious practices were not a true religion. This misinterpretation was due to the fact that "The Indian looks upon nature, upon all natural forms, animate and inanimate, from a different standpoint and he draws from them different lessons than does one of the white race." Even the academic community had yet to fully understand these beliefs (La Flesche 1905, 4–5).

To La Flesche, religion formed the intellectual core of a culture. If one does not understand the core beliefs of a society, then one cannot fully understand its other cultural practices, because other aspects of its culture are derived from these beliefs. Academic studies were only superficial accounts. La Flesche's objective was to explain the Indians to white Americans and, in so doing, demonstrate that Indians were not simple, ignorant savages but were as mentally capable and sophisticated in their thinking as were white Americans. In *The Omaha Tribe*, he did not merely describe Omaha culture; rather, he attempted "to get close to the thoughts that underlie the ceremonies and customs of the Omaha tribe" (Fletcher and La Flesche 1911, 14). In attempting to explain, not merely describe, the Omaha culture, he used the Omaha conceptual model of the universe to explicate their social and political organization. Later, he would use the Osage to illustrate the true complexity of Indian philosophy and culture.

Academic reviews of *The Omaha Tribe* were mixed. The most critical review was by anthropologist Robert Lowie, in *Science*. He objected that the volume contained no literature review, thus ignoring the earlier writing of J. O. Dorsey, "so sane, conscientious, and competent an ethnographer" (quoted in Mark 1988, 338). Further, he "criticized [Fletcher and La Flesche] for classifying the material in accord with 'aboriginal' rather than 'scientific' logic and for attaching historical value to the origin accounts of a primitive tribe, a 'tendency, now definitely abandoned by ethnologists.' . . . they slighted topics like material culture and decorative designs. . . . 'Every professional ethnologist may reasonably be expected to pay some attention to the points that have come to be of theoretical interest to his fellow students'" (quoted in Mark 1988, 338). *The Omaha Tribe* thus failed to meet what Lowie considered to be the "professional standards" of academic anthropology.

La Flesche's lengthier study, *The Osage Tribe*—more than sixteen hundred pages—was published in four separate volumes of the Bureau of American

Ethnology's (BAE) annual report, between 1921 and 1930. In addition, he published seven articles on the Osage, and after his death, two more unpublished Osage manuscripts were published as BAE bulletins. Although none of these works was professionally reviewed, in *Cultural and Natural Areas of Native North America*, Alfred Kroeber remarked, "Thanks to La Flesche we know several of [the Osages'] rituals in detail; but these give relatively few indications of the type of culture as a whole" (1939, 75).

In retrospect, Kroeber's dismissal of La Flesche's Osage studies should not be surprising. The two men had very different approaches to the study of the American Indian. Kroeber was concerned with describing and analyzing the tangible; his dissertation had been on Arapaho decorative art. La Flesche was interested in describing the metaphysical world of the Indian as a means to understanding their culture; in doing such, he was describing an Indian world that it is doubtful Kroeber could even imagine.

Throughout his career in Washington, La Flesche was involved in professional activities. In 1922, he was elected president of the Anthropological Society of Washington (Liberty 1978b, 46). In April 1923, his closest friend Alice Fletcher died, leaving him most of her estate (Mark 1988, 346–348). That summer, he visited the Osage for the last time. By then, most of the traditional Osage priests were dead, and he spent his time taking notes on Osage plant usage (Bailey 1995, 289 n55). Returning to the Smithsonian, he worked on preparing his final manuscripts for publication, and in 1929, he moved back to Nebraska to live with his brother. He died in 1932.

La Flesche's obituary in the *American Anthropologist* reflected the diminished status of Indian intellectuals in the discipline. Its author, Hartley Alexander, praised *The Osage Tribe* as "collectively . . . what is certainly the most complete single record of the ceremonies of a North American Indian people" (1933, 329–330). However, he asserted of *The Omaha* that "the text is from her [Fletcher's] pen" (1933, 329), and he did not list it in La Flesche's accompanying bibliography. I have never found any basis for this claim that Fletcher was the sole author of *The Omaha*. La Flesche was an accomplished and prolific writer, not only of academic articles, books, and monographs, but even of short stories and an opera.

The most telling aspect of the obituary was the accompanying photograph. In almost all photographs of him, La Flesche appears impeccably dressed in a coat, vest, and tie (for examples, see Bailey 1995, 8, and Fletcher and La Flesche 1911, plate 1). Yet Alexander selected a photograph for the obituary showing La Flesche bare chested and dressed in a buffalo robe (1933, plate

24). In death, La Flesche was treated as an oddity, a curiosity, a "wild savage," a mere informant who was not truly one of "us," not a fellow professional.

What happened to La Flesche and the other Indian intellectuals involved in anthropology during the first decades of the twentieth century is best summarized by Robin Ridington in his introduction to the 1992 edition of *The Omaha*.

> Lowie and others of his generation in the first decades of the twentieth century reversed the focus of anthropology from the world of the Native Americans to that of the academy. They valued the university programs they were founding above an interest in the lives of aboriginal people. . . . In the years immediately following, anthropologists became obsessed with a search for an "objectivity" that they envied in the physical sciences. As they began to train students and grant graduate degrees in anthropology, they rejected the . . . works of authors like La Flesche as "subjective" and "unprofessional." (1992, 5)

Professionalizing Anthropology

With the professionalization of anthropology in universities, the era of collaboration between white scholars and Indian intellectuals came to an end. Indians as Indians would and could no longer play a collaborative role; they could only be interpreters, informants, or subjects of research. In fact, their intellectual insights were not considered necessary to understanding native culture. As Margaret Mead stated, "In complicated civilizations like those of Europe, or higher civilizations of the East, years of study are necessary before the student can begin to understand the forces at work within them. . . . A primitive people without a written language present a much less elaborate problem and a trained student can master the fundamental structure of a primitive society within a few months" (Mead 1928, 14–15).

Academically trained anthropologists now asserted sole dominion over the Indian cultural past. William Jones (of the Sac and Fox nation) died in 1909 while conducting fieldwork in the Philippines for the Field Museum (Hall 1997, 42–44), and it would not be until 1952 that the second American Indian, Ed Dozier, a Santa Clara, would receive a PhD in anthropology (Norcini 2007). With no intellectual input from Native Americans, white academically trained anthropologists alone decided what was suitable for research, and they defined, evaluated, and analyzed the American Indian world. As Lowie stated in his 1935 preface to *The Crow Indians,* "The audience I have in mind . . . embraces anthropologists . . . sociologists, historians, and other social scientists eager to grasp the varied patterns of human societies." Although Lowie was speaking of studies in cultural anthropology, the same attitude applied to linguistics, archaeology, and physical anthropology. The audience for anthropological studies was other academics, not the members of Indian communities.

Anthropologists felt that they had an inherent right, as well as an academic "responsibility," to study and record whatever they wished or thought important. Leslie White made this clear in his preface to *The Pueblo of Sia, New Mexico*: "Whereas the pueblo, as a community, takes a firm stand on the question of secrecy [regarding their religious practices], there are occasional individuals who realize full well that the culture of their people is rapidly disappearing. . . . It is the ethnographer's task to 'scent out' such individuals" (1962, 7). Anthropological research on the American Indian was premised on the myth of the "vanishing Indian." White saw Indian culture as "inferior to that of the United States and Europe" (1962, 3). Indians as Indians could not be part of the modern world, and they were doomed to disappear. As Julian Steward noted in 1945, "Anthropologists are in general agreement that it is purely a question of time before all Indians lose their identity" (quoted in McNickle 1970, 6). Thus, what living Indians thought or felt about what was said concerning them, their communities, or their ancestors was irrelevant. Their "vanishing" cultural heritage was the exclusive domain of the professional anthropologists.

The White Man's "Indian"

In the National Gallery of Art in Washington, D.C., there is a painting by Henri Rousseau that serves as a visual metaphor for the problem of the Indian (see Strickland 1979). The Indian is portrayed struggling with something that never existed, a New World ape. So it is, and has been, with almost every facet of Indians' interactions with dominant white society—they have had to struggle with the "white man's Indian," an imaginary Indian that never existed. It is not just that every law passed and every legal decision handed down by the courts was and is based, in large part, on the mental image of an Indian who never existed; almost every encounter between Indian peoples and members of the dominant white society was and is, to some degree, conditioned by this myth.

La Flesche made it clear that his involvement in anthropology was to correct these misconceptions. Only anthropology was or is capable of directly challenging the core concept of this myth: that America before the white man was a wilderness occupied by mystical, uncivilizable savages who could not remain Indian and be part of the modern world. However, the potential for correction was extinguished with the professionalization of anthropology within the universities. Instead of challenging the misconception of the Indian that was, and is, pervasive in American popular culture, anthropology has served to give academic validation to this "imaginary Indian."

By the 1930s, cultural research had shifted. Little knowledge remained of what anthropologists perceived as "traditional" culture. It was impossible for field research to produce classic synchronic ethnographies. Most North American Indian specialists now changed to studies of assimilation and acculturation.

So, what did anthropologists do in the late 1960s when the natives announced they were not "vanishing" and had no plans to do so? It varied by subdiscipline. Physical anthropologists and archaeologists did nothing. Although their research was the most objectionable to Indian activists, they had little personal contact with Indian peoples, and most were not aware of any "problem." This started to change in the late 1970s, when Indian organizations began to publicly protest exhibits of the human remains and burial goods in research collections and museums. However, it was not until the passage of the Native American Graves Protection and Repatriation Act (NAGPRA) in 1990 that they fully realized they too had an "Indian problem."

The third subdiscipline, linguistic anthropology, was not particularly controversial. As a result, it was the cultural anthropologists who, in the early 1970s, responded by holding public meetings with Indian activists to confess their sins, verbally flagellate themselves, and promise amends. Academics expect at least some criticism from fellow academics on their research methods or theoretical approach or general conclusions. However, cultural anthropologists now found themselves in the awkward position of being forced to publicly defend their research findings against Indian college students who asserted that what they were saying was simply not true. I was present at a number of these meetings and was involved in many of the informal conversations, both with anthropologists and with their antagonists, which followed.

First, it may be noted, it is impossible to defend yourself publicly against a broad accusation that your research is simply incorrect or when, as one young woman put it, "My grandfather told me that he lied to the anthropologists." What surprised me at the time was that many senior anthropologists accepted these accusations uncritically, even at times questioning the veracity of their own research. As to the antagonists, they were a diverse group, not unlike the people with whom I had grown up and gone to school. Most were younger urban Indian college students; some were from "traditional" families and possessed some "traditional" knowledge, but most were not. A few were "New Age" Indians whose actual Indian ancestry was subject to doubt. More than a few were individuals whose Indian identities, even in their own minds, were in question, and they were using the opportunity to assert that they were "still Indian." A few actually spoke in "broken English," affecting the speech pattern of the older, traditional, non-native English speakers. Many of their criticisms were justified and should have been taken seriously, but others were not. To me, these meetings and conversations demonstrated that in conducting their research, anthropologists collectively had maintained such a high degree of social distance between themselves and the communities they studied that they had little understanding of the actual social and cultural dynamics and diversity of the younger contemporary Native American world.

What was the result? In Vine Deloria's obituary, Raymond DeMallie wrote, "Singlehandedly he had changed the culture of anthropology in relation to American Indians" (2007, 932). He had, but not in the positive way implied. Far too many cultural anthropologists now saw all Indians as hostile to their research. As a colleague remarked, "Indians are a pain in the ass to work with." Just as important was that, by this time, Indians had lost most of their exotic appeal to anthropologists; they were no longer "real Indians." As a result, the relative importance of North American Indian studies in cultural anthropology declined sharply. In the fourth anthology of papers from the *American Anthropologist*, covering 1971 through 1995 (Darnell 2002), only 10 percent concerned North American Indians. In 1969, 22 percent of the cultural anthropology faculty (by my count) at the ten departments granting the largest number of PhDs were North American Indian specialists (American Anthropological Association 1969). By 2008, however, only 6 percent of cultural anthropologists in these same departments were Native American specialists, and six of the ten departments had no American Indian specialist at all on their faculty (American Anthropological Association 2008). To the detriment of both the anthropological and the Indian communities, it seemed that

American Indian studies were no longer an integral part of the study of cultural anthropology.

Hero, Hawk, and Open Hand

In 1998, I was contacted by Richard Townsend of the Art Institute of Chicago, James Brown of Northwestern University, and Kent Reilly of Texas State University–San Marcos. They had an idea for a major exhibit on the Mississippian Civilization of 500 BC to 1500 AD, to be titled *Hero, Hawk, and Open Hand*, and they wanted it to be a truly collaborative project, with the active involvement and support of the living descendants of the Mississippian peoples. Recognizing that such an exhibit had the potential to challenge the prevailing myth that prior to European contact Indians were uncivilized savages, I agreed to organize a meeting between them and members of local Indian communities in Tulsa, Oklahoma. This meeting was critical, because we agreed that if they failed to gain the support of the invited Indian group, the exhibit idea would be dropped.

The initial problem was who to invite. There are twenty-eight federally recognized tribes in Oklahoma who are descended from the Mississippian peoples, with several hundred thousand descendants overall. The attendees had to represent the full range of possible concerns of the traditional communities, and there had to be individuals whom I felt would support the idea, as well as individuals whom I was certain would, at least initially, oppose it. At the same time, the group had to be small enough that all issues of concern could be fully aired. Finally, to keep internal tribal politics out, no currently serving elected tribal official would be invited. Forty individuals were contacted to attend, including traditional religious and social leaders, artists, educators, and appointed tribal officials. For various reasons, only twenty-seven were able to participate in the one-day meeting.

At the start of the event, I told the group that this was only a proposal for a possible exhibit. If they did not support the idea, then it ended with this meeting. If they liked it, and wanted to support it, the Art Institute of Chicago would proceed with planning and fund raising. Kent Reilly then presented the basic concept. Using slides comparing Mississippian materials to those of other early civilizations, he explained how the proposed exhibit would present the Mississippian peoples as a civilization comparable to early civilizations of the Old World. This idea was discussed through the morning, over lunch, and during the afternoon. All of the expected culturally sensitive issues were raised and aired. By the end of the meeting, a general consensus was reached. The majority enthusiastically supported the exhibit, and a few who for various reasons could not openly support it did not oppose it.

With the assent of these influential members of the traditional communities, planning for the exhibition began. Working with contacts from the meeting, Townsend and Reilly began approaching tribal officials. Because of NAGPRA, many of the objects they hoped to use in the exhibit were controlled by tribal governments, and their official permission had to be granted. Altogether, thirteen tribal governments formally endorsed the exhibit (Townsend 2004).

A second planning meeting was held in Chicago, involving individuals from the Tulsa meeting and, for the first time, the archaeologists who would write some of the chapters for the exhibit catalog. On the morning of this meeting, I had breakfast with a few of the archaeologists, one of whom stated that although the exhibit was a great idea, the Indians would never agree to it. I did not mention the prior Tulsa meeting. At dinner that evening, a close friend and tribal elder told me that during the day's meeting, she had overheard some of the archaeologists comment in surprise that the Art Institute had "talked to the Indians before they consulted us." My friend confessed that although she always trusted me, it was not until she overheard the archaeologists that she fully believed that what I had told them in Tulsa—about not proceeding without their support—was true. Many American Indians have an inherent distrust of the academic community, and there is good reason for their suspicion. They have a long history of being lied to by representatives of the dominant society, including academic institutions.

Descendants of the Mississippian peoples were involved in almost every stage in the exhibit's development—from the Tulsa meeting to writing chapters for the catalogue, to the making of films shown with the exhibit, to the creation of educational materials to accompany it.

As the largest and most important exhibition to directly challenge the white myth of the "simple-minded savage," it was important for it to travel as widely as possible. However, only one other museum hosted the exhibit, the St. Louis Museum of Art. The Smithsonian National Museum of Natural History initially agreed, only to cancel when objections were raised by their archaeological curators—some objects in the exhibit were from private collections, and the display of privately owned items was, by their standards, not professionally ethical or allowable. The Smithsonian's archaeologists asserted that they alone had the right to determine which prehistoric objects were or were not suitable for display in a public museum. (I was not involved in the negotiations; staff members of the museum later told me what had happened.) In effect, they were insisting that regardless of the opinions of the American Indian community, the academic community was the ultimate custodian and protector of Indian patrimony.

Art of the Osage

In 2001, I received a call from Charles Tillman, chief of the Osage. Representatives of the St. Louis Museum of Art were going to meet with the Osage elders committee to discuss an exhibit on Osage art, and they wanted me to participate. A planning committee was created consisting of Sean Standingbear, director of the Osage Tribal Museum; John Nunley, a St. Louis Museum of Art curator; Daniel Swan, an anthropologist; and myself.

The first issue was the design of the exhibit. We came up with the idea of creating the entry hall as a visual reconstruction of the Osage model of the universe, thus introducing visitors to Osage culture. Among other elements, there would be the symbolic Osage path of life, drawn through the middle of the hall. The exhibit would explain that the north, the symbolic sky, was the masculine side, and the south, the symbolic earth, was feminine. Along the north wall would be Osage painted shields and along the south side, Osage painted cradleboards. This visual arrangement would illustrate how the Osage equated the role of woman and mother with that of man and warrior. This design was based on La Flesche's Osage studies and was similar to the way he presented Omaha culture in *The Omaha*.

The design was submitted to the museum exhibitions committee, which rejected it as "offensive." Traditional Osage culture was, in effect, politically incorrect; there could be no opposition of "male" and "female." I found this response offensive, as I think did the other members of the planning committee. However, Standingbear, Swan, and I were participating at the request of the Osage community, and they wanted this exhibition. Accordingly, we redesigned the exhibit hall to give the museum committee what they wanted: some beautiful objects stripped of any meaningful cultural context.

A second issue arose when I submitted my introductory chapter for the catalogue to the museum's editorial staff. I began this chapter by stating, "Osage art can only be understood within the context of Osage culture" and proceeded to discuss Osage art and art objects in relation to Osage beliefs and concepts. The editorial staff objected to my approach, countering that to be "art" an object had to stand on its own and be judged solely on its aesthetic qualities. This time, I was adamant about distorting Osage art to make it conform to ethnocentric Western ideas as to what constituted "art." After several discussions, we agreed on a modified sentence: "While most people can readily appreciate the qualities of Osage material objects and technical skills used in their creation, they can only appreciate the full meaning and significance of such objects within the context of Osage culture and history" (Bailey and Swan 2004, x).

A Failed Relationship

These two examples illustrate some of the basic problems in the relationship between American Indian and academic communities. Indians may have trust and confidence in individual anthropologists they know, but they are suspicious of the academic community as a whole. Their suspicion is reflected in the research protocols recently adopted by several tribes. The Hopi have one of the most comprehensive statements. All research and other activities involving the study and recording of Hopi culture, past or present, is subject to the formal approval of the Hopi tribe, and approval depends on perceived benefits to the Hopi people. Further, the Hopi tribe reserves the right to review and prevent publication and to maintain control over any data or recordings collected. Why they are doing this is made clear: "The Hopi people desire to protect their rights to privacy and to Hopi Intellectual Property. Due to the continued abuse, misrepresentation, and exploitation . . . it is necessary that guidelines be established" (Hopi Cultural Preservation Office n.d.). It is important to note that these controls apply not just to anthropological and academic research but to popular media. It has not been just anthropologists who have violated Hopi privacy rights and misrepresented their culture; there is a vast popular literature on the Hopi as well.

In terms of control over the future use of research data collected, the most widely known recent case involves the Havasupai. In 1990, with the knowledge of the Havasupai, an anthropologist and a geneticist at Arizona State University received a grant to study diabetes. Looking for a genetic factor, they collected blood samples from about one hundred Havasupai between 1990 and 1994. After the DNA studies for diabetes were completed, the samples were placed in storage. At a later point, these samples were used in other DNA research, including studies of inbreeding, mental illness, and migration, and more than two dozen articles were published using these data.

When the Havasupai became aware of these new studies, which they considered damaging to their traditions, forty-one surviving individuals from the 1990 study sued Arizona State, claiming that they had not been "fully informed," and they were awarded seven hundred thousand dollars. One tribal council member said: "I am not against scientific research. . . . I just want it to be done right. They used our blood for all these studies, people got degrees and grants, and they never asked our permission" (Harmon 2010).

The same is true of cultural studies. As a group, Native American peoples are very proud of their past and present cultural traditions. Most Indian people realize that they have lost much of their traditional cultural knowledge and history and are interested in gaining a greater understanding of it. However, they want to be active and willing participants in the study and interpretation of their past.

The problem is the academic community. For more than a century, anthropologists have been the voice of the American Indian within the academic world. During this period, thousands of academic books and monographs and countless thousands of articles, chapters, lectures, and talks have been written or given. Although I can think of many individual exceptions, collectively, academic anthropology (as distinguished from applied anthropology) has done little to benefit the Indian. Anthropologists have succeeded in eliminating many of the more overt negative expressions of racism within academia, but we have failed to eliminate many of the implicit racist stereotypes. Collectively, we have not challenged the basic assumptions concerning the Indian expressed in the white myth of the Indian. The images of Uncas and Magua, of simple children of nature and red devils, still inhabit the collective mind of the academic community, and anthropology has failed to exorcize them. Academic researchers have taken their cultural knowledge, hospitality, and friendship and not only given little in return, but all too frequently, knowingly or unknowingly, we have misconstrued the data we have collected to reinforce and/or validate prevailing white stereotypes of the Indian. We continue to reconstruct the Indian past not as it was in any relativistic reality but as we, the intellectual agents of the dominant society, wish it to have been.

As if this basic educational failure was not enough, the academic community, of which anthropology is a part, continues to claim exclusive dominion over the study and use of the critical, tangible records of the Indian past—the archaeological and ethnological collections and archival materials such as notes, manuscripts, photographs, and audio and film recordings. The exclusive control and use of these materials are a violation of basic Native intellectual property rights and of the ability of a people to define their own past and not have it defined for them by agents of the dominant society.

The academic community is an elitist club, with membership based on formal academic credentialing, usually a PhD, and members of each discipline being the collective experts on a particular topic of inquiry. As a result, academic or professional activities are "club activities" in which academics communicate with other academics; experts can only increase their knowledge through research and ongoing dialogues with other academic experts. There is no place in the academic dialogue for uncredentialed novices. Indians as Indians, no matter how knowledgeable they might be on a particular topic, have no role in "professional" dialogues. We are the experts, not them. American Indians were only sources of raw data, not interpreters of their past. As Lowie insisted, "When a Crow tells me that his tribe and the Hidatsa have sprung from a common stock, this is correct but superfluous information, for I arrive at this result with absolute certainty from a linguistic comparison. In history, as everywhere else, our duty is to determine the facts objectively; if primitive notions tally with ours, so much the better for them, not for ours" (Lowie 1917, 163).

Fortunately, most anthropologists today are not Lowies. Many, if not the majority, have at times worked collaboratively with native communities on their cultural concerns, questions, and issues. Many, as individuals, have taken time to communicate their research findings with members of the communities they have studied, and they have valued the communities' input. However, the basic problem remains. The larger academic community collectively rarely considers such involvement "professional." As a young faculty member, after returning from Washington, D.C., where I had testified before the U.S. House of Representatives Subcommittee on Indian Affairs, I was told by a university administrator to "stop wasting my time" and that I needed to work on publishing "professional" articles. The problem is with the nature of academic institutions and how they evaluate professional achievements.

Academic Elitism

During the nineteenth century, the American public was fascinated by the ancient mound builders of the Mississippi and Ohio valleys. There were numerous theories concerning these "vanished" peoples, most holding that the builders of these mounds, the work of a highly advanced people, were not the ancestors of the Indians but were a separate vanished race.

The congressional appropriation for the new Bureau of Ethnology in 1882 required that 20 percent of its budget be used for investigations of the mound builders. As a result, a "Division of Mound Exploration" was established, and Cyrus Thomas was put in charge. In 1894, Thomas published his 728-page *Report on the Mound Explorations of the Bureau of Ethnology*, showing conclusively that the historic tribes of the region were the descendants of the mound builders (Judd 1967, 19, 68, 84).

Although anthropologists accepted Thomas's findings as obvious, the general public did not. The study refuted the myth of the Indian and established that America had not been a "wilderness" occupied by uncivilizable savages. Although archaeologists continued to research the mounds for the next century, they did little to try to change the misconceptions of either the public or of members of the American intellectual establishment. Thus, aside from its size and the publicity associated with it, there was nothing revolutionary about the 2004 *Hero, Hawk, and Open Hand* exhibit. To me and to other anthropologists, it only restated what we had long known.

Others did not see it that way. Edward Rothstein, in his *New York Times* review, "Who Should Tell History: The Tribes or the Museums?," compared *Hero, Hawk, and Open Hand* unfavorably to another exhibit, "Machu Picchu: Unveiling the Mystery of the Incas." The difference between the two was that Machu Picchu was the sole product of academic curators; it told us, Rothstein asserted, "what that past *actually* was" (emphasis mine). *Hero, Hawk, and Open Hand*, in contrast, was a collaborative project between academics and members of the Indian community, yet to Rothstein, "it seems as if the exhibition's purpose were to boost tribe pride" and that "the explanations of these societies' workings seem idealized, skewed by contemporary sensitivities." He concluded, "All this is a form of guilty overcompensation for past museum sins that themselves need re-examination and assessment. In the meantime, exhibitions like the one on Machu Picchu serve as reminders of what is possible. And the objects at the Art Institute can still be heard straining to speak for themselves despite the layers of promotional and political gauze in which they are wrapped" (Rothstein 2004).

One would think Rothstein had never visited the National Museum of American History in Washington or, for that matter, any museum of American history in the United States. As many have said, "history is myth," and in museum exhibits, someone's "myth" is always retold, using objects as evidence. The problem Rothstein had with *Hero, Hawk, and Open Hand* was wrong "tribe," wrong "sensitivities," wrong "myth." Rothstein, a PhD and a journalist, expresses the intellectual elitism of the academic community: if one is not a professional, one cannot contribute intellectually as an equal to a "professional" endeavor. In fact, such involvement "taints" the endeavor.

The problem is not with the members of the Indian communities. They are highly receptive to collaborative projects of mutual benefit. The problem is with the collective attitudes of the members of the academic institutions of the dominant society.

Important changes, however, are occurring outside these institutions. American Indians have always been far more interested in American Indians than have members of the academic world. Thanks to economic development, primarily casinos, many tribes have significant amounts of discretionary money available, and contrary to their federal, state, and local counterparts, tribal governments are far more concerned with educational and cultural concerns. Tribal museums, archives, and cultural and language programs are being expanded or created. Tribal colleges are being established, as well as tribal academic presses, in a few cases, so tribes can publish their own books. At the same time, the number of American Indians with graduate degrees in anthropology and other disciplines is rapidly growing. Many of these individuals, together with professionally trained non-Indians, are finding employment in tribally controlled academic institutions.

Collectively, academic institutions and professional communities remain highly protective of their elevated intellectual status and prerogatives. Only for limited purposes, such as a museum exhibit, are they capable of engaging in meaningful intellectual exchange with nonprofessionals. This is particularly true in regard to members of relatively powerless minority communities such as American Indians. Some American Indian intellectuals have long affirmed that to take any meaningful control of their past and challenge popular misconceptions of native peoples, they would have to create their own parallel academic institutions. Only then will American Indians be able to interact with the academic community on a basis of intellectual equality and to truly challenge the myth of the "white man's Indian."

Chapter 2

The American Anthropological Association *RACE: Are We So Different?* Project

Yolanda T. Moses

In this chapter, I address the intersection of race, racism, and education, my focus for the past two decades as an anthropologist and higher education administrator. Although today we reject the essentialist biological race concept of the early twentieth century as a valid explanation of human variation, racism as a structural reality remains alive and well in this country in the beginning years of the twenty-first century. As anthropologists, we must use our work to speak out against racism as well as to speak as accurately as we can about what "race" is and is not.[1]

The concept that "all people are created equal" is at the root of our Constitution. Yet we all know that the original definition did not include women, poor people, or people of color, and their rights were hard won over the centuries-long history of the United States. Even with those victories, it is evident in our society today that, because of systemic oppression and/or lack of opportunity, some groups have not achieved equality as measured by household income, wealth accumulation, education, employment, or access to health care. The bottom line is that despite 2014 marking the sixtieth anniversary of the *Brown v. Board of Education* Supreme Court decision—which declared "separate but equal" unconstitutional—the playing field is still not level for most students of color to receive a quality education in this country.

Today, race remains a ubiquitous feature of our daily lives. It is difficult to pick up a newspaper or hear a podcast without encountering references to people's racial identities and to the racial categories used to generate public policy and inform the design of social and medical research. U.S. Census officials continue to wrestle with the problem of how to classify the growing number of multiracial persons first officially enumerated in the 2000 Census. The identification of immigrants and refugees who have entered the United States usually involves the use of racial, or at least ethnic, classification. In 2017, the nation will recognize the seventy-fifth anniversary of U.S. internment of its own Japanese American citizens at the outbreak of World War II. With the election of an African American president of the United States in 2008 and again in 2012 (although some questioned whether or not he was really "African American"), Barack Obama, whose mother was an American anthropologist and whose father was from Kenya, is forging new ways to be a biracial and multifaceted American and, we can hope, helping many to approach the issues surrounding race in new ways.

In an article titled "Reestablishing 'Race' in Anthropological Discourse," published in *American Anthropologist* in 1997, Carol Mukhopadhyay and I challenged anthropologists to tackle the issue of race publically, using the discipline's four fields combined. We did so because we felt that, despite the knowledge generated by anthropologists over the years, little had been done to communicate what we had discovered in an accessible way. We were convinced that there was a need for a project that challenged the popular and what many researchers believed was the scientifically accepted view that races are biological entities. We argued that only an integrated biocultural approach could show both how race is a social/cultural construct and how the physical differences people see in each other do not define neatly bounded groups. We felt that, of all the disciplines, anthropology, with its four-field approach, provided the best integrated view of human biological variety and of the consequences that culturally constructed racial categories have had, and continue to have, on people's lives.

In 2001, the American Anthropological Association (AAA) began planning a public education project ultimately called *RACE: Are We So Different*? The project was designed around a museum exhibit intended to educate K–12 students and teachers, undergraduate and graduate students, scholars, and the general adult public about issues surrounding "race" and human variation. Because many adults in the United States continue to hold some version of the idea that race is based on biology and that therefore biology must explain racial differences in behavior, economic status, and disease, a major purpose of the project was to develop an effective educational program and curricular materials that would discredit these myths. The project aimed to show how culture actually creates race over time in a dynamic, ever-changing way. The information was disseminated through a national traveling exhibit, a website, and publications aimed at lay audiences, including guides for teachers and families.

Looking through the three lenses of history, science, and the impact of race on the everyday lives of people, this project demonstrates that

- Race is a recent human invention
- Race is about culture, not biology
- Race and racism are embedded in our institutions and everyday life

The *RACE: Are We So Different?* Exhibit

When we started, it was not clear that the Science Museum of Minnesota (SMM) would ultimately be the institution we would partner with to develop the exhibit. We were first turned down by the Field Museum in Chicago, the Smithsonian in Washington, D.C., and the American Museum of Natural History in New York, and the reality sank in of how deeply controversial the subject of race was to museum administrators. Perhaps I was naïve, but I thought the sophisticated approach we were taking with the topic would make it something these nationally prominent urban museums would view as a way to connect to new, more diverse populations.

When they awarded us funds for the *RACE* Project, the National Science Foundation told us the SMM had a wonderful reputation for producing exhibits that translated complex scientific information into programming the general public could understand. Once we approached the SMM, their new director Eric Jolly told us they were willing and eager to work with us, and with his leadership, their board of directors agreed as well. We already sensed from their vice president Paul Martin and chief curator Robert Garfinkle that they were passionate about undertaking this journey. They admitted they did not know much about the subject of race, and we anthropologists from the project's advisory committee, in turn, knew very little about curating a science-oriented exhibit for the general public.

The rest is history. Eventually, a smaller work team from the SMM staff and our advisory group coalesced to produce the exhibit, a process that changed us all. According to Garfinkle, he and his predominantly Euro-

American, midwestern staff came to embrace a deeper understanding of the concept of race and how it works in everyday life, at both individual and institutional levels. Moreover, the additional "wraparound" programming the SMM staff developed was as important as the exhibit itself for attracting and engaging diverse local communities. This would be the case for many of the other museums and institutions that hosted the exhibit and expanded their own programming to draw new audiences and to signal that they cared about topics important to the larger community. By working with Native American groups, social justice organizations, and educators, SMM was able to bring "talking circles" and community-produced original plays on the theme of race into their institution.

The AAA *RACE: Are We So Different?* public exhibit opened at the SMM in Saint Paul, overlooking the Mississippi River, on January 10, 2007. Although the temperature was minus ten degrees, it was the largest, as well as the most culturally diverse, turnout for an exhibit opening in the museum's history. As visitors entered the exhibit area, an opening video informed them

> Race is an enduring concept that has molded our nation's economy, laws, and social institutions. It is a complex notion that has shaped each of our destinies. . . . Europeans . . . traveled overseas and encountered, and then colonized or conquered peoples in Africa, Asia, and the Americas who looked, talked, and acted much differently from them. Naturalists and scientists then classified these differences into systems that became the foundation for the notion of race as we know it today. . . . Soon a new society emerged based primarily upon skin color, with those of European ancestry at the top and African slaves and American Indians at the bottom. . . .
>
> As our new nation asserted its independence . . . blacks and American Indians were viewed as . . . not deserving the same liberties as whites. . . . In the nineteenth and twentieth centuries, the notion of race continued to shape life in the United States. The rise of "race science" supported the common belief that people who were not white were biologically inferior. The removal of Native Americans from their lands, legalized segregation, and the internment of Japanese Americans during World War II are legacies of where this thinking led.
>
> Today, science tells us that all humans share a common ancestry. . . . The American Anthropological Association has developed this exhibit to share the complicated story of race . . . and to encourage

meaningful discussion about race in schools, the workplace, within families and communities. (Goodman, Moses, and Jones 2012, 5)

As visitors left the exhibit, they had an opportunity to speak about what they had seen and learned in "talking circles" facilitated by Native American volunteers.

Anthropologist David McCurdy of Macalester College in St. Paul described the exhibit in an appreciative illustrated "walk through" review in *General Anthropology* (McCurdy 2007). He noted that sections of the exhibit dealt with four overarching topics: "The Cultural Construction of Race," "The Consequences of Racial Discrimination," "Scientific Attempts at Racial Determination," and "Gene Flow and Adaptation: Why There Aren't Human Races." Each of these contained many charts, maps, timelines, images, videos, and interactive features. These components were accessible on the *RACE: Are We So Different?* website (www.understandingrace.org) and later appeared in the project's companion volume, *RACE: Are We So Different?* (Goodman, Moses, and Jones 2012), although the exhibit, website, and book also included content unique to each.

Several of the exhibit's elements attracted McCurdy's attention. He noted the large photograph of a diverse group in which each person wore a T-shirt indicating how he or she would have been classified racially by the U.S. Census—differently for several of them—at three different points in the past (see Goodman, Moses, and Jones 2012, 154). An interactive display allowed visitors to "vote" on how the Census ought to classify people by race and ethnicity: either "stay the course," "simplify," "have it your own way," or "no questions at all." A display board detailed the inequities that African Americans have faced in obtaining housing loans and GI bill benefits. Another described the controversy over the use of American Indian names and symbolism by college and professional sports teams. A map made the point that although people in widely distant parts of the world may look different from each other and might even resemble long-established stereotypical images of "races," in fact, visible human differences vary subtly as one travels geographically, for example from Oslo to Nairobi, and that no racial divides can be identified (see ibid., 96–97, 108–109). Another exhibit display made the point that sickle cell anemia, which occurs in areas where malaria is found and can confer resistance to it, is prevalent not only in Africa but in parts of Europe, the Middle East, and Asia (111–119).

More than 246,000 people visited *RACE: Are We So Different?* at the SMM during its four-month run, and within a year, more than one million had either seen the exhibit or accessed the project website (Overbey 2007, 2008). After leaving St. Paul, the exhibit began a journey that by 2015 will have taken it to forty-two museums and institutions in thirty states.[2] In a conversation with SMM officials in 2007 a few weeks after the *RACE* exhibit departed, they said they would miss the special connection they felt they had established with the greater Minneapolis–St. Paul community. Even more important, people were now asking: "What is your next project to involve the community going to be?" That was a recurring theme I would hear at many *RACE* exhibit venues.

In January 2007, the *RACE: Are We So Different?* website went online. In addition to a virtual tour of the exhibit and other content, the site provided free downloads of three guides to talking about race—one for families (ten pages) and two for middle school (sixty-eight pages) and high school teachers (seventy-three pages)—by project anthropologists and staff (Gomez et al. 2007; Jones et al. 2007a, 2007b). The teacher guides met national and select state standards for science, biology, social studies, and social science and provided lesson plans that addressed biological and cultural variation and the experience of living with race and racism. The guides included some of the background material and lesson plans in a related resource volume for teachers also published in 2007, *How Real Is Race? A Sourcebook on Race, Culture and Biology* (Mukhopadhyay, Henze, and Moses 2007). It has been gratifying to learn that the website has been used by people outside of the academy. For example, I have been asked twice to talk with health-care workers and officials at the Riverside County, California, health department about race and health disparities and about how to use material from the website to train their fieldworkers and researchers.

Funding *RACE: Are We So Different?*: The Backstory

The key to funding the *RACE* project was timing—having the right people in place and having the right national public message at the right time. In the final year of my 1995–1997 term as president of the AAA, I convened a group of biological, archaeological, cultural, and linguistic anthropologists to talk to each other about what race means in their subfields, furthering the initiative called for in Mukhopadhyay and Moses (1997). Concurrently, the AAA's lead journal, *American Anthropologist*, published a "Contemporary Issues Forum: Race and Racism," edited by Faye Harrison, with papers by eight scholars representing the four subfields plus genetics and African American studies (Cartmill 1998; Early 1998; Harrison 1998; Hill 1998; Orser 1998; Shanklin 1998; Smedley 1998; Sussman 1998; Templeton 1998).

While these efforts were occurring, Mary Margaret "Peggy" Overbey, the AAA's director of government relations, met with staffers on Capitol Hill and in federal funding agencies located in Washington, D.C. At one of these meetings, she spoke with National Science Foundation (NSF) Program Officer Al Desena, who was interested in innovative science projects aimed at public education. He agreed with Overbey that a scientific approach to race could be an excellent topic with which to engage the public about what science is and how it informs our everyday lives and identities.

Meanwhile, important things were happening at the Ford Foundation. They were launching a new initiative that would examine the importance of affirmative action in higher education, and they continued to support social justice goals at a time when other foundations were backing away from issues relating to race. I was aware of this because at the time I was a member of the Ford Foundation's board of directors. Although I could not personally apply for a Ford grant for an AAA project on race, I did facilitate an invitation for Overbey, AAA Executive Director Bill Davis, and anthropologists Faye Harrison, Carol Mukhopadhyay, and a few others to talk to people at Ford about the big idea. We also had two Ford program officers—Gertrude Fraser and Irma McClaurin, both anthropologists—who remained supportive of the project through its formative Phase I period (2001–2007).

Overbey and Harrison recall one meeting at Ford during which representatives from national social justice organizations, including the NAACP Legal Defense and Educational Fund and the Mexican American Legal Defense and Educational Fund, expressed skepticism about the ability of the AAA to produce anything critical about race in America, because we anthropologists had been the ones who helped create "race science" in the first place. One of the ways we surmounted this was to invite Theodore Shaw, then head of the NAACP Legal Defense and Educational Fund, to join the twenty-six–member *RACE* Project Advisory Board I chaired, which consisted mainly of anthropologists and other scholars.[3]

In 2001, Ford made an initial grant of one million dollars to the AAA, and the *RACE* Project's Phase I began, with Overbey serving as principal investigator and director at the AAA's Washington, D.C., office. Overbey, Harrison, Mukhopadhyay, AAA President-elect Alan Goodman, Michael Blakey, a few others, and I now shepherded several versions of a larger grant proposal to

NSF Program Officer Al Desena. In 2004, NSF granted the *RACE* Project three million dollars. Fraser and McClaurin from Ford and Desena from NSF remained with us every step of the way, attending advisory board meetings and other *RACE* Project events.

The input of the *RACE* Advisory Board and foundation program officers was augmented by more than two hundred conference and panel participants, consultants, and representatives of eight museums and science centers, as well as by fifteen scientific and professional organizations, all of which collaborated in honing the exhibit's message and content.[4] With our grant funding, we sponsored two interdisciplinary scholarly conferences: one in 2004 on "Race and Human Variation: Setting an Agenda for Future Research and Education" (Achenbach 2004; Overbey and Moses 2004), and another in 2007 on "Race, Human Variation, and Disease: Consensus and Frontiers." Six of the conference plenary presentations were later posted on the *RACE: Are We So Different?* website (di Leonardo 2004; Haney López 2004; Holt 2004; Johnston 2004; McGaghie 2007; Smedley 2007).

We were also active within the AAA, organizing a panel at the 2003 annual meeting, "Exploring the Nature of Human Biological Diversity: Myth v. Reality," with the Biological Anthropology Section and Committee on Minority Affairs (see Jantz 2003; Long 2003). In 2005, we sponsored two panels at the AAA annual meeting: "Exploring the Intersection of Race, Human Variation and Health," coorganized with the Society for Medical Anthropology, and a presidential session on "The Past, the Present, and the Future of Race and Health in Anthropological Perspective" (Jones and Beckrich 2006).

RACE Exhibit Dialogues

Project leaders and staff kept the AAA membership informed through frequent reports and updates in the *Anthropology News*, which all members received nine times a year. In 2005, the *RACE* Project invited AAA members to contribute short pieces based on their own research and experience for an *Anthropology News* special section on "Rethinking Race and Human Variation" (Jones et al. 2005). Nine contributions, selected by a group of advisory board members, were published in the February and March 2006 issues and later posted on the *RACE: Are We So Different?* website (Hangen 2006; Hart and Ashmore 2006; Hartigan 2006; Lee and Farrell 2006; Lee 2006; Pollock 2006; Simmons 2006; Takezawa 2006; Thompson 2006.)

As the opening of the traveling exhibit neared, the *RACE* project presented a panel discussion at the department chairs breakfast during the 2005 AAA annual meeting. I was on the panel, along with Joseph Jones of the *RACE* staff and Thomas Patterson, then chair of the anthropology department at the University of California, Riverside. One goal of the project was to encourage local departments to work with museums in those communities where the exhibit was scheduled to appear. The panel focused on telling the department chairs about the project's goals of reaching beyond the university to help people understand what race is and is not. Patterson and I spoke about the possibility of museums and departments of anthropology partnering on public programming, including cohosting community dialogues with local organizations. Jones described his work at a summer institute for middle and high school teachers on "Rethinking Race: Understanding Genetic and Biological Diversity Without Race," then in its third year (organized by Alan Goodman and Hampshire College).

At the Science Museum of Minnesota, the five-thousand-square-foot *RACE* exhibit, with nearly fifty components, was being designed by staff project heads Robert Garfinkle and Joanne Jones-Rizzi and their creative and resourceful team. Following a Ford-funded "difficult dialogues" conference with museum professionals hosted by the Field Museum and its curator Alaka Wali in Chicago, SMM had been chosen because of its reputation for dealing with complex issues, such as creationism and evolution, and for reaching and engaging young people. Ford asked us to partner as well with California Newsreel, which they funded to produce "Race: The Power of an Illusion," a documentary first broadcast on PBS stations in 2003. Members of our advisory board served on their advisory team, and clips from their three-part series were incorporated into the SMM exhibit, especially in the biological/genetic and history sections.

Overall, there was wonderful interplay among our many collaborators—academics, museum curators, designers of the exhibit and website, funders, community groups, policy researchers, and social justice advocates. All of these people, representing different standpoints, believed in the need for the project, even if I felt the creative process sometimes seemed like herding cats.

Following a successful opening and several awards (Overbey 2007, 2008), we wrote a proposal in 2008 and received a second Ford Foundation grant of $450,000 toward Phase II of the project (2008–2015). This involved (1) designing a condensed, fifteen-hundred-square-foot exhibit for smaller venues, which began circulating in 2010; (2) duplicating the existing five-thousand-square-foot version to meet demand through 2015; and (3) producing a trade book with images, charts, and timelines from the exhibit and website designed to complement the image-free *How Real Is Race?* (Mukhopadhyay, Henze, and Moses 2007) produced for teachers. This companion volume, *RACE: Are We So Different?* (Goodman, Moses, and Jones 2012), also includes short essays by a wide range of interdisciplinary scholars[5] and addresses public policy issues: the intractable nature of racial health disparities, the subprime mortgage industry and race, race and immigration, the educational achievement gap, racial and ethical issues of the Tuskegee Syphilis Experiment, and racist policies of the U.S. Department of Agriculture toward African American farmers, to name a few. In addition, Phase II co-principal investigators Alan Goodman and I completed development of a DVD/CD-ROM started by Peggy Overbey, which contained all exhibit videos and interviews. The DVD/CD-ROM became available for purchase, along with a *RACE: Are We So Different?* T-shirt, at exhibit locations and from the AAA website (http://www.aaanet.org/resources/A-Public-Education-Program.cfm).

Our one setback came when a proposal by Phase II Project Manager Joseph Jones and me to develop applications of exhibit and website materials for afterschool programs was turned down by the National Science Foundation. We then applied to the National Endowment for the Humanities (NEH) in 2007, and again in 2008, when our proposal made it all the way through the review process to the office of NEH Chairman Bruce Cole. In the George W. Bush administration, the chairman had final say in the approval process. He did not like the themes of the proposal or the plan to take the discussion of race to public libraries across the country, especially to rural and poor locations that would never see the exhibit. The feedback we received was: "Race in America? Why do we want to talk about race in a color-blind society?" What I found disturbing was the oppressive atmosphere at NEH among program officers who talked with me, off the record, about what they saw as a chilling political environment silencing any talk about issues that might show the Bush administration in a bad light. In that environment, the NEH chairman overturned the recommendations of a faculty peer review committee and the program officer and denied us funding.

RACE: Are We So Different? on the Road

Positive responses and increased community attendance and interaction frequently accompanied *RACE: Are We So Different?*, and, as at the Science Museum of Minnesota, other sites suffered "*RACE* exhibit withdrawal" when the exhibit at last moved on to its next location. Each sponsoring institution in turn gave the exhibit its own local flavor with added "wraparound" events and activities. At the Liberty Science Center in New Jersey, Peggy Overbey addressed more than one hundred and fifty K–12 teachers at a special exhibit preview and worked with two newspapers that each produced eight-part, full-color *RACE: Are We So Different?* feature series (Overbey 2008). The Mashantucket Pequot Museum and Research Center in Connecticut developed a concurrent "Race Matters in Indian New England" exhibit exploring how "Native peoples in New England have continued to resist and speak out [against racism], claiming their identities and living their lives—not as a separate race—but as indigenous communities" (Jones 2008). The Cincinnati Museum Center hosted its city's annual African, Appalachian, Asian, and Celtic Culture Fest during the exhibit run. They also added a *RACE* Story Kiosk, where visitors' impressions of *RACE: Are We So Different?* and thoughts about race in Cincinnati were video recorded (Jones 2009).

One of the more successful department-museum-community collaborations involved the anthropology department at Western Michigan University, the Kalamazoo Valley Museum, and social justice and civic organizations in the city of Kalamazoo. Dr. Kristina Wertz played a key role in involving students, university officials, and social justice leaders in conferences that began a year before the exhibit arrived. The *RACE* Project thus was the impetus for bringing together groups ranging from the Girl Scouts of America to the YMCA to the NAACP, groups that had not worked together before, to develop a community action plan on issues of racial justice based on material from our project. I was invited to speak at the university, and on a second trip, I addressed a community audience (Rietsma 2010).

In January 2010, the *RACE* Project came to Capitol Hill in Washington, D.C., and key components of the traveling exhibit were on display in conjunction with a conference on race and public policy. The event, "A New National Dialogue on Race," was sponsored by the American Anthropological Association; the Science Museum of Minnesota; and the Congressional Black, Hispanic, and Asian American Caucuses and was held in the U.S. House of Representatives Cannon Office Building (Dozier 2010). The several hundred in attendance included Representatives Barbara Lee (D-California), Sheila Jackson-Lee (D-Texas), and Bobby Scott (D-Virigina), plus dozens of congressional and senatorial office staffers.

The conference began with a keynote address, which I delivered, and included four panels of national advocacy and policy organization leaders, journalists, media activists, and anthropologists. The issues addressed included racial disparities in education, employment, health outcomes, and drug-use sentencing; media coverage of race; and expanding intergroup dialogue.[6] During the conference, AAA President-elect Leith Mullings joined me and AAA staff in conversations with several legislators about the *RACE* Project and other AAA initiatives. Anthropologists Johnnetta Betsch Cole, Marc Lamont Hill, John Jackson, Jr., and Maria Vesperi also played important roles in the two-day event.

When the smaller version of the exhibit opened at the Riverside Metropolitan Museum in June 2010, University of California, Riverside (UCR) anthropology chair Thomas Patterson, museum collections director Brenda Focht, and I were there to welcome *RACE* to our community. With us were ten UCR anthropology and history graduate students who had developed companion research projects on racial issues in Riverside and San Bernardino Counties:

- Isabelle Placentia, Richard Alvarado, and Steve Duncan focused on the predatory nature of the mortgage industry in targeting poor and vulnerable people of color.
- Zita Worley's project examined the rise of the Ku Klux Klan in Southern California in the nineteenth and twentieth centuries.
- Vlasta Radin highlighted the subject of allies and supporters of Japanese families interned during World War II.
- Michelle Lorimer presented a pictorial ethnohistory of the Sherman Indian Institute in Riverside.
- Jacqueline Gutierrez described the role of Mexican American women in the region since the early twentieth century.
- German Loffler and Jessica Gross researched and explained how people link evaluative statements to particular ethnic and racial groups.
- Michelle An told the story of the rise and fall of Riverside's Korean community through the life history of one Korean woman.

These student projects were displayed on campus during fall 2010. It was especially gratifying for me to see how these materials became a platform for people in my own institution and community, and from diverse racial and ethnic communities and social classes, to have frank conversations about what they saw at the *RACE* exhibit.

Perhaps the most surprising encounter was a request for *RACE* project resources from the Texas Department of Family Protective Services in 2010. Its Child Protective Services Office (CPS) is a national leader in addressing racial disproportionality in child welfare; its mission is to protect children, act in children's best interest, and seek active involvement from the children's parents and family members to solve problems that can lead to abuse and neglect. With more than eight thousand staff members, CPS can offer services in 254 Texas counties, and on any given day, CPS has approximately thirty thousand children in out-of-home care.

The Department of Family Protective Services was instructed by the state legislature to develop training programs to reduce the practice of removing black and Latino children from homes at a disproportionately higher rate than that for white children facing the same domestic conditions. Their head of training happened to access our *RACE: Are We So Different?* website and was intrigued by the way it explained the origins and operation of structural racism. Because they work with social workers, family providers, judges, child advocates, and others, they wanted to understand more about "race and human variation" and how assumptions about difference play out in the real world. The state trainers saw the value of our materials in enhancing and revamping their current diversity training framework. They said that *RACE: Are We So Different?* challenged them to think more broadly and unconventionally about what constitutes institutional and structural racism and how, as an agency, they should be examining all of their policies and practices by learning how to look through an anthropological lens.

In June 2011, *RACE: Are We So Different?* opened for six months at the Smithsonian National Museum of Natural History on the mall in Washington, D.C. Ten Smithsonian museums developed parallel exhibits and programs on race, and I helped train eighteen volunteers who underwent a two-month course to assist *RACE* exhibit visitors. In conjunction with the exhibit, the museum's Anthropology Outreach Office published a special issue of *Anthro-Notes*, its free online publication on anthropological research and resources, which is sent to nine thousand teachers. It featured articles by anthropologists Johnnetta Betsch Cole, Nina Jablonski, John Jackson, Jr., Mark Leone, and Joseph Jones and me (Cole 2011; Jablonski 2011; Jackson 2011; Leone, Knauf, and Tang 2011; Moses and Jones 2011).

For the exhibit opening, I was invited to address the Smithsonian Congress of Scholars on "Anthropology and the Cultural Construction of Race" and to present a public lecture at the National Museum of Natural History on

"The Making of the *RACE: Are We So Different?* Project," an enjoyable return "back home," as I had served on the museum's advisory board for nine years. Both talks were video recorded and made available on the National Museum's website (http://www.mnh.si.edu/exhibits/race/related-resources.cfm). These events, however, were somewhat ironic for me, because the Smithsonian initially had declined our invitation to curate the exhibit. Nonetheless, I was pleased that the National Museum of Natural History now wanted to house it for six months rather than the usual three-month tour period. This allowed us time to add a program for teachers. And, because this was our nation's own natural history museum, it was particularly pleasing to me that more than a million visitors would see *RACE* in this venue during its summer-fall stay.

The Impact of *RACE: Are We So Different?*

When I was a child in the 1950s, my grandparents used to take me, my sister, and our first cousin to the Los Angeles County Museum of Natural History on weekends—because it was free and we had little money—and that is when I fell in love with anthropology. I used to roam the aisles of that vast museum looking at the artifacts and thinking about the places that they came from. Later in my career, the idea of an exhibit in a museum had a particular positive resonance for me. I wanted it to be an exhibit that grabbed the imagination of children and young adults. The *RACE* project and traveling exhibit was therefore designed to bring an anthropological perspective of this controversial and important topic of race to today's young public. When we were asked by skeptics, "Isn't race too complex an issue to explain to the ordinary citizen?" we said, "No, it's not. People talk about it, but in an uninformed way." Kids of all ages, we learned, are interested—they want to know because it is about them, about their own identity, about who they are. They have to understand diversity, both biological and cultural, and our role as educators and parents is to help students become informed global citizens who are comfortable living in and understanding our diverse nation.

Even before the exhibit first opened, we interviewed high school students and museum visitors, held focus groups, and convened community meetings at seven museums to learn how people discuss race and what they wanted to know about it. We learned that people are fascinated by human similarities and differences. They wanted to know more and to talk about how race figured in their communities and lives (Overbey 2007). I was pleased with the many dialogues the exhibit created, especially as we learned how parents and high school and college instructors used it as a springboard to meaningful conversation and deeper understandings.

The *RACE* project's goal has been to enable students who view the exhibit to understand and talk about the concept of race in new and more informed ways—from K–12 classrooms to freshmen seminars to introductory anthropology courses to a broad range of social science and biology classes. Teachers who have used the materials from the *RACE* Project gave us feedback that they would like to have a more in-depth understanding of race and human variation and would like to come together to do this as professional development training. By 2011, the AAA Resource Development Committee had raised eight thousand dollars from AAA members to convene a pilot group of teachers to discuss the materials developed for teachers and students in an extremely productive meeting at the Science Museum of Minnesota that June. Following this event, we spoke with NEH Deputy Chairman Carol Watson, who was excited about the idea and arranged for a $25,000 grant (how times change) to the AAA and the Smithsonian National Museum of Natural History to bring more teachers who have used the *RACE* materials in their classes to a larger meeting in December 2011. We wanted to learn how to make our materials even more user-friendly for teachers. We have learned a lot from these meetings, and eventually we hope to have a national conference to share what we have learned with an even larger group.

I remain committed to conveying the message that biological race is not real—human variation is real, and the social construction of race is real, but there is only one biological race: the species *Homo sapiens sapiens*. The approach is a biocultural approach, and that is what continues to be unique about this project. It is only through an educated citizenry that understands the intersections of culture and biology that we can move toward a point where racism will not be part of the everyday lives of people around the world. We may not live long enough to see it, but we can be the architects of the changes that will make this a reality for our children.

Anthropology is a discipline well suited to carry out this project. The concept of race continues to be one of the most intractable and important issues in the twenty-first century. Anthropology's traditional focus on race, its multidisciplinary expertise, and its evolutionary and cross-cultural perspectives all position it as the appropriate discipline for replacing myth and folk beliefs about race with data and facts. It is only through educating our students that we can move to a point at which misunderstandings about race will be a thing of the past. Our classrooms are the place to start the process of transformation.

The project and its materials have been a catalyst for conversations about race not only in classrooms but in boardrooms, workplaces, homes, and diversity training programs. Now viewed by more than three million people (Mullings 2013), the knowledge and resources contained in the AAA *RACE: Are We So Different?* project are a giant step in the right direction.

Chapter 3

Mutuality and the Field at Home

Sylvia Rodríguez

> Can anthropology foster a critique of cultural dominance that extends to its own protocols of research?
>
> —James Clifford 1997b, 218

A few years ago, a community radio station in Taos, New Mexico, invited me to have a fifteen-minute spot every Wednesday morning to chat on the air with the host of a popular talk-show program, "Breakfast with Nancy." Nancy had googled for specialists on northern New Mexico and come up with my name—I had published *The Matachines Dance: Ritual Symbolism and Interethnic Relations in the Rio Grande Valley* in 1996 and *Acequia: Water Sharing, Sanctity, and Place* in 2006. The general topic of conversation was to be the history and anthropology of what goes on in Taos, New Mexico, and in the world.

I jumped at the chance to engage in a bit of public anthropology. For the first few months, we roamed over topics ranging from feast days to tourism, land and water issues, art and language, ethnic identity, history and current events, and the bitter controversies over "culture" that regularly surface in the media. We did this mostly by phone, although occasionally I traveled from the University of New Mexico in Albuquerque to the Taos studio so we could also answer calls. She gave out my university e-mail address for responses and queries. One Taoseña took exception to my claim that the annual summer fiestas of Santa Ana and Santiago were invented by Anglo boosters during the 1930s to promote tourism.

Eventually I asked Nancy if there were topics she or others might especially want me to talk about. She asked around and, unsurprisingly, the number one topic to come up was Taos Pueblo—not a subject I was eager to discuss on the radio. In our quick romps over the social landscape of Taos, the pueblo would certainly come up, but I never proposed it as a topic per se. As an anthropologist, I felt a certain obligation to comply with the request. I proceeded with trepidation, carefully avoiding the presumption of any substantive "facts," emphasizing the pueblo rule of secrecy, and raising the question of who had the authority to speak about Taos or any other pueblo. I talked about how insider and outsider accounts might differ and why this topic is so delicate. For a couple of shows we skated along, avoiding pueblo "culture" itself, discussing instead a series of color photographs published in *The Taos News* of an award ceremony that brought LaDonna Harris to the pueblo. Eager to move on to Taos as a contact zone where all sorts of differences meld, clash, and slide along, I mentioned the pueblo's twofold moiety structure and layout, divided by the Rio Pueblo into north or Winter and south or Summer People. That was it: common knowledge, nothing you would not find in a tourist brochure or the pueblo website. After all, how deep can you go in fifteen minutes?

Ten minutes after the show, I received the following email from a woman at the pueblo whom I did not know:

> Enough already.
>
> You talk of being an anthropologist who wishes to preserve culture.
>
> By discussing "culture" of Taos Pueblo you are not fostering the preservation of culture. Taos Pueblo prides itself on preserving their culture by not sharing information about their way of life with outsiders.
>
> Regardless of your occupation, please stop using Taos Pueblo as a talking piece while on the radio. It is very disturbing to hear a non tribal member discuss our way of life to a culture who is only looking to the Pueblo people to learn of a tradition they can only wish they had.
>
> Many people from Taos Pueblo do not appreciate your on-air discussion as if you are aware and versed in our culture. If you respect the Taos Pueblo, you will find other topics to discuss on the radio.

Unnerved, yet knowing I had gotten what I deserved by being foolish enough to say anything at all about the pueblo on local community radio, I promptly sent her the following message:

Thank you for your comments. I mean no disrespect to the people of Taos Pueblo. When I asked Nancy if there are topics she and others wanted me to talk about, of course Taos Pueblo came up as number one. I have tried to be careful by acknowledging at the outset the problem of who has authority to speak of pueblo matters and the rule of pueblo secrecy. If you have listened to this program for the past 2–3 weeks you will recognize that I have said nothing that isn't already commonly known, and have emphasized that outsiders including anthropologists have limited and imperfect knowledge that no doubt differs from what pueblo authorities believe. In any case, as you request, I will no longer focus on Taos Pueblo on the radio.

I would welcome any suggestions you might have about interesting or appropriate topics for the weekly radio chat.

Respectfully,
Sylvia Rodríguez

Shortly thereafter I received this response:

There is plenty of history and anthropological topics of the Taos area that do not surround the Taos Pueblo.

Your and [local history buff and tour guide] Peter M['s] commentary only leave more questions and intrusion from the outside public. Notice KTAO does not have tribal members talking about their own tradition and/or religion?

Appreciate your respect for our traditional values—this is what has kept us a vibrant living community.

Unable to restrain myself and hoping for dialogue, I sent her the following message:

I agree that pueblo people should be the ones to speak about their culture. I appreciate your request to dial it down and focus elsewhere. But does this mean that outsiders should never even mention the pueblo? How would this be possible? Wouldn't ignoring the pueblo or failing to acknowledge its importance in history or significance in the modern world be yet another form of disrespect? To leave the pueblo out of the larger Taos picture would seem to me a kind of distortion. As a native Taoseña whose family has been there for many genera-

> tions, I feel like the pueblo is part of my history too, and my people and culture have been affected by relations with pueblo people in deep ways. This has worked both ways, like it or not. I can try to keep my mouth shut out of respect, but I can't erase the pueblo from my mind or my heart. Do you think the [radio] station should invite a pueblo representative to speak, or would that be just another form of intrusion?

I received no response. In the weeks and months that followed, Nancy and I returned to an ever-expanding repertoire of topics related to New Mexico, borderlands, and world history, culture, politics, and current events—virtually everything *except* Taos Pueblo.

Mutuality

This vignette opens my response to Roger Sanjek's question about the role of mutuality in the professional practice of sociocultural anthropology: Why do we do what we do? It speaks to how I ended up as an anthropologist who studies her hometown. The short answer seems trite: I do what I do because I cannot do otherwise. The long answer, spelled out in this chapter, charts the trajectory of my career: away from its start in foreign extractive research into hometown or "native" ethnography and, ultimately, into collaborative and participatory action research with communities of interest. First I trace the source of my interest in anthropology to a circumstance of birth and childhood at a particular time, place, and social location. I identify several factors that shaped my path. The questions I have pursued for more than three decades of research in Taos spring from my experience and observations growing up and, later, periodically residing there. Each question arose out of conversations with other Taoseños and Nuevomexicanos about one or another aspect of the deep colonial structure of local society, which, despite four centuries of historical transformation, persists today in recognizable form.

The motivation behind my lifetime fascination with and curiosity about Taos sometimes seems to serve separate and contrary masters. I have sought not only to understand what goes on in Taos and why but somehow to influence the larger course of events as well. With whom does one make common intellectual and political cause? Should—or can—these be separate? Although I have never thought of it in exactly these terms before, one could say that the problem of mutuality resides at the heart of my lifelong intellectual struggle and journey within the discipline of anthropology.

What is mutuality? According to the online Free Dictionary, "*Mutual* is used to describe a reciprocal relationship between two or more people or things. Thus *their mutual animosity* means 'their animosity for each other' or 'the animosity between them,' and *a mutual defense treaty* is one in which each party agrees to come to the defense of the other. But many people also use *mutual* to mean 'shared in common,' as in *The bill serves the mutual interests of management and labor*" (Free Dictionary, n.d.).

The same source also defines mutuality as a legal principle that "provides that unless both parties to a contract are bound to perform, neither party is bound." Sanjek notes that mutuality is neither new nor intrinsic to anthropological practice. A continuum of mutuality exists in anthropological research. Anthropologists can engage in all three variants: reciprocity, interest in common, and contractual, and no doubt there are other forms as well. Its absence from ethnographic fieldwork is illustrated by the uncooperative attitude the Nuer showed Evans-Pritchard, or by the Zuni resistance to Cushing's rude intrusion into their kiva ceremonies. The most familiar form of anthropological mutuality is called reciprocity, as in "gifts for informants," or the small and sometimes not so small services, goods, and aid anthropologists routinely provide to their research subjects. To one degree or another, the devoted participant observer inevitably becomes enmeshed in the daily give and take of personal interaction. Herein lie the power and the frailty of ethnographic fieldwork.

The contradiction at the heart of ethnographic practice is, arguably, a crisis of mutuality. On the one hand, the ideal of detached objectivity proscribes familiar and passionate engagement. The investigator formulates the research question and method in an academic setting and directs her findings primarily to other academics. Yet successful—and nowadays institutionally approved—ethnographic research requires assent, consent, and/or permission; hence, some degree of toleration, if not cooperation, is necessary. Rapport and the development of mutual understanding is the wherewithal of successful ethnography—and *successful* does not mean limited to Geertzian interpretation. Today, research subjects require assurance that no harm will come to them if they participate and that they may expect some benefit if they do.

The reflexive, poststructural, feminist, postcolonial, postmodern turn in late twentieth-century Euroamerican anthropology showed how the Other is bound up with the Self and that all questions, along with subject-researcher relations, are historically situated and politically charged. Decolonization demands that anthropologists be held to account for their work by their past (or descendent), present, and prospective subjects. Today, no social research can reasonably be said to stand free of the messy entanglement of historical moment, political location, and moral relation. The very act of representation is recognized as an exercise in power.

What if mutuality were to become *one* measure by which anthropologists could consider and evaluate social—especially ethnographic—research? How would research questions be generated, by whom, and to what end? Who would do fieldwork, and how? Who would control the findings and have access to them? Would this approach derail or advance science? What is the purpose of science, and whom does it serve? Does mutuality offer a solution to the dilemma posed by a field science born of colonialism? What role should mutuality have in pedagogy and anthropological training? How does pedagogy foster or suppress mutuality in research practice? I will return to these questions after recounting the path that led me to search for answers.

Origins

My father's maternal family had been in Taos, my grandmother told me, for six generations before her, and prior to that, some family members had come from the pueblo of Pojoaque. Somewhere along the line, she said, there was a gringo from Missouri who deserted the U.S. Army, ate his chaps to get through the desert, and married in. My grandmother taught school when she was young, after attending Haskell, a government boarding school for Native Americans, for reasons that remain unclear, as no one in Taos, including herself, considered her an Indian. She chopped her own wood, drew water out of a well in her front yard, and irrigated a garden and fruit trees from an *acequia* (irrigation ditch). She raised and slaughtered her own chickens and rabbits in her back yard. In the last decade of her life, she relented and allowed her adult children to install indoor plumbing and a gas cookstove in her house.

My paternal grandfather came alone from Parral, Chihuahua, as a youth before the Mexican Revolution, running from something. Recently we learned that he abandoned a family in Colorado to elope with my grandmother and start another one in Taos. He died before I was born, so I never knew him, but there were vivid stories about his career as a professional gambler who ran a saloon in Rodarte and a meat market on the Taos plaza. He worked my father, the only one of his sons who lived to adulthood, brutally hard. My mother told me that her in-laws were deeply ashamed of my grandfather's sometimes public epileptic seizures. He was an outsider, she said, like herself. Like so many Taoseños born in the late nineteenth and early twentieth centuries, my father's family went from *vecinos* who worked their land to wage laborers in the space of a single generation. Like his sisters, my father struggled to make it into the middle class. He became a pharmacist who had a drugstore on the plaza, and much to his mother's dismay, he married an Anglo Protestant who came from Texas.

My mother came to Taos as a young woman to study art and escape the stifling atmosphere of upper-middle-class Austin society. Her father was a Kentuckian who worked as a superintendent on the Southern Pacific railroad. Her mother's people were of Scots-Irish descent; they came to Texas from the South. A few were prominent, college-educated businessmen and professionals. One of her maternal uncles, she suspected, belonged to the Klan. Although she grew up in Austin, accustomed to being served by black and colored live-in servants, my mother was born in Douglas, Arizona, right on the border. Her earliest memories included the fiery glow of smelters at night and a fenced back yard with a gate she once wandered through as a toddler. "And there," she recalled, "was Mexico." She reminisced about digging bullets, randomly fired by Pancho Villa's men, out of the rear adobe walls of their house to mix in a cup with dirt, nails, and bugs for a poison to kill Villa.

There can be little doubt my parents married for love, because neither family was thrilled at the match. In the early 1930s, theirs was an interracial marriage that crossed class lines. In order to receive my father's family's blessing, my parents had to agree to raise their children Catholic. My mother refused to convert and gradually strayed from her own Episcopalian roots to become agnostic. Even though he grew disillusioned by what he called the hypocrisy of the church, until the day he died my father got down on his knees to pray before he went to bed. My sister and I grew up very much in the bosom of his extended family, not far from La Loma, where my grandmother and the rest of the Trujillos lived. We had friendly but infrequent visits with my mother's family in Austin, whom my father wryly referred to as "the white folks." He insisted that our first language be English and later agonized because our Spanish was so fractured. We attended a convent school and were taught to read and especially to pray by Loretto nuns, who referred to the public school, located on the other side of their fence, as the "devil's school." Ultimately, after many heated family arguments, we both ended up in the devil's school, where my eighth grade science teacher proudly refused to teach about evolution.

The Devil's School

Her flat refusal piqued an interest in evolution that gradually led me to the devil's school of anthropology. This impetus nevertheless seems minor compared to the experience of growing up *coyote* (Spanish-Mexican/Anglo or some other biethnic combination) in Taos during the 1950s and 1960s. By the time I was thirteen, all I wanted was to get out of Taos as soon and as far away as possible, not unlike most kids today. Much of the adult world of Taos across all social boundaries had drifted into alcoholism, my parents and their friends included. My chance to escape came when a wealthy friend of my mother took me to visit a boarding school in Arizona where her daughter was enrolled. Thus began my career as a minority scholarship student in elite institutions. It was at this small, progressive boarding school deep in the red rock country that I received permission to indulge my egghead proclivities and took my first anthropology class. My classmates included offspring of the Hollywood Jewish left. Everything looked smaller when I came home after my first semester and discovered that my parents had wildly disparate accents. Visiting my roommate for spring break our junior year at her lavish Westchester home, I took one look at Manhattan and knew I wanted to be there.

Immersed for four years in the cultural, social, and environmental shock of West 116th Street and Broadway in New York, I became a New Mexican. I majored in anthropology at Barnard and applied to graduate school, which, I imagined, would lead me to fieldwork in Asia or South America. Moments occurred at each institution when crucial information about my social location was driven home to me. My student counselor at boarding school told me the admissions dean had cautioned her that I might be "sensitive about being half Mexican." In the deep exile of New York City, I finally understood just how much Taos, New Mexico, the Southwest, the West itself, were *not* the norm. The dazzle, noise, vastness, and grime of the city slowly depressed me and made me homesick for the mountains, clear high-desert air, and people of New Mexico.

When I arrived at Stanford, my faculty advisor looked at me and said, "I thought we were getting a *real* Chicana!" My gringa phenotype notwithstanding, I received a Ford Foundation minority fellowship that paid for my—and my generation of Chicana/o scholars'—doctoral education. Another illuminating moment came when the newly formed Stanford Movimiento Estudiantil Chicano de Aztlán (MEChA) brought Cleofes Vigil to campus from San Cristóbal, New Mexico. I had known Cleofes simply as some old guy who was a friend of my father. It turned out that Cleofes was a revered icon of traditional rural Chicano/Nuevomexicano culture, celebrated in Stan Steiner's book *La Raza* (Steiner 1970). Cleofes sang *alabados*, carved cedar sculptures, and recited poetry about his beloved "*nacioncita*" of northern New Mexico. He ranted against Anglo racism, land loss, and the American occupation of Aztlán—in a way my father would never have dreamed of. A few years later, after completing my fieldwork and moving to San Cristóbal to write my dissertation, I got to know Cleofes and his wife Frances much better. He became my first and only professor of Chicano studies.

Feminist and Chicano, Black, and Native American studies did not exist when I was at Barnard, and they were just emerging during my first years at Stanford. My introduction to feminist anthropology came when Shelly Rosaldo and Jane Collier taught the first course in women, culture, and society. When the time came to go into the field for my dissertation research, the only one who warned me that fieldwork would involve political complications was the avowed Marxist in the department. When I was ready to pack up and head for southern Mexico to study shamanism and its relation to the 260-day divinatory calendar, I realized that despite seminars in theory, methodology, and ethnology, I had no clue what to do when I actually walked into a village. I went around to my professors and asked their advice. Only Bridget O'Laughlin reminded me that my ability to walk into a village was dependent on the history and unequal power relations of colonialism.

The Field Is Where?

One of the lessons my father impressed on me as a child was never to ask Indians any questions about their religion or anything else they did at the pueblo. He had grown up, as I had, not far from the pueblo village, and he had many friends as well as customers from the pueblo. He spoke what must have been a pidgin Tiwa as a trade language, which he easily conversed in when Taos Indians came to our house or the store or when we went to the pueblo to visit friends and enjoy the feast-day dances. He sometimes took me with him when he visited friends at the pueblo and neighboring communities in the area, and he inculcated in me a very different sense of etiquette for these occasions than my mother did for the middle-class Anglo settings familiar to her. Such lessons sink to the level of *habitus*, and we are often unaware of their power until they come into conflict with competing demands. Basically, in keeping with the norms of proper northern Nuevomexicano as well as pueblo social comportment, my father taught me to show respect to everyone but especially to elders, always keep a low profile, and talk as little as possible.

Educated among the sons and daughters of affluent professionals at elite institutions and caught up in the political and countercultural turmoil of the late 1960s and early 1970s, I rebelled against these values as antiquated and repressive norms designed to keep the downtrodden, especially women, in their place. And not only that: my father's cultural guidelines would spell professional suicide in a system that rewarded standing out, speaking up, and making sure to show everyone how much I knew and just how smart I really was.

I took great pains at Stanford to locate as remote a village as possible for my fieldwork, and after expeditions to two different mountain regions of Oaxaca, selected a village about four days' walk from the nearest road, deep into the rugged cloud forest of the Sierra Mixe. The little-studied Mixe were famous among their more assimilated Zapotec neighbors for being "*muy retirados*" and, in the past (it was rumored), cannibals as well. The Mixe themselves proudly claimed they had never been conquered, "*ni por los Aztecas ni los Españoles*." The people of Cotzocón were largely monolingual, and few of the women had traveled outside the sierra. The sudden appearance of a young solitary white woman was enough to cause *susto*, or spiritual fright, in the first child I encountered at a water hole on my first day there. Apart from a serious case of parasites, the crisis I experienced in the following months was essentially moral. It came down to this: I would be ashamed to walk into Taos Pueblo to try to investigate magical-religious beliefs and practices or, for that matter, anything else. How then, could I justify doing it in San Juan Cotzocón? I struggled to survive and carry out research while my hosts reluctantly tolerated my intrusion. Two or three gracious souls even went through the motions of cooperating with my effort. But I never managed to shake the conviction that I was doing something fundamentally wrong. My arrogance and naïveté in going there felt inexcusable.

After ten miserable, disease-ridden, transformative months, I returned to New Mexico to recover my health and shattered sense of who I was or should be and began my dissertation. I read feminists and Marxists, chopped wood, learned to irrigate and grow vegetables, and underwent a political and ideological sea change. I saw Taos with new eyes. It was as interesting, problematic, and "exotic" as any other place anthropologists are keen to study. Like all such places, it was also deeply troubling. When my fellowship money ran out, I was lucky to find a temporary teaching position in the Sociology-Anthropology Department at Carleton College, where they were happy to hire a "twofer" in a non–tenure-track replacement position that lasted four years. In addition to introductory anthropology and subjects in which I had training, I was asked to teach a class on women because I was a woman and in Chicano studies because I was Chicana, the first ever on the Carleton faculty. Thus began my education in feminist theory, Chicano and borderlands history, Southwest ethnology, and the rewards and perils of professorship.

After Carleton, I decided to undertake ethnographic research on social change and interethnic relations in Taos. Taos had undergone rapid social, economic, and demographic change since I left for high school. The tension, resentment, and century-old memories that had simmered pretty much beneath the surface since 1847, when Taoseños murdered the first American governor, had begun to seep back into the open. However much they might rejoice in the privacy of their hearts, my father's contemporaries, with a few exceptions like Cleofes, were scandalized by the heated, confrontational rhetoric of land-grant and Chicano activists. The inevitable assimilation that social scientists had predicted for Native Americans and Mexican Americans in the Southwest simply was not happening. Something more interesting and complex was going on. On the one hand, Indians, Hispanos, and Anglos seemed to share more linguistic and cultural common ground than they had when I was a child. On the other hand, the material and symbolic boundaries that separated them were becoming more explicit, self-conscious, and openly defended. The story unfolding in Taos was just one micro version of the greater story playing out all over the modern world: the agonistic, seemingly unstoppable advance of capitalism. I hoped that greater Taos (but not the pueblo!) would be the one place I could do nonintrusive ethnographic research. For a moment, I even believed that the political and moral dilemmas encountered in Mexico would be less acute at home.

Home Field

Anthropologists traditionally defined "the field" in opposition to "home." The rationale for ethnographic fieldwork in small-scale exotic cultures held that being an outsider fostered objectivity and that simpler social structures were more clearly discernible than the complex ones anthropologists come from. Postmodern critics now question the role and nature of fieldwork as well as the implicit field/home dichotomy. They reconfigure the "field" as a disciplinary habitus or "cluster of *embodied* dispositions and practices" rather than as a distant and exotic place where difference is found (Clifford 1997b, 202, 199; Gupta and Ferguson 1997b). Postexoticist anthropology defines the field as more a matter of "shifting sites" than of "bounded places" and envisions the pursuit of anthropological knowledge as "a form of situated intervention," working, sometimes, in political alliance with communities of study as well as of action (Gupta and Ferguson 1997b, 38–39). Feminists have led the way in deconstructing the "native," as in "native anthropologist" (Narayan 1993), arguing that "halfie" ethnography works against cultural objectification (Abu-Lughod 1991); explaining "homework" as a struggle that simultaneously betrays and empowers (Visweswaran 1994) or as a way to gather information on which to base one's moral choices as a citizen (Williams 1995); and proposing that the excluded, invisible status of the "virtual" ethnographer working at home is best suited to the practical task of "retooling anthropology" (Weston 1997).

These new perspectives helped name my need to understand the local as part of global process; they vindicated my inalienable sense of alienation inside the ivory tower and illuminated the uneasy path of "outsider within" through home/field on the one hand and academe on the other (Weston 1997, 178, citing Collins 1990). My study of Taos investigates the place that has shaped me and others so that I may communicate my understanding to one or more communities of interest, and together we can create an intervention against the prevailing order of things as it continues to unfold. The problems that animate me are shared by others of the native as well as the anthropological variety. To put it another way, they are mutual problems, or problems of mutual interest—to which we bring a range of practical and theoretical perspectives. In coming home to the field, I seek an inner ground where the organic and the traditional intellectual come together and where ethnographic skill can serve the practical needs of a mobilized community of action, as well as theoretical inquiry in a discipline.

Nevertheless, the heresy of studying my hometown would consign me, I knew, to the margins of anthropology. Once given into, however, this endeavor became a profound intellectual luxury that even now holds my attention. My first, most extended period of fieldwork, in the early 1980s, lasted about twenty-six months. Thereafter, I devoted summers, term breaks, and sabbaticals to research in and around the town of Taos. Fieldwork involved interviews, photography, and participant observation across a range of public and private events, including all town and county government, political, and other organizational meetings, rituals, civic celebrations, and myriad social/cultural occasions. I examined five decades of tax rolls and newspaper archives and collected maps, reports, publications, photographs, and other documents. The newspaper archives and tax rolls were housed in the county courthouse, where I spent many months of "deep hanging out": getting to know staff, officials, and those who passed through their doors, listening to daily gossip, banter, and jokes. Here beat the political pulse of Taos. I watched and got drawn into grassroots mobilizations by coalitions of natives and newcomers against escalating resort and associated developments that polluted a river, promoted water right transfers, and transformed rural agricultural patterns of resource ownership and use.

Several projects yielded publications over the years; these dealt with interethnic relations, tourism and art, ritual, and conflict over land-water issues (Rodríguez 1987, 1989, 1990a, 1990b, 1992, 1994, 1997, 1998, 2001, 2002, 2003, 2007, 2011). The first research phase focused on interethnic relations and social change from 1930 to 1980, and from this baseline flowed other studies. Later projects arose out of events and phenomena that compelled deeper investigation. Two were about the Matachines Dance and the Taos summer fiesta, both ritual traditions that symbolically encapsulate aspects of the region's deep colonial structure, evoking individual and collective expressions of identity and attachment to place.

My status as a coyote town daughter, whose paternal family was genealogically "wired in" to the Hispano-Mexicano community, gave me entrée to some but not all sectors of Taos society. Insider and outsider anthropologists alike can never expect otherwise, because positionality structures all social access and interaction. Native familiarity helps enormously, but privileged insight often carries a blind spot. Every door that swings open in a divided and polarized community causes another to slam shut, especially for a displaced local who has become identified with particular causes. I tried to maintain an appearance of objectivity, impartiality, and detachment, but no one was fooled. This gave me an inside track with some parties but made it harder to gain access to their adversaries. More than once, it took me years of humble supplication, met with stinging rejection, before a key individual would grant me an interview.

Acequia, or traditional community irrigation associations, around northern New Mexico began asking me to do research and provide expert testimony on their behalf for water-right transfer cases. I felt honored to be asked and was glad to help; then there was no turning back. A large federation of acequia associations in the Taos basin commissioned me to conduct an ethnographic study of water sharing and related cultural meanings and practices. The acequia project became a culmination of my fieldwork, because it was community initiated, collaborative, and perforce brought me full circle to the kind of behavioral invisibility my father had preached so long ago. It was one component of a larger multidisciplinary effort to document, for a court of law, historical and contemporary irrigation practices on local river systems. The circumstance surrounding the protracted, pretrial phases of the Taos Pueblo water-rights adjudication, or Abeyta, case, required me to carry out the research in strict confidentiality, with no public disclosure of my findings and no publication. The price for privileged access to the community of study was silence, invisibility, and the appearance of mysteriously unproductive research. Ultimately, this glacially slow and overwhelmingly complex case was resolved in a negotiated settlement between the parties (Taos Pueblo, the Taos Valley Acequia Association, the Town of Taos, and others) that took seventeen tortuous years to reach. At last I received permission to speak publicly and publish articles and a book based on the project.

Mutuality is selective and yet fluid over time, an evolving relationship with communities of interest that I grew into as my work matured. Ethnography's "continuous dialectical tacking" between "experience-near," or native, and "experience-distant," or external perspectives (Geertz 1983a, 57–58, 69), sometimes poses a challenge to mutuality. A crisis of mutuality can arise also when circumstances polarize one's dual or multiple accountabilities. The contradiction at the heart of ethnographic practice must be constantly negotiated rather than resolved once and for all. My publications are for interested New Mexicans and other nonacademics as much as they are for scholars, and although they have grown increasingly clear and accessible, mostly the latter read them. Having now retired, I continue to spend time in Taos and to join participatory and collaborative projects—much more freely and fully than before—with acequia activists and researchers around the state.

Mutuality, Method, and Pedagogy

The achievement and degree of mutuality in ethnographic practice depends on how the research questions are generated and by whom. Interesting and important questions are formulated every day in academe without anyone directly consulting the populations they concern. Typically, subjects are consulted later, as required by the IRB process, based on a biomedical model. This model can even decree that prior consultation with the population of study compromises objectivity, an attitude inimical to much ethnographic—not to mention decolonized, dialogical, collaborative, and participatory—social research. I do not wish to argue that all anthropology should follow a mutual paradigm or that nonmutual research should cease. Nor do I claim that all "native" or "home" ethnography is necessarily mutual, or vice versa. The mutuality continuum is a function of method, attitude, and ethics: from initial formulation of a research question and objective through the collection, analysis, write-up, and dissemination of data. Although mutuality seems most compatible with inductive, qualitative approaches, we must also consider whether and how to incorporate it into deductive and quantitative research.

After thirty years of teaching anthropology in one college and two universities (University of California, Los Angeles and University of New Mexico), I have concluded that the traditional pedagogical techniques of lecture and seminar promote, and indeed model, asymmetrical, top-down, extractive, nonmutual social research. Why would they not? Conventional institutional pedagogy, from the first grade through college, employs what critical popular educators call the "banking" method of knowledge transmission, in which teachers deposit knowledge or wisdom in the minds of students who passively receive it (Shor and Freire 1987). As students progress upward through the grades, educators endeavor to cultivate "critical thinking" and the development of analytic skills by enabling active engagement with the subject matter. Graduate school imparts theory, technique, and mastery of content, with the dissertation the ultimate professionalizing exercise of designing, executing, analyzing, and writing up original research. Formulation of the research problem and objective takes place safely within the confines of the institution and academic department, under the oversight of one's doctoral committee. Applied and public anthropology programs promote consultation, cooperation, and collaboration with communities of study, but by definition, the successful completion of any academic course requires submission of a properly formatted written thesis or report within an allotted time frame. One's primary master must always be the institution that confers and affirms professional standing.

Professorship, not to mention graduate study, at an institution of higher learning typically impedes a high degree of mutuality in one's research. Several features of academic life militate against participatory research with an external or "public" community of interest. Apart from problem/objective formulation and the constant pressure to "publish or perish," the greatest deterrent to mutual participatory research is the academic calendar itself. A rigid academic schedule does not mesh easily—or perhaps at all—with the temporal rhythms and practical concerns of community or citizen-researcher-activist coparticipants caught up in the situation they seek to address. It is ironic that the very institution that fosters a life of the mind and enables free inquiry can also come to curtail them.

Some consider participatory research to be about action, not about investigation or the pursuit of "pure" science, knowledge for the sake of knowledge. But is science a purposeless endeavor? To what end do we seek to understand the world? Who is motivated to pursue questions that have no bearing on the conditions of our lives? Apart from the narrow strictures of academia and the colonial legacy of top-down extractive research, anthropology—especially ethnography—is well suited to participatory action research on a problem or topic of mutual interest with a self-identified community of coparticipants. Such interest can be simultaneously practical and theoretical, because it transcends the antiquated theory/praxis or theoretical/applied dichotomy. The full mutual approach may become a kind of guerilla anthropology in that the first master is the research community or team itself. In submitting to this process, the anthropologist must unlearn or relinquish much of what academia has taught her. The second, inner master remains the theory building intrinsic to sociocultural anthropology as a critical endeavor. Such pursuit is never neutral. I do not mean to imply that any of this is easy, but I do consider it possible and worth attempting.

Chapter 4

"If You Want to Go Fast, Go Alone. If You Want to Go Far, Go Together"

Yup'ik Elders Working Together with One Mind

Ann Fienup-Riordan

For the past forty years, I have worked as an anthropologist in southwest Alaska. Perhaps the happiest have been the last fifteen, when I have been working with the Calista Elders Council (CEC), a nonprofit organization representing the 1,900 Yup'ik tradition bearers of southwest Alaska. CEC is the primary heritage organization in the Yukon-Kuskokwim delta region, an area the size of Kansas and the homeland for more than 23,000 Yup'ik people, 14,000 of whom speak the Yup'ik language. Our organization is small. Mark John is CEC's executive director, Alice Rearden is our principal translator, and I am their anthropologist.

Mark, Alice, and I have worked together on a variety of CEC projects, all of which were initiated by CEC's board of elders. The nine Yup'ik-speaking men on the board, representing villages throughout the region, actively support the documentation and sharing of their oral traditions, which they view as possessing continued value in today's world.

CEC's primary information-gathering tool has been the topic-specific gathering. The CEC pioneered this format working with elders between 2000 and 2005 during a major Yup'ik knowledge project funded by the National Science Foundation's (NSF) Arctic Social Science program. We found that meeting with small groups of elder experts, accompanied by younger community members, for two- and three-day gatherings devoted to a specific set of

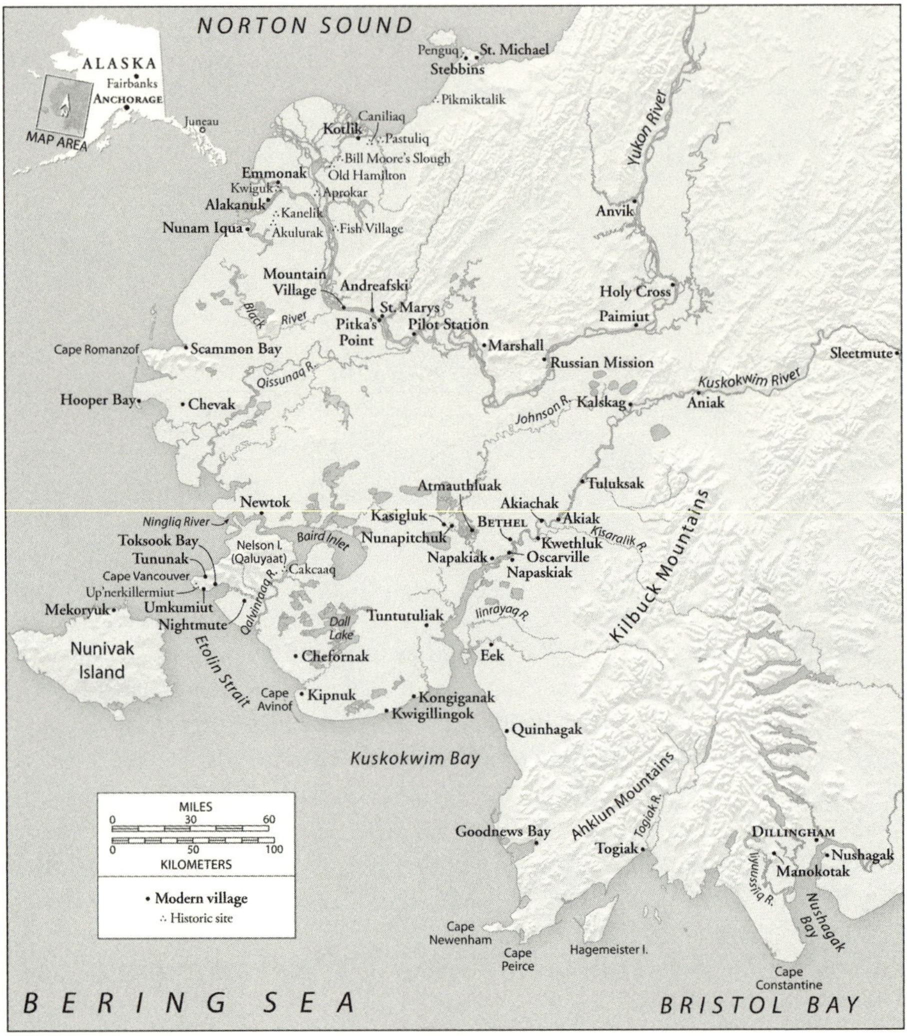

Figure 1. Map of the Yukon-Kuskokwim delta region, 2010. Cartography by Patrick Jankanish.

questions, was an effective and rewarding way of addressing topics. We use the term *gathering* to describe these open-ended exchanges between generations as opposed to the term *meetings*, which are more often viewed as goal-oriented, decision-making events. Gatherings are also unlike interviews, during which elders answer questions posed by those who often do not al-

Figure 2. Mark John and Alice Rearden (center) looking over archival photos with Barbara Joe of Alakanuk (left) and Maryann Andrews of Emmonak (right) during an elders' gathering in Anchorage, April 2012. Photograph by Ann Fienup-Riordan.

ready hold the knowledge they seek. Gatherings (like academic symposia) encourage elders to speak among their peers at the highest level. John Phillip (October 2006:284)[1] of Kongiganak observed during one gathering: "Hearing the story you just told, I learned what I didn't know. As we are sitting here one explains what we did not know, while another one explains something else. It is like we are still learning."

Our gatherings always take place in the Yup'ik language, which Mark says I speak well enough to beg for food. Alice Rearden then creates detailed transcripts of each gathering, and we work together to turn these into bilingual publications and accompanying English texts. It is important to emphasize that these gatherings build on each other, and long and careful listening provides unique perspectives on Yup'ik knowledge. Over the past ten years, CEC has hosted dozens of gatherings, resulting in more than eight hundred hours of recordings and fifteen thousand pages of transcripts.

Finally, in gatherings, elders teach not just facts; they teach listeners how

Figure 3. Elders and youth discuss place names during a CEC gathering in the Chefornak community hall, March 2007. Photograph by Ann Fienup-Riordan.

to learn. They share not only what they know but how they know it and why they believe it is important to remember. CEC staff and Yup'ik community members value topic-specific gatherings not merely as tools for documentation but also as contexts of cultural transmission. The gatherings themselves are meaningful events that enrich lives locally at the same time that their documentation has the potential to increase cross-cultural understanding globally. Gatherings are both very social and very spiritual experiences, with prayers, thoughts of the sick and dying, remembrances of ancestors, and expressions of concern for today's young people. During one gathering, Camilius Tulik (March 2007:596) of Nightmute declared: "Your work here causes one to be grateful. It seems like for the sake of our children and grandchildren, we've revealed those things that were out of their reach."

Qanruyutet/Wise Words

The Calista Elders Council's early efforts were devoted to documenting the *qanruyutet* (wise words or instructions, from *qaner-*, "to speak") that guided interpersonal relations in southwest Alaska in the not-so-distant past. Our first books—*Wise Words* (Fienup-Riordan 2005a) and its bilingual companion volume, *Yupiit Qanruyutait/Yup'ik Words of Wisdom* (Rearden, Meade, and Fienup-Riordan 2005)—explore the relatively small number of memorable adages elders used to communicate the basic tenets of Yup'ik moral instruction. Elders "thingafied" knowledge for their young listeners, presenting it as something that one could put in one's pocket, take out, even steal, for use later in life. In the past, elders used formal adages and metaphors to objectify complex and essential life lessons, and today they share these same adages to educate listeners of all walks of life, especially their young people.

Much has been written about the importance of observation and practice in learning the techniques necessary to thrive in the subarctic. Less well-known is the importance placed on verbal instruction. The narrative repertoire, including detailed rules for living, was vast, and children could only master it through constant listening. In fact, among Yup'ik people, a stated ideal was that elders speak and young people listen. Elders who did not speak publicly about what they knew, but only shared it privately with their own children, were considered stingy and "jealous." Conversely, children who "failed to pay attention to the speaker's mouth" or left the room before the speaker was done were admonished that they would someday be found dead in the wilderness, "with their teeth gleaming at the end of a snowdrift."

Elders explained every aspect of their lives with reference to these "rules for right living." Many qanruyutet are stylized sayings, often including the phrases "they say," "they said," or "it is told." In Yup'ik, this attribution to an ancestral voice is denoted with the enclitic *-gguq*, used to report what has been said by others if the speaker cannot claim complete authority for his or her statements (Jacobson 1984, 621). For example, "*Ciutek-gguq iinguuk*" ("Ears, they say, are eyes") is shorthand for the admonition that people follow the rules lest they be talked about in other villages and known by strangers for their misdeeds.

The basic tenets of Yup'ik moral instruction comprise multiple memorable phrases, both elegant and picturesque. This is no accident, as elders wanted them spoken and remembered from an early age by everyone. These adages include short, graphic phrases such as "boys are like puppies," "women are death," and "a tongue hurts, even though small." All are considered qanruyutet or *qaneryarat* (words of advice, sayings), like their lengthier counterparts. Nick Andrew (November 2000:124) of Marshall noted that elders tried to keep admonishments short: "When a person hears an instruction that is not long, it sticks inside the head." In her description of the adage "an idle person gets approval from sloth," Theresa Moses (June 1995:64) of Toksook Bay noted, "These were some of the things they told us to get our attention."

Though many elders remain committed to sharing qanruyutet, opportunities to do so diminish with each passing year. Contemporary elders are the last to have grown to adulthood in *qasgit* (communal men's houses) where the men and boys of a community lived and worked together, an arrangement since replaced by single-family dwellings and schools. In the qasgi, they received oral instructions that they continue to view as the moral foundation of a properly lived life. Paul Kiunya (May 2003:93) of Kipnuk recalled: "When I was old enough to go to the qasgi my mother would say, 'Okay, go over to the qasgi and try to steal something.' She apparently meant that when I listened to men teaching, though the instructor wasn't talking directly to me, if I learned something, it would be something that would help me for the rest of my life."

Raised on Nelson Island, Mark John (April 2001:78) testified that the reason for educating young people on qanruyutet is far from academic. Such knowledge, he believes, can change their lives. He, too, spoke from personal experience, recalling how his grandmother's words had given him strength later in life. Frank Andrew (September 2000:13) of Kwigillingok agreed that qanruyutet are the tools that can change their world: "Qanruyutet change people's behavior. All of our material belongings can be fixed with our arms. But a person's nature can only be fixed by qanruyutet." John Phillip (March 2000:17) echoed this view of the instrumental value of qanruyutet: "The teachings are like something that pushes one to a good life. Those who listen and apply the teachings will live good lives."

Ellavut/Our Yup'ik World and Weather

Just as qanruyutet guided relations among humans, they guided humans' relations with the world around them. And just as elders "suffer" over the fact that their young people lack knowledge of qanruyutet that could help them care for one another, they regret that youth lack knowledge of qanruyutet that can keep them safe in a sentient world. In 2006, funded by the National Science Foundation's Bering Ecosystem Study Program (BEST), the Calista Elders Council set to work with elders from five Nelson Island communities to understand these connections, and what we learned has been published as *Ellavut/Our Yup'ik World and Weather: Continuity and Change on the Bering Sea Coast*, which Alice and I coauthored (Fienup-Riordan and Readen 2012).

Our work with Nelson Islanders was not conceived of as a study of climate change. Rather, elders initiated these conversations to teach their youth not merely the physical features of land and sea but ways in which one's actions elicit reactions in a responsive world. Paul Tunuchuk (March 2007:216) of Chefornak shared: "They mention that we must treat our world with care and respect, but these days, it's as though the land has become a dumping ground. What will become of us if we don't treat *ella* with care?"

Among the richest, most evocative words in the Yup'ik language, *ella* can be translated as "weather," "world," "universe," or "awareness," depending on context. Contemporary Yupiit may use *ella* to denote "atmosphere," "environment,"

Figure 4. Simeon Agnus points out a land feature near Arayakcaaq at the mouth of the Qalvinraaq River, July 2007. Michael John sits to his right and Theresa Abraham to his left. Photograph by Ann Fienup-Riordan.

and "climate." Clearly, the Western concept of an ecosystem as an integrated system is not new to Yup'ik people.[2] By some accounts, *Ellam Yua*, the Person of the Universe, watches the world with boundless sight, observing transgressions and meting out punishment. It is not simply that the universe is aware but that universe and awareness are synonymous.

Throughout our discussions, elders have been eloquent not only in what they say but also in how they say it. The most striking feature of our conversations is the integrated way in which information is shared. For example, elders do not distinguish between human impacts on the environment, including the effects of commercial fishing or overhunting, and the "natural" effects of climate change. During recent gatherings on weather, at least one elder always repeated the well-known *qanruyun*, "The world, they say, is changing, following its people." This adage captures the Yup'ik view that environmental change is directly related not just to human action—overfishing, burning fossil fuels—but to human *interaction*. To solve the problems of global warming, elders maintain, we need to do more than change our actions by reducing by-catch and carbon emissions: we need to correct our fellow humans. Elders encourage young people to pay attention to qanruyutet, believing that if their values improve, correct actions will follow.

Finally, elders do not dissociate themselves from observed changes in their homeland but accept personal responsibility. They relate the negative impacts of change to their failure to instruct their younger generation in proper behavior. Now, they say, is the time to reverse this trend. John Eric (January 2007:26) of Chefornak remarked, "We must talk to them, to delay them from becoming like dogs." Elders view our work together as much more than passive documentation of change; they see it as part of an active solution.

Sharing Knowledge on the Web

Building on our work with Nelson Islanders, in 2011, the Calista Elders Council began an environmental knowledge project, also funded by the National Science Foundation, focusing on four Yukon delta communities 150 miles north of Nelson Island (see figure 5). Activities included both community gatherings and traveling with elders on the land. Natural scientists accompanied us on our trips and attended village gatherings, both to share their work and to have an opportunity to listen to the elders' perspectives on changes in sea ice, snow, and weather patterns. Local residents are also carrying out weather and sea ice observations.

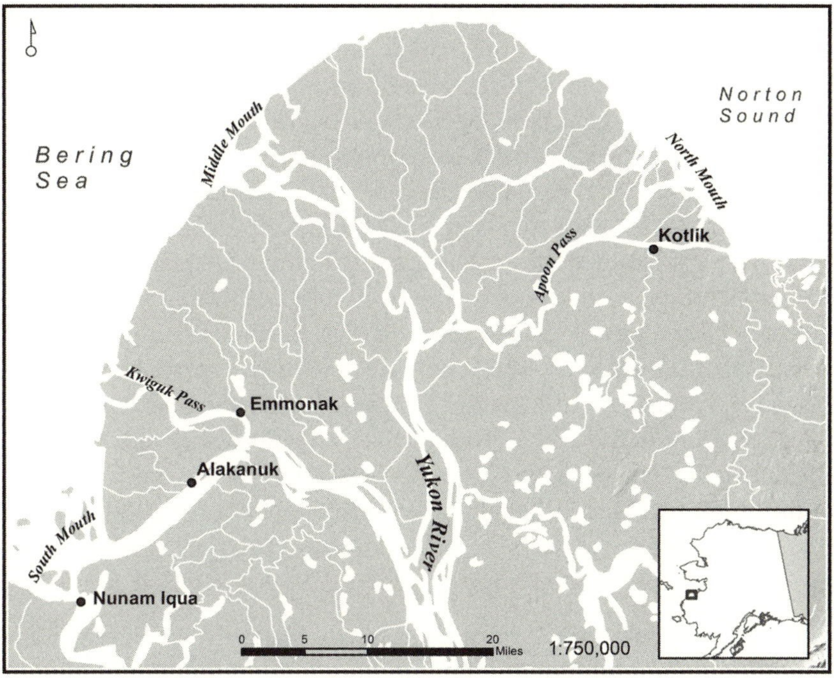

Figure 5. Lower Yukon communities, 2011. Cartography by Nicole Braem, Alaska Department of Fish and Game, Division of Subsistence.

Our work on the lower Yukon has gone beyond all expectations in revealing still vital and meaningful relations between local people and their coastal homes. Yukon elders, like their Nelson Island counterparts, are dedicated to documenting traditional knowledge, especially place names. As Denis Shelden (August 2011:272) of Alakanuk said, "If our young people especially forget about the land and the names and the hunting places and those rivers, it's like they will lose some of their body parts. But if they learn more about their identity, their minds will be stronger." Lawrence Edmund (August 2011:271) of Alakanuk agreed: "When they travel [without knowing place names], it's like they are lost [in a storm]." Unlike Nelson Island, where the majority of names are attached to points and historic sites, in the Yukon, names are focused on routes, in what Emmonak resident Ray Waska described as the "highway of puzzles" that comprises the delta. Moreover, whereas Nelson Island elders want young people to learn the Yup'ik names for places before they are forgotten, Yukon elders fear the new English names and nicknames youth are attaching to the old places, names like Ukulele and KK Slough for *Yuuqernarli* and *Qerqertulli*, which they cannot pronounce. Young men use these names freely on the VHF radio, and elders hear them with dismay. Whereas for elders all places have names, young people know few places well. Today, the elders say, "they don't recognize places but only bump into things" (Mike Andrews, March 2011:580). According to Alakanuk elder Fred Augustine (March 2011:1042), good map work will save lives.

Following work on the lower Yukon in 2011, the CEC staff has focused on translating elders' narratives as well as on transferring the place-name information we recorded to ArcGIS, a geographic information system for working with maps. The question before us is how best to share what we have learned. In January 2012, our project steering committee—including elders and representatives from twelve coastal communities—met in Bethel with CEC staff and Chris McNeave of the Exchange for Local Observations and Knowledge of the Arctic (ELOKA, based at the National Snow and Ice Data Center in

Figure 6. Lawrence Edmund, Mark John, and Denis Shelden at Akuluraq. Photograph by Ann Fienup-Riordan.

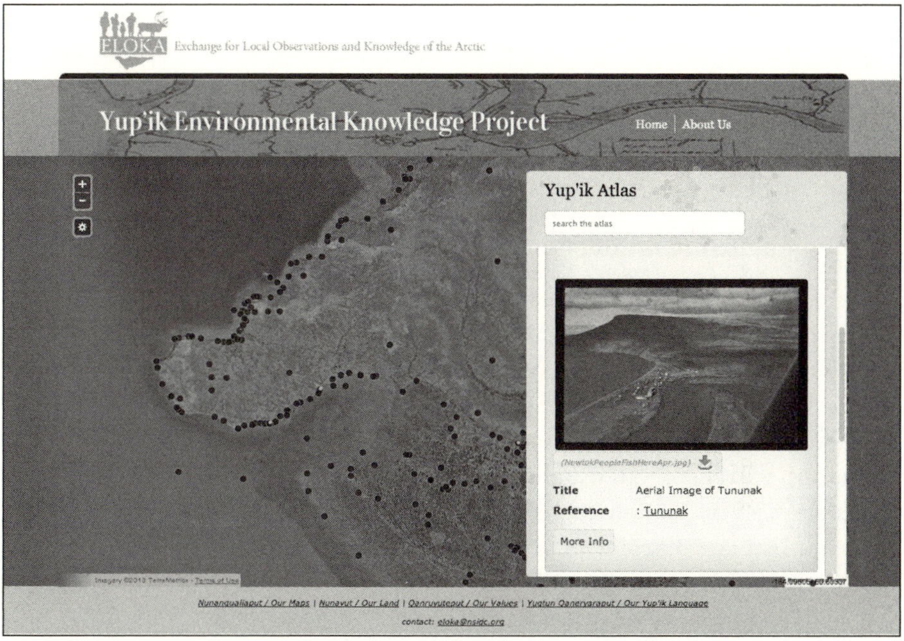

Figure 7. ELOKA website home page. The site is now available at http://eloka-arctic.org/communities/yupik/. Screen capture by Chris McNeave, ELOKA.

Boulder, Colorado), to discuss creating a place-based "Yup'ik Environmental Knowledge Project" website to link separate mapping efforts in these communities into a comprehensive map web service covering two hundred miles of Bering Sea coastline.

During our meeting, Chris showed our group how such a website might look, as well as the kinds of information that could be linked to each mapped location—bilingual texts, photographs, video footage, and audio recordings. The group voted unanimously for open and free access to their website, arguing eloquently for the importance of making their history and traditions available to all. Today, Yup'ik young people—the elders' primary audience—are spread throughout the globe. Moreover, elders believe that increased respect for their view of the world by non-Natives can only be gained from a deeper understanding of what they share.

Elders hope that young people will use the site to learn about their history, but they are well aware of the limits of sharing knowledge on the web. Noah

Andrew of Kwigillingok spoke of mapping efforts in his community, where elders not only worked with youth in schools but took them out on the land to show them the places they spoke about. All agreed that although a website is no substitute for such interactions, insofar as it engages youth, it is of value.

Yukon elders, like those in other coastal communities, are also much less concerned with potential misuse of the information shared than with the consequences for young people of ignorance. For example, part of our discussion concerned how accurately to present place-name information. The database includes cemetery and historic site locations. Some regional landowners are concerned that a website that reveals such locations could potentially result in looting or damage to particular sites. Yup'ik group members, however, were much more concerned with the consequences of people *not* knowing site locations than with the dangers of knowing them. Their fear is that graves, especially, will be forgotten and thus potentially disrespected. The importance people place on acknowledging these past relations led directly to their consensus that our mapping efforts accurately display as much information as possible.

Last, group members suggested that once we have worked with ELOKA to design the site, Yup'ik student interns, working with CEC staff, should be the ones to add to and maintain its content. Over the past year, all our geographic information system (GIS) place-name work has been done by Yup'ik engineering student Amy Berlin, who also traveled with us on the Yukon, listening to the elders whose history she is helping to transfer to a map.

As we continue working in communities with elders and youth, the question also arises concerning to what extent recording tools such as video cameras and digital recorders should be put in the hands of youth so they can do their own documentation. During CEC gatherings, elders have preferred to have youth listen while CEC staff document proceedings. During summer fieldwork in Kotlik, however, Isidore Hunt's granddaughter used her smartphone to record the place names he shared. By trip's end, she put away her phone and he tested her. She knew the names. It has always been traditional for Yup'ik people to use the best available technology. That elders not only support using new technologies to communicate a lived tradition but also approve young people using these technologies to "steal knowledge" in innovative ways should come as no surprise.

During a recent trip with Nelson Island elders to work in museum collections in Washington, D.C., we were accompanied by a Yup'ik college student, Abby Moses, who helped with social media, letting people back home see in real time what we were seeing. Hurricane Sandy left us stranded in our hotel rooms for several days, and Abby used the time to create the one-minute YouTube hit "Yup'ik elders gang," communicating the fun we were having in ways no text or photo ever could. Elders take their role as teachers seriously, but not without humor and grace.

The Paradox of Talking on the Page

Yup'ik elders with whom we work are fluent in their Native language, and they were privileged to hear stories from their parents and grandparents as part of an oral tradition thousands of years old. In their article "The Paradox of Talking on the Page," Tlingit scholars Nora and Richard Dauenhauer (1999) aptly compare this vibrant narrative tradition to the salmon running upriver and berries growing on the tundra—an abundance with the power to sustain us. But contemporary Yup'ik elders recognize that their younger generation is moving away from the rivers and tundra. It is for their sakes the elders support sharing knowledge in new ways.

Although the Yup'ik language remains strong in coastal and lower Kuskokwim communities (with more than 14,000 first-language speakers), language loss has been severe in Yukon and middle Kuskokwim villages, where few young people are fluent speakers. Golga Effemka (January 2006:139) of Sleetmute sadly declared: "Upriver they don't comprehend in Yup'ik but only in English. It's because we elders don't teach them. When our parents raised us, they spoke to us in Yup'ik. They no longer speak [in Yup'ik] nowadays. And when speaking to them [in English], some get angry because they can't speak in Yup'ik." Although Yup'ik is second only to Navajo in numbers of speakers of an indigenous language in the United States, its long-term survival is far from assured.

"Much of great importance is lost and added in translation," linguist A. L. Becker (2000, 90) reminds us. The truth of his words captures both the strengths and weaknesses of the bilingual books and websites that CEC has worked to produce over the past decade. Each translated text is at once less than the original telling—devoid of the shapes and sounds of the narrator's voice—and more. Through the double process of translation from Yup'ik to English and from oral to written form, something is inevitably lost. At the same time, readers and viewers gain access to a unique and compelling perspective on the world around them as well as on their place within it.

Calista Elders Council staff and the elders we work with are enthusiastic about both the books we publish and the website under development with ELOKA. They are quick to point out, however, the importance of acknowledging the men and women who have contributed to our work, as well as of ensuring that their communities and youth benefit fully from their contributions. Although sharing knowledge is highly valued, responsibilities attend the process. Stories are not objects to be collected, classified, paginated, and sold for personal profit, and writing them down does not confer ownership. Elders also remind us that words are inherently powerful, with the capacity to create that which they describe. Words have never been used lightly within Yup'ik oral tradition, and CEC staff take seriously the challenge of how best to translate and share these oral traditions in written form.

One important issue is how much interpretation to include with bilingual accounts. All recognize that the context of a narrative is essential to grasping its meaning and that many non-Yup'ik and younger Yup'ik readers require some cultural and linguistic information to fully appreciate what is shared. Yup'ik elders, however, are reluctant to assign a "moral" to their narratives. When asked whether questions were appropriate in storytelling contexts, many said no, that stories should be "just told." Yet, in our topic-specific gatherings, we have found elders ready and willing to answer our questions, especially when these questions show that we have listened to what has gone before.

CEC topic-specific gatherings and work together with the elders out on the land are ultimately shaped by the concerns and choices of individual participants. It is difficult to adequately convey the compassion and loving spirit that shape their accounts. Mark John's father, Paul John, once told me that children should never be talked to harshly, as it blocks their minds and prevents them from learning: "If those who are giving them advice speak with compassion, it would be like giving them strong, healing medicine and would help bring them happiness." We remain deeply grateful for the gifts these elders have given us and their trust that we will treat these gifts responsibly and respectfully and share them in our turn.

The instrumental value of what we do is in the forefront of our work together. The image of the igloo-dwelling Eskimo still smiles out from many a gift-shop window in Alaska. Although few elders directly confront this simpleminded and insidious stereotype, they sense that sharing their detailed narratives strikes its foundations, destabilizes it, and sends it crumbling down. Their contemporary narrative references to the past, both on the web and on the printed page, are active efforts to shape the future—a future in which they believe Yup'ik knowledge should be recognized and valued.

The Value of Working Together

I have briefly described what we do, how we do it, and why. I will conclude with the potential of this way of working to inform Western science in meaningful ways. Our work on Nelson Island was funded by NSF as part of a larger, integrated Bering Sea Project, funded jointly by NSF and the North Pacific Research Board. Although the primary concern of the Bering Sea Project was oceanographic, a significant effort was made to understand the impacts on coastal communities of changes in the eastern Bering Sea.

In my work with the Calista Elders Council, my primary role is facilitating community-driven projects. In the Bering Sea Project, however, I also work as an anthropologist and social scientist. Within CEC, I never view my voice as authoritative in the old pith-helmet–wearing anthropological sense, but given my background and training, I find it important to look for connections between Yup'ik and non-Yup'ik knowledge and for how the two ways of knowing can inform each other. I have come to the following conclusions:

1. *There are many fruitful connections between Yup'ik knowledge and Western science.* My goal for many years now has been to use Western science to better understand Yup'ik knowledge. Working with CEC, we have sought out natural scientists to help us answer questions raised by what elders share. Yet, as we have become better known, scientists are starting to come to us with questions. In fact, beginning in 2011, CEC has employed topic-specific gatherings to bring together elders and natural scientists from the Alaska Geophysical Institute in CEC's most recent environmental knowledge project to approach collectively topics such as changes in sea ice, snow, and weather patterns. We are finding that the use of topic-specific gatherings is both an effective and a culturally appropriate forum for sharing information, "teaching listeners how to learn," and demonstrating the embeddedness of knowledge systems. Moreover, like their Yup'ik partners, participating scientists have indicated that they value these gatherings not only for the knowledge shared but also for the relationships fostered among knowledge holders.

2. *One excellent way to understand the connections between Yup'ik and Western knowledge is through collaborations with communities, and this takes time.* I am reminded of the proverb "If you want to go fast, go alone. If you

want to go far, go together." These deep collaborations go beyond consultation and cooperation to the true co-conceptualizations of knowledge. My advice to both young anthropologists and to natural scientists is to begin to work with a community and, if you can, stay with them and follow their lead. You will be richly rewarded.

3. *Along with these connections, it is important to recognize and respect profound differences between worldviews.* In documenting Yup'ik knowledge, we work hard to ensure that the direct voice of individual elders always comes through. One young man visiting our Yup'ik science exhibit in 2008 asked me why I did not do anthropology anymore. He was referring to my use of quoted statements from elders throughout the exhibition to tell the story. My short response to his query was, "Why should I rephrase Yup'ik knowledge when elders can express it better than I ever could?" In fact, I carefully crafted the exhibition text to communicate that knowledge of the elders that was based on personal experience. The anthropologist does have a role to play, but not as expert: as translator, editor, and good listener.

Yup'ik knowledge and Western science operate with different paradigms—the latter largely quantitative and generalizing and the former intensely observational, holistic, and incorporating a spiritual dimension into interpretation. One technique we have developed as a way of sharing Yup'ik knowledge is to always do two books: one in English for the general audience and a bilingual companion volume (without index) in which quoted statements from individual elders are contextualized and shared at length.[3] Our most recent bilingual book, *Qaluyaarmiuni Nunamtenek Qanemciput/Our Nelson Island Stories* (Rearden and Fienup-Riordan 2011), won a 2012 Before Columbus Foundation American Book Award, a literary award recognizing both the eloquence of the elders' oratory and the power of Alice's translations. My role as editor, and what in many places is the new, challenging, and extremely important work of anthropology, was well described in a review of the book appearing in *Arctic*, in which Elizabeth Marino wrote:

> This book likewise represents an operational paradigm of anthropological research that is new, though it has often received lip service: that is, a serious effort at the co-creation of knowledge by academic researchers and Alaska Native research participants and communities. The research methods, presentation of content, and authorship, and publication itself (by the Calista Elders Council), all speak to this partnership. In this way, this book provides an important example of how

> Alaska Native communities can take the lead in research projects and how academic researchers can act as important facilitators for these projects. A great compliment to Fienup-Riordan throughout this book is her ability to do what must have been significant amounts of work and then get out of the way. (Marino 2012)

I firmly believe that the Yup'ik view of the world has independent, standalone value, not just insofar as it informs Western science. As anthropologist Julie Cruikshank (2005, 9) points out, "local knowledge has become a common-sense term, couched in acronyms like TEK (traditional ecological knowledge) or IK (indigenous knowledge), gaining new visibility in management science studies, but too often depicted as static, timeless, and hermetically sealed." In fact, Yup'ik knowledge is dynamic, changing, and socially situated, with continuing value in today's world.

Our experience is that elders and knowledge holders want to collaborate with researchers, as they do in topic-specific gatherings, to better understand their past and present and so inform their future. The multiple viewpoints expressed in these contexts are critical for understanding this complex contemporary situation. To gain indigenous observations and information that will inform natural science research, so-called local and traditional knowledge (LTK) components are increasingly added to natural science studies. Yet no oceanographer would try to understand the Bering Sea ecosystem as a whole without considering the biology of individual species and their links to other organisms. How can we then expect to understand coastal communities through LTK in isolation, without a fuller understanding of the historical and cultural context of the contemporary situation?

As noted, in gatherings Yup'ik elders are not just trying to *say*, but to *do* something. They know they possess a narrative tradition and knowledge system second to none, and they want others to give it the respect it deserves. Nelson Island leader Paul John (April 2009:32) stated that our documentation efforts can help provide Yup'ik young people with the tools they need to gain respect comparable to that earned by President Obama: "If white people see these books, they will think, 'These Yup'ik people evidently are knowledgeable about things and know how to take care of their affairs independently through their traditional way of life.' Like the African American who has become president, our young people will be able to carry out their desire to independently practice their way of living. These [books] will prepare our younger generation for the time when they will start to take care of their own affairs."

If we really want to understand Yup'ik community vulnerability and sustainability today, it is not sufficient to say that changes are taking place, even rapid change. We need to understand how community members interpret these changes—not just *what* is occurring but *why* people believe it to be so; not just what social and economic circumstances are in flux but how these situations are perceived. Local knowledge taken out of context cannot provide such an understanding. Long-term collaborations with communities, combining our insights and observations, can help us move in that direction.

PART II

ROOTS

Chapter 5

The Invisibility of Diasporic Capital and Multiply Migrant Creativity

Parminder Bhachu

In India today, *jugaad* is a buzzword of economic success. In Hindi (and also Punjabi), it denotes "an innovative fix; an improvised solution born from ingenuity and cleverness . . . quite simply a unique way of thinking and acting in response to challenges; it is a gutsy art of spotting opportunities in the most adverse circumstances and resourcefully improvising solutions using simple means . . . *doing more with less*" (Radjou, Prabhu, and Ahuja 2012, 4). Yet jugaad as "frugal engineering" has a specifically Punjabi origin. "Many years ago, innovative Punjabis mounted a diesel irrigation pump on a steel frame with wheels creating a vehicle they called *jugaad*. It was ultra-cheap. . . . Over time, *jugaad* came to mean grassroots innovation to overcome any constraint" (Aiyar 2010).

In this chapter, I focus on the ability to create the new without knowing what the contours of that creation will be. This is a central feature of Punjabi diaspora sensibilities as immigrants tread new terrain by dialogically responding to the moment as it transpires and collaboratively negotiating the next move. The experience of exploring territories that are unknown in advance fosters a powerful aesthetic among diasporic peoples, one involving both discovery and skill.

Using the past and present global Punjabi Indian diaspora as my lens, I will examine deep-rooted sensibilities and aesthetics that have been honed in pioneering settings over a long period. I focus on supremely durable diasporic capital that has been in the making for centuries, especially on those artisanal and craft skills that continue to have enormous generative power in many twenty-first-century arenas. I show that diasporic aesthetics and collaborative sensibilities are aspects of a deeply rooted legacy transmitted transgenerationally to progeny, who may in turn deploy it in new contexts. I examine particular traditions of craft—ways of doing and making—and an improvisational aesthetic that are rooted in the homeland and have been rerouted, reinvented, and reimagined in successive diasporas and multiple individual migrations. Thus technical and artisanal diasporic capital is central to my argument.

Edward Said reminds us that the starting point of critical engagement is the consciousness of what one is, of "knowing thyself," and of being cognizant of the historical processes that have deposited in us, to quote Antonio Gramsci's *Prison Notebooks*, "an infinity of traces . . . without leaving an inventory" (Said 1979, 25). Said underscores Gramsci's injunction to actively compile inventories of these traces that history and biography deposit. To accomplish this for diasporic communities, we must identify those continuities, sensibilities, and aesthetics developed in the past that remain significant for diasporic cultural values and production in the present. To do this, I will traverse a wide-ranging historical canvas, one that includes the experiences and mutualities of my own family members.

Enduring Diasporic Capital

Diasporic capital is a product of movement and marginality; class capital mostly emerges from staying put for generations. Both are generationally transmitted and reproduce themselves durably. The creative reach of diasporic capital has increased dramatically in recent decades as a result of hyperconnection and of the sophisticated ways in which the progeny of migrants are coming of age in a time when Old Europe and the United States are declining and the transnational influence of diasporic peoples is rising. Although much of the attention to cultural capital in general originated with Pierre Bourdieu's influential conceptualization of the social, economic, and cultural capital that undergirds class domination (1984, 66–69), the diasporic manifestation of generationally transmitted cultural capital has been underappreciated. This is a capital that arises with and grows through transnational movements and runs parallel to established territorially based class capital. This capital is becoming more powerful than ever as contemporary globalization increases its creative reach. I will demonstrate how this innovative creativity of diasporic peoples has emerged not all of a sudden but from origins in the locales from and through which they migrated. Their skill bases were developed in different sites and over several generations, as people improvised to recreate their lives in new contexts and built the infrastructure of pioneering communities.

People in the diaspora transformed the older cultural and social capital they inherited as they seized opportunities and then later deployed this legacy in new professions. Their specific cultural capital strongly conditioned their disposition to improvise and invent, thus refashioning the skills of their parents, grandparents, and ancestors. Pierre Bourdieu describes this persistence of *habitus*, or dispositions that reproduce themselves in multifarious ways, as a deeply rooted "spontaneity without consciousness or will" perpetuated in the future. It constitutes an accumulated cultural capital with "infinite capacity for generating products, thoughts, perceptions, expressions and actions—whose limits are set by historically and socially situated conditions of its production"; it indexes the "active presence of the whole past of which it is a product" (Bourdieu 1990, 55–56).

In the twenty-first century, the enduring traditions of diasporic capital have been reimagined in the realms of film, fashion design, architecture, art, science, music, performance, and other arenas (for discussion of the first and second of these, see Bhachu 2003 and 2004). To appreciate this, we need to think about "craft" in new ways that are as relevant to the contemporary world as to the past. I follow Richard Sennett, who suggests that craftsmanship is alive in many domains of life as "an enduring, basic human impulse, the desire to do a job well for its own sake. Craftsmanship cuts a far wider swath than skilled manual labor; it serves a computer programmer, the doctor, and the artist" (Sennett 2008, 9). As Sennett reminds us, "Every good craftsman conducts a dialogue between concrete practices and thinking; this dialogue evolves into sustaining habits, and these habits establish a rhythm between problem solving and problem finding. The relation between hand and head appears in domains seemingly as different as bricklaying, cooking, designing a playground, or playing the cello" (ibid.).

I will show that the deep-rooted artisanal inheritances that developed over many centuries in places of origin and in sites of migration are alive and vibrant in today's global landscapes. In fact, through new conduits of connectivity, they are defining features of the current century. This artisanal diasporic capital has been transnational for the last millennium, but it remains largely invisible to the vast majority of the world, along with many of its current generation of diasporic youth (see Bhachu and Bhattacharyya 2009). In *Dangerous Designs: Asian Women Fashion the Diaspora Economies* (Bhachu 2004), I described innovative fashion entrepreneurs in London's global markets who used this legacy in creating new micromarkets of highly democratized design and style that are mutually improvised and co-constructed, in the moment, with diverse customers. In a later section of this chapter, I will show how these generative legacies and bequests are flourishing in other new ways across a range of technical and cultural fields, including in the work of architect Amarjit Kalsi, artist Bhajan Hunjan, and physicist Tejinder Virdee.

The Punjab Background

Sennett's conceptions of the relationship between hand and head—"making is thinking"—and the use of hands to do a job well resonate with powerful Punjabi sayings about the hand:

hath kul javay: the hand becomes fluent through practice
hath taang hai: the hand is tight and not generous
hath saaf: a clean hand that can work with finesse and clarity
hath waylay nah rahan: hands should not be idle doing nothing
pakka hath: a strong hand (refers to doing a job well)
kaccha hath: a weak hand (a job handled badly, without care)

From the earliest phases of consciousness and socialization, these metaphors are drilled into all of us who are the progeny of Punjabi craft castes, and we are reminded of them on a daily basis. We learn that work done in the past is encoded in hands and gives them the facility to move with fluidity and skill, almost without thought, making appropriate gestures to get things right, to create work of quality and finesse. These bodily practices of the hand produce skill sets and habits of work embodied in the "making of things" with precision and perfection.

The Punjabi artisans I speak of included Tarkhans (carpenters), Lohars (blacksmiths), and Raj (bricklayers). These upwardly mobile groups consolidated in the nineteenth and twentieth centuries as Ramgarhias (Bhachu 1985; McLeod 1974; Saberwal 1990). In rural villages, they were employed by landowning caste patrons as woodworkers and furniture makers; builders of technical equipment, farm implements, armaments, and machinery; and constructors of buildings.

Their skills also included production of the Persian water wheel used for irrigation. "In Punjab it appears to have been in extensive use by the twelfth century, but south of Delhi it was infrequent even in the twentieth" (Saberwal 1990, 97). In the mid-nineteenth century, Baden-Powell observed, "The Persian wheel [is] used in most wells in the Bari Doab . . . and but little used in those parts of the Punjab bordering on Hindustan [Hindi-speaking North India]. . . . Every peg and bit of iron or other material used in making up these implements has its appropriate and distinctive name" (1872, 243, quoted in Saberwal 1990, 97).

Most Punjabi immigrants all over the world are from the Doab, or Doaba region, in the Punjab. Their ancestors were subjects of the Sikh kingdom of Maharaja Ranjit Singh, which included the Doab and was the last independent area of India annexed by the British.

> Ranjit Singh's kingdom [earlier had] achieved self-sufficiency as regards the production of weapons and munitions. . . . In 1810, the *mistries* [master craftsmen] in Punjab were capable of manufacturing flints [for guns]. The government established cannon foundries, gunpowder magazines and manufactories of arms in Lahore and Amritsar. . . . The equipment (matchlock cannons, mortars, howitzers, shots, shells, ammunition, spears, daggers, boots, belts, saddles, tents, etc.) required by the *Dal Khalsa* [Sikh army] was manufactured in the foundries and workshops maintained by the state as well by various private individuals. (Roy 2011, 143)

The kingdom's technological base matched that of the British East India Company, which did not defeat it until the second Sikh war of 1848–1849 (Roy 2011, 164).

British colonial administrators in the later nineteenth century thought highly of the skilled craftsmen of the Punjab, viewing them as enterprising, industrious, and innovative. They were brought to build the colonial infrastructure of the British summer capital in Simla and the main capital, Delhi. "During early British rule, these skills were harnessed to new purposes: making high quality furniture for the British [and] producing cutlery and doing other fine metal work" (Saberwal 1990, 90). Punjabi craftsmen were recruited for the Indian railways, to lay track and build rolling stock, and as engineers and skilled artisans, to build and operate the extensive canal irrigation system of North India, in which the British Empire invested heavily, and develop large tracts of semiarid land. The quality and efficiency of their work also recommended them for migration to build railways in Assam in eastern Indian (Sharma 1996), as well as in East Africa.

Many moved within the subcontinent, from agricultural settings to urban areas including Calcutta, Delhi, Simla, Phagwara, Jalandhar, and other cities. There, late nineteenth and early twentieth-century industrial development attracted them, as did overseas opportunities in British colonies. The demand for their skills removed them from oppressive village caste hierarchies, in which upward mobility was restricted. Saberwal (1990) argues that they benefited from the status dissonance that migration to Indian cities and overseas produced, as their artisanal and craft skills flourished in new urban and global diaspora niches. Another consequence was that kin in Punjab gained from remittances sent home in the early days of diasporic success, when the myth of return (Bhachu 1985) was still strong.

In 1885, Mayo College of Industrial Art in Lahore, named for Viceroy Mayo of India, was established to harness and professionalize the expertise of Punjabi artisans through formal education. John Lockwood Kipling, an Englishman who promoted indigenous craftsmanship, and the father of Rudyard Kipling, was its first principal. His star student, Ram Singh Sohal, later vice principal of Mayo College, became the architect of the elite Aitchison College in Lahore and Khalsa College in Amritsar, both in Punjab. Recognizing his exceptional skills, in 1891 Queen Victoria invited him to design the Durbar room at Osborne House, her summer palace on the Isle of Wight, where he built intricately carved wooden fireplaces, ceilings, and cornices, drawing on traditional Punjabi motifs (Ata-Ullah 1998).

With growing prosperity, the technical skills of a number of Punjabis of artisan background were further enhanced through university educations. The possibility of such an education arose from the migration and remittances of successful diaspora elites. Nand Singh Sehra, a son of craft-caste parents, obtained a mechanical engineering degree from the University of California in 1910 and later taught at American universities before returning to India to represent the Ford Motor Company in the 1930s. He; Sohan Singh Thekadar, who struck it rich in the oil fields of Assam; and Mohan Singh Hadiabadi, a wealthy building contractor, were driving forces in establishing an engineering and technical college in Phagwara, Punjab, where students from artisanal castes found educational opportunities unavailable to them elsewhere. Members of my family who became architects and engineers were educated at this college in the 1940s and 1950s before they migrated to London and Kenya; my two great-grandmothers, who owned a foundry business in Jalandhar, Punjab, were among the top donors to this institution. Dalip Singh Saund, the first Asian U.S. Congress member, who served from 1967 through 1973, was from this same Ramgarhia artisanal group; he earlier had earned a PhD in mathematics from the University of California, Berkeley in 1924. His brother Karnail Singh, a prominent engineer whose legendary technical skills were featured in the Indian press, became the chairman of Indian Railways.

Artisanal Creativity in East Africa

In *Out of Africa* (1937), her memoir of life in Kenya, the Danish Baroness Karen Blixen, whose well-known literary pseudonym was Isak Dinesen, evoked with admiration the artisanal skills of Punjabi migrant Pooran Singh, the *Fundee* on her coffee plantation in the Ngong hills outside Nairobi, the British colony's capital. Fundee, or *fundi*, is Swahili for the skilled artisans and mechanics employed in the workshops, railways, British government–owned institutions, and private enterprises of East Africa. The term derives from the Swahili *ku-funda*—to pass on knowledge, to teach; a form of pedagogy. Punjabi artisans were well-known for transmitting their skills to Asians and Africans alike, a reflection of the diasporic sensibility of collaboration and co-construction. This generosity, in contrast to Asian mercantile groups, held them in good stead, and they were not seen as exploitative capitalists.

As Dinesen portrays him, Pooran Singh could make or repair anything needed, an expertise not uncommon at that time among artisanal migrants who arrived in East Africa with technological skills attained in the Punjab or previous sites of sojourn.

> Pooran Singh worked at a superhuman pace, as if his life depended upon getting the particular job of work finished within the next five minutes. . . . He was our Fundee of the farm, which means an artisan of all work, carpenter, saddler and cabinet-maker, as well as a blacksmith; he constructed and built more than one wagon for the farm, all on his own. But he liked the work of the forge best, and it was a very fine, proud sight, to watch him tiring a wheel. . . . He had taken much pride in our machinery, such as it was and was now for a while as if nailed to the steam engine and the coffee dryer of the factory, his soft dark eyes consuming every nut in them. . . . When he went away [after

> she sold the farm], he carried no luggage with him but a small box of tools and soldering outfit. (Dinesen 1937, 318, 320, 376)

My recent fieldwork concerning early Punjabi migrant families in Kenya included an interview with the daughter-in-law and grandson of engineer and master craftsman Jivan Singh, who, like his sister's son Arjun Singh, was part of my grandfather's circle in Kisumu on the shores of Lake Victoria. The daughter-in-law, in her eighties, related the story of Jivan Singh's repair in the 1920s of the airplane of Lord Maurice Egerton, a colonial landholder in Kenya's White Highlands, and the grandson provided the following details and family history.

> My father tells us the story when Lord Egerton's water plane engine failed. One of the pistons had cracked and getting parts during the World War would have taken a very long time, and he asked around if there was anyone who could do the job locally. The word passed that a competent Indian engineer could have a look. My grandfather Jivan Singh was summoned, and he said he will give it a go. So, in short, he took measurements, made a die-cast, and molded a new piston, piston rings, et cetera, and accurately machined the piston to the right size. He put the engine back together and there was a sigh of relief when the engine fired and got going. Lord Egerton was impressed and offered him a full-time job at Ngata Farm workshop [in Njoro in the Kenyan highlands near Nakuru]. He was in Njoro for a few years, and my father was in fact born in or near Ngata Farm.
>
> Later on my grandfather was head-hunted by Onslow's in Kisumu to manage the workshop. Later on he built his own successful engineering business, Nyanza Engineering Works, in Kisumu. [Jivan Singh's son Harbhajan Singh Nagi inherited this firm, and operated it until 1970, when he moved to London; it was later sold to a relative of Kenyan political leader Oginga Odinga.] Jivan Singh was a pioneer who brought as many as eighty to one hundred people over from Punjab to Kenya [whom he also trained and found jobs] for [in] the labor force required in Kenya.
>
> Jivan Singh's nephew, Arjun Singh, was also taught by Jivan Singh. He had his workshop in Kisumu, where they made grinding crank shafts for cars and lorries to keep them moving, and also did welding and made car body parts. He also repaired farm machinery of all kinds, especially in Kibos where a number of Asians owned farms and

> saw mills, and grinding machines for sugar cane, flour, and wood mills. He himself owned flour mills to grind *posho* [maize] flour that the local Africans and also Asians used for making *ugali*.
>
> There was a cinema called Silver Cinema whose owner came to see him because a projector part broke. This was an urgent task and if he had sent for the part from Europe it would have taken months to get it, and the cinema had to go on showing films. Arjun Singh examined the broken part and was able to not only copy it, but also make a spare part for the cinema owner in case there was future breakage.

The artisans of my grandparents' and parents' generation had an intuitive feeling for how things worked and could "make, repair, improvise" machinery and parts. They worked long days, from seven A.M. to eight P.M., seven days a week, with occasional Sunday afternoons off. Their wives shared the same innovative skills and culture of inventiveness, deployed in different domains. The polythene liners of tetrapak milk cartons were used to make tea cozies and cushions, and fishing net string was used for crocheting bed sheets and table cloths, thus demonstrating the aesthetic of recycling everyday objects and making do with materials at hand. This form of women's jugaad, or improvisation, utilized ingenuity acquired in village and small-town India, where dowries displayed the craft skills of brides and their kinswomen, and many things were made at home.

My Grandfather's and Father's Artisanal Stories

My earlier work (Bhachu 1985) emphasized the movements of East African Asian twice migrants from India to Africa to the United Kingdom (from where younger generations later moved to the Americas, Europe, Australia, and elsewhere). But at the time, I was not fully cognizant of extensive prior multiple migrations. What I have discovered from recent fieldwork is that my grandparents' generation had already moved multiply before they moved multiply again. That is, many had moved from rural to urban India—the trajectory of my maternal grandfather, who moved to Simla and back—and others had moved from Punjab to Shanghai, Assam, Burma, and Basra in Iraq. They had fought as Sikh troops in Egypt and Italy in World War I and in other British regiments during World War II, in locations all over the world. Their pathways were more complex than in my previous analysis.

Many of them lost the desire to return home fairly quickly after arrival in East Africa, even though they continued to send remittances to kin in Punjab. From the early stages of his arrival in Kenya, my paternal grandfather, Sant Singh Bhachu, never wanted to return to India, but he did send money to help his brother and sisters still in the Punjab. My grandfather had first migrated to work in Shanghai, where in the late nineteenth and early twentieth centuries there was a significant presence of Punjabi Sikh men recruited for the British police service and for skilled construction work. He next worked in the shipyards of Yokohama, Japan, where he learned Japanese woodworking techniques and absorbed the aesthetic of finessing tasks to perfection. He later worked in Malaysia, Burma, and Basra before moving to employment in the British colonial steamship yards in Kisumu on Lake Victoria.

He invested in Punjab, in houses, land, and foundries that flourish to this day. Such expatriation of acquired wealth was common in East Africa, especially in the early stages of settlement, but had declined considerably by the end of the 1940s. It reintensified in later decades, especially now to Britain, as East African governments implemented Africanization policies that displaced Asians. Those involved in the diaspora who did return to India found it difficult to negotiate local caste and class hierarchies and the high levels of corruption in the Indian economic and political systems. East Africa was considered to be the "Africa of the Hindus," where Asians acquired wealth and enormous upward mobility, both in terms of caste and social status. In India, they were often considerably more prosperous than were local Indian landowners, entrepreneurs, and power brokers, who thwarted their enterprises and innovations. They felt discriminated against in India, especially by the caste system in rural areas; at the same time, their presence disturbed the established order in both rural and urban settings.

My grandfather worked for the East African Railways and Harbours authority in Kisumu, crafting the elaborate woodwork that was an essential component of early twentieth-century shipping vessels. He was known as a perfectionist in his work and for his refined artisanal aesthetics in general. He was vigilant about the condition of his toolbox, the *sandh* box, and he knew instinctively if someone had touched his tools, even whether they had been moved by one millimeter. No one was allowed to touch this box, which had sacred and magical qualities. My grandfather's toolbox was his most precious possession, and he had made many of his tools himself, as was expected of mistries, or master craftsman. My mother told us the story of my mischievous uncle, my father's younger brother, who as a boy used to play with the toolbox when my grandfather was out of the house, despite being banned from touching it. He would put things back exactly as my grandfather arranged them, but my grandfather knew immediately when he arrived home that someone had touched them.

My definitive memory of my grandfather was of his close examination of a first class railway carriage we traveled in after 1964 when my father, Kartar Singh Bhachu, was promoted to "European Grade 2," a position restricted to British colonial whites until the early 1960s and held by a only a few Asians until independence in 1963. When my father reached this grade, we could travel first class and enjoy the attendant luxuries. As we were about to leave Kisumu for Nairobi, where my parents lived at that time, my grandfather's fingers followed the woodwork in our compartment and examined every detail of its workmanship.

I have never forgotten this interrogation of the woodwork. As a master craftsman, he demanded things be done perfectly. His clothes had to be perfectly sewn and ironed with trouser creases just right. The seams of the clothes that my mother made for him had to run in the same direction. Once a cousin sewed a garment for him that he would not wear because the machine-sewn seams did not all run in the same direction. My cousin was shocked that he could notice this. To most of us, the seams looked the same, but at a glance, he could see flaws invisible to an ordinary person. The cobbler who made my grandfather's moccasin shoes was expected to craft them perfectly according to the exacting design template my grandfather provided him. Once this cobbler elongated the top beyond my grandfather's design and had to remake the pair of shoes. I remember many such incidents of his expectation of everyday perfection that, as a child, I read as dictatorial rules but, as an adult, have come to appreciate, especially as I am now more knowledgeable about the background of craft and artisanal aesthetics.

This level of perfection, including the direction of the hand movements and the rhythms used for varnishing and polishing wood, was incorporated in his teaching of those African workers to whom he passed on his expertise. My grandfather instructed them in the precision cuts needed for fine woodwork, about how to use each tool, and in which direction to move the body and hands to get the right finish. Today an East African artisanal class is continuing these traditions as a result of the sharing and transmission of such skills by Punjabi craftsmen.

Although he worked in the administrative sector of East African Railways and Harbours once he migrated to Kenya, my father arrived skilled in ironmongery. In fact, he carried the mark of his artisanal heritage on his person—the top bit of his index finger was missing. It had been hacked off on an anvil when his hammer hit the iron piece he was working in the family foundry in Jalandhar, Punjab. My grandfather's brother's grandchildren there still manufacture steel and iron implements, gates, agricultural equipment, coolers, and other objects in foundries started in the 1920s by my two great-grandmothers, who negotiated a contract for a quota of iron from the Tata Steel and Iron Company. These enterprises, run by their two sons, would not have succeeded without the help of remittances sent from Kenya by my grandfather to his brother.

A Feeling for Buildings, Art, and Machines

The jugaad sensibility, similar to American "Yankee ingenuity," well characterizes the multiply migrant people I have lived among and write about. It is the modus vivendi and operandi of this artisanal diaspora, and it is the aesthetic that has been transmitted to a contemporary generation of creative agents for whom it is second nature.

Architect Amarjit Kalsi is a codirector of Rogers Stirk Harbour + Partners, a globally influential architectural firm created and led by multiple award–winning architect Richard Rogers. Kalsi was a team leader for designing Terminal 5 at Heathrow Airport, which opened in 2008. His other projects included the Lloyd's building, London; the European Court of Human Rights in Strasbourg, Germany; Madrid-Barajas Airport, Spain; the Centre Georges Pompidou, Paris; and law courts in Antwerp, Belgium, and Bordeaux, France. Currently, he is director in charge for two new subway stations in Naples, Italy.

Kalsi was born and spent much of his childhood in Kenya, where his maternal and paternal grandfathers both migrated as carpenters. Like many Kenyan Asians, they worked in the railways as artisans before they established their own workshops and enterprises. Growing up in in a rural area, Kalsi learned to fix his father's truck when it broke down while traveling to the Kenyan coast. He also absorbed craftsman values from his grandfathers in Nairobi. "As a kid, at my grandfather's workshop in River Road, Nairobi, outside the Ramgarhia Sikh temple, I used to play with the wood after school. I remember the smell of scotch glue used for carpentry and the wood pieces that we were given. You got used to dealing with wood—you had an affinity to it."

Kalsi moved to Slough, United Kingdom, in 1970. While a teenager, he was entranced by eminent art historian Kenneth Clark's BBC television series *Civilisation*, which traced the history of European art, architecture, and philosophy from the Dark Ages to the present. He loved the descriptions of "the Renaissance period, the height of human creativity," and also Sir Kenneth's accessible and engaging way of conveying information. Later he watched Jacob Bronowski's 1973 television series *The Ascent of Man*, designed to complement *Civilisation* by focusing on the development of human society from the perspective of science.

These two series persuaded Kalsi to find a profession that combined art and science, and architecture seemed the answer. He studied physics at night school and took art classes in technical college before he enrolled at the Architectural Association School in London. His sensibility, drawing on art and science, combined with his diasporic inheritance of craftsmanship, is significant for his architectural work, in which repetition of design and of lighting, of utilizing the same components multiply, is significant.

This is evident at Heathrow Terminal 5. As Kalsi explained to me, "The trick is to reduce the design to three or four elements and harness repetition for the sake of economy. If you take the airport, you have to find some sort of order that you can repeat. So the trick is to reduce the number of aspects you are representing. There is an economy in this. You can harness repetition for the sake of economy. It is like a mathematic technique. You do a small sample and then you repeat that." Kalsi and I also discussed how this same technique is used in crocheting: you make a hexagon or a square and repeat it to create multiple designs.

The diasporic aesthetic influence encoded in his high-profile European buildings is not often noted, yet it can be read there as a product of migrant creativity. The son of a highly skilled East African Asian carpenter and builder, Kalsi makes use of new materials and sidesteps establishment architectural norms in designing his buildings. In his work, he brings together people of diverse ranges of expertise collaboratively, he melds elements in new ways, and he designs buildings in which repetition and improvisation are highlighted.

The use of repetition is also a fundamental aesthetic for Bhajan Hunjan, an artist trained at the prestigious Slade School of Fine Art in Bloomsbury, University College London, who specializes in public art. Her work includes the floorscapes of the Belgrave Behano Peepul Centre in Leicester, the High Street Town Square in Slough, and the metal frieze work on the Three Mills

Pontoon gates in London's 2012 Olympic Park. As she told me, "Whenever I have worked on a piece, repetition is there. It is like *simran*, meditation. You repeat and you repeat, and what happens at the end is you feel elated as it comes together through reducing an image, and—like the *tikkis* in crocheting, the oblongs, the squares, the rectangles—a unified form emerges . . . by putting these units together in different patterns again and again."

Hunjan was born in Kenya, where her father, of craft-caste background, was a building contractor who also owned a quarry and hardware store in Nanyuki, in the foothills of Mount Kenya, where family members still reside. As a child, Hunjan watched buildings being constructed by her father and became familiar with cement, stone, and the kinds of wood in her father's storage yard. In her art, she utilizes materials often not seen as usable by artists—such as cement, which she molds by adding adhesive as a reinforcing agent. She feels confident constructing innovative forms with this material, which she has been familiar with since childhood, and she enjoys producing art that will not easily disintegrate. She also uses colored cement in her floorscapes, because Indian homes in Kenya often had red and green floors: using a technique from India, people added color to the plaster, and floors were polished with coconut husks.

She first worked with cement when she made a concrete and ceramic wall collaboratively with a women's community group. "Cement is not considered to be a woman's material. It is a building material and it is a masculinized material because of the stereotypes. [But] cement tiles are made like making biscuits." In her art, Hunjan feels closest to the work of her builder father, but she readily acknowledges being "influenced by the strong women in our household, who were work orientated [*sic*] and very skilled at the crafts at home. They made everything they needed, and sewed, embroidered, made objects of decoration for the home, and all the clothes for everyone, including the men's coats and jackets."

The women of her house were powerful and creative. They did not work outside for wages, but they worked all the time.

> There was enormous emphasis on the skills naturalized in the hands—*hath khulay ho jaan* or *hath khul javay*, that you should have practiced hands that could do and make things with ease and fluency, that you did not leave hands free and idle. You made and worked on a craft, like knitting, embroidery, crocheting, hemming stitched garments, or you did a bit of the craft preparation to get on with the actual job when you

> gossiped, conversed, listened to the radio or television. And you did your work neatly, fast, and with care, not with *shoosti* [laziness]. You had to be *fortilli* [sharp, smart] and attentive to your job and pick it up fast. You could not sit around doing nothing.

Her female childhood experiences also provided direct inspiration for her artwork. "I wanted to take the patterns that I saw on my mother's sheets with embroidery, *phulkaris* [sheets and shawls embroidered with green, orange, and red silk thread] and tablecloths of crochet, and wanted to show that this was art. They were art forms, by any standards, found in our homes. It is thinking of these that I started to make prints from these sheets with *disooti* [cross-stitch embroidery] on metal plates which I could reproduce endlessly."

The migrant improvisational aesthetic continues with Hunjan. She has spent a great deal of time in Barcelona, Spain, and is inspired by Catalan artist Antoni Gaudi's use of recycled materials in famous Güell Park.

Punjabi diaspora values of technical mastery, creative improvisation, and mobilizing and managing people underpinned the July 4, 2012, announcement at the Conseil Européen pour la Recherche Nucléaire (CERN), the multinational European organization for nuclear research in Geneva, Switzerland, that its Large Hadron Collider particle accelerator had detected compelling evidence for the existence of the elusive Higgs boson subatomic particle. Although European and American media coverage focused largely on white scientists in reporting this scientific breakthrough, the lead scientist for the project was twice-migrant Tejinder Virdee, professor of physics at Imperial College London and Fellow of the Royal Society.

Virdee was born in Nyeri, Kenya, also the birthplace of artist Bhajan Hunjan. Virdee's father had moved from the Punjab to Kenya at the time of his marriage and settled in Kisumu, where my family lived. Like my grandfather and father, Virdee's father worked for East African Railways and Harbours. The family moved to Birmingham, U.K., in 1967, when Tejinder was fifteen, and he attended King's Norton Boys Grammar, where his physics teacher inspired him to pursue the subject. He began working at CERN while a graduate student in the 1970s, and after receiving his PhD in physics from Imperial College London, he continued at CERN almost until the Higgs boson announcement, commuting between Geneva and London.

The Large Hadron Collider is a $10.5 billion particle accelerator filling a circular tunnel seventeen miles in circumference. Virdee led an international team of three thousand scientists from thirty countries in developing this most expensive machine ever made. He designed as well the Higgs boson, or "God particle," experiment and the Compact Muon Selenoid (CMS) technology that detected its existence. During my interview with Virdee in January 2012, he spoke of the challenges of building the collider and the CMS detector.

> The project is very successful now and working well. But when we started there were only a handful of us who actually designed the experiment. We had cut our teeth on a previous UA1 . . . proton/antiproton experiment. There were a couple of Frenchmen, a couple of German men, and myself. We learned a lot from this experiment and wanted to learn much more still. We needed to build an experiment, and there was nothing in existence that would work. We did not know if we would succeed or if the technologies that were necessary could be found.
>
> The challenges were enormous. There are bunches of particles, each bunch contained one hundred billion protons. . . . It was not clear whether [the detectors] would be damaged by radiation and cease working. We had to think of techniques of survival. We worked with the electronics industry, and at that time the electronics existed in the military industry. So it was extremely costly and the technological challenges were enormous, leaving aside [that] you had to get the finance and the people. . . . One of the great lessons we learned from this exercise is that half of the effort required to solve the problem is knowing that you have a problem. . . . There was not a single problem we faced to which we didn't find a solution.

Virdee explained that there were "many calculated risks, and we had to have the courage to take them."

> Remember, there are three thousand scientists. They are individuals, have big egos. In the end you are trying to understand nature, so you have to have no prejudgment about what you think. That is why you do the experiment, to find out what nature has actually done. . . . People have ideas, but the good thing is that the ideas are tensioned and tested, and that flattens the egos in a manner, because people come to recognize what the right answer is. They argue forcibly, but ultimately

> we all want to succeed and to do physics. They cannot succeed on their own; they will have to do it collectively. So you have to understand the ideas of the others, and compare the ideas and compare their performance.

We discussed how consensus had to be created, how each idea had to be tested by using prototypes to shoot particles and see how they behave. Virdee continued, "So you compare results, and then you convince people that what you say is actually better. These are very bright scientists, so you had to convince them about what was the right thing for the experiment as a whole. That is how things happened, and sometimes people did not want to let go—and that is why senior people made a call to say: we are going in a particular direction."

At the start, they had to create a team to build the detectors. The skills needed included not only management of hardware and software programs for this biggest machine in the world but also highly developed people management skills. Virdee recognized early on that the resources required were not only funds but also talent. "One of the big things we had to do was to match the capability of the countries, and the scientists in these countries, with the requirements of the experiment, which were severe. The objects required for the experiment were produced in different countries and then put together." Virdee's many trips to Russia to help develop the crystals for the CMS furthered Russia's mastery of crystal technology. This led to technical advances in image and photo devices, as well as in scanners to detect cancers.

The development of CMS took ten years and was critical for the experiment in which the Higgs boson particle was confirmed. In a BBC Radio World Service interview, Virdee explained, "It is a very elegant detector. The beauty lies in the intricacy and in the technologies pushed to the limits and all put to a pattern. They are like a work of art" (BBC World Service 2012).

Anthropologists as Decoders of Traces and as Sages

People may do remarkable things in diasporas when horizons open that replace closed hierarchies in their place of origin or site of last settlement, and they must learn to create new infrastructure from scratch. People may flourish and take up new opportunities, and new ways of improvising and creating may emerge. This can release imaginations and innovative and inventive ways of crafting, making, and thinking. The people I study and write about today are some of the leading filmmakers, designers, architects, artists, scientists, and musicians of the emerging twenty-first century. They bring a strong ethos of improvisation and collaboration. Their defining hallmark, jugaad, is making do with whatever you have and sharing skills with generosity.

We must take seriously Edward Said's injunctions about "knowing thyself" and investigating the uninventoried "infinity of traces" that are deposited in ourselves and in the experience of the communities and biographies that precede us. Anthropologists can help reconstruct these inventories and convey them to contemporary generations, which may thus reimagine the invisible legacies bequeathed to them. We can also make visible to the world at large the innovative, diasporically generated sensibilities that are products of movement, improvisation, mutuality, and living and working in the present moment.

I believe that young people can find in anthropology different messages from the teachings of older people, priests, and community leaders who are carriers of cultural capital or even its innovators in prior multiple movements, locations, and dislocations. The pedagogical role of anthropologist as detector of traces and interpreter of cultural dynamics can aid today's second- and third-generation migrant offspring to recover their histories and to draw out the complexities and deeper roots of their contemporary lives. This may permit contemporary generations to understand that much of what happens in our hyperconnected world has connections with the past.

Even sophisticated young people are not always cognizant of how deeply determined their lives are by the cultural capital, technical expertise, and deep-rooted aesthetics fought for and secured by the earlier generations on whose shoulders they rest, which may remain submerged and invisible to the majority of the world. They assume they are inventing life anew, which indeed they are, but they are also reproducing traces innovatively in the dissonant worlds in which they are dynamic agents.

Chapter 6

A Savage at the Wedding and the Skeletons in My Closet

My Great-Grandfather, "Igorotte Villages," and the Ethnological Expositions of the 1900s

Deana L. Weibel

When I was a child, my mother told me stories about her grandparents, who had traveled the world with a band of "pygmy headhunters" she referred to as "Igoroadies." She was certain that they had come from Africa, that they were dark skinned, and that they feasted on dog meat. I am not sure how much of an influence these tales of family contact with the exotic were, but as a young adult, I decided to study anthropology. I got my PhD after thirteen months in France studying sacred sites, their residents, and the pilgrims who visited them. There were no headhunters in my research plan.

Still, as time passed, my view of these stories evolved. First they sounded preposterous. As I became better educated, I came across a group of Philippine mountain people known as the "Igorots," but my mother insisted the "Igoroadies" had come from Africa, not Asia. Later, as the Internet developed I picked up traces of information: I learned about the way Philippine peoples and others were displayed at world's fairs in the late nineteenth and early twentieth centuries. I found my great-grandfather's name, Richard Schneidewind, in articles and books linking him to these "shows." Finally, I found the name of an anthropologist at the Smithsonian, Patricia Afable, who had done research on my great-grandfather and was an Igorot herself.

It was in 2007, while I was an assistant professor of anthropology at Grand Valley State University near Grand Rapids, Michigan, that I first made contact with Pat. My early e-mails were apologetic; hers were reassuring. "[Don't] be too hard on your ancestor," she wrote. What I have learned in these past few years, almost entirely in partnership with Pat, is that my great-grandfather's work as an impresario shuttling Bontoc Igorot men, women, and children from one "Igorrote Village" to another was not an isolated incident of a European American man exploiting other human beings to make a buck. Instead, the history of my family interweaves in numerous ways with the history of my chosen profession. Any guilt, misplaced or not, about my connection to the Schneidewind family is compounded by the complicity of the discipline of anthropology. As Pat and I have conversed, cowritten, and collaborated over the years, blending her knowledge of the Philippines with my family stories, the relationship between the *Nikimaliká* (American-traveled) Igorots, my great-grandfather and his family, and the anthropologists and ethnologists of the early twentieth century has proven to be much more complex and nuanced than it first appeared. In this chapter, I will tie my family history to the history of anthropology, discuss the relationship between the fairs and their varied participants, and discuss how work that blurs the lines between researcher and informant can be a fruitful contribution to the profession.

Richard Schneidewind and the Fairs

Richard Schneidewind was born on December 17, 1876, in Detroit, Michigan. His parents were Karl Schneidewind and Minna Hoppa, immigrants from Germany who had made their way to the United States shortly before he was born. Older sisters Elma and Anna completed the family. The Schneidewinds, like many first-generation immigrant families, spoke their mother tongue in the home.

Schneidewind joined the U.S. Army in June 1898.[1] Perhaps because of previous work with a druggist, he was made a nurse in the Field Hospital Corps. His first assignment was at Camp Merritt, located in San Francisco, where he cared for patients under quarantine, most of whom had measles or mumps. A training session at the Presidio led to his being made the head nurse of Ward I and exposed him to patients with the more serious illnesses of spinal meningitis and typhoid. While traveling on the USTS Scandia to Manila, Philippines, Schneidewind was discovered to have contracted typhoid himself. He came very close to death but recovered well enough to be placed on Corregidor Island during the early days of the construction of a convalescent hospital. Photography seems to have occupied some of his time, as he recorded disturbing images of war, including mass burials and executions, as well as medical pictures of people with leprosy. He was still on the sick list when he left the service as a private in the Hospital Corps in July 1899.

Upon his discharge from the Army, Richard Schneidewind decided to remain in the Philippines. On March 7, 1900, he married a Manila local, a woman called Gabina Dionicio R. Y Gabriel, who died later that year during or soon after the birth of a son, Richard Schneidewind, Jr., on December 16, 1900. The following year, Schneidewind found work as a post office employee but strayed into some questionable practices. According to a Bureau of Insular Affairs (War Department) memo from 1907, "About the latter part of 1901 the Schneidewind referred to was employed for some months as a clerk in the Manila Post Office. He was dismissed from that service, one of the charges against him being complicity in a smuggling scheme. He mailed many packages of valuable jusis and pinas [types of embroidered fabric very popular with Western visitors to the Philippines[2]], etcetera, to a confederate in San Francisco, who sold them there and in Los Angeles. . . . My recollection is that Schneidewind did not deny the charge" (McKay 1907).

This event seems to have been the spur to Richard Schneidewind's departure from the Philippines. Apparently leaving his son in the temporary care of the boy's maternal family in Manila, Schneidewind returned to the United States. His attraction to the Philippines remained, though, and when the St. Louis World's Fair (more accurately referred to as the Louisiana Purchase Exposition, or LPE) was held in 1904, Schneidewind was there, working the cigar concession that was part of the Philippine Reservation. He must have been drawn to the "Igorot Village" run by impresario Truman K. Hunt, because soon after the LPE, Schneidewind entered into partnership with Edmond Felder and founded the Filipino Exhibition Company as direct competition to Hunt's Igorot Exhibit Company (Parezo and Fowler 2007, 384). He and Felder set off to the Philippines in early 1905. (Schneidewind had made one earlier trip to Manila and returned to the United States with his young son in October 1904, placing "Dick" in his family's Detroit home.)

Felder and Schneidewind began to tour the United States in 1905 with a group of men and women from the Bontoc Igorot tribe, traveling from Oregon to Ohio, Toronto to Tennessee, and having their Igorot charges build so-called "Igorrote Villages" in amusement parks and expositions. (The use of the Spanish

Igorrote rather than the English Igorot may have been a way to distinguish Felder and Schneidewind's group from Hunt's.) These "villages" would charge additional admission and were places where paying guests could, it was claimed, see Igorot "savages" or "barbarians" in their natural environments, performing rituals, doing war dances, making crafts, and so on. These exhibits were extremely popular.

During this time, Truman Hunt's competing villages were disbanded and his charges put in Schneidewind's care after the Igorots traveling with Hunt took him to court in Tennessee for mistreatment and withholding money. Afable writes that Hunt lost the cases against him, perhaps surprisingly, "given the social attitudes in the southern United States at the time." Although the presiding judge set aside the juries' verdicts, Hunt did spend several months imprisoned in Memphis (Afable 2004, 465). The Igorots who had been part of Hunt's show traveled with Schneidewind's troop for the rest of the tour, which ended with a stint at Riverview Park, an amusement park in Chicago, Illinois.

Selma Eichholz, a young woman of eighteen, was working as a ticket taker at Riverview. She had been born in Germany, and she and Schneidewind became romantically involved. They were married on October 4, 1906, in Detroit. A newspaper wedding announcement at the time undoubtedly scandalized readers (although simultaneously providing advertising for Schneidewind's business) with its headline "Honeymoon to be Spent with Band of Filipino Savages." Something of Schneidewind's flamboyant nature and success as a showman can be gleaned from the announcement, which reads, in part, that Schneidewind "attracted considerable attention in Detroit last June, when he came to attend the wedding of his sister and brought with him his favorite Igorrote" (the "favorite Igorrote" was very probably Antero Cabrera, who worked for Schneidewind as an interpreter and was a darling of the press).

Selma Schneidewind was an adventurous woman in her own right. Not only did she head to the Philippines on her honeymoon, but returned, five months pregnant, with her husband and a new group of Bontoc Igorots (including some who had traveled with Schneidewind previously), on the *Nippon Maru* in May 1907. She gave birth to my grandfather Carl in August and continued to travel with the Filipino Exhibition Company (FEC). Young Carl frequently played with the Igorot children (many of whom, like him, were born during the tours), and Selma gave birth to Carl's sister, named Gabina Selma, just before the opening of the 1909 Alaska-Yukon-Pacific Exposition. Schneidewind's older son, Dick, remained in Detroit attending school while his younger half-siblings traveled with the FEC.

Schneidewind (along with Selma, Carl, and Gabina) returned to the Philippines in 1911 and recruited a group of Igorots for a tour of Europe. The destinations were to include London, Paris, Ghent, and Lyon, among other places. Some accounts state that while in Ghent in 1913, Schneidewind, struck by financial difficulties, abandoned his Igorot charges, leaving them to fend for themselves and leading to the death of at least one member of the troupe, Timicheg. Other accounts suggest some disagreement between Schneidewind and certain Igorots in the group, who brought the consul of Ghent (and eventually the U.S. government) in to intervene. Apparently some of the Igorots wanted to continue touring; others claimed mistreatment and wanted to be returned home. Newspaper reports from Ghent in December 1913 stated that despite this division, all of the Igorots were sent back to the Philippines, and none of them continued on to Lyon (Capiteyn 1913). According to Afable, legislation by the U.S. government in the Philippines passed in 1914 prohibited further exhibitions of Philippine people, and the era of such tours came to a close (Afable 2004, 467).

A few years later, in 1915, Schneidewind participated in San Diego's Panama-California Exposition, this time exhibiting a Samoan group. His career as a showman ended around this time. My mother recalls that during the Great Depression, he and her father used a machine to punch out industrial disks, working from their backyard. In his life as a retiree, Schneidewind listened to the Detroit Tigers on the radio, told tales of his past, and drank San Miguel beer.

As for Schneidewind's first son, Dick, who was born in the Philippines but came to live with his German-speaking aunts and grandmother in Detroit, he attended school while his father, stepmother, and half-siblings traveled the world. After the era of the fairs had passed, the family reassembled in Detroit, and Dick ended up being the pride of the Schneidewinds. He graduated from high school in 1917, then went on to earn a bachelor's degree in chemical engineering from the University of Michigan in 1923. He earned both his master's degree and PhD in engineering research at Michigan and was hired there as a professor in the College of Engineering. His specialty was metallurgical engineering, and he produced many publications and patents having to do with such topics as chromium plating and iron casting. All told, he spent forty-three years in research and teaching positions before retiring from the University of Michigan in 1967.

Dick Schneidewind never had any children of his own. Rebuffed by a fiancée's parents when they discovered their daughter's intended had a darker complexion than they had imagined, he held off marrying until much later in life, and he married only on the condition that the union not produce children. Apparently his mixed Spanish-Philippine and German ancestry was problematic for him throughout his life, and one can only imagine the impact of his awareness as a child that his father displayed people from the Philippines as a form of entertainment. He told my Aunt Ann in an unguarded moment that he considered himself a "half-breed." He passed away in 1970.

The Igorot People and the Fairs

The various "tribes" often (but not always) included under the ethnonym *Igorot*, which loosely refers to people from the Cordillera Mountain region of the island of Luzon, Philippines, are the Isnegs, Ibaloys, Kankanaeys, Kalanguya, Ifugaos, Kalingas, Aplai, Balangao, and Bontocs.[3] The term *Igorot*, because of many negative past associations, is avoided by some groups, although others are currently seeking to reclaim it. The most complete and detailed information about what the era of the "Igorotte Villages" was like for the Igorot performers in these exhibitions comes from Patricia Afable, an Ibaloy linguistic anthropologist who conducted interviews with the descendants of Bontocs who traveled to America during the early years of the twentieth century.

In contrast to some who portray the experiences of the Igorot performers in an overwhelmingly negative light, Afable focuses on the agency of these travelers, dubbed *Nikimaliká* by those back home because of their connection with America. She writes that "northern Philippine highland people entered into business arrangements to travel to North America to perform cultural activities in expositions and other fairs" (Afable 2004, 445) and argues that her interviews with contemporary Bontocs reveal that "the most important outcome of the journeys was the overwhelming desire among their ancestors for education for their children" (469). Although she does not sugarcoat the obvious exploitation involved, Afable conveys how these extraordinary experiences were seen emically and sheds an interesting light on the Igorot perspective.

Their home region in the Cordillera Mountains, by the middle Chico and upper Abra Rivers, was well traveled in the days of Spanish rule for purposes of trade and the attempted Christianization of the inhabitants. After the Spanish-American War, several Americans came to this area and offered local youth, mostly teenaged boys, the chance to interact with Americans, learn

English (in addition to the Spanish many had learned from schools set up by the prior colonial government), and increase their educations in the years just prior to the 1904 St. Louis fair.

Anthropologist Albert Ernest Jenks arrived with his wife in 1902 and conducted five months of fieldwork, resulting in the ethnographic monograph *The Bontoc Igorot* (Jenks 1905). The Jenkses employed many young people to work in their household and act as interpreters, including "Antero Cabrera, Pitapit, Falikao, Bugti, Maklan and Sitlanin" (Afable 2004, 451).

When the Reverend Walter Clayton Clapp, an Episcopalian missionary, arrived in the Bontoc region to set up a mission school and write a Bontoc-English dictionary, many of the same ambitious young people worked with him. This dictionary, published in 1908, acknowledges the assistance of Antero Cabrera, James Amok, and Tainan, among others (Afable 2004, 452). These young men, used to contact with Americans and quite fluent in English (particularly Antero Cabrera), were among those selected to go to St. Louis by Jenks, the fair's director of Philippine ethnology. When Truman Hunt came to Bontoc on his recruiting mission for St. Louis' Louisiana Purchase Exposition, he put Antero Cabrera in charge of finding ten older men, ten older women, ten younger men, and ten younger women who would be able to travel to America (462).

The name Antero Cabrera is mentioned frequently because Antero (who eventually dropped the name Cabrera and used "Antero" as his children's family name) was an essential member of the fair enterprise. The best interpreter in the group, Antero was also charismatic and became something of a "star" in the press coverage surrounding the LPE and later venues. Afable reports that he traveled to America at least three times and, after Hunt's group was put in Schneidewind's care following Hunt's arrest and trial, was one of only three in the group (along with Bugti and Felingao) to receive some access to Western education when Schneidewind enrolled the three young men in a Los Angeles elementary school during their stay at Chutes Park (Afable 2004, 453).

Antero returned to the United States with Schneidewind's group in 1907 and brought with him his new wife, Takhay (Isting/Cristina) Ulapan. Like Schneidewind (also traveling with his new wife at this time), Antero found his family expanding during his travels. Antero and Takhay eventually had ten children. Afable reports that after the time of the fairs had passed, Antero worked as a government interpreter and helped conduct a census of Bontoc in 1911. This latter employment prevented him from being able to travel with

Schneidewind's last group, which went to Europe and left the tour under a cloud in 1913. Antero died in 1940, and Afable's interviews with some of his daughters reveal a man who continued to network with people he had met from a variety of local tribes during the St. Louis fair, who was talkative and curious, and who encouraged all of his children to seek education (Afable 2004, 455).

Afable addresses the agency of other Nikimaliká who traveled with the impresarios but were able to stand up to them. She discusses Julio Balinag, who was employed by Truman Hunt in 1905 and worked as his assistant until Hunt revealed himself to be "corrupt and unscrupulous" (Afable 2004, 464), defrauding his charges and apparently even assaulting some of them. It was Balinag who contacted the police, leading to a suit against Hunt, a jury's guilty verdict, and jail time.

Afable describes the memories the Igorot hold of these times as generally happy. She mentions "Schneidewind's cordial relations with Bontoc people" (Afable 2004, 465) and the Igorot perspective that Americans were, in general, both "kind and indulgent" and "gullible." Although the Nikimaliká who had experienced the outside world were sometimes seen as "spoiled," Afable writes that, for the most part, "the Bontoc people speak of their ancestors as mostly young adventurers who 'ran away' to Malika, teaming up with their neighbors, families, and other relatives, in the hope of bringing back money and White people's goods" (462). The Igorot performers were certainly exploited, portrayed unfairly, and used by anthropologists and the American government to justify imperialism. But the emic perspective reveals a bit more complexity by showing that the Bontoc travelers and their children and grandchildren also saw the experiences abroad as a unique, desirable, educational opportunity.

Anthropology and the Fairs

The story of my great-grandfather's days recruiting Igorot performers and working as a showman is both colorful and disturbing, suggesting a time when a pro-empire American could profit from his nation's entwined fascination and fear of "the other." My family's collection of newspaper clippings from the time (now housed as the "Schneidewind Papers" at the Bentley Historical Library at the University of Michigan) demonstrate a recurring theme in the press coverage of the touring village—the "wild Igorrote" who escapes from the fair into the neighboring community and terrifies an innocent housewife. Journalists describe nearly naked ax-wielding savages who eat dogs and climb trees, tempting readers to come to the local fair or park and witness these relics from time past. Anthropologists of today may wonder how their counterparts of the 1900s responded to these inflammatory and largely inaccurate portrayals of tribal peoples. The truth is that their reactions were mixed.

The 1904 Louisiana Purchase Exposition, in fact, provides a clear example of how certain anthropological ideals and imperialism went hand in hand at numerous world's fairs. Anthropology was a relatively new discipline at that point, moving from a more amateur to a professional status. Universities were beginning to form anthropology departments, and anthropologists began to debate whether groups like the American Anthropological Association (AAA), founded in 1902, should be limited to professional experts only or should welcome anyone who showed an interest. Many anthropologists believed it was necessary to demonstrate anthropology's status as a science. As Nancy J. Parezo and Don D. Fowler write, "participation in expositions was the most public way anthropology . . . could present itself as socially useful and authoritative" (Parezo and Fowler 2007, 8). W J McGee, then president of the AAA, was chosen to direct the Louisiana Purchase Exposition's Department of Anthropology, and McGee's ideas, described by Parezo and Fowler as "filled with the bombast and racialist assumptions of nineteenth-century unilineal anthropology" (14), were a driving force behind how various indigenous peoples were portrayed there.

Fostering anthropology in a similar vein was Albert Jenks, the ethnographer who, as noted above, studied the Bontoc Igorots of the Philippines from 1900 to 1903 and was selected to run the Philippine ethnological section of the LPE. Jenks and his wife had lived among the Bontocs and had recruited several young people in the community to work as help in their household. Jenks encouraged some of these youths, such as English interpreter Antero Cabrera, to participate in the fair's "Igorot Village," run by Truman Hunt, and Jenks's presence as an expert who was able to provide both artifacts and people did a lot to validate the Philippine Reservation as a scholastic enterprise.

In the years after the LPE, anthropologists were less likely to run enterprises like the Philippine Reservation, and these kinds of traveling shows were mostly managed by promoters like Richard Schneidewind. However, these exhibitions were still seen as having genuine educational value, especially in areas of cross-cultural comparison. Famed anthropologist Alfred Kroeber, for example, in

1906 published an article in *American Anthropologist* detailing his measurements of the inhabitants of the Igorot Village set up in San Francisco. Kroeber measured several Igorot individuals, noted skin color, and took down other features, all "courtesy of Mr. R. Schneidewind" (Kroeber 1906, 194). These exhibitions, although deeply racist and troubling from a contemporary perspective, were also places where the academic work of the period could take place.

Another anthropologist who took advantage of the educational opportunities provided by the popular expositions was Alfred Cort Haddon, a reader in ethnology at Cambridge who had studied populations in the Torres Straits Islands, New Guinea, and Borneo. Haddon was brought to teach a summer class at the University of Washington during the Alaska-Yukon-Pacific Exposition of 1909 in Seattle. This course, "Stages of Cultural Evolution around the Pacific" (Stein, Becker, and Historylink Staff 2009, 30), used the proximity of the exposition to introduce students to the great variety of "savages" and "barbarians" that had been assembled for the public's delight but sought to provide an academic perspective.

Another academic whose research had some anthropological bearing was linguist Carl Wilhelm Seidenadel. Afable writes that Seidenadel, who hailed from St. Louis and was once employed on the University of Chicago's German faculty, tracked down Schneidewind and Felder's group during their 1906 stay at Riverview Park in Chicago. Seidenadel, in close collaboration with members of the group, including Antero, who had assisted Jenks and Clapp, spent five months studying the Bontoc language and produced a 592-page English-Bontoc dictionary in 1909, one far superior to that published previously by Clapp. Afable writes, "Antero's prior experience with dictionary work in Bontoc proved to be crucial to Seidenadel's project, and he was responsible for editing out texts that had numerous Ilocano borrowings" (Afable 2004, 459).

Much of what went on in the "Igorrote Villages" was spectacle, intended to draw the largest audiences and to shock and delight fairgoers. To that end, ceremonies were taken out of context and, in some cases, changed or invented to appeal to the public. A sham "Igorrote Village" constructed over a few days with the sole purpose of depicting an image of an exotic, primitive, and potentially dangerous habitation was no more authentic than a Hollywood movie set. The people on display, however, were authentic when they were, as Afable puts it, "offstage," and these offstage Igorots were occasionally able to convey their culture authentically to scholars who, like Seidenadel, were willing to collaborate with them.

The Personal Meets the Professional

As a scholar used to writing within the traditional frameworks of anthropological description, it is strange indeed to tell the tale of myself. Reflexive ethnography is one thing, but describing what goes on away from the field is something else.

My mother, Carlyn Schneidewind Weibel, spent her early childhood in Michigan. She was born in Detroit and lived with her parents and paternal grandparents in her grandparents' home from 1933 to 1941. The attack on Pearl Harbor and my grandfather's subsequent career in the U.S. Army pulled my mother from Michigan and into the life of the peripatetic Army brat. She returned to Michigan to earn her degree from Michigan State University, then settled in Southern California to join her parents, who had moved there after her father's retirement. I was raised in Santa Ana, California. Despite never having visited Michigan during my childhood, I ended up moving there when I accepted my position at Grand Valley State University (GVSU). This geographical switch is likely what made my research into the "Igorrote Villages" possible.

In 1992, preparing to apply to the doctoral program in anthropology at the University of California, San Diego (UCSD), I decided to volunteer at the San Diego Museum of Man, which is dedicated to anthropology and was constructed, along with most of the rest of the park, as the setting for the 1915 Panama-California Exposition. I had a number of duties at the museum, but many of them had to do with maintaining records and entering data from note cards into a computer. One day I came across a description on a note card of a basket made by a tribe called the "Igorots" from the Philippines. The name did not sound exactly like the "Igoroadies" mentioned by my mother when she talked about her grandparents, but it was close enough that I made a point to ask her about it. No, she told me, they had no connection to the Philippines.

I was accepted into the program at UCSD, went to do research in France, and never gave the Igorot people of the Philippines much thought. While employed part-time at California State University–Fullerton years later in 2002, I found mention of Philippine "dog eaters" displayed in the United States and encouraged a small group of Filipino students taking my course to conduct some research into this. I began to realize, very slowly, that my family had perhaps been involved in some of these displays, and I was conscious of embarrassment as the students angrily described what had taken place to the rest of the class.

When the new academic year began in 2003, I was at GVSU, starting my first year as an assistant professor. I met relatives who still lived in the area, including my great-aunt Gabina, then in her nineties and very frail, suffering from dementia (she died in August 2006); her son Doug; and another great-aunt, Ann, who had been born in 1920, after the fairs. In the years that followed, I became more adept at Internet research and, in 2006, located a mention of my great-grandfather in Robert Rydell's *All the World's a Fair* (1984). I experienced an odd combination of pride and shame—there was my great-grandfather in a book, but a book that portrayed him as being of deeply suspect moral character in a way that was in strong conflict with my values as an anthropologist.

I discussed my findings with my mother, fretting about whether to let Great-Aunt Ann know about this description of her father. Mom thought it would upset her, so I held back and shared the information instead with my mother's cousin Doug in an e-mail message. Doug's immediate reply was, "Ohmygod. . . . to think I have all those scrapbooks down in the basement." At that point I was unaware of the treasure awaiting me.

I began to search more urgently for information on my family's past and finally came across an article about a decision made in the city of Ghent, Belgium, to construct a railroad underpass and name it for Timicheg, an Igorot who had died while in my great-grandfather's charge. (The tunnel, named *Timichegtunnel*, opened in May 2011.) The article mentioned an anthropologist named Patricia Afable, who worked at the Smithsonian. I searched for her contact information to no avail. Finally I asked a newly hired colleague who had worked at the Smithsonian if she could locate it. Success! An e-mail address was obtained.

I sent a missive to Pat on February 1, 2007, identifying myself as an anthropologist who was also the great-granddaughter of Richard Schneidewind. I rather defensively described myself as "indignant" about his career, and misspelled Igorot as "Igarot." Pat responded two hours later, describing herself as "sitting here in a state of shock." She continued that she had "known Richard Schneidewind's name since Rydell's book came out and [had] many times wondered what he looked like, whether he had any children, or descendants, and so on." Pat was excited and so was I. There was a flurry of information back and forth. She supplied me with history and context and answered many questions. I provided photographs and stories, and a family tree. Pat "introduced" me (via the Internet) to Keith Eirinberg, who was working on a novel about a showman much like my great-grandfather, and he sent me a collection of photocopied documents from the Veteran's Administration in Washington,

D.C. I shared this with my mother, and she broke down and in turn shared the information with her Aunt Ann, the only surviving child of Richard Schneidewind. Ann said she did not want to talk about the past. Of course I did, and a whole new area of research began.

In August 2007, I visited Doug and saw the scrapbooks he had mentioned. Much to my surprise, he turned them all over to me. On August 27, 2007, I wrote to Pat with the details:

> There are literally hundreds and hundreds of newspaper articles. My great-grandfather (or maybe his wife) apparently liked to keep track of every mention in the local papers and even the tiniest notices . . . are included. Many of the articles are glued to the pages of the scrapbooks, others are squished and folded between the pages. Most of them are in good condition and a few of the ticket stubs and exposition passes are in amazing condition. There are several cartoons, editorial and otherwise, that mention the "Igorottes." . . .
>
> There is a ton of stuff here and I'm not an archivist and I don't quite know what to do with it. Lots of it is on the verge of crumbling. Very little of it is family oriented, although there's a pretty amazing wedding announcement about my great-grandmother and great-grandfather marrying and having their honeymoon with savage headhunters. There are also a few photos of RS here and there, but everything is very jumbled and old and fragile. The scrapbooks are quite big and the largest, which is falling apart, is a good 19 inches long. There are some really amazing photographs of what appears to be the Yukon-Pacific exposition in Seattle.

I was able to visit Pat and Keith in Washington, D.C., during a trip for my cousin's wedding in January 2008, and Pat flew to GVSU the following March. She spoke to my "Language and Culture" class about her research, and we gave a joint presentation about Igorot voyages with Richard Schneidewind to the GVSU Anthropology Club. I brought a cardboard box containing the scrapbooks to her hotel room and let her peruse the collection during her trip. After that, our real collaboration began.

Pat and I spent the next few years presenting our collective work to different audiences. We spoke at the Asian Symposium during the Alaska-Yukon-Pacific Exposition Centennial in Seattle in 2009, gave a joint keynote talk at the Eighth Igorot International Consultation (IIC-8) in Burnaby, British

Columbia in 2010, and participated in a discussion of World's Fairs and Expositions at the American Association for the Advancement of Science meeting in San Diego in 2011. At each of these events I followed where Pat led, meeting her friends and contacts and growing slowly more familiar with the subject matter at hand. I felt pretty comfortable, being an academic in an academic setting, during the 2009 and 2011 events. The Igorot International Consultation, put on by the Igorot Global Organization, however, was more of a personal challenge.

The Igorot People of Today

The biennial IICs are one of the more important cultural events that occur for contemporary Igorot populations, particularly given the current Igorot "diaspora," with Igorots living throughout Asia, the Americas, Europe, Oceania, the Middle East, and Africa. Liezel C. Longboan argues that despite the wide geographic spread of the Igorot population, "Igorots have constructed their indigenous identities within and through an expanded diaspora of chosen, rather than forced, migration" (Longboan 2011, 325). Technology and regular meetings permit Igorots to maintain an ethnic identity and a sense of collective solidarity, despite the reality of physical separation from the Cordilleras and each other.

Longboan's choice of words, contrasting the voluntary movement of today's Cordillerans with an idea of "forced" movement that is probably associated with Igorot participation in the fairs, illustrates how the stories of the past may be painful to Igorots living today. In fact, writings by and about the indigenous peoples of the Cordillera Mountains often acknowledge a past (influenced by the Spanish and American colonists in addition to the traveling "shows") in which the term *Igorot* was used to portray them as different from the rest of the Philippine people—as "savages." The Cordilleran resistance to conversion, long adherence to traditional practices, and time spent as objects of curiosity abroad all contributed to the term *Igorot* becoming pejorative. According to Igorot anthropologist Albert S. Bacdayan, "The exasperating effect of this prejudice on the part of our lowlander countrymen is that it drives many birthright, red blooded Igorots to deny that they are Igorots and to argue or resist the label 'Igorot' when applied to them" (Bacdayan 2012, 41).

The organizers of the first IIC were well aware of the controversy connected to the word *Igorot* when they named the event the Igorot International

Consultation. Rosalynda Teckney-Callagan states that the IIC "was deliberately titled 'Igorot' to inspire pride among the inhabitants of the Gran Cordillera Central," despite the fact that there was disagreement among those involved. She continues that during the first IIC, held in West Covina, California, in 1995, "It was a struggle to discuss how, outside of our ethnic group, others perceive us. The group was divided between those who wanted to be identified as Igorots and those who did not want to be called by that title. In the end, the word 'Igorot' was agreed upon, regardless of previous negative connotations" (Teckney-Callagan 2012, 5–6). The founders of the IIC and other Cordilleran groups have, like disenfranchised groups the world over, sought to weaken the negativity of a pejorative term by making it their own.

IICs continued to be held every two years and have embraced the participation of a loose grouping of tribes known as BIBAK, which initially stood for the provinces of Bontoc, Ifugao, Benguet, Apayao, and Kalinga. Bontoc is now Mountain Province and Abra has been added to the regions included in the acronym, although BIBAK is still used. (BIMAAK, a variation that incorporates the A for Abra and M for Mountain Province, is sometimes used instead.) During the third IIC, held in Baguio City, Philippines, in 2000, the General Assembly made the decision to validate the constitution and bylaws of a new body—the Igorot Global Organization. According to their official website, "The Igorot Global Organization is a non-profit entity based in the United States with members from across the globe who trace their indigenous ancestry from the Cordillera Administrative Region of the Philippines," and its mission is to "preserve for future generations the diverse heritage of the Igorot people and proactively promote their upliftment, advancement and interests and those of related people." IGO represents a proud ethnicity that is aware of its history and the way it is sometimes misunderstood by others in the Philippines and by the world at large. In the preface to *Igorot by Heart*, the editors state simply, "Much has to be done to correct people's perception of the Igorots" (Dyte et al. 2012, xv).

When Pat and I were invited to speak at IIC-8 in 2010, I was enthusiastic about attending but also acutely aware that many incorrect perceptions of the Igorot people had been encouraged and exacerbated, if not directly brought about, by my great-grandfather and those like him who earned a living by exploiting a certain mostly inaccurate image of them. After the initial invitation from Cliff Belgica, the president of BIBAK for British Columbia, I asked if my mother, who had been following my new discoveries about her grandparents and father with intense interest, could also attend. Belgica assented enthusiastically.

Attending IIC-8, held at Simon Frazer University in Burnaby, British Columbia, was one of the most unusual, uncomfortable, exciting, and enlightening experiences of my life. Although in some ways it resembled academic conferences I had attended (it had panel discussions and was held at a university), it also had an element of "family reunion." This made sense. Given the wide range of countries where Igorots now reside, IICs provide a chance to get together with family and tribe, catch up on people's lives, and celebrate one's culture. It was a joyful event, full of music, memories, and plans for the future.

I have worked as an ethnographer since 1995 and am used to being an outsider. I had been invited to the IIC, and I was giving a keynote speech. Still, I have never felt so much like an intruder. It was not the people. Everyone I met was incredibly friendly. However, the theme for the consultation in 2010 was "Keeping Our Heritage Alive," and in remembrance of the Igorot past, BIBAK British Columbia had taken a covered, outdoor courtyard at Simon Frazer University and turned it into a reproduction of the kind of "Igorot Village" Truman K. Hunt and Richard Schneidewind used to run. (It struck me at the time that this was, ironically, a replica of something fake.) Posters were placed upon temporary walls depicting photographs of the "villages" at various world's fairs, including my great-grandfather's "Igorrote Village" at the Alaska-Yukon-Pacific Exposition in Seattle. The opening ceremonies of the event even included my mother, described in the program as the "Hon. Carlyn Schneidewind Weibel," doing the ribbon cutting. Finally, during the ceremonial dances meant to recall the dances done during the expositions and fairs, my mother and I were pulled from the audience to dance with the Bontoc Igorots.

On one level, I was thrilled and delighted. This was a dream come true, after all, a chance to connect with a people I had heard so much about and who were so entwined with my family's history. There was something beautiful, on a symbolic level, about dancing with the Bontoc people, wondering what Richard Schneidewind would have made of it all. On the other hand, I was mortified. Participants who did not know why we were there looked my mother up and down, trying to determine whom we looked like and whether we had any Igorot ancestry. Far worse was my constant awareness that my ancestor had exploited the ancestors of some of the people there. What is more, my family had engaged in a career that had helped damage the reputation of the Igorot people as a whole. All around me were reminders that the

Schneidewinds had used the Bontoc Igorots, and here we were as invited guests!

Some of Antero's descendants were present at IIC-8, but our paths never crossed. Was it just bad luck, or were some wounds still too painful to be examined? I was able to speak to quite a few other people, including a physician who told me in no uncertain terms that the tours had been beneficial because they made his ancestors more sophisticated about the world, brought education, and had led to their conversion to Christianity. I found myself trying to make an anthropological argument for cultural relativism, suggesting that perhaps the Igorot community would have been better off had the tours never happened, but he disagreed. I felt baffled. Who was I going to listen to—contemporary anthropologists and historians, or a member of the "exploited" group?

I was reminded of a certain tension between Patricia Afable's assertions of Igorot agency during the fairs, which have been strengthened by the knowledge she gained from me of the close interactions between the Schneidewinds, their children, and Bontoc families during the tours, and Robert Rydell's contention that the so-called "performers" were really victims. "It is worthwhile remembering the terrible episode from the 1904 St Louis exposition," Rydell writes, "when a very famous anthropologist from the Smithsonian Institution severed the heads of several deceased Filipino performers, removed their brains, and sent them to the Smithsonian for future study—a harsh and extreme way to treat people who are regarded primarily as performers" (Rydell 2008: 21.3). As for me, I am unable to make either argument in a reasonable way. I am not a neutral party, and my experience at IIC-8 made me all too aware of this.

Whether or not the fairs were a major factor, the Igorot people are a minority in the Philippines, one seen by many as inferior to the majority populace. Since I began to work with Pat, I have come across non-Igorot Filipinos who complained that the fairs made outsiders think *all* Philippine people were dog-eating headhunters. A Philippine doctor I met in Michigan, hearing about my research, was stupefied that I was working with Pat. "I've never heard of an Igorot with a PhD!" she exclaimed. "When I would go to Baguio City with my family, they would just come down from the mountains and play music for spare change!" A young Kalinga woman I met in California, who worked as a police officer in Manila, described how astounded her coworkers were when they learned she was Igorot. Igorots today are still commonly afflicted by prejudice, especially within the Philippines.

Despite this, or because of this, groups like IGO have come into existence. As the Igorot diaspora spreads, however, there is a continued identification with their indigenous roots. Analyzing the online presence and self-identification of the global Igorot population, Longboan notes that the Internet has turned into an accessible-from-anywhere *dap-ay*, which refers both to a community decision-making procedure and the physical structure where it takes place. Longboan points out that "Igorots continue to be framed by colonial-era discourses more than a century after they were displayed in America as dog-eaters during the St. Louis World's Fair" but argues that in contemporary times, via community boards such as Bibaknets, "indigenous peoples are reconfiguring indigeneity and modernity in translocal places, both online and offline" (Longboan 2011, 335, 338).

Mutuality and the Future

As an anthropologist, it would not be out of the question for me to turn to the Igorot community as a focus of new research. Given my family identity and the history of anthropology vis-à-vis the Igorot community, any steps in that direction have to be carefully considered. I would not want to enter any situation that could be considered a form of exploitation, an echo of the past. At the same time, my work so far on this topic has been alongside Pat, and I have tried to remain constantly sensitive to the Cordilleran frame of mind. In the preface to *Igorot by Heart*, the editors write that one of their major goals is to provide "a reference for understanding the Igorot culture from the perspective of the people themselves" and to educate the "non-Igorot and/or Cordilleran audience" (Dyte et al. 2012, xv). It seems to me that there may be an opportunity here for an anthropologist with a guilty conscience.

Although I could possibly serve a role educating non-Igorots about the Igorot population (there are BIBAK groups representing Igorot populations in Chicago, somewhat close to my home in Grand Rapids, and in Los Angeles and San Diego, where I travel frequently to visit family), the Igorot "diaspora" is very different from the refugee situation of the Somalis with whom Catherine Besteman works (Chapter 16; Besteman 2009). Igorots abroad seem to be, on the whole, settled, organized, and fully capable of advocating for themselves. At IIC-8, I met a large number of politically active and engaged people, many of whom held advanced degrees and were involved in the project of assembling their history, documenting their culture, and participating in the necessary steps to keep the widespread Igorot community intact and informed.

Patricia Afable, of course, is an example of an Ibaloy Igorot woman who was called a "savage" in her childhood but went on to study chemistry and then anthropology, eventually earning her PhD from Yale and working in the Smithsonian's Asian Cultural History Program. Sanjek wrote two decades ago that the profession of anthropology at the time was limited "in terms of training and according professional recognition to ethnographers of colour who study their own peoples" (Sanjek 1993, 16), but Pat and others, including anthropologist Albert S. Bacdayan, a retired University of Kentucky professor who studied such topics as irrigation and gender dynamics in Igorot populations and has served as cochair of the Igorot Scholarship Program, as well as Australia-based applied anthropologist Minerva Chaloping-March, whose work examines the impact of mining and mine closures on the residents of the Cordilleran region, demonstrate that for the Igorot population, no lack exists.

One of my goals, as I continue to study my family's history, its connection to anthropology, and its impact on the Igorot community, will be to undertake ethnographic research of some kind in this area, but with an applied, mutualistic focus. Part of understanding a culture and creating a lasting, accurate ethnographic record is providing information that fills in details, retrieves lost information, and supplies new perspectives. My background and worldview differ from those of the early, cultural evolutionist anthropologists such as Jenks and Haddon but also from those of contemporary Igorot ethnographers Afable, Bacdayan, and Chaloping-March, so perhaps my contribution to a better understanding of Igorot culture and its value, starting with the steps I have already taken with Patricia Afable, may be of service.

Chapter 7

Thinking About and Experiencing Mutuality

Notes on a Son's Formation

Lane Ryo Hirabayashi

A key assumption of mainstream anthropological fieldwork is that the researcher, as an adult raised in a different culture, must grapple with learning a new worldview and all the intricacies of an unfamiliar design for living. One enters the field with a tool kit containing the tried and tested methods of firsthand data collection, including the critically important technique of participant observation.

As a neophyte in the PhD program at the University of California, Berkeley, where we were still exposed to Malinowski's *Argonauts of the Western Pacific* as a model of how to do fieldwork, even I—a rather naïve twenty-two-year-old who had grown up in the suburbs of Marin Country, California—felt skeptical about the apolitical context that such a model implied. Even, however, with all the critique surrounding the United States' wars in Southeast Asia, I remember that we were still warned not to say anything in our first-year graduate seminars about what Talal Asad had termed anthropology's "colonial encounter" (Asad 1973).

What I came to understand over the next decade was that mutuality, as Roger Sanjek situates it in the Introduction, does not overtly displace this anthropological tradition; rather, it repositions and reorients the researcher in terms of why, and possibly how, social research is initiated, as well as how it is carried out and disseminated.[1] Unlike "distanciation," once valued in some scholarly quarters for its clear (and supposedly clean) separation between researcher and subject or topics—which ostensibly promotes objectivity—mutuality essentially posits a compatibility of perspectives and implies, at the very least, an overlap, or even shared identity, of researcher and subject.[2]

As a viable approach to anthropological research, mutuality resonates with my career-long experiences. Like Sanjek, I do not necessarily place mutuality in opposition to traditional mainstream anthropological research, but for heuristic purposes, it is convenient to compare and contrast the two, as he does in his introduction to this volume.[3] At a practical level, mutuality can entail common ground in the sense that all parties involved in a research initiative may hold shared interests regarding information (specifically, what kinds of data are produced and who is given access), interpretations, possible organizing efforts or actions that may result, and larger outcomes or goals. In this sense, mutuality would appear to generate a distinctive approach to social research that goes well beyond the phenomenology of shared experience, or feelings of mutual regard and friendship, that previously have been scrutinized by anthropologists.[4]

In this context, I propose that mutuality is simultaneously an ideal, at least for some researchers; an approach to research, if not a method in its own right; and, thus, a mode of social research practice. And, as many of the essays in this volume indicate, it is also ultimately a kind of epistemology—that is, although the ideal of mutuality entails some risks, in its best instances it can also generate forms of knowledge, including insights, hypotheses, and outcomes, that go beyond what mainstream approaches to social research can offer.

Teaching Through Instruction

Where and why was I exposed to this version of mutuality? Although a year as a postdoctoral scholar at the University of California, Los Angeles in 1981–1982 reinforced my interest in how mutuality could be used to ameliorate what I perceived to be the negative impact of power relations to shape fieldwork,[5] looking back, I would have to identify the prior influence of my father, James A. Hirabayashi, as I grew up, attended college, and began my graduate training in sociocultural anthropology. From a pedagogical perspective, Jim's approach and influence was clearly didactic in nature, but now I realize that as I reached my early twenties, it was also, at the same time, tacit in many ways. I would like to use this chapter as a vehicle to reexamine what my father, an anthropologist intimately involved in the creation of the fields of Asian American and ethnic studies, imparted to me. My hope is that beyond allowing me to place a major debt on record, this account will reveal an alternative for scholars concerned with finding better ways to negotiate the ethics and politics of data collection in sociocultural anthropology.

Family was highly important to my father, and his commitment was conveyed largely through an oral medium. Although my parents had divorced while I was in the sixth grade, from as early as my high school years my father made a point of inviting me to his home in San Francisco so that we could spend time together. On these occasions, he often told me stories about his family's history. Because I was interested in the Hirabayashis, it felt easy and natural for me to pursue this topic, and I used independent study units, an integral part of Sonoma State College's Hutchins School of Liberal Studies undergraduate curriculum, to carry out projects related to my family's history. In 1973, I collected an oral history of my step-grandmother, Sadako, also known as Sadie. Both of my parents vetted the original interview as I worked for weeks to transcribe it and break it into analytic themes; I even wrote a play loosely based on the story of Sadie's second marriage to my paternal grandfather, Shungo.[6]

Another occasion I remember quite clearly had to do with a sad development, around 1970, when my paternal grandfather became terminally ill. My father took time off from work, went to Seattle, and spent a couple of weeks with his tape recorder at my grandfather's bedside. During my grandfather's last days, my father was able to record a detailed oral history focused on why Shungo had come to the United States and on his initial experiences working for a railroad company in the hinterlands of Seattle. This oral history became the topic of numerous discussions I had with Jim over the years, especially during my undergraduate years, when I was becoming more interested in Japanese American history writ large. In particular, this was the first time that I remember my dad talking about the role of Mukyokai, a unique non-church-based Christianity that was originated and led in Japan by religious philosopher Kanzo Uchimura, following his sustained period of studying Christianity in the United States in the early 1900s.

This was the point at which my father also started sharing memories with me of his own childhood. Jim had grown up on a small farm in the White River Valley, close to the present-day towns of Thomas and Kent, Washington.[7] Among other stories, I remember Jim telling me about his boyhood hijinks and a number of episodes related to his teen years "in camp" during

World War II. One of the latter stories had to do with my father's disappointing educational experiences in the U.S. government's Tule Lake camp. I never forgot Jim's account, and years later, the two of us developed and presented joint testimony at the U.S. Commission on the Wartime Relocation and Internment of Civilians hearings in San Francisco in 1981. Both in written and oral testimony, my father recalled his and his parents' dismay at the Tule Lake high school curriculum and resources and how, in the end, this became part of the reason the Hirabayashis tried to leave Tule as soon as they could. My addition to my father's personal account was to scour the available literature in order to assess the damage that *Nisei* (the "second generation" born in America to Japanese immigrant parents) children in general had incurred as a result of both the conceptual foundations of the school system in the War Relocation Authority camps and the substandard conditions that plagued these schools, especially in the first and second years of confinement.[8]

Beyond family history, Jim's didactic instruction about social research took a decidedly serious turn after I entered the doctoral program in anthropology at the University of California, Berkeley in 1974. While I went through the required graduate seminars, including "the classics" (e.g., Bronislaw Malinowski and A. R. Radcliffe-Brown) and key ethnographies (e.g., Edmund Leach's *Political Systems of Highland Burma*, E. E. Evans-Pritchard's *The Nuer*, and others), my father began to supplement my formal training by suggesting themes and giving me books that were important to him in terms of his own training as well as to his ongoing work. I began to hear more oral history about my father's interdisciplinary social sciences training at Harvard University's famed Department of Social Relations and his classes with luminaries such as sociologist Talcott Parsons, social psychologist Gordon Allport, and anthropologists who included Cora Du Bois and Clyde Kluckhohn. Concurrently, I became more aware of my dad's huge library and began getting a sense of his current interests, which included Claude Lévi-Strauss and French theory in the social sciences more generally.

Jim's discourses on *Objectivity in Social Research* by Gunnar Myrdal (1969) made a particularly strong impression on me. Jim spoke to me a number of times about the significance of Myrdal's thesis—that social values are an integral part of any and all social research and that we handle bias only by explicitly presenting our own, especially as these impact our work. He eventually gave me his heavily underlined paperback copy of this book, which I have kept in my personal library for decades.

Another influential piece of writing that my father frequently mentioned to me in our talks about social research was a seminal article by Mina Davis Caulfield, "Culture and Imperialism" (1972). From this progressive vision of what was required in order to "reinvent" mainstream anthropology, my father especially highlighted Caulfield's idea of "cultures of resistance" as a perspective on how a group's design for living could be harnessed to combat the vicissitudes of colonial and neocolonial intervention. A companion idea was Caulfield's concept of "culture building," a theoretical tool that Jim greatly valued in his community-based work.

Jim's appreciation of Caulfield's ideas was probably the major, and lasting, influence that he transmitted to me. I have used it as a touchstone in pursuing my various research endeavors. At one level, a "cultures of resistance" perspective sensitized me toward understanding why and how vernacular beliefs and practices were a kind of "cultural capital" that communities of color and communities forced to deal with oppression employed to obtain a modicum of self-determination.[9] At the same time, the concept of "culture building" provided a practical, political agenda for anthropological fieldwork. Here, one could certainly apply the fundamental tools of ethnography but with a specific goal of trying to delineate how sociocultural institutions could be drawn upon, strengthened, or supplemented in their efforts to enhance the resources that supported their worldview and self-determination.

Teaching Through Example

Apart from these specific discussions that exemplified his didactic approach to our family history or the discipline of anthropology, I now realize that my father also taught me a great deal through example. As it turns out, this may be a family pattern—toward the end of his life, my father related that his father had taught all of the Nisei children in our family about Christian values and ethics through the course and example of daily life, not by preaching or even by talking about Christianity per se.

The timeline of my tacit learning is intertwined with my last years of high school and my undergraduate and graduate education during the late 1960s and the 1970s.[10] In 1968, my father completed a year-long stay in Nigeria and returned to the department of anthropology at San Francisco State College (now university), where the seeds of the ensuing "Third World Strike" had already been planted. Because of his incarceration experience as a Nisei during World War II and his fieldwork with communities of color at home and internationally, my father was disposed to listen seriously to the message of students active in the Asian American Political Alliance (Asian American Studies Department 2009; Nakatsu 2013). He joined the American Federation of Teachers and walked the picket line with his faculty colleagues in support of the student-run Third World Liberation Front in 1968 and 1969. Subsequently, when the strike resulted in negotiations that included the creation of a new School of Ethnic Studies (SES), my father took a leave from the department of anthropology to become the first dean of SES, a position he held for the next seven years.

Although my parents were divorced by that time, I remember that the strike and subsequent developments were the topic of many discussions I had with both of them. Increasingly, because he was busy keeping up with developments in each of the constituent departments of SES, my dad ended up taking me with him to various community events in the Bay Area. Standouts I recall were a Native American urban powwow, held in a community auditorium in South San Francisco; a Chicano/Latino theater performance at the Galería de la Raza in the Mission District; and a Black Panther rally in Oakland, where, for the first time, I heard the Reverend Jesse Jackson speak.

As part of this expanded educational exposure, my dad also introduced me to a number of community organizations. At this point in my life, I was heavily involved in music and was playing with musicians in both Marin County, where I lived, and San Francisco. My dad encouraged me to consider offering free lessons for youth so I could utilize the one actual skill I then possessed.[11] Unfortunately, I was a little too young to market my skills effectively, and perhaps because suburban Marin County was a more sheltered environment than San Francisco, I always felt out of my league when dealing with urban youth raised on the other side of the Golden Gate bridge. Nonetheless, the message from Jim was clear: the Third World Movement was about identity—identifying as a "Third World person," as we put it in those days—and, beyond that, about exploring what you could give to community organizations seeking empowerment and working for the benefit of all people.

In 1972, when I began my sophomore year at Sonoma State, I arranged through Chicano studies to enroll in a nine-unit independent study course offered by Asian American studies at San Francisco State. This was an innovative class led by a senior professor of social work. It met in San Francisco's Japan Town, in the Japanese Community Youth Council building on Sutter and Buchanan Streets. There were no formal lectures, but once a week, leaders from one or two community-based organizations would come to class and talk about their group—their mission, their target populations, the services they provided, and how their work related to the history of Japanese Americans attending to needs within their own community. This was a wonderful exposure to what was going on in Japan Town, and we learned about groups and activities as varied as "Nisei Singles"; the Japanese American Citizens League, a long-established civil rights organization; social work clinics and their clients in the J-Town Western Addition neighborhood; and men's and women's service committees at the area's Buddhist temple and Methodist church.

A major requirement of the course was to select one of the organizations we learned about; do volunteer work there for a certain numbers of hours; and with this foundation, write a term paper that identified a community need, developed a means to assess that need, and proposed an innovative way to respond to it. I volunteered at the Japanese Community Youth Council and worked at that agency's community newspaper, *Rodan*. This commitment led to additional community organization work in the Japan Town area.

The independent study course became the vehicle that allowed me to find a place within the San Francisco Japanese (and Chinese) American communities. Although it was obvious to everyone that I was biracial and clear that I had grown up in Marin County apart from any Bay Area Japanese or Asian American community, I experienced a degree of warmth and acceptance that made J-Town a more pleasant and enjoyable social environment than any I had encountered since high school. It was "a matter of comfort," as one anthropologist (Kendis 1989) described the subjective feel of belonging within a Japanese American community, and once I experienced this, I felt at ease and "home."[12] This deep-seated sense of mutuality is something I have repeatedly sought and found in places that have enough of a numerical critical mass to form a Japanese American community. It is also the root of the mutuality I seek to establish when I initiate a new research project and negotiate an agreement with individuals and organizations to work with or for them.

Research Work Together

In the mid-1970s, I worked with my father on two projects in San Francisco that had a profound impact on how I see and do research to this day. While he was still dean of SES, Jim was invited by a Japanese American community organization to do an analysis of its institutional decision making. It was a fascinating project, because this organization had evolved within the context of the Third World Strike and thus was egalitarian, nonhierarchical, and democratic, and it operated with the assistance of many volunteers of all ages. Because it was a service organization concerned with the medical needs of its clients, there were increasing pressures to professionalize. There was also pressure to formalize many aspects of its operations, not only to provide services more efficiently but to generate data that could be used for state- and federal-level grant applications as well.

In a nutshell, these pressures were leading to decision-making struggles, and one faction of the organization's leadership invited my father to assess the situation and offer recommendations about how decision-making impasses could be ameliorated. My father was able to collect much data on the group's operations and difficulties, but, as he explained the situation to me, he did not have the time to undertake analysis and write up his conclusions. So I worked with him over the period of a year to produce a finished report (Hirabayashi 1974).

The second project, five years later, concerned a Japanese American organization offering bilingual, bicultural education to secondary school–level students. One segment of its leadership invited Jim to assess its performance and offer suggestions for improvement. As before, my father collected qualitative data onsite, and then asked me to work on its analysis and to draft a report for the school's administrators.

The underlying problem was that the school was trying to serve two different groups—first, Japanese students, many of whom would be returning to Japan to live and continue their education there, and second, a cohort largely of third-generation American children of Japanese ancestry with some children of other ethnic backgrounds. Serving the needs of both these contrasting groups was the key difficulty in adhering to the overall mission of the school. We delivered our report, although I do not recall that we met further with any administrators, nor were we updated by them about how our information and recommendations were utilized. This lack of follow-up was an oversight that I now regret.

Looking back, I can see that these two studies carried out with my father in the 1970s were the key to how I conducted my doctoral fieldwork in Mexico,[13] as well as how I have done research within the Japanese American community in the years since I was awarded my PhD at the University of California, Berkeley in 1981. The critical features of this joint work were as follows:

1. The agencies were having internal difficulties and wanted "outside" input about these problems and about possible means to ameliorate them.
2. My father was invited to carry out the research by the agency leadership. I was drafted after the initial invitation to help with analysis and writing up the findings.
3. My father was given access to "inside" information quite readily because he was well respected by the agency leaders, no doubt because of his role in the San Francisco State strike and because of his reputation of supporting community-based organizations. Jim did not have to create fieldwork rapport, let alone overcome issues of mistrust. These concerns were answered from the start.
4. Although we were invited because of our status as "insiders" (or insiders enough), we consciously tried to offer an objective analysis and present it in such a way that the agency leadership and concerned members could understand and evaluate our work themselves. Rather than attempting to produce *the* answer, we tried to offer options for their consideration and then leave decisions about follow-up action to them.

A final dimension of these projects has to do with mutuality. We took these two research projects very seriously. Jim invested weeks of precious time in collecting data; I contributed months of pro bono effort working with Jim to develop analytic schema for data analysis, doing literature searches to supplement the primary material, and drafting and redrafting numerous versions of each report. Why all this effort? This was the first time that I harnessed my skills for the intended benefit of Japanese American community-based organizations that were trying their best to serve the people. In a few years, I had gone from being a kid whose major offering was guitar lessons to a budding social scientist who felt he might have something tangible, in the form of analysis and advice, to give to an agency trying to do good in the larger community.

My own approach to mutuality remains centered in this vision, in the focus on working with or for a community-based group seeking to empower an ethnic minority population that had been excluded from the mainstream in terms of resources and services, whether for the elderly, for women, or for youth.

In short, these organizations were manifestations of a "culture of resistance." At the same time, this was occurring precisely during a period when, as a biracial kid from the suburbs, I began to find and assert my own identity as a Japanese and as an Asian American, *hapa* boy though I was. So the mutuality in my case had a decidedly ethnic dimension, and I willingly plunged in, even though I was scarcely a bona fide Asian American community insider.

Perhaps as a result of the mutualities involved, we did not seek to publish either of the two reports, even when an editor of a prestigious educational journal asked me to submit a manuscript about the school project. In effect, our research findings were privileged, and we did not share them with the Japanese American community at large, let alone with anthropologists, other researchers, or the general public. Although I cannot remember whether confidentiality was requested from the organizations' leadership at the time, the fact was that Jim was invited because each organization was experiencing internal difficulties, and publishing or otherwise disseminating our analyses might have revealed problems that would cause embarrassment for the research participants, at the very least, or that could have resulted in funding being curtained or denied the next time a grant was submitted. We could not know this for sure, but confidentiality was a correlate of mutuality as we practiced it. This was our basic logic: it is our community, and we are dealing with a community-based organization that is serving our ethnic compatriots; we should not seek self-promotion through the publication or dissemination of information that could damage individuals or the community-based organization. We would not circulate potentially negative information about a group any more than we would do so about each other or about the Hirabayashi family.[14]

How do the two cases relate to the question of bias? Bias is always an issue in social research, and this was where Jim reminded me of the lessons we had learned from Gunnar Myrdal: no social research is "God's truth." The best that a responsible practitioner can offer his or her readers is to be as forthright as possible in delineating where he or she is coming from in terms of background values and commitments, the relationship one has with a particular topic or community of research subjects, and the theoretical and methodological tools that one utilizes. I believe we tried to carry out Myrdal's injunction in both our studies.

Mutuality as Means and End

I end this chapter by returning to the basic dialectic that Sanjek identifies in his introduction between the analytic and professional academic and the engaged, all-too-human practitioner. I have tried to account for the reasons and the manner in which this dialectic was bridged for me in the advice and the practices of my father, especially in terms of the mutuality that he felt with the Japanese American community and that I inherited and absorbed through my ties to and the respect I had for Jim.

Perhaps another way to think about this dialectic is by posing an ideal hypothetical case: to be fully "native" and conduct fieldwork on that basis alone would assume a perfect coincidence between subject and object that is theoretically possible, but it is not a situation I can recall any anthropologist ever professing.[15] Anthropology, rather, inherently encourages an analytic disposition, and its tradition, theoretical resources, techniques for data collection, and analytic tools all propel practitioners in this direction (although I have wondered if it is also those people who are inclined to step back and observe social situations who are disposed to become anthropologists). In sum, mutuality does not fully resolve this dialectic, but it is worth considering in the sense that it may provide a way to think about the bridging of these two ideal poles.

Beyond this, as I look back on my training as an anthropologist, I can see that I was the beneficiary of a unique historical moment. My father was exposed to a remarkable tradition of interdisciplinary social sciences at Harvard University. He did his best to pass on the high points of that tradition, as he understood it, to me. Jim was also deeply involved in and deeply influenced by the Third World Strike at San Francisco State College in 1968 and the subsequent formation of the School of Ethnic Studies. My father's efforts to teach me about mutuality in this context were largely tacit but were manifest through his (and then my) identification with and participation in Japanese American community-based organizations. These linkages, in turn, led to a methodology that privileged mutuality but also, I would argue, to an *epistemology* that had its base in practice (explicit and tacit cultural knowledge) and in action. Subsequently, based on this conceptual foundation, Jim and I were able to work together quite easily on a number of projects. These included three books: an anthology resulting from a transnational multiresearcher project about *Nikkei* (persons of Japanese ancestry) in the Americas (Hirabayashi, Kikumuro-Yano, and Hirabayashi 2002); a second on the innovative philosophical approach to community engagement of the Japanese American National Museum (Kikumura-Yano, Hirabayashi, and Hirabayashi 2005); and a volume about my uncle Gordon Hirabayashi's life during the 1940s, when he was jailed for resisting the mass removal and incarceration of Japanese Americans (Hirabayashi, Hirabayashi, and Hirabayashi 2013).

The invitation to think about mutuality that gave birth to this book, then, has presented me with an opportunity to revisit and rethink this personal history and the research activities it generated. In doing so, I have tried both to share what was given me and to invite readers in turn to rethink and sharpen an approach that can be an integral tool in ethically and politically informed social research leading to engagement and empowerment as part and parcel of creating cultural knowledge.

Chapter 8

Cartographies of Mutuality

Lessons from Darfur

Rogaia Mustafa Abusharaf

Recent years have witnessed a major shift in anthropological engagement with contemporary urgent predicaments. This shift is to be expected, for as Clifford Geertz put it more than a decade ago, "the ways of the world and the ways of anthropology" dictate it (2002, 3). Reconciling the myriad meanings and significances of the concepts of mutuality and "anthropology's changing terms of engagement," as Roger Sanjek invites us, is timely and critical. I see mutuality and urgency, a concept now gaining currency in British social anthropology, as complementary, propelling us to both interrogate our subject positions vis-à-vis the interlocutors we encounter in fieldwork situations and move beyond detachment and other "persuasive fictions of anthropology" (Strathern 1987, 251).

In this chapter, I reflect on who I am as an anthropologist by drawing on my experiences living and studying in diverse locations in the north, south, west, and east: in my native Sudan and later in Cairo, the United States, the United Kingdom, and the State of Qatar. Writing this chapter raised an important question as to my position vis-à-vis my subjects. My interviewees themselves brought tremendous depth to the issues I was exploring and helped sharpen my theoretical and analytical tools. Their worries and concerns shaped the kind of research I pursued in the past and continue to track in the present.

In 2011, the southern region of Sudan seceded following a Southern Referendum in which the overwhelming majority of southerners voted for independence. This occurred exactly six years after the signing of the Comprehensive Peace Agreement (CPA) between the Government of Sudan and the Sudan Peoples' Liberation Movement/Army (SPLM). The CPA brought an end to the protracted war, both boosting morale and restoring confidence and trust between south and north Sudan. This 2005 power-sharing agreement between the Government of Sudan and the SPLM, one of the movement's primary demands, paved the way for formation of a government of national unity. For the first time, Sudanese citizens saw the foundation laid for the reinstatement of some semblance of normalcy.

The 2011 secession, a critical factor in Sudan's present weakness, has deep historical roots in the years of British rule. This fact must be abstracted neither from an oppressive colonial history nor from a postcolonial environment that has negated the successful implementation of a viable nation-building project. In the critical matter of identity, Sudanese politics have now reconfigured my subjectivity, as they did earlier for the larger segment of Southern Sudanese whose trials and travails I tried to unravel in *Transforming Displaced Women in Sudan: Politics and the Body in a Squatter Settlement* (Abusharaf 2009b). As a Sudanese writer, my subject position changed as of 2011. Now, inescapably, I write as a northerner, and key anthropological debates on "the re-identification of the ethnographer" vis-à-vis ethnographic writing (Marcus 1998, 6) have arrived at the forefront of my subject role. This involuntarily acquired identity does not diminish my interest in issues of national self-definition, displacement, borders, political violence, and cross-cultural mediations (Abusharaf 2002, 2009b, 2010a, 2011), nor does it limit my concern with competing narratives of the situation in the Sudan (or both Sudans) locally, regionally, and transnationally.

In this chapter, I begin with issues related to my experiences growing up in Khartoum. I hope to impart some insight as to how I see mutuality and urgency in various ethnographic scenarios. I hope as well to show how my surrounding environments over time have contributed to forming my views and my fieldwork concerns in and out of Sudan, including its Darfur crisis.

Formative Years of Childhood in the 1970s and Beyond

Three distinctive memories of Darfur's difficulties have helped to shape my interest in the ethnography of conflict and mediation and my view of mutuality, which I see as reciprocity and acknowledgment of the very real influence that interlocutors bring to bear on what we study. In retrospect, these scattered autobiographical experiences significantly impacted my understanding of the anguish of the region, a crisis observers such as Colin Powell have depicted as "the first genocide of the twenty-first century" and an "African Holocaust."

The first memory was formed in primary school at Teachers' Training College in Omdurman, Sudan. Founded by the British in the 1930s, the college was located near the Tomb of Imam Mohamed Ahmed Al-Mahdi, a revered revolutionary who fought colonization. To me, its location represents a sublime irony of history and politics in the city that many would prefer replace Khartoum as the national capital. The colossal, majestic copper bells in the college's schoolyard always heralded the end of the day, as well as marking the beginning of holidays. I remember the loud clank at the start of the four-day religious holiday, Eid Aladha, or Feast of the Sacrifice, which follows the end of the annual pilgrimage to Mecca, the Hajj. Eid is celebrated to give thanks to God for providing a lamb to sacrifice instead of Abraham's son Ishmael.

In 1975, the headmistress called all the pupils for an important announcement before we dispersed. As I recall, she spoke about how we could contribute to a project then called "Fighting Thirst in Western Sudan Provinces of Darfur and Kordofan," regions hundreds of miles away in what, until 2011, was the largest country in terms of territory on the African continent. She asked us to convey a message to our families to donate the skins of their sacrificial lambs as water containers to help people dying of thirst. Sheepskins and hooves, with other less desirable parts of the animal, ordinarily would have been bequeathed to the butchers who slaughtered and skinned each animal. Volunteers would come to collect the sheepskins, she told us.

Sure enough, Eid Day arrived, and so did the butchers with their sharpened knives and axes. The butchers roamed from one house to the next in their bloody clothes, ready to utter a short prayer before they cut the throats of the sheep. All in all, this event was traumatic for children. For three days before their slaughter, we watched these animals moving around, eating grass, drinking water, and sleeping when night fell. The slaughter brought only horror to us, but not so to the elders, who exulted at fulfilling a pillar of the faith.

Eid brought families and neighbors together, and relatives from each nook and cranny joined to feast in celebration of the solemn commemorative sacrament. On that cold day, trucks piled high with the skins of lambs in variegated colors, their fatty tails intact, drove through one neighborhood to the next, picking up these remains. For me, the cause of saving the thirsty and the dying in a drought-stricken land did not mitigate the horror of the frightful events I witnessed. My memories, even as I write today, stir emotions of horror. In retrospect, the slaughter helped concretize the political economy of scarcity for me. As I reflect on why I am interested in Darfur's anguish, I see that scarcity was stacked on those trucks dripping with blood, spewing exhaust from loud mufflers, as they drove through the narrow alleys and bumpy roads of Omdurman Street.

As years wore on, the narrative of Darfur's suffering shifted from roaming butchers to human catastrophe in desert regions ruined by drought and desertification in the early 1980s. Hundreds of thousands of people from Darfur and Kordofan were propelled to flee famine. They arrived in droves at Khartoum, seeking refuge and abode. From that time on, they inhabited an ad hoc camp called Al-Muailh in the southern part of Khartoum, separated by many miles from the national palace where President Gaaffar Nemeri lived in luxury and extravagance, oblivious to the tragedy of those living in plastic tents under sweltering heat in yet another merciless desert.

My family and neighbors started discussing how best to provide immediate help to the refugees, particularly to women and children. In due course, clothes, mattresses, bedsheets, food items, and over-the-counter medicines started to be amassed. We, the young volunteers, were instructed to inspect donated clothes for suitability of use before folding and packing them neatly in carton boxes. I enjoyed the task. I basked in an atmosphere brimming with a sense of purpose and industry. Although we took pride in the philanthropy of kith and kin, my family emphasized that such effort is necessary but not sufficient. What would have been sufficient was a systematic effort by the state to perform its responsibilities toward citizens who fell on hard times.

These memories remain indelibly engraved on my mind because they allowed my thinking about the relation of politics to the appalling disparities afflicting fellow Sudanese to slowly mature. At the time, the government took no responsibility. Rather, the country's leaders opined about natural disasters over which the government had no control. This served to hide the underlying indifference of the ruling regime, whose lust for power and accumulation of capital superseded its concern for a disenfranchised people. "Mother nature's wrath" was the language used to obfuscate questions of governance and accountability. All the while, citizens were left thirsty, hungry, and adrift. In a rare ethnographic account, *Famine That Kills: Darfur, Sudan, 1984–1985*, Alex de Waal (1989) described the complex stories of despair, at the same time engaging with the politics of humanitarianism. De Waal (1989, 2007) also noted the power of those afflicted to overcome adversity through mobilizing strategies of survival and carefully measured steps toward easing their suffering.

Upon graduating from college, I joined the Sudan Development Corporation (SDC), the largest development organization in Africa, founded by the late Ambassador Mohamed Abdel Majid Ahmed. I was appointed as a junior development information officer, and my job was to maintain contacts with national, regional, and international partners and donors and create a trilingual (Arabic, English, French) newsletter to report progress on all three phases—feasibility, appraisal, and implementation—of development projects. I participated in field visits with international teams, an experience that exposed me to the logic of international development economics, discourses, and practices. Against incalculable odds, the SDC ventured forth into providing assistance and loans ranging in scale from small microcredit to large sums for projects such as iron-ore foundries, marble quarries, agricultural equipment, and the like.

The SDC allowed me to see how some European companies viewed Sudan at the time. For example, when we received persistent requests from a European country to market asbestos products to Sudanese building contractors, our CEO responded with a resounding "No!" Although this example may appear tangential, it was not, and institutionalized disparities on a world scale became obvious to me. Profit outweighed serious health risks to Third World people. Permanent lung damage and pleural disorders were of no concern to the company in question.

With respect to the scale of development projects in Western Sudan, including Darfur, efforts by the SDC were important but, unfortunately, could not alone reduce poverty or change decades of institutionalized neglect. Western Darfur, like the south, was an incubator of grievances. Little is mentioned about the situational analysis of indices of poverty in north and east Sudan, however, but they too fell below the poverty line. My SDC experiences compelled me to engage in a sustained effort to understand the disparate voices, practices, and representations through which the stories about Sudan are told. Later, as I embarked on my Darfur project, these memories propelled me to ask myself: Was my fear of the piles of bloody sheepskins on the backs of the trucks misplaced, or was it a sign of horrors to come?

Family Reminiscences and Their Connection to Mutuality

As I consider "the values we bring from the wider worlds in which we grow up and live" (see the introduction to this book), I want to mention the role my father, Mustafa Abusharad, and other family members played in my upbringing. The connections are clear between my childhood and the topics I have chosen to pursue as a "native" anthropologist, including the dilemmas of Darfur.

I grew up in a northern Sudanese political family of intellectuals and freedom fighters and with a father who exposed me to a wide variety of literature from around the world, ranging, early on, from Taha Hussein's *The Days* and Charles Dickens's *Oliver Twist* to works of comedy and irony, including Denys Parson's popular "Funny" series, which began in 1969 with *Funny Ha Ha* and *Funny Peculiar*. In later years, my father gave me books of a more complex sort, both in Arabic and English, such as *Cashmere, The Dubliners, Season of Migration to the North, Children of the Alley, Chambers' Cyclopedia of English Literature, The Ten Problems of British Statesmanship, Christianity in Old Nubian Kingdoms*, and translated works from Hebrew (such as *The Yellow Wind*), Russian, and French. My father's exceptionally satisfying introduction to the mythological world of the imagined city of mirrors, Mocandu, in Gabriel Garcia Marquez's *One Hundred Years of Solitude* (which I read in Arabic) alerted me to a world of narratives of myth and reality. I now see the conflation of myth and reality of this great literary work in the chronic maladies of Sudanese politics, particularly in the construal of "secularism" as apostasy and disdain and the construction of "religion" as a driving force in politics.

My father influenced me by his principled work and values, as well. He held prominent jobs and founded schools for children who could not afford an education. He lived in southern Sudan and spoke several of that region's languages proficiently. He cultivated in me his respect and affection for the people of south Sudan. He was an Arab unfriendly to Arabizing the South and maintained that Arabic be taught as a second language and only on a voluntary basis. Later, when I began my work on the Sudanese diaspora to the United States and Canada, my father was the first to introduce me to the Sudanese sailors who earned American citizenship by virtue of their service in World War II (Abusharaf 1998; 2002, 33–43). He also told me the story of Sati Majid, the first Sudanese to set foot on American soil in 1904, and through my father's unwavering support, I managed to marshal resources within Sudan National Records and craft a narrative about Majid and his lasting impact on African American and Caribbean communities in Brooklyn (Abusharaf 2002,

17–32). I would be remiss not to mention his close reading, substantive comments, and scrupulous copyediting of articles and books I finished before his passing in 2009.

I was also fortunate to live in a home with my late uncle Abdel Khaliq Mahgoub (1927–1971), whose life's work and writings compare with his contemporaries Franz Fanon and C. L. R. James. Banned by successive military and civilian governments alike, the voluminous literature Mahgoub authored is still arguably among the best work on colonial governance and postcolonial surrogacy (see Abusharaf 2009a, 2010b, 2010c). As one of the first to articulate the magnitude of postcolonial violence, as well as providing a theory and method for understanding it, Mahgoub stands among Africa's most important public intellectuals. A Marxist, he was elected to parliament in 1965, after the 1964 October Revolution. He was expelled in 1966 on charges that, as a leftist, he disdained religion, because he advocated the imperative of secularism in a religiously plural society. He was imprisoned, exiled, and finally executed because of his political valor and commitment to Marxism as a frame of reference for thinking and writing about Sudanese political transformation. In solitary confinement, he consecrated his time to writing about the vexations of Sudanese politics and to forecasting the impending failure of the state.

His classmate, and our family friend, El-Tayeb Salih, author of *Season of Migration to the North*, noted in remembrance that Mahgoub was a genius with a thunderous mind; he recounted how, during their literature lessons, twelve-year-old Mahgoub challenged the teacher on an assignment. Mahgoub maintained a keen sense of justice and an absolute faith in the Sudanese people. His military trial and execution deprived us of his charismatic presence and blanketed our home and our entire neighborhood in unbearable sorrow. (I recall even now the guilt and regret I felt for taking apart a matryoshka doll he brought me from Moscow and losing many of the smaller dolls within.) But in the midst of bereavement, we took solace in his brave statement to the military judge's question, "What have you contributed to the people of Sudan?" Refusing to bow, Mahgoub firmly replied, "Consciousness, as much as I could."

I bring Abdel Khaliq Mahgoub's vision to bear in my work as an anthropologist. He ably employed the dialectic in his philosophy of vernacularizing leftist politics. He had a powerful impact on my approach to studying my own society and on the choices I make about the simplicity of writing in plain language so that Sudanese with no training in anthropology can read and digest the material. I see this as a form of mutuality. His lessons about avoiding self-censorship and refusing to "lean in" are ones I try to carry out in my work.

Another uncle, Mohamed Mahgoub, who died in exile in Sweden in 2011, also left an indelible memory. He, too, fought with valor and dignity and wrote about the meddling of the army in politics. A third uncle, Ali Mahgoub, worked for Sudan's agricultural cooperatives. He declined promotion to higher rank and, because of his principles, resisted a salary increase that he believed came directly from the already burdensome taxation of the Sudanese people. Osman Mahgoub, one more uncle, a brilliant historian and former cultural attaché, after his retirement taught evening classes at a nearby Teachers' Union high school in an enrichment program that prepared girls for college admission. This was a low-paying job, but he excelled at it. The women in my family were and are also strong, direct, and averse to accepting reality at face value. At times, they are brutally honest, a trait I resented when directed at me but that I value.

By sheer accident of birth, I am privileged. With family members such as these, my experience growing up was unusual. When Holy Eids arrived, instead of joining friends at the magnificent fun fairs or at the Khartoum Zoo by the River Nile, we visited my uncle Abdel Khaliq Mahgoub in prison, bringing baked goods, candy, and Rothmans cigarettes. We treasured our prison visits as much as our friends cherished their holidays at fairs and zoos. We learned pride, as well as how to celebrate sacrifices and to value Mahgoub's life and thought. What remains pertinent to me is that keeping the best interests of the people around me at heart is the gift I received from my father and uncles. It opened my eyes at an early age to the political lay of the land.

Glimpses from University Years

After attending college at the Cairo University School of Economics and Political Sciences, I went to graduate school at the University of Connecticut, which canalized my thought with scholarship and a commitment to mutuality as I studied with James Faris, Seth Leacock, and the late Bernard Magubane. I recall my journey to America and Storrs, Connecticut, where, upon arrival, I experienced a crushing burden of loneliness and longing for my family and friends back home. Entire days passed without a chance to speak to anyone. Whenever a person of color passed by, I thought to myself: *He or she reminds me so much of so and so in Khartoum.* I called this *ghorba*, or alienation, in my book *Wanderings: Sudanese Migrants and Exiles in North America* (2002).

I watched the *CBS Evening News with Dan Rather* religiously and felt a great sense of gratitude to him in training my ear to the American accent. Upon Faris's return to campus from Arizona, where he had been doing research for his book *Navajo and Photography* (1996), my solitude came to an end. I found myself in the presence of a truly progressive individual. Faris had done fieldwork in the Nuba Mountains in Sudan and taught for several years at the University of Khartoum. He introduced me to key works in anthropology and the critique of anthropology and assigned readings from Foucault, Lévi-Strauss, Raymond Williams, David Harvey, and Karl Popper. He brought Talal Asad, James Clifford, and Brackette Williams to the campus lecture series he organized. I was challenged at every turn, one essay and one visitor at a time. And to this day, I continue to be challenged by the many paradoxes of the anthropology of my native Sudan and by the discipline's location in the world.

Faris had taught Sudanese anthropologist Sharif Harir (see Harir 1983), and he introduced me to him at a Sudan Studies Association conference. Faris pressed me at that early stage to become a teaching assistant and to present papers at American Anthropological Association and African Studies Association meetings. I cherished his assignments on "the political relevance of anthropology" (Magubane and Faris 1985). He placed high expectations and an enormous sense of accountability on my shoulders while instilling a can-do spirit. My discussions with him about location and position led me to continue my graduate training with him. To me, this was a rare opportunity.

My studies with Faris deepened my appreciation for my interviewees, whether Brooklyn Sudanese sailors and recent migrants and exiles in the West, refugees and internally displaced persons (IDPs) in Sudan, or Darfur migrants in Qatar. I emulated Faris's belief in the Navajos "as subjects of their own history," as he put it in his coauthored piece with Magubane (Magubane and Faris 1985), believing that Sudanese people at home and abroad were "subjects of their own history" too. My forms of engagement with Sudanese in and out of Sudan arose from their larger communal worries and hopes. When called upon to work with activists from Darfur, I saw this work as an opportunity to improve my listening skills and, at the same time, serve as conveyer of messages to wider publics but with explicit recognition that they alone could speak about their fraught worlds with rigor and authority.

Darfur: Brief Context

The great diversity of the people of Darfur and the intercultural experiences in which they have lived are a product of long and complex sociopolitical processes, including migratory movements, which have influenced intergroup politics in many dynamic and reciprocal ways. Migratory streams from localities within Sudan (Abdul-Jalil 1988) and from neighboring countries (Chad, Libya, the Central African Republic) augment the variety of Darfurians. The notion of *Dar*, or abode/haven, is linked to population density. The Arab sultan of Darfur granted land to the largest indigenous groups—Fur, Zaghawa, and Masaleet. Smaller non-Arab ethnic groups were not Dar owners. Nonetheless, all coexisted. The environmental crisis that swept the region in the early 1980s brought radical changes in political dynamics and socioecological forces. The resulting hunger, thirst, and environmental erosion led to intractable hostilities (Abdel Ghaffar and Manger 2007).

Notwithstanding the diversity in Darfur, common denominators are consequential. Cultural backgrounds, modes of livelihood, and ethnic identities are the most obvious markers of difference, but the many ethnic groups that consider Darfur their homeland are not isolated from one another. They mix, mingle, and marry and, in the process, contribute to Sudanese hybridity, belying any notion of Arab and Zurga (black, or "African") as contrasting biological facts. Common denominators also exist in relation to political economy, for instance in modes of production. Nomadism and agriculture were once seen as complementary rather than competitive. Farmers traded their products in the marketplace, and the livestock of nomads fertilized everyone's land (Abusharaf 2011).

Yet, in spite of these intersections, the Sudan is a place where history has a way of repeating itself in the most dreadful and rancorous manner. The Darfur conflict exploded in early 2003 when two main rebel groups, the Sudan Liberation Movement/Army and the Justice and Equality Movement, both Darfurian, decided to strike national military installations in Darfur with the intention of sending a hard-hitting message of resentment and bitterness about the region's sociopolitical and economic marginality and exclusion. The conflict devastated the region's economy, shredded its fragile social fabric, drove millions of people from their homes, and created an unstable environment filled with fear and misery. Reports issued since the eruption of the conflict find the majority of IDPs reluctant to return to their villages of origin. The lack of security has caused large numbers to transition into extended vulnerability. And, finally, UN Security Council Resolution 1593 has referred the situation in Darfur to the International Criminal Court (ICC).

The scenarios that follow are intended to illuminate my role as a reporter, one I see as valuing reciprocal engagement and mutuality. Concurring with the argument that "informants," as Mills (2008, 21) phrases it, "constitute themselves as speaking/viewing subjects," I continue to value my encounters with the people from Darfur in Khartoum and Qatar who surrounded me as mentors and interlocutors and to appreciate the valuable education I received from them.

Fragments from Fieldwork

Since the onset of the Darfur crisis, I have conducted systematic ethnographic fieldwork and participant observation in diverse contexts and situations: in Sudan, Egypt, Addis Ababa, and Doha, Qatar; in camps for displaced persons, shantytowns, and forums and college campuses in the United States and the United Kingdom; in Central Park in New York City, the United States Congress, and at the United Nations and the UN Security Council. Since 2003, I have amassed a considerable number of ethnographic materials, and here I highlight two excerpts that inspired in me a sense of urgency to become involved in whatever capacity I could.

I have felt a personal responsibility to amplify the voices of those directly affected by the crisis and to tell the story through the lens of personal narratives from IDP locations. I interviewed Asha Ali in Dar Al-Salam, Sudan, on August 14, 2004:

> Our situation is a real catastrophe. When the fighting started we all tried to run away with our children. The men fled after seeing others get killed and beaten by the Janjaweed. These people acted like devils. They don't have good hearts. They burnt villages, attacked and kidnapped women, and caused a lot of pain and misery. We fled on foot in a very difficult journey. Now we are staying with people from home who came to Khartoum a long time ago. Like us they don't have a lot, but they allowed us to stay with them in these small houses. We don't have money to buy food. We are also very worried about work. We cannot find work since this place is very far. Now the rainy season created added problems because this area is flooded. We depend only

> on Allah to change our situation. Our children are in danger too. Our situation is extremely terrible. We don't know what had happened to other relatives and neighbours. We hope that they are still alive. We are also worried that we will not be able to go back. We have no hope that we will get assistance. Not in this place anyway.

Khadija Yagoub, who arrived at Khartoum in May 2004, explained:

> We used to farm back home in our village. We did not extend our hands or beg for food or anything else. The poverty and want we see in Khartoum is causing us a lot of worries and stress. We have to think about the little children because at least the adults are strong enough to bear hunger. Our life in the village was merciful. Here in Khartoum there is no assistance. We are here in this faraway place where we cannot move to find work, especially the majority of women who have little children. There is no food and our hosts are struggling and are themselves in trouble. This fighting destroyed our lives there and caused us humiliation and hunger here. I don't know what the future holds. Now, I have no hope.

The Problems of Women in Darfur: Reflections on Mutuality in Washington, D.C.

In 2003, Swanee Hunt, Ambassador to Austria during the Clinton Administration, invited me to join her Women Waging Peace initiative. I gladly obliged. I have always been aware of the harsh reality of women and girls as victims of sexual violence and torture. My involvement in the initiative has had profound bearing on my thinking about the expectation that scholars must uphold a contemplative distance. I see my scholarly work and my involvement in war and peace issues in the Sudan as one of complementarity, of mutuality, and of recognition that my role helps gives voice to the dispossessed and those who find themselves in constant confrontation with "[an] authoritarian institution with a large stake in women's bodies" (Sered 2000, 17). My participation in both scholarly and nonscholarly forums organized by Ambassador Hunt was significant, in part because it brought my multiple subject positions front and center. These pursuits are mutually inclusive and not amenable to compartmentalization.

One event organized by Women Waging Peace, "Understanding the Crisis in Darfur," brought sixteen Sudanese women peace builders to meetings, presentations, and events in Washington, D.C., and New York City in 2006. Despite a cease-fire agreement and the presence of an African Union peacekeeping mission, pervasive violence and an unyielding humanitarian crisis persisted. Tens of thousands of people had been killed and more than two million driven out of their homes. Women from all over the Sudan attended the conference, but the majority were civil society activists from Darfur. The week-long meeting pivoted around concerns predominant at the time: supporting inclusive peace negotiations, greater involvement of women in refugee and IDP camp planning and administration, return and resettlement efforts, creating gender-sensitive accountability and reconciliation mechanisms, and establishing security and keeping the peace.

My mandate was specific: to take notes and to report on problems and recommendations. As the Darfur delegates started to speak about how women have been disproportionately affected by the violence in Darfur, it became obvious that the victims themselves were at the forefront of the efforts to alleviate the crisis. Through networks, informal groups, and as leaders of nongovernmental organizations, they were involved in trying to reconcile with rebel groups and stop the rampant sexual violence against women and girls. As in other conflicts around the world, women are integral to ensuring successful peace negotiations, providing humanitarian assistance, creating accountability, establishing security, and maintaining peace.

The final report of the meeting yielded important recommendations, including one advising that the women from Darfur pay visits, facilitated by Ambassador Hunt and in conjunction with me and other staff of Women Waging Peace, to the National Council on African Affairs, the State Department Women's Division, the United States Institute of Peace, and the World Bank, as well as having a session with members of the Congressional Black Caucus plus U.S. senators and other policy makers working on Darfur. In these meetings, and in the final report, the women of Darfur articulated their recommendations for a solution. The experience overall was important in shaping my view of mutuality.

Scenarios of Mutuality in the State of Qatar

The context of my ethnographic work in Doha warrants comment. Qatar's government promotes a strong vision of its place in the region and the world.

Given its meteoric rise to world prominence and its extraordinary economic power, Qatar today holds tremendous credibility as a third-party mediator. This small peninsula, which in its pre-oil past perfected the industry of pearl diving and held impressive knowledge of celestial navigation for deep-sea voyages, is today exhibiting shrewd diplomacy.

Since I moved to Qatar in 2007, I have been fascinated by its cosmopolitanism as well as by its tolerance, embodied in a philosophy of "live and let live," which governs everyday life. Qatar has been the recipient of the largest number of Sudanese migrants, many of whom have been living there for years and consider it the paradigmatic home away from home. The country's journey from diving to diplomacy leads me to believe that a new form of ethnographic navigation was warranted as numerous Sudanese continued to arrive in Doha in search of wealth and peace.

In 2008, the emirate of Qatar adopted the Darfur situation as a principal foreign policy focus. The Qatari leadership sponsored ongoing dialogues on the Darfur crisis with the intention of facilitating a durable resolution. The contending Darfurian parties who arrived at Doha as part of mediation had their own ambitions and were not amenable to compromise. Qatar has espoused civil society as the engine of all peace efforts, including the rehabilitation of communities and those persons who are not formally active policy makers in Darfur. I began to conceive of my project as interweaving two ethnographies—one of Qatar and the other of Sudan.

Since 2008, my fieldwork, paradoxically, has been mostly in extravagant Doha hotels—at concerts, town hall meetings, *tabaq al-khair* (charity bazaars), and formal dinner events held at the Gulf Cornice, the Four Seasons, the Ritz Carlton, the Sheraton, the Millennium, and the Swiss-Qatari–owned Movenpick. Beyond their glamorous allure, these locations raise questions of what is at stake, as these gatherings assemble an orchestra of voices and offer an opportunity to reflect on the contingency of a "field" that is not confined to territorially bounded spaces.

As I reflect on these locations, I find myself asking, where exactly is "the field"? My experience resonates with discussions crystallized by anthropologists Akhil Gupta and James Ferguson, who argued that "anyone who has done fieldwork, or studies the phenomenon, knows that one does not just wander on a 'field site' to engage in a deep and meaningful relationship with 'the natives.' The 'field' is a clearing whose deceptive transparency obscures the complex processes that go into constructing it" (1997b, 5). Both in the IDP camps and in five-star hotels, I became educated about firsthand perspectives on the conflict, epistemologies of remediation, and community-crafted dispute solutions, such as Rakoobat Ajaweed Darfur (a forum for mediation and conflict resolution). In sum, my notion of the field changed dramatically when Doha metamorphosed into a site of Darfurian mediations.

The complexity and urgency of the Darfur crisis has shaped my understanding of the interactions between Qatari and Sudanese populations in Doha. I have worked intensively with the Sons of the Greater Darfur's Peace. In this capacity, I have interviewed delegates arriving from Darfur—traditional chiefs, civil society participants, leaders and spokespersons for major armed movements, and people who testified before the International Criminal Court. All were invaluable interlocutors. Sudanese migrants attest to the fact that the intersecting agendas of "the state" and "non-state actors," which permeate the prevalent political discourse around Darfur, do not exist as such in Doha. Prepared to dispense with the discourse of victimization, Darfurians in Doha exhibit greater commitment to dealing with problems of local politics and with the prospects for reconciliation and citizenship. They also address Islamism; disputes among Darfurians; banditry; and issues surrounding water, land, and the environment. I have been afforded the opportunity to formulate a perspective on migrants in Persian Gulf nations that foresees an increasingly sophisticated political society rather than reducing Darfurians to mere economic migrants.

I also encountered mutuality in the classrooms at the institutions in which I taught, Qatar National University and the Georgetown University School of Foreign Service, Qatar. I taught public anthropology as part of a course on society and cultures in Qatar's national university. At Georgetown, via digital technologies, I taught "global classroom" courses that included students both in Doha and at the Washington, D.C., campus. Both these experiences enabled me to ascertain how Qatari students see their state's burgeoning role in the Gulf Cooperation Council and around the world. They were interested in a wide range of issues related to Darfur—the role of the international community, the United Nations Resolutions vis-à-vis Darfur, the UN Security Council, the International Criminal Court, the Janjaweed "militia," theories of protest and the politics of culture, ethnic cleansing, imperialist ambitions in the region, representations of sociocultural structure, and the underlying political economy of resource distribution.

When occasion arose, I invited Dr. Tigani Sese Ateem, president of the Darfur Transitional Authority (launched in 2013), and Sharif Harir, former professor of anthropology at the University of Bergen, Norway, who abandoned the classroom to bear arms with his Zaghawa compatriots from Western

Sudan, to speak to my students. Both Ateem and Harir were excellent interlocutors, sharing their expertise. My students told me that these encounters would have a long-lasting impact on their understanding of Darfur. A junior remarked: "I was so drawn to every word uttered by Sharif Harir. Listening to his smoke-cured voice telling us how reading Edmund Leach's *Political Systems of Highland Burma* had changed his perspectives on politics just blew my mind."

In the Corridors of the Millennium Hotel

In 2009, I volunteered to be rapporteur for the Arab Democracy Foundation at a six-day Darfur Reconciliation conference at Doha's Millennium Hotel. The purpose of the gathering was to bring together major players from government and civil society in the Sudan and in Darfur and, in particular, to discuss and envision a plan for implementing transitional justice and lasting peace. In-depth discussions, workshops, and presentations on truth and reconciliation commissions, with a focus on the applicability of the Moroccan Equity and Reconciliation Commission and on the prerequisites, fundamentals, and prospects for peace resulted in guiding principles for establishing a Truth, Equity, and Reconciliation Commission for Darfur.

Organizers hoped the gathering of diverse leaders and social activists would be a "defining moment" in the crisis and serve as a catalyst for achieving justice and building lasting peace. As highlighted in the opening speech by the secretary general of the Arab Democracy Foundation, Mr. Muhsin Marzouq, the prospects for peace are never simply based on signing treaties between rivals but rather depend on addressing and resolving the causes of conflict. To this end, the meeting attempted to examine the complex social, cultural, and economic, as well as political, factors rooted in the Darfur crisis. This depended on the active participation of all the major stakeholders and a promise to respect differences in perspectives in order to facilitate and enhance political will, trust, and agreement.

Worldwide experiences with truth and reconciliation commissions and the concept of transitional justice were discussed on the first day. Participants then examined the major issues of the Darfur conflict in seven workshops, ranging from how to use Darfur's traditional cultural heritage in support of transitional justice to how to engage all affected parties in dialogue. The diverse groups of people tackled issues of weapons, compensation, and reparation. They scrutinized mechanisms for establishing accountability and ways to build and consolidate trust between adversaries, particularly in relation to the grave violations of women. They searched for ways to activate and rebuild local government bodies, and they addressed the repatriation of refugees and the displaced. After discussion, each workshop came up with guiding principles, suggestions, and recommendations. These were consolidated in a final report endorsed by the general session.

In the workshops focused on reconciliation, normally considered the master of all provisions, the attendees made note of Darfur's ancient and very rich history of conflict resolution, which had allowed for peace among diverse tribes for centuries. That history, they argued, should be mined for solutions to the current conflict. But first, they agreed, identification of root causes of the crisis was essential: disputes over natural resources due to environmental degradation, land-use conflicts, armed rebellion, robbery and assault, the political appointment of leaders at the local level against the will of traditional tribes and leaders, underdevelopment, and youth unemployment.

A workshop focused on security defined the concept broadly, as embracing public peace of mind—including economic well-being—and public order. Again, participants agreed that land-use issues contributed to the causes of a breakdown in security, as did international arms smuggling, conflict in neighboring Chad, and the divestment of power in local government. The group discussed violations of human rights, including random killings, rape as a weapon of war, and destruction of property. It became clear that without considerably strengthening the role of local government and implementing judicial bodies and the rule of law, the situation would not improve.

Two workshops tackled issues of female victims of gross human rights violations and the importance of engaging women in the process of instituting peace. It is well-known that young girls in Darfur have been circumcised as a perceived precaution against rape. The participants argued that education and women's roles in creating peace were key to reconciliation, as was holding perpetrators accountable.

Beyond the Glamorous Allure: Listening to the Voice of Sheikh Musa

On February 13, 2011, a blogger on the website Sudaneseonline.com posted a link to an article titled "George Clooney Fails to End Genocide in Darfur."

But where the Hollywood actor failed, a Sufi leader from Darfur may be headed toward success. Since 2003, efforts to end the crisis have tended to ignore local knowledge and neglect customary practices of conflict resolution. Joining forums in Doha as a moderator in town halls and other peace-related occasions has afforded me the opportunity to become familiar with a 2007 Sufi call for peace in Darfur issued by Sheikh Musa Al-Husseini (Abusharaf 2011).

Sheikh Musa was born during the 1930s in Queraida, south Darfur, and when a youngster, accompanied his father to Nyala, where he has lived since the 1940s. As a disciple of the Grand Mufti of Nigeria, he learned the Quran, its jurisprudential core, the prophet's life history, and Arabic language arts. His mastery of these subjects enabled him to establish religious schools that were seen as laboratories for democratization and conflict resolution. I interpret his perspective as a form of citizen diplomacy that places significant weight on dialogue, intercultural communication, and recognition of difference in the process of reconciliation; at the same time, it circumvents essentialist binaries that impede constructive approaches to the crisis in Sudan.

Sheikh Musa belongs to the Tigania Sufi Brotherhood in Darfur, which derives from one of the most influential Sufi movements in West Africa. Sufism is Islamic mysticism, practiced pervasively among Muslims. It originated in North Africa and traveled via migratory currents to Sudan as well as to Mauritania, Senegal, the Gambia, Nigeria, and Egypt. With an orientation toward inner and outer peace, a vision of universal humanity, and recognition of cultural diversity, Sufism offers a powerful resource for peace negotiations.

With his Sufi call for peace, Sheikh Musa undertook a double movement. First, he sought to deracialize the conflict by questioning a dichotomy between "Arabs" and "Africans" (as had Abdel Khaliq Maghoub; Abusharaf 2010b, 4) and by interrogating the recycled tale of their long-standing enmity toward one another. Second, he sought to utilize Sufism to facilitate intercultural communication, demystify mysticism, and correct its scholarly representation as a purely subjective experience. Contrary to such discourse, Sufi practices actively engage society; contemplative Sufi practice is not as much physical isolation as it is a form of inner withdrawal that allows for an action-oriented spirituality to influence worldly affairs in profound ways. It accomplishes this by offering a variety of initiatives that attempt to mend a badly torn sociopolitical fabric.

Although I was an observer-translator at the 2009 Arab Democracy Foundation conference, I am neither a Sufi scholar nor an expert on Darfur's intricate ethnocultural configuration. However, I hope to shed light on this distinctive approach to the question of Darfur by presenting readers with this example of how anthropologists can expand the realm of knowledge by treating our subjects' perspectives as central to the rendering of their own lives. As a Sudanese anthropologist from the northern Sudan, not Darfur, my role is primarily the prismatic one of translator.

Other peace initiatives have lacked comprehensive "native" answers to local problems, and thus I see great importance in Sheikh Musa's approach to healing a festering political wound. His inspiration for peacemaking derives from a personal philosophy that unites Sufis. (Halliday's work [1976] on antilanguages is applicable to grasping Sufism, in all its diverse elements, as a powerful challenge to the authority of institutionalized religions.) Uncompromising in its adherence to monotheism, Sufism resists any notion of prophets and views most forms of religion as incarnations of divine wisdom, thus prompting each seeker to continue on his or her own spiritual path. Scholars have illuminated an intriguing set of commonalities among Sufis, including the *Dhikr*, or remembrance, of the divine presence in expressions of love, piety, meditation, ecstasy, chanting, music, and whirling trance (J. M. Nasr 2007; S. H. Nasr 1989, 2008; Touma 1996). (Further discussion of Sufi devotional rituals and cosmology falls outside the purview of this chapter.) What makes Sufism matter in the Darfur context is its principled opposition to carnage and cruelty, in addition to its emphasis on reconciliation and clemency across cultural differences. From Sheikh Musa, I learned invaluable lessons.

Inspired by Tigania, Sheikh Musa set out to construct a strategy for dialogue crafted within an imaginative framework of citizen diplomacy in his native land. He has advanced the possibility of compassion among the many ethnic groups in Darfur. He has gained trust, both inside and outside Darfur, for the multiple roles he plays in the learned society of south Darfur, the Dhikr, the high commission of Ulmaa Al-Sudan, the Organization of Muslim-Christian Understanding, and the Peaceful Coexistence Conference in Darfur. His efforts to build bridges across ethnicities and cultures have been celebrated in public ceremonies. Due to the respect he has earned as a man of charisma and courage, communities of youth, women, learned religious leaders (Ulmaa), and missionaries from all regions of the country flock to hear his message of solidarity and hope in the face of catastrophe.

My education by Sheikh Musa directed my attention to Sufi approaches to political reconciliation. (We may draw useful pointers from Anthony Cohen and Nigel Rapport's anthropological analysis [1995] of collective consciousness and their interpretation of cultural dynamics that concretely formulate our self-understanding vis-à-vis the cosmos.) Linking Sufi notions of consciousness to an awareness of sacredness and divinity makes their pertinence to peace readily apparent.

Participants in a Sufi forum in Darfur were told that "the call," which referred to Sheikh Musa's "Call of the People of Allah" for peace (Abusharaf 2011), was written and orally recorded in 2007, when, starting in Al-Fashir, Al-Geinana, and Nyala, more than ten thousand cassette tapes were distributed. The call addresses distinctive, but mutually inclusive, sets of stakeholders: the grass roots, the political elites, parties, civil society, the government, and the armed forces. From Sheikh Musa's call, we learn about differences and convergences in the Darfurian mosaic: there are at least 156 ethnic groups who speak more than one hundred distinct languages and dialects. In addition to being the language of the holy book, Arabic is the lingua franca throughout Darfur and thus occupies a special place in Darfurians' discursive and communicative strategies. Although many recognize Arabic as their mother tongue, other languages are also spoken, and the relatively recent radicalized discourse has not instilled any aversion toward bilingualism.

Without romanticizing pre-2003 Darfur, Sheikh Musa identifies the main causes of conflict and mass violence as rising numbers of IDPs and refugees in Sudan and Chad; the proliferation of weapons; the illegal acquisition of land and the collision of nomads and agriculturalists who abandoned customary laws that governed their mutual interests prior to the atrocities; illiteracy and poverty among the majority of youth; weakening and politicization of native administrations that used to enjoy moral authority in resolving day-to-day disputes; the emergence of new faces in Darfur whose interests are intimately linked to the continuation of war; and border politics with Chad, Libya, and the Central African Republic (Abusharaf 2011).

Disputes between Darfurian ethnic groups over pastures are also important because of the genealogies of conflict in a region that has pitted humans and the environment against each other. The invisible political economy that produces enmity and competition over scarce resources has been a powerful causal force in the politicization of ethnicity. Sheikh Musa thus took the environmental crisis into consideration and did not become preoccupied with the ubiquitous Janjaweed, the soldiers of fortune, comprised of those with an appetite for mercenary activities, banditry, and the capacity to commit acts of brutality.

I deal further elsewhere with the social processes outlined in the Sufi call (Abusharaf 2011). Most succinctly, Sheikh Musa's task is to embrace principles such as citizenship, justice, and compassion. The call asks that, after minds are purged of vengeance, mutual trust be cultivated. Solidifying what is known as *zat a bain* or *al nafs al wahidat*, the collective self, in Darfur, is sine qua non for apology and exculpation. To Sheikh Musa, neither government nor insurgent groups will succeed in peacemaking without a deep-seated belief in the fundamental unity of the collective self and its security, freedom from fear, and relationship to its maker. A fundamental conviction that peace must live within each citizen and that goodwill is the only desirable foundation for making peace inspired his essential understanding.

Conclusion

What I have described in this chapter reveals my keen interest in interweaving memories and making sense of the past and how these have compelled me to tackle difficult topics. I have attempted to knit several strands from these disparate locations and show how, as an anthropologist, I harbor no qualms about undertaking prismatic roles. In this respect, I hope to highlight wider "parallels and paradoxes" (Barenboim and Said 2004), even if the task of illuminating my understanding of mutuality warrants an autobiographical account of who I am. On taking a closer look, I can see that multivariate contexts and situations, across several axes of north and south, east and west, have influenced me as I remember Sudanese Communist Party Secretary-General Abdel Khaliq Mahgoub's legacy and speak about Sufi mystic Sheikh Musa's whirling trance for peace.

PART III

JOURNEYS

Chapter 9

On the Fault Lines of the Discipline

Personal Practice and the Canon

Robert R. Alvarez

Anthropology renders a unique sense of belonging for practitioners, because they enter and discover new social worlds and the rich humanness of the people we anthropologists choose to study. Here, practice, guided by the canon of professional goals and methods, produces a mutuality between anthropologist-as-learner and subject. We seek deep ethnographic understandings in our questioning of power, belief, human strategy and survival, social change and justice, and other foci embedded in the canon. The anthropologist is empowered by this experience, and the canon itself is also nourished. This is a fundamental mutuality in the give and take of anthropological praxis.

Yet, there is more to mutuality in anthropology than this harmonious give and take. Each of us brings a nuanced interpretation of the canon, as our theoretical discussions illustrate. We practice our trade independently and with individual creative passion (see Bernard 2000; Robben and Sluka 2006; Sanjek 1990b; Vogt 1994). This is particularly evident in that no one can really replicate our individual research, even if all our efforts begin with and contribute to the canon. Those of us engaged in the anthropological life each experience our own connections to the "field" (the traditional geographic and ethnographic foci of our studies) and discipline. As individuals, we bring varied and nuanced versions of mutuality to the collective canon.

As implied above, the notion of mutuality encompasses a variety of implications and usages in anthropology. As a topic of anthropological inquiry, mutuality has not been widely explored. Anthropologists, however, have focused on reciprocity, a concept that encapsulates one form of mutuality. Marcel Mauss's *The Gift* (1990 [1925]) was fundamental in delineating reciprocity among peoples and cultures of the world. Rather than being received "freely," gifts are imbued with meaning, power, spirituality, and value that transcend the actual material gift itself. This reciprocity conditions the relationship between giver and receiver and extends beyond the dyadic relationship of giver to receiver. In reciprocity, givers give a part of themselves. Such is the mutual relationship of anthropologist with and to the discipline's canon and praxis. Anthropologists give to and take from the canon in a mutuality imbued with power, values, and meaning.

Anthropology's transformation from a principally white male discipline to one with recognizable (although still spotty) diversity makes mutuality even more complex. Unlike most of the discipline's history, in which the native and nontraditional anthropologist (female, queer, ethnic, foreign) was a rarity, today anthropology touts its growing numbers of nontraditional anthropologists. The discipline has been forced into accommodating this internal difference. The change has nurtured the canon, producing mutualities that have changed the relationships of anthropologists to their discipline.

All anthropologists bring to and share their uniqueness with the discipline. Yet, the nontraditional anthropologist and the native/insider enter the anthropological pursuit with different baggage than others: they might be community members, or they might study their own kind. This introduces questions that, I would argue, are germane to the professional canon and differences that contest the hallowed anthropological quest. What is the anthropological meaning of the anthropologist who not only studies but also personally represents the studied? How is reciprocity enacted within the anthropological encounter by the practitioner who never leaves the field (Weston 1997)? How does personal attachment—proximity—to the subject of study challenge the canon? Ignited by critical gender studies and feminist and native anthropologies, anthropology has come a long way, yet the mutual reciprocity and friction of practitioner to discipline, especially of those practitioners who belong to and continue to work in the social-cultural worlds we study, is in need of analysis.

It could be argued that the impact of the native anthropologist is now part of the standard literature. This literature, however, focuses primarily on the validity of nontraditional anthropologists and their work (Abu-Lughod 1991; Narayan 1993). There is little focus on how nontraditional praxis contributes to the deeper meaning of the anthropological. There is a give and take here, a mutuality with both benefit and friction, that is inherent in all anthropological praxis.

This chapter is not intended to be a proclamation but rather a query that explores the oblique relationship of an anthropologist on the fault lines of the discipline to its canonical practice and an examination of its generative dimension. Gazing back at episodes in my own career and life, I ponder diverse meanings of mutuality in a particular anthropological experience, one that at times has intersected with personal passion and belonging. I aim to illustrate how mutuality provides value to not only personal endeavors but also to the canon. And let me stress that it is not solely the native anthropologist who experiences such mutualities—mutuality may be encountered in all anthropological effort.

The 2009 Association of Black Anthropologists Legacy Award

At the 2009 American Anthropological Association meetings in Philadelphia, I attended the first Association of Black Anthropologists (ABA) Legacy Awards ceremony. One award was presented to Johnetta B. Cole, a living legend in the anthropological world; George Bond, my close colleague and friend, received the other. I have a strong affinity to both Dr. Cole and George. Their work, legacy, and intent are close to my own sense of purpose in anthropology and in life. The award ceremony fostered a spirit of belonging, a sense of celebrative mutuality in anthropology, in the ABA, among the sisters and brothers present, and, curiously, in the life role of being an anthropologist.

This sense of mutuality was especially evident as I listened to Dr. Cole's acceptance talk. Rather than on her own accomplishments, Dr. Cole focused on anthropology. She acknowledged a personal tie with colleagues and friends in the room but insisted that it was anthropology, and specifically the anthropological perspective, that had brought her to this place in life. Here, I thought, is an accomplished woman, a former president of Spelman College, a person who has engaged the powerful circles of the nation, a Black woman who has created opportunity for people of all colors, one who has been keenly involved in change, and who is now director of the National Museum of African Art/Smithsonian Institution, yet she is speaking personally of anthropology's value. She spoke with a passion that rekindled the feeling I had when I was a newcomer to the field. Dr. Cole made it clear that how she "sees" the world—through an anthropological lens—has led to her accomplishments. This simple yet profound confession raised questions about how my own life and career fit into the anthropological domain and, conversely, how the anthropological pursuit fits into my personal life. How has the anthropological lens affected how I see and interpret the world? How do my own values and those of the people to whom I have sought to give voice reverberate in the anthropological world? What do individual perceptions and values have to do with the discipline?

Once again, as throughout my professional career, I was in a position between the anthropological and the personal—inside the discipline, yet also looking into it from the outside; understanding the canon, but questioning its dogma. It is here at the crossroads of the personal and professional, attuned to the fault lines of the anthropological canon, where a creative tension exists, where anthropological fellowship renders support, and where the voices of those with whom I have worked echo clearly. And it is here where one can also fall through the cracks as diverging boundaries of the personal, the scientific, the emotive, and the objective shift. This is not about taking one road or the other but about a substantive convergence—a mutuality that exists between our anthropological and our private selves.

I first met George Bond, the second 2009 ABA awardee, in 1980, when I held a postdoctoral fellowship at the Institute for Urban and Minority Education at Teachers College (TC), Columbia University, and a visiting slot at the TC Program for Applied Anthropology. This was my first academic appointment, where I met and formed lasting ties with Jerry Wright, Leith Mullings, Roger Sanjek, Alaka Wali, and others. At Teachers College, George and I debated issues of race and hierarchy, worked for inclusion in the discipline, shared daily tasks and tribulations, and learned from one another about the deep meaning of our pasts. Mine was a Chicano/Mexicano experience of the West Coast, George's an African American tradition fostered east of the Mississippi. Both our histories were couched in family and community, but we acknowledged the legacy of nation state and racism that framed our mutual existence. We shared the intellectual goal of a proficient and rigorous anthropology aimed at social change. It was a mutuality from which we, along with other colleagues, formed lifelong friendships that engendered a generation of intellectual challenge to enduring social inequality and the discipline's white patriarchal posture. This mutuality stemmed not solely from our thirst for knowledge about our pasts but also from recognizing the worthiness of anthropological understanding. Historical context, social relevance, and anthropological commitment framed our discourse.

The significance of this mutuality, a personal and professional sharing, became especially evident for me with Dr. Cole's acceptance presentation and with George's absence due to illness (Roger Sanjek graciously and eloquently accepted the award on behalf of Dr. Bond). Here at an award ceremony within the anthropological canon were passion, collegial appreciation, and deep-seated personal relationships.

Mutuality includes friendship and the other enduring interpersonal consequences of how we do anthropology—how we collect our information and interpret and report our conclusions. Mutuality, personal and anthropological, includes the ways we conduct ourselves as professionals. It embraces not only the intellectual curiosity of the social scientist but the passion and grit of personal lives. Like C. Wright Mills's (1959) dialogue of engaging the past and present, it answers to our dedication to understanding the context of social life. The mutuality of which I speak encapsulates the many tensions underpinning anthropological perception; we acknowledge the persistent hierarchy that pervades the discipline, but we also practice the ethic of placing those whom we study first. This guides our understanding and draws on the power of belonging, not just in disciplinary venues and fellowship but also as community members and participants.

Critical Ethnic Studies: The Anthropologist as Devil

This professional-personal dialogue has another dimension that became especially evident to me when I joined an ethnic studies department some two decades after my TC beginnings. We anthropologists live with the stigma of our discipline's past and its hierarchical posture. How we deal with this is reflected in how we conduct ourselves as anthropologists.

In 2001, I moved from Arizona State University and a traditional four-field anthropology department to the University of California, San Diego (UCSD) Department of Ethnic Studies (ES). I was returning to my birthplace, San Diego, to fulfill a dream of working in the community in which I had grown up. Also, ES was a place where diverse ethnic scholars and students were the majority, a rarity in academia and particularly so in departments of anthropology. In all, it was a welcome change.

The UCSD department differs from traditional ES departments in that the histories and experiences of specific groups (African American, Asian, Chicano, Native American) are not the focus. The department "is committed to the interdisciplinary study of race, ethnicity, indigeneity, gender, sexuality, class . . . dis/ability . . . power, [and] inequality, including systems of knowledge that have emerged from racialized and indigenous communities in global contexts" (Ethnic Studies Department 2012). This focus corresponds to what is, in fact, practiced by many anthropologists, yet the mere mention of the anthropological in ES raises eyebrows.

As an anthropologist, I have often been perplexed by the common ES characterization of anthropology. In critical ethnic studies, the anthropologist becomes the devil-colonist that preys on the ethnic community and person. Anthropology often draws snickers in regard to its seditious involvement in the privilege of whiteness and institutions of control. In this ES gaze, anthropology embodies and reflects social injustice and the institutional racism of the academy. However, numerous ethnographic and anthropological texts are widely used in a substantial portion of ES scholarship. Nonetheless, a negative stereotype of anthropology is strong, and especially one of its methods, in which the anthropologist is seen as the expert and the native as his indentured informant. This is coupled with a racist past in which anthropological knowledge triumphs over savagery. At graduate student receptions, I was humorously introduced as a "recovering anthropologist."

Although I acknowledge anthropology's dark history, I continue to embrace the goals and methods of its canon. The 2009 ABA Legacy Award ceremony symbolized for me the conflict I felt as an ES scholar and anthropologist. The irony of an anthropologist, Johnetta Cole, a highly successful and admired ethnic scholar, expressing anthropological passion rankled against the vision of anthropologist as devil. I defend anthropology's canon and values, but like many of my colleagues, I have experienced the deleterious, often noxious, repercussions of the discipline's shunning of native scholars' personhood and the privileging of whiteness (Alvarez 1994; Harrison 1997; Lipsitz 1998; Medicine 2001). I find objectionable such elements as the "staging" of the native (for examples, see Asch and Chagnon 1974; Chagnon 1968), the controlling power of the anthropologist's word that becomes accepted knowledge, and an "expertise" authenticated by disciplinary hierarchy and history.

At USCD, the critical dagger of ES intensified my long-held rancor against racism, inequality, and white privilege but also reified the bond I maintain with ethnography and anthropology. Critical ES tested me, confronting those values I held that opposed the racial core of the social but also reaffirming the necessity of employing the anthropological lens in the search for understanding, of pursuing sound research and practical application, and of empowering our subjects.

Our normal understanding and usage of *mutuality* refers to something shared in common, a commonality between two or more people or parties. Yet mutuality is not solely beneficial or cooperative; it also bursts with friction and a clashing of values. Reciprocity is not necessarily harmonious. Anthropologists are well aware of the tensions and political oppositions nurtured in reciprocal relationships. The outcome may be effective continuity, but there is also underlying imbalance. My critique and my defense of the anthropological exemplify such imbalance. It is part and parcel of the discipline, of the very relationship of practitioner to canon.

When I began my long trek into the discipline's canon, I was clear about wanting to be an anthropologist. I loved reading ethnographies, learning how archaeologists reconstructed prehistoric social orders, and absorbing anthropologists' renderings and deep understandings of the world. I became passionate about anthropology, and as a novice, I was enthralled with its history of practice. Later, I also learned to appreciate sound theory. I became eager to enter "the field" and practice the trade, to use anthropology to engage the world.

In the process of becoming a practicing anthropologist, I began to see the belly of the beast. My experience in the discipline produced a critical tension that stemmed from friction between learning the anthropological trade and my personal life. Rather than subsiding as I became a more proficient professional, the friction became more intense and the tension more precise. To review this personal versus disciplinary story, let me return to a time when anthropology was not yet part of my existence. I do so to explain how my deep relationship with the anthropological canon emerged and evolved. My aim is to reveal how the resulting tension challenged my embrace of the anthropological, on the one hand, and on the other, helped make my chosen work more productive.

A Life and the Anthropological

I was born in San Diego, California, into the produce trade, where it was understood that as eldest son I would follow my father's charge over the family wholesale business. I was raised in the heyday of San Diego's Market Row, which we knew as "las marketas" (the markets). Market Row was a world of three o'clock mornings, the bustling activity of trucks and fruit loading, bright lights, and clear, cold daybreaks. It was an exciting world where San Diego's anonymous ethnic entrepreneurs competed and engaged with one another. My father, Roberto Alvarez, Sr., took me there as a young boy and had me sorting fruit by the time I was nine. We went on road trips to purchase oranges in the foothills of California's Central Coastal Range, in Porterville, Riverside, Merced. I worked through high school and, later, for my college tuition. On vacations, I spent my time on the produce docks. After I graduated from college and served in the Peace Corps, I returned to the business. I had a passion for the fruit business—as my father said, "it got in your blood."

The produce life I had lived was in stark contrast to the career I later had in mind—becoming an anthropologist. But the passion and effort of those familial endeavors would eventually enrich my anthropological quest. Ironically, the family pull became a primary force that would guide and steer my work and career. When I first went to "the field," it was a return to my home and to the personal. Anthropology opened a life's work that has revolved around my own family, my experiences, and the world of which I am part.

When I encountered anthropology as an undergraduate at Arizona State College (ASC, now Northern Arizona University), I frankly did not know what anthropology meant. Yet, at a meeting about majoring in the subject, the anthropologists I met captivated my interests. Their goodwill drew me to southwestern archaeology and cultural anthropology. I graduated with a BS in anthropology (at ASC, anthropology was part of the sciences), but I was also keenly interested in Latin America, pulled to that area of the world because of my personal history and Mexican/Chicano heritage.

When I graduated from ASC, although the family business still beckoned, I had a different plan. At that time, the U.S. Peace Corps was recruiting volunteers for Latin America, and this caught my attention. I applied, was accepted, and was trained in community development in Puerto Rico. In December 1965, I left for the Republic of Panama.

Panama, 1966–1969

The three years I spent in Panama as a Peace Corps volunteer (PCV) changed the course of my life and ultimately steered me into an anthropological career. From 1966 to early 1968, I lived in Santiago de Veraguas, in the heart of Panama's interior. In Santiago, my experience in the produce world served me well. I was working in agriculture with campesino farmers and became a cooperative extension agent with other Peace Corps volunteers and a group of idealistic, energetic Panamanians. We organized campesinos into a multiservice cooperative: La Cooperativa de Servicios Multiples, Juan XXIII, which, now self-sufficient, continues to provide services today. I identified closely with Panama and the people with whom I worked, in large part because of my Mexican background. They were Latinos, and we had much in common. In Panama, I learned to appreciate the values of mutual goals, cooperation, and respect, values that have steered my professional work in social change and my engagement in anthropology.

In 1968, when my volunteer service term was ending, the Vietnam War was raging, and my male fellow PCV friends were leaving for military service. On a visit to the U.S. Canal Zone, I decided to join the Coast Guard and applied to Officer Candidate School. Just days before I enlisted, Peace Corps Panama asked if I would consider participating in a new cooperative project among the Kuna Indians of San Blas, Panama.

The Kuna, an indigenous people of Chibchan ancestry, live on idyllic palm-studded tropical islands that float in deep blue seas. Kunayala, the Kuna name for their reserve, and the strikingly distinctive culture of the Kuna changed my life trajectory. Not only was this the gateway to a career in anthropology, but it was then that I met and married my life partner, Karen Anne Hesley, a fellow PCV. We worked together in San Blas and were married in late 1968 when we left Panama.

In contrast to Santiago de Veraguas, the Kunayala community was not an easy fit for me. In Santiago, I was part of the crowd: I was Latino, spoke Spanish, even looked Panamanian, and shared culturally explicit values. Being among campesinos was akin to being in Mexico, and I often felt like I was among my own family. The Kuna world was different. Here, I was under suspicion as a "waga," a Kuna term for outsider and non-Kuna Panamanian. Soon after my arrival, a local rural educator accused me of being a communist who was trying to usurp Kuna resources for the Peace Corps. I became the *mergi sichiti*, or the black American, a term used to distinguish me from other PCVs who were fair skinned, blond, and Anglo. The San Blas cooperative project was also composed of Kuna women, with whom the female volunteers worked, and I was the only male. Hence, I was viewed as an outsider in multiple ways.

The Kuna social world challenged my prior position as the Other. The

Kuna speak their own Chibchan language and speak Spanish only secondarily (see Sherzer 2001). Like other PCVs, I often found myself perplexed by cultural misunderstandings. Among other things, I could not figure out why in a world of communal behavior Kuna women were not participating in a cooperative project for their own interests. As I would learn, it was the Kuna social order that structured women's participation (see Alvarez 1972; Salvador 1997; Tice 1995). Ethnography became key not only to my understanding the Kuna world but to the realization that anthropology could be a profound tool in effecting positive social change.

Utilizing the most basic of conceptual notions and methodological tools, I learned how the Kuna themselves approve and conduct social obligations. Asking relevant questions, watching how things were done, and participating in daily activities and "council" gatherings (see Howe 2002), I learned rules of behavior and accompanying social norms and utilized them in our work for the cooperative. Like the Kuna, I learned to approach the town councils to seek approval for travel and to explain thoroughly the cooperative's goals and benefits for the Kuna. In one important meeting before the town council and the entire village on the island of Tigre, I debated with the young agricultural agent who had accused me of conspiring to usurp profits from the proposed cooperative for the benefit of the Peace Corps. When this confrontation ended, the *saila* (chief) arose from his hammock and summarized the gist of the disagreement. I still recall his oratory and his approval for the cooperative project. He described the value of Kuna women as holders of Kuna tradition. (My challenger and I, by the way, eventually became close allies.)

My readiness to accord respect to Kuna wisdom and knowledge stemmed from a sensibility I now see as ethnographic. I did not understand what ethnography really was at the time, but I learned not just to understand but also to live and work in the Kuna world. My experience was anthropology at its most basic. When I returned to the United States, I was sold on anthropology as a tool for social change, and I carried these newfound values into my life and career.

Graduate School, 1970

When I returned to San Diego, I worked once again in the family produce business. My father was retraining me according to family custom: from the ground up. I was a floor worker, unloaded semitrucks, made deliveries, dispatched long-haul drivers, and worked night shifts, relearning and being resocialized into the produce business and family structure. The produce world was a challenge and a responsibility, but I felt a nagging passion to pursue anthropology further, to employ the values and tools I had learned in Panama.

I enrolled in graduate classes at San Diego State University (SDSU), wrote papers "against" theory, and relished the thought of practical involvement in engaging social change. I wrote an MA thesis (Alvarez 1972) under the guidance of John Young, based on my experience with the Kuna, and looked forward to entering a PhD program and returning to Latin America. In 1973, I was admitted into the social-cultural anthropology doctoral program at Stanford University.[1]

As I look back on those years, I realize that two parallel tracks—mutualities of different sorts—fed my personal development. The first revolved around being trained formally as an anthropologist. At ASC, SDSU, and Stanford I had excellent mentors and classes. I grew as a person and in my intellectual engagement with the canon. I continued to be passionate about my trajectory into the world of social change. My training built upon my experiences with campesinos and the Kuna and underlined the value of anthropology. The produce-world life I had lived at first contrasted sharply with the values I found in my new career in social anthropology, but it also provided a strong impetus to seek the human dimension of lives different from my own. This personal-career mutuality, however, was influenced and strengthened by some unanticipated aspects of my graduate student years.

In addition to formal training, there was an informal dimension of becoming an anthropologist that encompassed a mutuality of collegiality and friendship. At SDSU, I met colleagues who to this day remain fundamental influences in my life. At Stanford, I was admitted into a large incoming class that included a number of "nontraditional" Chicano/a, African American, and Native American, as well as Anglo, students.[2] These colleagues brought a different reality to Stanford's PhD program. We were not a typical straight-out-of-college cohort: many of us had practical experience outside of the academy; some of us continued to be active in civil rights struggles. We all were committed to challenging social injustice and enacting social change. During this time, the impact of the civil rights movement continued to reverberate in academia, as it did in the nation at large. This graduate cohort gained much from the PhD program, but we also reinforced our mutual interests in social change and social justice and in the communities from which we originated.

In addition to our ongoing discussions and challenges, we received an especially forceful boost when Beatrice Medicine entered our lives as a visiting professor. Bea Medicine illustrates the collegial mutuality of which I speak. She was a Native American Sioux; lived in Wakpala on her home soil; was committed to the underserved, especially in academia; and was both a proponent and critic of the anthropological. She aimed her criticism not only at the discipline but at her own community. She stood her ground relentlessly as a Sioux woman and as an anthropologist, and she understood the relevance and strength of the canon (Medicine 2001). In her short time at Stanford, she impacted our lives. Bea taught classes but viewed us as equals, respecting our views. She maintained a fierce stance against the hierarchy and ingrained racism of the discipline and the academy. Her students forged an alliance that, even without Bea's physical presence, continues to this day. In addition to working toward our professional goals, we coalesced and acknowledged the worlds from which we had come.

Social Change and Immigration: A New Challenge

In preparation for my qualifying examination, I defined my geographic specialty as Mesoamerica and the greater Southwest. This encompassed my interests in the U.S.-Mexico borderlands, the United States, and Latin America. I chose social change as my theoretical topic, including within it social ecology and education.

As I prepared for "the field," I wrote a dissertation research proposal to study Kuna economic strategies in meeting the challenges of modernization. I received a travel-research grant, returned to Panama, and began preparing for extended fieldwork there with my partner and our son Luis. While preparing for my comprehensive exams, I was surprised and disturbed by the academic literature on immigration that I was reading, and unexpectedly, I changed my research direction. My commitment to social change and application did not waiver, but I now focused on immigrant lives and voices. This turned me toward my own family and personal history.

While reading for the exams, I reviewed current literature on migration, an area I had not studied systematically before, as I had never thought immigration might become a focus of mine. As I read through this literature, I realized that in the analytical descriptions and theoretical treatments of global human mobility, a crucial variable was absent: people, the migrants themselves. The literature described immigration as patterned social movement, as "waves" and "stages" in which "populations" were "pulled and pushed." It was "the host society" that received immigrants and, conversely, "the home society" that forced them out. "Laws of migration" were proposed and accepted by theorists. I was highly critical of this portrayal because it did not mesh with my own family's experience.

In my response to the literature, I asked: how does this fit my own family's immigrant past? How does it explain how we settled and survived along the border? What does it say about the human values and sentiments that were engrained in such a process? How, I wondered, might anthropology enrich this view and provide deeper meaning about migrants, about the voices and agency that were missing in the literature? I became passionate about setting the overly sociological record straight, about representing the lives of those people left out of the picture.

My goal was no longer Kuna or Mexican "culture," nor was it about "Latin America." It was about a part of the world I was from. My anthropological query now reached into my own past. It was personal, yet it was stimulated and refined when I looked through an anthropological lens. I began interrogating my own history and sense of belonging in the context of social change and social justice. My revelation while I prepared for a graduate exam became the gateway to my subsequent work on the border, on Mexican settlement and Chicano survival, on my community and family. My commitment became steeped in the personal, in the awareness of who I am. But importantly, it arose and would be explicated via the professional goals and methods of the canon.

A mutuality emerged between anthropological canon and query, one that encompassed debate about the human quality of life, the absence of voice, and in particular, the absence of people like those with whom I had lived and whom I had known and respected. I turned my attention to a new puzzle that was both anthropological—the meaning behind immigration—and personal—my own family history.

The Field: San Diego and Baja California

When I left Stanford for "the field," I returned to the place of my birth to do fieldwork among the people with whom I had been raised, and where, intellectually, I was engaging theoretical questions about immigration and human mobility. I was excited not only about finding my personal roots (my colleague and good friend Leo Chavez termed this "Up from Baja," by Booker T. Alvarez) but about reconstructing a history that was embedded in Baja California and along the Mexico-U.S. border. I sought to portray a particular migration north, beginning with my own family members and their pasts, and to connect their trajectories to the places where they had originated and lived. I had been to Baja California as an adolescent and visited Loreto, Comondu, Santa Rosalia, Cabo San Lucas, and San Jose del Cabo, and I had always wished to know more about the peninsula. With my dissertation work, I had the opportunity to document not only that familial legacy but also a larger set of communal memories. As I engaged the peninsula more deeply, I discovered nuanced histories of movement. I learned to know more intimately many of the kin with whom I had grown up.

As an anthropologist, I utilized the methods of our trade: collecting oral histories, perusing handwritten records, scouring the documentary literature, and putting into words the rich meanings of the world from which I had come. Equally important, as I excavated family history, I found deep ties among a set of families that, over time, had meandered with the ebb and flow of economic forces through Baja into the United States and, as immigrants, had challenged the legality of the then-segregated school system. I learned that as a child, my father had been the plaintiff in the first successful school desegregation court case in the United States, *Roberto Alvarez v. The Board of Trustees of the Lemon Grove School District* (Alvarez 1986). This was but one of the community's struggles, and they formed a strong communal organization, La Union de Campesinos y Obreros de Lemon Grove, in the early 1930s. Before my research, these efforts were unknown to me, and they had been neglected as components of the larger history of the United States and its border region. This story of arrivals, settlement, and struggle by Mexican immigrants in our society emboldened my own sense of purpose in contributing to an anthropology of social justice and social change (Alvarez 1986, 1987, 1995a).

Going to the field was thus also going home. In many ways, this was a violation of the edicts of the anthropological canon. The ultimate goal of being "in the field" is to get as close as possible to the native subject, to live like the natives long enough to report what they think, how they see and interpret the world. Becoming an anthropologist demands that we enter a new dimension, that we truly enmesh ourselves and go beyond being outsiders. The ritual requires that we enter as novices and be born again under native eyes, emerging with new emotive, sentient, and intellectual strength. Fieldwork is required to experience the anthropological.

Gupta and Ferguson, as well as others, argue convincingly that "the field" has defined the discipline, that fieldwork is the foundation of our science (Gupta and Ferguson 1997b; Stocking 1992). Fieldwork, archetypically, is embedded in ritualized performance; it initiates and categorically creates the genuine anthropologist; without it, there is no anthropology. Fieldwork is central to the canon, yet its practice involves bewildering tensions for its practitioners. A primary tension in fieldwork lies between distance and proximity, both in the personal relationships we foster in the field and in our relation to "the field" itself (Alvarez 1997).

In our personal lives, "the field" is embedded in our lifelong journeys; in our disciplinary practice, we enter and exit "the field" as an extended event in itself. Proximity in fieldwork is part of the personal connections we establish as anthropologists. It also defines how we do our work—proximity to our subjects, as part of our canonical values, lies at the heart of anthropology. Yet, proximity contains its own contradictions. On the one hand, anthropologists strive for proximity, but practice also demands distance. To get close to our subjects, we first must go far away. We thus distance ourselves from our personal histories, from our immediate social and cultural milieus. In canonical fieldwork, we engage a separate reality. This separation and distance allow us a needed objectivity, we are told. They allow us to distinguish our own perceptions as individuals from those of the worlds we wish to describe. With this separation, the anthropologist is born. Fieldwork in the far away is genuine fieldwork. This yin and yang is another facet of anthropological mutuality, another tension along the fault lines of the canon.

Although the notion and importance of "the field" has been debated, critiqued, and redefined (see Gupta and Ferguson 1997a), there continues to be a stigma attached to those who do not leave for distant geographical and cultural areas of the world and who choose to focus on people and places close to home. Hence, at the canonical extreme, real anthropology is based on distance, on a remoteness in which personal lived realities are cast aside and scientific objectivity prevails. Distance, moreover, does not begin and end in the field. Leaving the field allows us another kind of distance. It imposes a distance that separates us from our field sites and from the people we study. When we leave the field, we immediately separate the sentient and emotive experiences of the field from the reality we return to as professional anthropologists. Once back home, now unencumbered by the experience of the field, we can allow objectivity to prevail. Only then are we able to write anthropologically about our people, our subjects.

Striving for closeness, and then for distance, separation, and scientific detachment; these are hailed as the desired catalysts that underpin the experience of being an anthropologist. I am exaggerating, yet we all realize the ritualized importance of fieldwork in becoming an initiated anthropologist. The canon instructs us to ultimately separate ourselves, distance ourselves, from the people we study. Proximity, closeness, and the personal connection are simply for creating "rapport," an important but instrumental part of the fieldwork process.

Like other anthropologists, I entered "the field" armed with sound anthropological questions. And like other fieldwork episodes, my sojourn into the depths of my own family history became a life-changing experience. Anthropology helped me explore this world in both canonical and personal ways. I posed broad theoretical questions about migration, global politics, the border, human strategy, and the nation state (Alvarez 1995), yet I was focusing on individual lives and communal experience from a personal and intimate vantage point. I see this as a "deep" proximity in which the anthropologist is well versed in knowledge of the "subjects" and conditions of the research focus prior to arrival in the field. Rather than being a disability, this is a positive factor in gaining understanding and insight into social lives and processes.

Another Mutuality: The People We Study

Anthropology puts us in special places, among special people. In my own career, I have been privileged to know my own kin in a way I might not have in a different career. I saw meaning in a world of immigrant lives, of connection and survival, and of the Mexico-U.S. border, that I had taken for granted. I came to know the early pioneers and their life experiences that formed the community in which I was raised, and this provided a broader interpretation for me of Mexican settlement and struggle in the United States (Alvarez 1995a, 1995b).

I have also experienced deep proximities in other "fields" in which I have worked. In 1981, I was recruited by the Cross Cultural Resource Center (CCRC), a grassroots bilingual education program at California State University, Sacramento.[3] I was attracted by the diverse communities it served and the center's applied focus. My roles there included research coordinator, codirector of the College Advancement for Migrants Program (CAMP), and teacher and leadership trainer in ethnographic evaluation. The center, led by Latino professionals, including three Chicano PhD anthropologists and a Cuban sociologist, had a field staff that worked in schools and community educational settings with Asian, Chicano/Mexicano, Native American, and other groups, and the staff mirrored the populations we served. At CCRC, we were challenged, as well as often embraced, by the people with whom we worked, in part for our work but also because we were Chicano, Latino, community members, and nontraditional scholar researchers. Here was another mutuality, between we anthropologists and our subjects.

The long-term relationship of anthropologist to a single community is becoming, for many, a thing of the past. Yet, contemporary stories of "the field" still include personal anecdotes of living and working with the people we study and of the personal associations that may form. This relationship is often taken for granted, viewed as an expected process of mutual acceptance as the anthropologist becomes recognized and known as a person by those people whom she or he similarly recognizes. Rarely discussed as complimentary to the canon's strictures, this is a central reward we receive as anthropologists who are privileged to work with the people we come to know.

I was fortunate to be part of a CCRC outreach team that provided community educational workshops throughout Micronesia at a time when many of these island nations were becoming independent from the United States. We provided resources for workshops; led community educational programs on curriculum, teacher training, and ethnographic evaluation; and participated in workshops for educators from diverse Pacific Islander communities in which we CCRC anthropologists were often the only non-Anglo outsiders.

At one seminar on the Republic of Belau, a personal assistant to a Belaun congressman invited my CCRC colleague Steve Arvizu and me to a barbecue hosted by the Belau Revolutionary Front. Eight off-island Anglo participants in the seminar were pointedly not given invitations. The typed invitation indicated that we were to speak about our work with the communities from which we originated. We were not sure what we were in for.

That evening, we were driven to a beautiful part of the island where, among tropical trees and vegetation, the young congressman and his spouse greeted us. Two other men were present, dressed, like the congressman, in colorful sarongs, and we spoke about Belau, the food, and the events of the day. Later we were shown a video on U.S. nuclear testing in Micronesia (a video I would later use in classes at ASU and UCSD). At its conclusion, a group of elderly women community leaders in bright, colorful, long dresses arrived and sat with us on the floor of the house. They were there to learn from us, we were told, and for the next several hours, they asked us questions about who we were and the work we did with our communities. A spirit of mutuality emerged during the evening, and it was anthropology that made this happen, even if the event was more than an anthropological fieldwork experience. It was not pursuit of the canon and its disciplinary practice that placed me there but, rather, my own community background and the values and experiences that brought me to my anthropological training in the first place. And it was our Belaun community leader hosts, not anthropology, who made it happen.

El Mundo del Chilero

In 1985, I returned to the world of produce and spent the following five years engaged in the trade (see Alvarez 2005). I left CCRC under immense pressure, due to federal government defunding of educational outreach programs. CCRC was basically dismantled. I was offered an eclectic set of interdisciplinary teaching opportunities at California State University, Sacramento, but this did not fit my personal values or anthropological goals. I was burned out, unable to find employment as an anthropologist in the type of work I had conducted, and I decided to leave academia. But I never left anthropology.

Beckoned by my family, I began working once again in "las marketas," the produce markets. This was yet another "field," and this time, PhD in hand, I worked in the Los Angeles Wholesale Produce Terminal (LAWPT), a vast market that distributes global product throughout the United States, Canada, and Mexico. Here I was cast into new ventures where I used my anthropological skills to learn the Mexican entrepreneurial and marketing system. I became a chile specialist, sourcing and distributing Mexican chile peppers into the LAWPT.

My objective was to indeed learn the "culture" and to understand how Mexican *fruteros* (fruit specialists) operated through the LAWPT. However, this episode was not solely for the sake of ethnographic understanding and analysis—I was now learning skills used for the subsistence and survival of my own household. With a Mexican partner, I eventually opened a chile-packing shed, named TijuaMex, in Tijuana. We sourced chilies and other tropical produce throughout Mexico, processed and packed it at TijuaMex, and sold our product in Los Angeles. Like other *chileros*, I became a principal intermediary between the packing shed and a number of large Los Angeles wholesale distributors specializing in Mexican produce. As noted elsewhere (Alvarez 1994, 2005), I became known as "el del cuaderno," he of the notebook, among other chileros and fruteros. I took copious notes about the market, strategic relationships in buying and selling, crossing the Mexico-U.S. border, and the logic and system embedded in "el mundo del chilero," the chile-trader's world. I became proficient in my knowledge of this world, not solely because of my produce heritage but because of the anthropological lens, the lens extolled by Johnetta Cole. My life was a blend, a mutuality, of my person and my continuing growth as an anthropologist. The people with whom I worked became colleagues and intimate friends. When I speak now of the chile trade, of that period in Mexico, on the border, and in the markets of Los Angeles, it is not about "the field" but about a life experience.

Un Chilero en la Academia

In 1990, I decided to leave the produce world and reenter academia. In this journey of reentry, I experienced inquisition and critique. I was denounced for having been involved in business by some and by others, ethnically profiled as an undifferentiated Chicano anthropologist who studies his own kind (Alvarez 1994). I eventually took an academic position in the Department of Anthropology at ASU, where my colleagues understood my earlier and recent work and supported the value-determined trajectory that I had undertaken. Importantly, my produce experience provided me with deep, dense understandings of the border, of Mexican markets and fruteros, and of a host of related topics. My life as a chilero became foundational for my continued work on the Mexico-U.S. border, markets, entrepreneurs, transnationalism, and the vested power of the nation state (Alvarez 2005, 2007, 2012a, 2012b). While writing on these topics, I have also conducted community ethnography in educational settings throughout Arizona.

Full Circle

In my career, I have been in and out of multiple "fields," beginning with my extended family and community in Baja California, Logan Heights, and Lemon Grove. While I was at CCRC, the field was Micronesia, the Northern

Marianas, and the Republic of Belau. The produce world became my field as I worked throughout Mexico, and at ASU, the field was defined by community work in Southwestern and Native American educational settings. In all these places, I was doing anthropological fieldwork defined, in part, by who I am and by the values I had developed as both anthropologist and individual. I was often recognized and allowed entrance into these "fields" because of my community origin and background. Yet anthropology led me to these places and provided requisite rules to follow in approaching people and making queries. This mutual process has shaped the work I have done and continue to pursue.

Like other anthropologists, I have been a part of numerous differing "fields." My work has taken me into places where people I have met and communities I have been fortunate to work with have embraced my efforts and my person. I once believed that I was living parallel careers. In one, I strove to apply anthropological know-how to practical problems, to rupture and challenge social injustice, and to work for community empowerment. In the other, my interests in Mexico-U.S. borderland studies, broader questions of the nation state, and issues of sovereignty seemed a world apart from the family histories embedded in my book *Familia* (Alvarez 1995a). Yet, the anthropological perspective draws these value-laden themes together as mutually inclusive, as well as productive contrasts, along a range of personal experiences satisfying both the canon and the anthropologist.

This chapter has focused on career experiences, on various forms of personal proximity, and on how the practitioner reflects and affects the anthropological quest. This involves the collaboration of those we study, even if this is often not acknowledged. When I conducted interviews with my great-aunts, friends of the family, and individuals who were part of my extended family throughout Baja California, I did so as a family member but also as an anthropologist studying immigration to reconstruct and reinterpret the past. I was received as kin in places where no outsider would be welcome. My place in this particular world provided me entry. Similarly, in the world of the Mexican fruit trade, my family background played an important part in the work I accomplished. Still, in each of these situations, it was the tools of the anthropologist I used in both query and interpretation.

I have come to realize that the field is not simply a place but the realm of human issues and problems that I engage as both a person and an anthropologist. In the past, I often defined my anthropology as eclectic, because my work was all over the map—in Mexico, the United States, markets, schools, communities, institutions. Looking back, I see the personal as being the catalyst and instigator of all my interests and professional work. My personal values are the thread that runs through them all. But the personal has also placed me in ethical quandaries about my position as an anthropologist and ethnic scholar.

Throughout my career, I have been in marginal positions as an anthropologist. This was the case in ethnic studies and even earlier in the choice of doing work in my own community, where I became marginal in regard to canonical strictures. This kind of marginality in fact pervades the situations in which I have worked. It is not a negative aspect but rather profoundly positive, because it has fed both my personal growth and my engagements with the canon.

In many senses, I have been a marginal native: marginal to anthropology, marginal as a social scientist in my own community, and marginal in the many fields—at the border, as a chilero, as a Chicano in Micronesia, in educational and community settings, and in other areas—in which I have been fortunate to work. This marginality has been a productive force, conditioned by the mutuality of personal values and canonical persuasions. At times, I have found myself at the fault lines of the canon, confronting the tensions and conflicts between person and discipline. But this, too, has revealed the creative possibilities and potential of our field.

Chapter 10

Listening with Passion

A Journey Through Engagement and Exchange

Alaka Wali

As an anthropologist, I have wanted my research to matter to the people whose lives and cultural practices I was mining for the understanding of human social behavior. I have wanted the research to help them change their structural conditions. I believe that because of this desire, I have listened to collaborators in the widely different settings where I have worked in a manner different than that of the traditional mode of academic anthropology. I was not listening to record and analyze but to more actively participate in the construction of a better world. As a result, I have changed my perspective on the nature of collaboration, and it is this more activist mode of collaboration that defines mutuality for me.

Mutuality must be an act of passion. Mutuality as a research strategy implies that the researcher is guided by the concerns and questions of importance to the research subjects. For the research to be successful, these concerns and questions must also be one's own. Over the forty years I have pursued a career in anthropology, from early days as an undergraduate to my current work in creativity, arts, and resilience, I have come to understand the importance of mutuality as central to my growth as an anthropologist. In this chapter, I reconsider my trajectory in anthropology with an eye to the growth of mutuality in my practice.

Anthropology at Harvard in the early 1970s was in ferment, as it was everywhere, when I was studying there as an undergraduate and decided to pursue a career in it. The process of decolonization was in full swing, and the junior faculty and graduate students who were my mentors and teachers were fully involved in the anti–Vietnam War efforts, feminist struggles, and campaigns to get Harvard to divest itself of stocks in companies supporting Portugal's colonialist vestiges in Africa. They connected anthropology directly to these struggles, as did I. In my case, I do not exactly understand what made me passionate about the struggles of indigenous peoples and their quest to secure their homelands. Shelton "Sandy" Davis, my undergraduate mentor and a leader of the radicalized faculty and graduate students, certainly raised our awareness of these concerns. We felt a special responsibility to indigenous peoples because of anthropology's historical entanglement with them. Sandy brought to light for us not only their struggles but also their immeasurable capacity to survive and reconstitute themselves. I think that Sandy's perspective resonated with me because of the wider context of my youth during the civil rights struggles and antiwar protests. My passion for anthropology was sparked by the potential it held for social activism.

Even in this context of the decolonization of anthropology, to agree to enter into relationships of mutual learning or establish common ground and mitigate the inequality between researcher and researched was to agree to accept marginalization from the established mode of academic practice. The academy, certainly in the 1970s and even today, has not been friendly to approaches that privilege mutuality in the researcher-researched relationship. The long history of tenure denials, lack of funding for anticolonialist methodologies, and other suppressions or dismissals of unorthodox work has been well documented (Harrison 1997; Jones 1970). Marginalization was not, however, a new condition for many of us who wanted a mutual approach to engagement with our research subjects. Accepting marginalization makes the decision to pursue mutuality a political act.

Marginality, however, does not necessarily entail mutuality. Inherent to mutuality are collaborative processes that ensure that the researchers and researched establish common ground in the methodology and design of the research project. Ethnographic methods have, by design, contained elements of collaboration. Ethnographers seek "entry" into the hearts and minds of their subjects of study. Such entry is not possible without the willing collaboration of the subjects, who ask in return that ethnographers share something of themselves. We ethnographers ask about marriage patterns and are asked, in turn, "Are you married?" However, this type of collaboration is guided by the desires of the ethnographer who has determined the parameters of collaboration. In my early work with indigenous peoples, although I was researching issues of concern to them, I did not include them in my "up-front" work designing the research or determining the specific questions I wanted to ask.

For example, my earliest work in Mexico with the Maya people of Zinacantan concerned the changing status of women—a subject not of great interest at that time to the Zinacantecos. I had a difficult time connecting with the women, because I could not speak Tzotzil. The women were not very forthcoming; they were reluctant to talk with a stranger. Despite my intentions, I could not establish the necessary bond that would allow me the collaboration I desired. And again, when I arrived in Panama to do my dissertation work on the social and economic impact of a large hydroelectric project on the dislocated people of the Darien region (Wali 1989), I fell short of a mutual exchange. I explained to the different communities what my project was, and they agreed that it was in their interest to have me tell the story of their experiences with the dam and their dislocations. On returning home and writing up my results, I attempted to send back information to the various groups I had worked with, but by then, their struggle had moved on.

Stress and Resilience in Harlem

Mutuality must also be an act of patience. To create deeper collaborations requires more time-consuming work that does not always fit with the research or funding cycles. It was only much later that I started experiencing this type of collaboration. Starting in 1993, I worked with anthropologist Leith Mullings in a research project investigating the social context of reproduction in Harlem (Mullings and Wali 2001). We wanted to understand the underlying causes of the higher rates of infant mortality among African American women. The project was funded by the Centers for Disease Control (CDC) and required a "participatory" approach. The CDC was quite aware of its bad reputation in the African American community due to the Tuskeegee "experiments" and other problematic research projects. The program officer who initiated this research, herself African American, did not want to create more distrust in the black community, especially over reproduction and birth outcomes. One reason that Mullings and her colleagues were awarded the grant is that they presented a strong strategy for community participation in the research. Mullings had more than twenty-five years of experience living and working in Harlem by the time we started the research, so she (together with her colleagues—an interdisciplinary group of medical and epidemiological researchers) was intimately familiar with the complexity of Harlem as a research site (see Mullings 1997, 2005).

We decided to construct several avenues for participation that recognized the diversity of those we wanted as collaborators. We formed a community advisory board constituted of civic activists, political leaders, and public health and social service professionals, among others. The board provided general oversight of the research project, including the initial research design, field sites, and public communication strategies. However, for deeper insight into specific issues (such as number of people and themes for the focus groups and how to discuss sensitive issues, such as infant mortality and the design of a survey questionnaire), we formed "topical dialogue groups" with a mix of people, including people from the field sites. Finally, in several large public meetings, we presented our research plan and preliminary findings and listened to comments from those who attended. All of this required more time than the CDC officers had anticipated, and when our report was delayed, they became irritated and nervous. For us as well, it was at times difficult to adjust the research design to what we were hearing from the advisory board and the dialogue groups. Ultimately, however, working through these issues provided us with deeper insights into the complexities of women's lives.

Looking back, I realize that the patience required of us in using the participatory approach spurred us toward an approach compatible with mutuality. Patience, however, is not normally considered in discourses about participatory research. Only recently have new theoretical insights begun to emerge about the nature of collaborative processes (Rappaport 2008) that might have important implications for how we can begin to use patience to centralize mutuality in anthropological work. In the rest of this chapter, I examine a specific benefit of mutuality practices, the enhanced capacity for resilience—most simply put, the capacity to recover from repeated adversity.

Creativity, Art, and Resilience

Anthropological interest in the quality of resilience is long-standing and primarily associated with research on social contexts of disaster and postdisaster events (Button 2010; Hoffman and Oliver-Smith 2002). It focuses on characteristics of social organization (such as strong social networks) that are necessary to enable affected people to recover from disaster. However, resilience is now being studied in much wider contexts of social life. Relatively understudied is the role of the aesthetic dimension in the production of resilience.

If mutuality is a political act executed with passion and patience, I was challenged in my current work to apply it to the study of resilience and creativity. Although I could have studied resilience and creativity in nonmutual ways, I could not have *valued* it as I do now. The interconnection between creativity, art, and resilience is intuitively obvious but more difficult to rigorously delineate. Creativity in humans is the capacity to imagine beyond the immediately perceived reality. It arises from our unique ability for symbolic thought, which evolved with the emergence of our species, *Homo sapiens* (Damasio 2001; Nowell 2010).

In the first exhibit I curated for the Field Museum of Natural History, we tried to present this anthropological understanding of human creativity. We wanted our visitors to form a connection between themselves and the cultures represented in the collections, to erase the dominant natural history trope of "us" and "exotic other." The link between creativity and human cultural evolution provided a visceral reminder of the temporal depth of this capacity. The exhibit's central message, "Common Concerns, Different Responses," encapsulated the perspective that all humans create life ways, material goods, and forms of social organization under the constraints of their circumstances (shaped by history and the environment). Using comparative examples organized into thematic common concerns ("Home," "Community," and "Image"), we showed that creativity characterized all cultural processes and that it was a principal reason for cultural difference. The exhibit used objects from the museum's collection but also included objects and examples of material culture and cultural processes from Chicago.

The thread of understanding the relationship between creativity and resilience had begun for me with the Harlem project. We were instructed by the community advisory board to avoid characterizing Harlemites as "victims." Over and over, we heard that people wanted to be acknowledged for their capacity to overcome oppressive circumstances. For that reason, Mullings and I titled our monograph *Stress and Resilience* and documented the creativity with which Harlem women devised coping strategies to confront the daily injuries of structural racism. Women's resilience depended on their capacity to strategize, make effective use of their support networks, and innovate new forms of social relationships.

We found that under the tough conditions of the early 1990s (the recession, Mayor Rudolph Giuliani's law enforcement policies, the residue of the crack epidemic), women had to piece together livelihoods for their families by relying on work and family combinations that could overcome the uncertainty of holding on to a job, cracks in their networks if members could no longer share resources, and the eruption of crises (conflicts with children's schools, health issues, housing problems). Although my fellow ethnographers and I were depressed and frustrated as we witnessed and shared the daunting conditions, we also were awed by the strength of women to keep on devising protective strategies for themselves and their families. I wondered if I had such strength in me.

I spent three months working in a Harlem McDonald's to capture the impact of low-wage work. One particularly hard day, I dispensed sodas for a non-stop flood of customers, standing on my feet without a break. Later, during the commuter rush, I took the train home to New Jersey, also standing, and then cooked dinner for my family. The visceral experience of physical stress and fatigue was humiliating and numbing, and it was different from any other fieldwork I had done. This experience spurred us to engage in further discussions with the women about their own experiences, but when we talked to them, we discovered that they did not define themselves by the work. They put the work in a deeper context of other parts of their lives and relationships. They took pride in their attention to detail in the performance of tasks and in their capacity to take advantage of the "part-time" nature of the employment (for example, working shifts) to attend to other needs. I found this a hard lesson to learn. I was used to having my work, my "career," define me, to be the driving force in my life. Learning the lesson forced me to accept that academic success by the usual measures might not be attainable or desirable, a lesson learned from the active practice of mutuality.

Members of the advisory board were not surprised by our findings but, in some sense, expressed vindication that their experiences, their analyses of social conditions, had been affirmed by research. They gained insights into the relationship between that experience and the stress pathways that contributed to high rates of infant mortality and to women's poor health outcomes. This mutual exchange affected me deeply and sent me further on the journey to using mutuality as an approach to both research and life.

Museum Collections

Although we analyzed these resilience strategies, we did not associate them with an aesthetic dimension, something that I began to do gradually after joining the Field Museum. This Chicago museum holds one of the largest anthropological collections among natural history museums. Reflecting the early history of museums, its holdings span the globe. The bulk of the collecting was done in the latter part of the nineteenth and early twentieth century, when wealthy merchants and industrialists financed expeditions to collect objects of peoples thought to be disappearing. Coming as I did from the activist bent, and wanting to pursue the approach we took in the Harlem research, I initially distanced myself from the collections and focused on conducting participatory action research with community organizations (see Wali 2006a).

In 2007, more than ten years after arriving at the Field Museum, I made my first collection acquisition. These were ceramics and textiles made by women in the Shipibo communities situated close to the Cordillera Azul National Park, in northern Peru. I had been working in this region since 2001 as part of a broader initiative to engage local people in the stewardship of the park and in their own natural resource base (see del Campo and Wali 2007 and Wali 2012).[1] The collections project was part of the effort to create a greater sense of value for the artistic work, to generate pride in the local knowledge and practices. The Shipibo, like so many Amazon indigenous populations, have been subject to massive displacement and assault on their lands and identities. The hunger for natural resources on the part of the industrialized world has resulted in successive cycles of boom and bust, with the latest "boom" centered on extracting timber and oil. In order to gain access to these resources, the extractors have insistently pushed indigenous peoples into joining the cash and market economies, making the argument that a subsistence-oriented life is inadequate, backward, and perilous for modern times. In the hope of countering the relentless discourse of money, we sought to strengthen the alternative value of home production, which is so closely linked with subsistence lifeways. The objective of validating a subsistence mode of livelihood was part of the broader strategy for environmental conservation. Clearly, subsistence-oriented modes of production produce significantly less forest degradation than capitalist modes that rely on intensive and extensive extraction of natural resources.

Visiting Shipibo communities on the Pisqui River, I was struck by the high anxiety people manifested over their lack of money, their remoteness from market sources, and their dismissal of the healthy intact forests that surrounded their villages. Yet, in contradiction to this anxiety, there also existed a more vibrant production of ceramics and textiles, more so than in the Shipibo communities that were closer to major cities. Everyone acknowledged the beauty of the vibrant colors and geometric patterns that made them so distinct from other indigenous groups' handcrafts. The aesthetics of the pieces encoded their relationship to place and to the history of Shipibo occupation of that place (Belaunde 2009). The geometric patterns represent the geographies of rivers, mountains, and forest paths. The designs come to women in their dreams or when they place an herbal potion in their eyes. The very persistence of the knowledge that enabled Shipibo women to make these pieces over the centuries had also created their strong bond to place and to each other. Without the designs, I am not sure that the Shipibo would have remembered the ways in which their values and beliefs differed from those of the national society into which they were forcibly integrated.

Yet, there was a deeper connection between the objects and the social relationships through which they had been produced. We learned this through the production of a documentary film on the ways in which Shipibo men and women thought about their past, changes in their cultural practices, and current conceptions of their own identity. The film, *Shipibo . . . the Movie of Our Memories*, was a component of the collections project. My colleague Claire Odland had found footage of Shipibo life taken in 1953 in the archives of the American Museum of Natural History. She edited this silent footage and we showed it to people in the communities, and they commented on what they saw in relation to their own lives. Peruvian videographer Fernando Valdivia collaborated, as did anthropologist Luisa Belaunde, among others.[2] The objects permitted the creation of these relationships and also created ties between object producers and the place where they lived—the Shipibo homelands. Making the film and building the collection was the first time I had experienced mutual exchange centered on the materiality of daily life. The film provoked for the Shipibo an intense nostalgia for the lifeways of their grandparents and reinforced the value of making the effort to maintain the knowledge and skills of making ceramics and textiles. For me, it sparked a new awareness of the deep connection between materiality (the making of things) and spirituality.

I was very influenced by what I had learned from the Shipibo women whose artwork we collected for the museum. I began to spend more and more time walking through the collections rooms, which were organized like library stacks—tall shelves and drawers and cabinets in rows, filled with objects. Every object, no matter how mundane its function (a spoon, a cup, a pouch, a basket) had a design to it, an aesthetic element that exceeded its functional necessity. For example, there were spoons, all with different curvatures in their handles or with carvings and engraved designs; baskets, woven with different colored bark or with geometric figures; pouches, painted and given a fringe—all of these and more. Clearly, aesthetics mattered. Time, labor, and effort had gone into the making of these objects and into giving each its unique look and feel.

Most of the ethnological objects in our collections date to the late nineteenth and early twentieth century, when the peoples who made them were experiencing the hardships wrought by colonial upheavals. For example, we have a number of objects made by Native North Americans during the times when they were living in a U.S. military fort. Fieldnotes from the curators and expedition leaders who acquired the objects describe states of near starvation and desperation. Yet, people were continuing to make things. The attention to design, to craft, is remarkable, given the pressures that were burdening people, and it seems counterintuitive. But I would suggest that it is in these worst of circumstances that people seem to most need to hold on to aesthetic and creative expression. The objects in the museum's collections reflect the same pattern I experienced with Shipibo artisans and their commentaries on their relationship to their art.

Resilience and Aesthetics in Chicago

The lessons from the objects in the collections and their resonance with my Shipibo encounters hit home even more when I wandered outside the museum walls and into Chicago neighborhoods. It was easy enough to identify aesthetics in material objects, but what of other cultural practices, not so materially manifest? What other "mundane" acts might reflect aesthetic principles? It was not until I moved to Chicago and undertook a study of "informal" artists (Wali, Severson, and Longoni 2002) that I began to understand that aesthetics could underlie the "design" of social relationships. It was during this study that I began to pay attention to the aesthetic dimension of everyday life, attempting to understand the link between creativity and art.

In anthropology, the study of art has largely focused on cross-cultural comparison of aesthetic principles and the documentation of artistic practice in different cultures. Nearly all anthropological research on art remains centered on description and contextualization of the artistic "language" of a people (Ben-Amos 1972; Bebb 1988; Geertz 1983b; Ingold 1996; Ward 1997).

Additionally, most anthropological research continues to concentrate on non-Western societies. Only recently have social scientists started examining the impact of art making on social interaction and other aspects of social life and on the performative practices of urban industrial cultures (for example, Stern and Seifert's 1997 research on nonprofit art organizations in Philadelphia).

Recently, however, anthropologists have started to deepen their understanding of aesthetics as an "operational force" in human social life, following the influential work of Alfred Gell (1998). Gell points out those anthropological studies of art have focused on the evaluation of the meaning of art objects at the expense of consideration of the social aspects of art production and circulation (3). Sociologists, for their part, Gell states, have attended too closely to the "official" institutions of the art world, an approach that Gell finds limiting because it overlooks the social relationships surrounding art production (7). The solution for Gell is to study art "as a by-product of the mediation of social life and the existence of institutions of a more general-purpose kind" (8–9), an approach that seeks out the social relationships and effects of arts practice beyond the official "arts world." Gell's position resonates with that of philosopher John Dewey. In his 1934 volume *Art as Experience*, Dewey suggests that art is a process rather than merely an object; it is part of and influenced by the social environment. Art is best understood simply as an "enhancement of the *processes* of everyday life" (6).

Our study of Chicago artists concentrated on people who were not considered "legitimate" or professional artists but, rather, people who participated in art making in more "informal" circuits—joining drum circles, quilting circles, choirs, and basement theater companies, for example.[3] My fellow ethnographers and I discovered an amazing range of people who were doing these things and investing into them great amounts of time and effort. Of all the ethnographic projects I had ever done, this was the most joyous, because our study's participants were invariably happy, engaged in art making, and stated without hesitation that they loved this part of their life more than anything. As I participated with them in making art, I felt the same happiness.

Although many recognized that they would never be taken "seriously" as artists, that they were considered "amateurs" or to be pursuing a hobby, they themselves were dedicated to perfecting their craft. We discovered that the desire to practice art led people to cross deep social boundaries of gender, class, and even, at times, race. We discovered that the serious dedication to the craft led people to overcome their fear of each other, to develop trust and engagement in ways that were not possible in their workplace or home place.

In our report, we pointed out that in the very process of mastering skills for their arts practice people acquired the skills of listening to each other, thinking critically about their own work as well as that of others, and imagining a different reality. Stepping outside the "safety zone" of their everyday life, these people had taken the risk of exploring a dimension of themselves for which there was no standard form of recognition. That risk taking eventually permeated other aspects of their lives.

It was during this study that I began to understand the benefits of participation as a research methodology. Outside this research, I would never have taken the risk of joining a music group or other arts activity, because I had had painful experiences with art making in childhood. As I played with a gamelan orchestra, I experienced the warmth of acceptance and patience with my lack of skill. The gamelan players never judged my ability but strove hard to make sure I felt included. This, in fact, was a central tenet of the informal arts—to be universally inclusive of any who wanted to participate, infusing their actions with mutuality at its most fundamental level.

I believe that understanding this aspect of art making in this visceral way led me and fellow ethnographers to craft a convincing case for paying attention to this undernoticed phenomenon. The report we produced (Wali, Severson, and Longoni 2002), although not published in a peer-reviewed format, had a strong impact on the arts policy community. It was widely disseminated and sparked further studies. More important, the work contributed to a shift in resource allocation. For example, the National Endowment for the Arts, in 2012, launched the "Our Town" initiative, which recognized that art making was happening outside of institutionalized venues and allocated funds to cities to encourage arts in neighborhoods. In Chicago, in 2013, the city's Department of Cultural Affairs released a new cultural plan that resulted from a consultative process allowing a wide variety of artists and neighborhood residents to showcase their arts practices. The informal arts are specifically recognized for funding.

Aesthetics Matter in Chicago

Although we expanded the category of "art making" in our study beyond that accepted in arts policy circles, we were still limiting our investigation to the standard genres—music, visual arts, theater. Dewey, however, challenged the notion that art is bounded by these forms. He sought to abolish the distinction between "artistic" (used as a description of a production or producer) and "esthetic" (the enjoyment of the product) (1934, 47). The process of creation, he argued, should be approached from an aesthetic perspective. It is this process of "doing and making" (253), and not simply the objects produced, that Dewey valued.

More recently, Dewey's position has resonated with another useful theoretical strand emerging from the examination of "relational aesthetics" (Bourriaud 2009) and performance in everyday life. Bourriaud, an art critic and curator, attempts to characterize trends in conceptual art that emerged in the 1990s, suggesting that certain artists are positioning art as a form of social activism in ways that emphasize social interaction and its context. Relational aesthetics is defined by art that is more participatory, collaborative, and activist. Following Foucault and Guattari, Bourriaud posits that this type of art works at the "micro-political" level, focusing on individual or localized transformation rather than striving for grander-scale social movements.

Although Bourriaud deals specifically with conceptual artists, relational aesthetics could be applied more broadly to the understanding of social life. This is, in effect, the direction being taken by the burgeoning field of performances studies, an increasingly important interlocutor for anthropology. Here, building on Goffman (1959) but moving beyond his "frame analysis," the emphasis is on uncovering the manner in which people construct social relationships within "staged" settings and on identifying events that encode the "acting out" of social relationships (Drewal 1991; Dunford 2009).

Both relational aesthetics and performance frame the creation of social relationships as agentive acts that capture the constant ebb and flow of interaction across time and place, as people navigate through the "arenas"/theater of daily life. We see social behavior unfolding before us as a drama of great improvisation and constant experimentation. This framework allows us to consider the significance of the aesthetic dimension in everything we do. It permits us to ask the question: why we are so careful to design things, stage events, provide narrative structure to our life? I contend that the infusion of aesthetic qualities into the practice of culture builds our capacity for resilience, because it secures a constant pathway to creativity and imagination.

As we moved beyond the informal arts study, we began to document more and more the aesthetic dimensions of the construction of social life, especially as it affected public space (see Wali and Tudor 2010). Our work at the museum had grown progressively more collaborative, and we were working with a wide variety of organizations to implement projects that, although they included ethnographic assessments, were principally about addressing the concerns of residents in regard to quality-of-life issues—affordable housing, access to green space, and adaptation to climate change.

During the research on arts practices in Chicago and in other collaborative research projects with community organizations, we documented the variety of ways in which neighborhood residents used and appropriated public spaces. In addition to discovering that parks and libraries were used for drum circles, poetry readings, and creative writing groups, we noticed the ways in which the streets themselves were appropriated. Informal economic activities, such as the selling of food, clothes, shoes, books, and the like by street vendors, dotted main neighborhood thoroughfares and contributed to the aesthetic terrain. They created a different sensibility of social commerce, complementing economic transactions that were happening inside traditional retail outlets. Although the city officials judge this as "clutter" on the streets, vendors' presence creates a distinctly urban feel on the street, a sense of adventure and delight at encountering the unanticipated bargain. Also, throughout Chicago neighborhoods, murals cover walls and graffiti marks bridges, underpasses, and other transit zones. We also noted the use of public space for protest—public marches, banner hangings, and impromptu signs or memorials marking zones of violence. These neighborhood-located protest performances, sometimes spontaneous, sometimes well organized, made visible the daily indignities that residents face and their resistance to quietly tolerating assaults on their quality of life.

The neighborhood uses of public space take on the distinct character of the residents and reflect the diversity of histories, cultural practices, and demographic composition. They stand in contrast to the aesthetic cultivated in the Loop, Chicago's "downtown," where city officials and civic leaders have concentrated resources to create attractors for a global elite by embracing new architecture and public art. The neighborhood aesthetics, although seemingly disconnected from the downtown, are connected to it by economic and political vectors. As the city continues to adjust to a global economic realignment, trends such as gentrification, shrinking of affordable housing stock, and migration of low-wage workers to the suburbs are shifting the claims on public spaces and increasing tension between the two aesthetic circuits. Although some city officials (for example, the commissioner of cultural affairs) want to empower neighborhood aesthetics, others pushing economic development are attempting to erase the diversity (Wali 2011). As we continue our work and research in this arena, we are mindful of the contradictions and diversities of strategies across the lines of stratification.

A second example of the aesthetic dimension of social life comes from research that looked at both "domestic" and "public" spheres. This was a study of the social and artistic networks of recent Mexican immigrants (people who came to Chicago between 1997 and 2007). Our study data showed, for example, that men principally engaged in workers' center activities and in social, cultural, and artistic organizations and that they increased their social cohesion, knowledge, and civic participation as a result. We found that the community organizations and the social networks that form when people get together to address issues they care about—whether workers' rights, health information, housing, or art—helped people to mobilize and make their voices heard. Integral to organizing were traditions of public displays of religious devotion, such as the performance of the *Via Crucis* (stations of the cross) every spring in Pilsen, which helped immigrants to more boldly stand up for their rights in other situations by explicitly linking the religious procession to sites of struggle for better housing and protection of immigrant rights. When we made visual models of the networks, they revealed the ways in which arts and cultural practices work to create social ties across gender, neighborhood, and kinship lines.

The formation of dance clubs, mariachi bands, tamale making for fiestas, and costume sewing for children's school performances all worked to facilitate new immigrants' abilities to access resources from social service organizations, labor rights activists, and kinship ties to long-time residents. Such networks spread the connections of migrants across the city, creating a pattern, in the words of network analysts, of *nodes* and *threads* that seem to take on distinctive designs. Specific churches, for example, become large nodes, as do social service organizations that offer arts programs or performance spaces. Through the design and activation of these networks, the new migrants build their capacity for resilience as they seek to gain a foothold in their new location. Art and aesthetics are at work at different levels: the act of creating art and then the use of these acts of creation to establish social ties, themselves with deliberate design elements.

Finally (and not surprisingly), we found aesthetic dimensions in domestic spaces beyond the arrangement of furniture. We conducted action research on how people in different neighborhoods could be engaged in climate change mitigation in collaboration with the City of Chicago Department of the Environment, which had developed a "climate action plan" to counter the regional threat of impending changes in the weather system, as predicted by sophisticated climate models. The plan heavily emphasized reductions in residential energy use, as well as recycling and other "environmentally friendly" practices. We conducted ethnographic assessments to create social asset maps[4] in nine neighborhoods throughout the city (Hirsch and Malec-McKenna 2011), with the goal of identifying entry points for residents to become engaged in climate change mitigation. In each neighborhood, we found distinct practices that could serve as "springboards to action" for climate change mitigation (see figure 8).

In South Chicago, which has a large Mexican immigrant population, a common practice was for men to drive through alleys and pick up clothing, furniture, and other reusable items. The *junqueros*, as these men were called, were engaged in a form of recycling, filling a void left by the city, which has yet to institute a comprehensive recycling program.

Recycling as a cultural practice is intricately woven into Mexican beliefs about the relationship between the dead and the living—as was made evident to us in a work of art displayed at a South Chicago community center, in which recycled objects (such as glass and plastic bottles) were intermingled with figures of the iconic skeletons used in Day of the Dead celebrations (figure 9). This

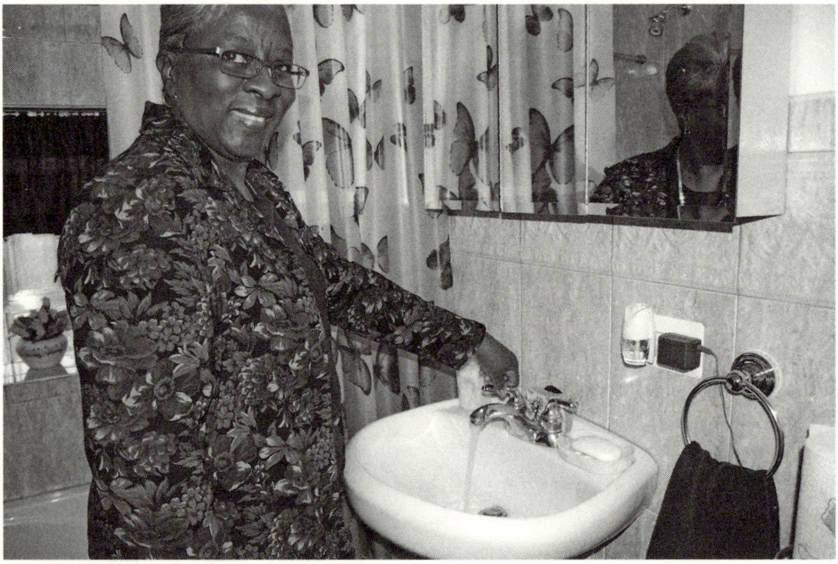

Figure 8. This woman demonstrates pride in the act of turning off water—something she has always done to save money but now recognizes as mitigating the impact of climate change.

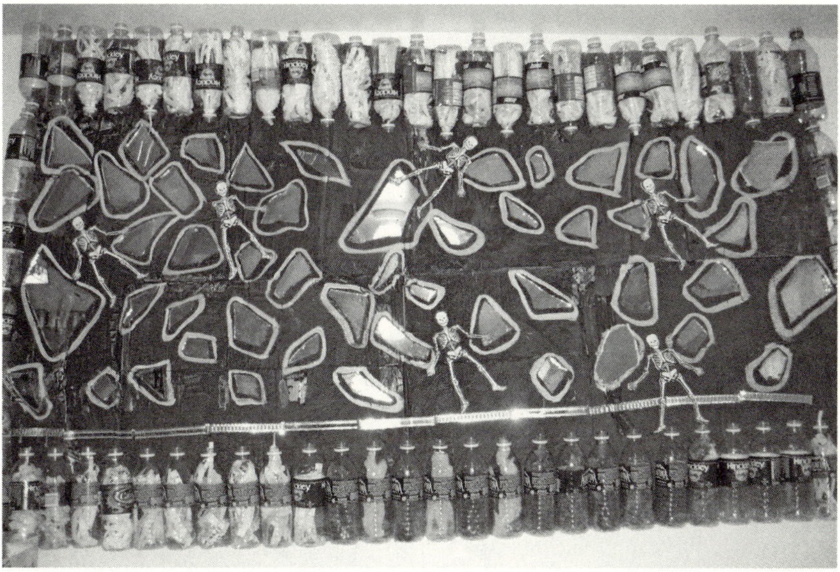

Figure 9. Artwork using glass and plastic bottles for the Day of the Dead at the Centro Comunitario Juan Diego in South Chicago attests awareness of a link between recycling and the "cycle of life and death."

tying of the mundane to the sacred is a resilience strategy that stimulates people to act to take care of their home places, even as those places are systematically neglected by the wider society. The sense of agency and the deliberateness of design reflected in this form of "recycling" permit one to consider its aesthetic dimension. As the ethnography identified these practices, it became clear that in some instances, there was a deeper connection between these acts and distinct belief systems.

Conclusion

These three examples of recent work represent for me a personal shift in my thinking about culture and social change that began with the informal arts study and grew through the work with the museum collections. The shift happened as a result of my deepening attention to mutuality and the kinds of engagement it entails. Although, intellectually, I began to see the concern with design in all these projects—in the objects residing in our collection, the work of Shipibo artisans, public use of space in Chicago, the establishment of immigrant social networks, and the cultural practices associated with energy saving—it was when I emotionally connected to the ways in which these designs were creating spaces of change that I understood how aesthetics activates resilience. I found these connections between aesthetics and resilience through acts of mutuality in my practice. My emotional connection in all these cases stemmed from the desire to participate in the change making and to afford to my collaborators the insights I was gaining.

To be an act of mutuality, collaboration has to be about risk taking on all sides. It requires that the researcher take to heart the lessons learned from the experiences of the researched. It requires that researchers let the different experience change their life course or, at the least, some aspects of the way they behave. Understanding that aesthetics permeates our lives has changed how I view myself in relation to others. I strive for a more deliberate, better crafted approach to building relationships, for a better stewardship of the place where I live, and to pay more attention to the stories we all tell, which I hope will afford me the continuing delight of discovering new pathways to creativity. But I now know I will not be able to do any of this without continuing to build mutuality into my work.

Chapter 11

Why? And How?

An Essay on Doing Anthropology and Life

Susan Lobo

Well, give me fifty years or so to think about this: the whys and hows of doing anthropology well.

Graffiti in Montevideo, Uruguay gives us a hint: "For humanity, more bridges and fewer walls."

This chapter encourages thought and discussion regarding the powerful potential within anthropology to create sturdy and long-lasting bridges. Anthropology, as a social science, always has had this potential via theories and methodologies that transfer and clarify knowledge and understandings between cultural contexts. We anthropologists are the technicians—yes, technicians—who facilitate this process. As a young student and later a practitioner of anthropology, I sensed and later recognized the power of anthropological methodologies and theories. They felt right and useful in my hands and in my thinking. Over the years, they became the principal tools of my professional life and also, to some extent, in the most personal aspects of my life. Years of work and many projects and collaborations later, it has slowly become clear how the tools of anthropology can indeed "build bridges . . . for humanity."

Writing this chapter was an opportunity to look back in order to think about the future of anthropological work and to make clear, through specific examples, some of my learning process in regard to the possibilities and potential that are an integral part of the science of anthropology. Being so intent on recognizing and analyzing patterns and processes in the actions, thoughts, and cultural life of others, anthropologists only rarely have occasion to reflect on the profound "whys" of our own work beyond the theoretical or methodological level. Now, looking back, I wonder why it has taken me so long to have an introspective look at the manner in which I view and utilize anthropology in my work. (I must admit, however, that I still feel a little twinge of—is it guilt?—when I write "I.")

There is an image that I strongly recall from the past. There, in an auditorium-sized class at the University of California, Berkeley in the 1960s, is Laura Nader, hands on hips, in her stylish outfit, looking intently at the very large class and saying (I paraphrase), "Any anthropologist worth her salt knows how to ask questions, and the right sorts of questions!" I like to think, now, that she included asking questions of ourselves regarding the profound *whys* and *hows* of the tools of anthropology that we were, at that time, learning about.

Uruguay, where I currently live and work, is a country with a long national identity as a racially "white" country and with a national history that envisions a population descended only from those who disembarked from the European boats that docked at her shores. I am often tempted to and, occasionally, among friends, do ask: "Have you ever taken a good look in the mirror?" to discern and address the indigenous and African roots that are so evidently (to me) a part of the people's heritage and of their contemporary culture. Of anthropologist friends, I have asked a similarly prickly question: "Have you recently thought, really thought, about why anthropology exists and how, as a discipline, it can realistically make genuine contributions to the lives of human beings now and in the future?"

As an undergraduate student in anthropology at Berkeley and at the University of California, Davis, with a two-year period as part of a "junior year" at Mexico City College and the Universidad de San Marcos in Lima, Peru, and later as a graduate student at the University of California, Santa Barbara, and then at the University of Arizona, I was fortunate during the 1960s to late 1970s to have mentors who encouraged delving into the profound reasons for the existence of anthropology. Among many others, these included Edward Spicer, Bernard Fontana, Laura Nader, and Wes Huss. I began to envision myself as a scholar, out hiking in the rolling hills of northern California. I pause there for a moment, and, taking my backpack of technician's tools in my hands, I toss it over the barbed-wire fence separating academia from the rest of the world and then bend down and crawl under that fence myself. What a sense of liberation! I have worked from that perspective ever since, "at home" in urban and rural communities in the United States and in Latin America, trying via collaboration with many to accomplish work with integrity as a scholar and as a human being.

The majority of my work has been as an independent scholar, an anthropologist working as a contract employee for a variety of primarily community-based, Native and non-Native groups, organizations, and nonprofits, as well as in government programs or academic institutions that serve the interests of Native peoples. I have always felt that this positioning, working side by side with other community members or staff, is a good fit for me, one that allows me to be the most productive and effective in selecting or creating projects or contexts within which to work. This positioning "on the other side of the barbed-wire fence," with my constantly evolving anthropological technician's tool kit in hand, has worked for me. It is in contrast to being primarily embedded within an academic or other institutional structure, where I might become involved in research or other projects "in the community" or "in the field" but in which the research or projects are primarily and ultimately linked to that institution's interests, sponsorship, and support.

For more than forty years, this decision to place myself and my work primarily in the world outside of academia has given me the wide-ranging independence and flexibility to be able to set priorities based on my values and my vision of the potential found within anthropology, to exercise my skills in the most creatively productive and appropriate ways, where they can be the most useful in "building bridges." In setting and ordering priorities, the first consideration for me has always been recognizing how my work could best contribute to answering the needs expressed by the community or organization that I am working for. When I remove myself from the employ of a university or other large institution and become an employee or even a volunteer at a community-based nonprofit organization, the starting point of the work and of my relationship with the people I work with shifts and collaboration is initiated. I now work for and with the people with whom I collaborate. I am not working on a project related to X community or carrying out research about or on X community or Native nation but am working as an employee of that community or Native nation.

Often I charge for my work on a sliding scale that goes from what might be considered the normal commercial rate for contract work all the way to zero. This depends on what my employers and I work out, based most often on the contractor's resources and ability to pay. We all make many choices in life; I have always been conscious and explicit in shaping my work, research, and project choices so that the goals express the values and priorities that I hold and have evolved over time and that these are appropriately suitable for each new circumstance.

I now recognize clearly, particularly when talking to other anthropologists, as we reflect on our professional choices, that the principal priorities in my work never have been in consideration of career advancement, of publication access, or even of finances. These have always been secondary, or not even under consideration, in my decisions about how I could carry out project or research work collaboratively with members of a community or organization. Strange? Not really, if the primary rationale for doing the work is that the results will be the best use of our joint or collaborative efforts and that this will result in an effective contribution. There is a practical note here. Often in talking to students or others and describing this philosophy and practice of anthropology, I am asked, "But how can you support yourself, and how can I support myself, with this 'patchwork'?" It is very possible. I have done it for years through flexibility, hard work, and strategic planning, the details of which are another essay in themselves.

During all these years, I have found it useful to maintain a marginal affiliation of one sort or another with an educational institution or other non–community-based organization or agency, choosing those with faculty or staff who share my interests. This has given me the ability, for example, to teach a class from time to time and to engage with and learn from students and other faculty. At times, this short-term "outside" work serves to subsidize my community-based work or gives me additional free time to write. However, in my affiliations with academia I have always stayed on the margins, looking in from the outside, accessing resources, and enjoying and appreciating the intellectual interchanges. Although I aim to do a good or excellent job in, for example, teaching, I have at the same time continued to be mindful that I must participate only to the extent that my participation adds to and does not distract from my work in engaging with issues and needs in the world outside of academia. In the same way that I have sought marginal affiliations with educational institutions, I have looked for affiliations with a wide range of organizations, nonprofits, and institutions, such as museums, libraries, and government agencies. I have done this because of a similar desire to interact with others with whom I share mutual interests, for interchange, to learn, to access resources that will enrich my anthropological technician's tool kit, and often to assist the communities for whom I work.

Collaborative community-based work is not easy, but the rewards in terms of outcomes are worth the additional stress, time, and energy. The collaborative process initiates a multiperson interplay that can refine thought and action and jointly polish a concept, strategy, or exploration. The varied levels of engagement in collaboration can enrich the diversity of perspectives derived from individual life experiences and the nuances of cultural differences.

The following are examples of some of the projects that I have worked on and some of the organizations or other entities that I have worked for. These give an idea of the variety and time range of these projects and, importantly, the necessary role of collaboration. Collaboration can be very short, an instant, such as with a shared idea or thought that becomes a thunderbolt of inspiration, or collaboration can continue for many years, as did my work with the Community History Project at Intertribal Friendship House in Oakland, California, a relationship that spanned three decades.

Collaborations

Far more than with the books and journal articles that I have authored or coauthored, my bookshelves and folders are filled with all sorts of project planning papers, reports and proposals, evaluations, maps, radio program scripts, photographic essays, community-based activity and event plans and posters, and conference presentations. These result from work on a broad range of topics, as well as from varied contract work. Some of these originate from work on behalf of the Violence Against Women Act, the California Indian Basketweavers' Association, the Children of Tamayowut, the South and Central American Indian Information Center, the International Institute for Human Rights (Costa Rica), the United States Census Bureau, SRI–Cultural Resource Management, KPFA Radio, the National Park Service, the Center for Substance Abuse Prevention, Intertribal Friendship House, Tohono O'odham Community Action, La Comunidad de Caroma (Bolivia), and El Grupo de Desarrollo de las Quebradas de Laureles (Uruguay). These are examples of the existing physical evidence that remains from years of wide-ranging project work in which the intent and results have been on "building bridges" through communication and action, both on my own and in collaboration with others, to create and strengthen capacities and structures and to remove barriers so that the bridges are sturdy and long lasting.

The Community History Project at Intertribal Friendship House in Oakland, California is a good example of some of the ways that a project can grow and shift, expand and contract, and make a number of contributions along the way, some of them surprising and unplanned. Living in Berkeley in the 1970s, I and my family frequently attended the Wednesday Night Dinners at Intertribal Friendship House. Intertribal was founded in the 1950s as a response to the many Indian families moving to the Bay Area, primarily as a result of the United States federal government's "relocation program." As my then husband and my daughter are Indian (I am non-Native), we were yet another family that had recently moved to the Bay Area. Intertribal was and continues to be a welcoming home spot for Native families of many tribal nations, who come originally from many parts of the United States. Over the years, Intertribal has offered social services, workshops and meetings, space for family and community events, and the Wednesday Night Dinners.

Word came to me that there was interest in starting an oral history project focusing on the original families that had established and created Intertribal. Since I had recently completed my PhD and was looking for a short-term project, I went to meet with the directors of social services, Marilyn St. Germaine and Geri Martinez, both of whom were members of early-relocating families. We made a plan, applied for funds, and were somewhat amazed and delighted when we received enough funding to get started. I was designated the project coordinator, because I would work almost full-time on the project. The fact that I had a doctorate was of little interest to anyone, and I believe that over the years, it was, for practical purposes, forgotten.

Recently, thirty years after we had started the project, Marilyn, Geri, and I laughed at what we had accomplished working together and with many others in our little "short-term" project. In the first few years, we taped and transcribed multiple interviews with forty-six community members and took photographs. Obviously, this project was here to stay. We then began collecting old photographs, documents, news clippings, artwork, ephemera, and other things that depicted the Bay Area Native community. More funds, more projects—soon it became a "community resource archive" that provided materials for exhibits, curriculum development, radio programs, Intertribal's lecture bureau, and general Native community use in looking at, learning about, and contributing to the contemporary "history" of the Bay Area Indian community. The office and archive has served as the birthplace of a myriad of projects, in most of which I was involved one way or another.

Depending on project timing, funding, and my other responsibilities and opportunities, I juggled my time working at Intertribal. Some years I worked there more, some years less, but I was always engaged and put my thoughts and efforts forward alongside the ever-shifting sets of people working on the Community History Project's activities. I usually tried to keep a low profile, focusing on necessary project work and avoiding the inevitable "politics" the best I could, knowing that my ultimate usefulness and that of the Community History Project was the long-term contribution to which we all were committed.

The establishment of the South and Central American Indian Information Center was one of the offshoots, and we also spent years working on and providing information for Berkeley's KPFA Radio's weekly "Living on Indian Time" program series. During the thirty-year period during which I collaborated with Intertribal Friendship House, I was often also teaching: one year in American Indian studies at the University of California, Davis, two years as coordinator of the Center for Latin American Studies at the University of California, Berkeley, and off and on at Merritt Community College in Oakland. I continued to spend my "free time" at Intertribal, working with others on Community History Project activities. I also continued to do short-term contract work and write during this period.

As with other aspects of my work at Intertribal Friendship House and in other community settings, my research and writing skills were recognized as useful, more so than anything labeled as anthropology per se. Frequently I was asked to put these skills to use in proposal and report writing, in public representations, and in producing research-based documents needed by Intertribal Friendship House. One of the suggestions that continually surfaced at Intertribal was that we should write a book about the Bay Area Native community. Slowly, over a fifteen-year period, we compiled the manuscript that became *Urban Voices: The Bay Area American Indian Community* (Lobo and Editorial Committee 2002). Although I was pressed to become the book's "coordinating editor," each of the photographs and each of the accompanying oral history quotations were selected after long discussion and community consensus. This was a very slow and laborious process, but the resulting book met with wide approval in the Indian community and beyond, and it continues to be useful.

After we finished that book, I vowed to myself never again to take responsibility for a book written collaboratively, especially with the collaboration of an entire community. I envisioned just sitting down and writing a book by myself—so much easier and quicker. However, I now recognize that collaboration for creating a book very often brings the richest results and may even be not only the best way to create certain books but the only way. A few years later, I started working jointly with Leonard F. Chana, a Tohono O'odham artist, on a book about his art, his life, and his Tohono O'odham culture (Chana, Lobo, and Chana 2009). After his death, the book could only be completed through collaboration with his widow, Barbara Chana. The three of us are listed as the book's coauthors.

Also a product of this Intertribal Friendship House period and experience, an article I wrote, "Is Urban a Person or a Place? Characteristics of Urban Indian Country" (Lobo 1998), later became a chapter in a book I coedited (Lobo and Peters 2001). This piece derived from a well-placed question by an elder at Intertribal (Laura Nader would be pleased!) that I thought about and mulled over with many others for twenty years: "What characterizes our urban Indian community and how do we explain it to the non-Indians?" Working on a research project for the U.S. Census Bureau around the time of the 1990 census, I tried to explain to the Census Bureau staff in Washington, D.C. (patiently, I thought) that most urban Indian communities are, structurally, networks of relationships, with dispersed residential patterns, rather than residentially clustered neighborhoods, as one often characterizes, or imagines, Chinatowns or Chicano barrios. Remembering the esteemed elder who ten years earlier had asked the essential question regarding the nature of urban Indian communities and the need to explain this to non-Natives, I saw that the enumeration methodology used by the Census Bureau, which was based on census blocks, was undercounting the urban Indian population. I tried to explain this, but apparently to little avail; as one census official responded to me, "No, all of our data indicates that all immigrant groups in cities live in clustered neighborhoods!" Where to begin? "Immigrant groups"—hardly! Or that thorough "data" and in-depth research regarding urban Indians was almost nonexistent at the time?

The article was finally published in 1998 (Lobo 1998, 2001). In 2000, I once again carried out a research project for the Census Bureau. At an early planning meeting in Washington, D.C., a census staff person rose to make an announcement, "We have discovered that there are some populations such as American Indians, living in cities, who live residentially dispersed, which means that we will have to adjust some of our enumeration methodology." At last! The elder at Intertribal Friendship House would be pleased, and I did mention it to him. Sometimes persistence pays off, I learned. Later, I wrote a book chapter, "Urban Clan Mothers: Native Women Activists" (Lobo 2009), which was also based on thinking about that elder's well-placed question from thirty years prior regarding the nature of urban Indian communities and about the ways that Indian people in cities make their communities work for them in answering their needs. (These are a vivid example of "structure and function," concepts that ring a bell from my graduate school training in anthropology and demonstrate that some beautifully foundational concepts still can be useful today.)

Were my years working at Intertribal Friendship House "research"? Not in the conventional anthropological sense, but we certainly did gather data and find means to analyze those data and communicate the results. And, very importantly, it was collaborative work. Thanks to those with whom I worked, I came away from those Intertribal Friendship House years having learned and gained a profound and detailed knowledge and understanding of the Bay Area Indian community and of other Native urban communities. I should add here that my dissertation topic, *Kin Relationships and the Process of Urbanization in the Squatter Settlements of Lima, Peru*, as well as the books derived from the dissertation research (Lobo 1977, 1982, 1984), focused on rural to urban migration of Quechua and Aymara migrants from the Andean highlands to urban squatter settlements near Lima-Callao, Peru. So, as with many things in all of our lives, there is a thread running through the years, connecting and interweaving ideas and actions.

Another example of long-term collaborative work of a somewhat different nature was the seven years (until 2011) that I worked for Tohono O'odham Community Action in Arizona (TOCA).[1] This is a Native nonprofit organization on the Tohono O'odham nation that functions separately from the nation's political structure. Its focus is on community well-being through strengthening and restoring long-held food and other cultural traditions. Since its founding in 1996, TOCA has had a number of programs, many concerned with youth and elders. Officially, I was the evaluator for a number of the grants, but as new projects emerged and my set of technician's tools became known, I was asked to write an ethnography and to participate and contribute my part in a wide range of this dynamic organization's activities.

Some Thoughts on Writing

So much of the shape that the work carried out by anthropologists ultimately takes is in written form, as books or articles, and, additionally, in the work that they produce as reports, updates, newsletters, proposals, or evaluations. Some of what I had to learn, unlearn, or relearn in my own work has been to write in a variety of styles, sometimes avoiding and undoing the formality and stiffness of academic writing that I had so carefully nurtured during my academic training. I had to learn to write in ways that could reach the range of intended audiences or readers if these anthropological skills were to be used to truly "build bridges." Now, looking at some of my graduate student papers and articles and that stately dissertation, I see how hard I had tried to express my research findings in an academic style that, admittedly, was necessary in that time and context. I wonder now if more than a few people ever waded through that difficult-to-read prose. These early written pieces of mine, I now see, are a lifetime of projects, research, writing, and life experience away from what I now know about the utility of writing.

I also learned to appreciate the National Writers Union's little handbook for writers of all sorts that taught me to think about negotiating with publishers over contractual details (National Writers Union 1995). I was surprised and amused at the shocked reaction of some publishers that were accustomed to working only with academic authors. These authors evidently do not go point by point over their book contracts as I do, but presumably they are happy and relieved to have yet another publication to their credit, leaving the details to the publisher. It is important to me that the publication has the look and presentation that I, or our collaborative group, have envisioned and that all visual details, not just those in the written content, are correct and have the look and "feel" that conveys the message we as collaborators have envisioned. It is also important that all contributors, including artists, are fully credited and that, when possible, biographical information about them is included.

I also now know how crucial it is to follow the entire editorial process once a manuscript is submitted to a press. For example, during the editing process of one of the editions of *Native American Voices: A Reader* (Lobo and Talbot 2001), we decided that a decorative motif was needed to set off informational boxes from the central text. I was told by the Prentice Hall editors that there was no need for me to see and approve the design, which would slow the process, and that the design department professionals had selected something "lovely" that had been used previously in a geology textbook that was selling well. I insisted on seeing and approving the design, as our contract stipulated. What they sent me for review was a row of little skulls and pickaxes! This was certainly not appropriate for a textbook focusing on contemporary topics in American Indian Studies. I also have learned to appreciate the use of art, photography, and other visuals, as well as poetry, in telling the story that some of my and our contributors' writing is intended to tell. This helps to communicate to a wide audience that may often perceive messages best via these media rather than by text alone. I have also had to learn how to write proposals and funding requests, as well as reports to funders and for evaluations, both efficiently and effectively, because our community-based work has depended on a flow of funding to support it.

Looking at my first book, *A House of My Own* (Lobo 1982), then at two more recent collaboratively written volumes, *Urban Voices* (Lobo and Editorial Committee 2002) and *The Sweet Smell of Home* (Chana, Lobo, and Chana 2009), and finally at my contributions to the third edition of *Native American Voices: A Reader* (Lobo, Talbot, and Morris 2010), the change in my writing style over time is shockingly evident. Did the same person write the early book and the later ones? One reviewer of my 1982 book referred to it as "uncluttered by . . . the jargon usually employed by social scientists," which secretly pleased but also surprised me.

Over the years, in numerous project reports, newsletters, radio scripts, lectures, interviews, and photographic exhibits, evidence of subtle changes has unfolded not only in my writing but in my thinking and in my approach to my work as an anthropologist. I slowly let fall away the static anthropologist's role as the expert who interprets or translates a reality from one context to another. I can now, when appropriate, step aside and into the background so that others' thinking and voices can be clearly heard and respected.

Evidence as to how far I had traveled was a comment published on the dust jacket of *The Sweet Smell of Home*, in which Bernard Fontana remarks, "Leonard Chana spoke and painted from his heart and deep cultural roots. His shared insights into the past and present of the O'odham, leavened by his gentle humor and unsullied by third party interference, have no peer in the published literature of his people." This was a comment for which I was openly pleased and greatly thankful. Bernard Fontana understood my stance in working with Leonard Chana. He had recognized and honored my efforts to place the words and knowledge of Leonard Chana front and center via my technician's skills as an anthropologist, and it was clear to him that these facilitated the complex process through which this sage intellectual and artist's thoughts and cultural insights, as well as his life story and art, could become a book.

A Final Thought

How and why have the walls grown around anthropology? How and why has some of the profession moved away from the goal of building bridges? Perhaps the answers can be found in the colonial roots of anthropology; perhaps in the professional priorities maintained in educational institutions; or perhaps in racism, class prejudices, and stereotypes. I do not know. I can only give examples from the way I have shaped my life as an anthropologist and what I have learned.

Where do we go from here? How can we maintain this science of anthropology as a powerful tool for humanity?

I suggest we answer this question together, through collaborative thought and action.

Chapter 12

Embedded in Time, Work, Family, and Age

A Reverie About Mutuality

Renée R. Shield

> We are caught in an inescapable network of mutuality.
>
> —Martin Luther King

I think I should start with the idea of time. For me, time pushed into prominent consciousness soon after I became a parent. Before that event, time seemed infinitely ahead of me, and I felt inviolable, in a time-proof bubble. I was young! I would always be young! Now, though, I remember my infant daughter gazing at me some months after she was born, and I had the random thought that I was separated from her by a generation. As her mom, there was a divide, and she would always see me differently than I see myself, a generation removed from her. Further: I was the age my mother had been when she had me. My mother was another generation above me, forever and far removed from me in time. Did my new insight imply that I might become my mother's age one day? A dizzying thought.

With these musings, I became fascinated with the passing of time and with my aging. It was as though I had entered the life cycle rather than being stuck in endless youth. I was a grad student in anthropology. I felt the same age as the other grad students but now with a difference: as a pre-parent student in the liminal student role, I had been able to maintain the fiction of being timeless and young. As a parent now, I had traversed a rite of passage and had a time barometer in my daughter's physical growth, and consequently, if I considered it honestly enough—my own aging. This new awareness made me feel different from the other grad students, in addition to the fact that I had responsibilities at home that I had to run back to, usually at inconvenient times that rudely interrupted school activities.

As one who had long been straddling borders, I was attracted to anthropology and topics connected with liminality. All my life, I had felt emotionally like a semioutsider, observing any new social situation from a self-conscious distance and tentatively venturing in with caution. My innate reserve kept me apart, somewhat unsure, and vigilant about my surroundings, as well as about myself. I had been an anthropology major who hung out in the music department; the anthro department hardly knew I was one of their majors. I knew that anthropologists often characterized themselves as *in* as well as *out*; even when feeling comfortable with people one studies or immerses oneself among, one has to deliberately pull back to observe and consider. This self-conscious stance made for an essential discomfort and an alert unease that, over my career, I have only become more familiar with rather than more comfortable about.

Now, as a grad student with a baby, juggling family and school, I was observing myself and the role of parent as an anthropologist exploring a strange culture, and I was also deciding what to study for real. I considered ethnomusicology, which would provide continuity in the relationship I had with music, but I was looking for something of practical use as well as of theoretical interest—for which, read, not *too* applied. In the 1970s, we heard glimmerings of the demographic deluge that would soon be upon us: hordes of aging Americans would descend, and what would we as a society do about it? It was also about *us*, the baby boomers. Time and age were thorny theoretical constructs with (probably, I surmised) great cultural variation. If I was examining my notions of my relationship with time, maybe I could design research to explore how people vary in how they think of and experience time and age. Although newly enlightened to the importance of age as a new mother, I did not really understand or embrace my own aging. Like everyone else, I "othered" the old. I was moved by Simone de Beauvoir's observation that it is easier to think oneself dead than old (de Beauvoir 1970). For the former, you take your current idea of yourself and X it out. To accept the idea of aging, you need to fundamentally alter your idea of yourself. I often think about the struggle this internal competing mutuality entails and find it continues to motivate me to "think myself old" (see, for example, Shield 2012).

I think of mutuality as reciprocity and, to a lesser degree, as about sharing things in common. This essay is my take on how mutuality has played out in the anthropological and personal projects I have undertaken during my life's career. It attempts to clarify my evolving relationship with these subjects, both human and academic, over time. Finally, it focuses on personal aging and on how my sense of time and age have changed and affected my sense of mutuality.

Looking back, it appears that I deliberately avoided a separation between what I am calling my project to create a family with my husband, Paul, and my project to develop a stimulating and productive professional career. I rejected the idea of "now we'll have kids, and then I'll focus on school and career, and I'll do each in sequential order and devote my full time to each." This notion seemed unworkable at a gut level. Instead, I attempted to blend these projects so that they would have a mutual impact on each other. Benefiting from my physician husband's ability to provide sufficient economic sustenance for the family and emotional support to me, I underwent graduate school and then worked in academic and nonacademic jobs on a part-time basis for the next decades. I was able to pursue these activities in my role as first responder to family needs. Thus, I ran home to nurse the baby, relieve the babysitter, take a child to the doctor, go to the cross-country meet or the school field trip—and later, visit my mother and mother-in-law in their assisted living and nursing home facilities, which were near our homes.

Negotiation and Roles

As Sanjek notes in his conclusion to this book, mutuality involves negotiation. Negotiation characterizes many of my activities and my considerations. Internal negotiation entails my willingness to reflect on a situation and stance by engaging in conversation with myself and others to determine how to accept the need to adapt, consider input, and weigh and respond to challenges. In my case, the threads that comprise mutuality, reciprocity, and negotiation weave through time and involve debate with myself almost or just as much as with others.

Negotiation with my husband resulted in the decision for my anthropological projects to take place at home rather than abroad. I had pictured uprooting us to go to an ideal "other" place and practice "real" anthropology away from home. His commitment to the long-term relationships with his psychiatric outpatients, however, was a fundamental challenge to this notion and entailed active conversation and my eventual reconciliation to the idea that anthropology could take place at home as well as elsewhere. Although I acknowledged that I might have preferred doing "real" anthropology outside the United States, I came to terms with what encounters with others, whether elsewhere or here, entail. This mutuality provoked me to scrutinize my relationship with Paul and with the field and helped propel my thinking toward the identification of a project that would be practical and applied, as well as local. Anthropologists in the 1970s were challenging the idea that American scholars intuitively knew their own cultures, against which we could compare with those of others. I was affected by the essays in *Reinventing Anthropology* (Hymes 1972). Paul and I together realized a preference to raise our children in the United States, relatively near extended family members. As a result of this thinking and negotiation, I located my projects at home and integrated them with our New England life.

Negotiation is contingent also on navigating multiple roles that entail the use of varied aspects of self. I think of negotiation as if it is on two simultaneous axes, synchronically occurring across roles at any one time as well as evolving over time. A reason Catherine Bateson's *Composing a Life* (Bateson 1989) resonated so much with me was that it helped me reconcile the naïve ideal that, on the one hand, there is one optimal way to plan and execute one's life against the unfolding and practical daily realities of a lived life that is typically interrupted, nonlinear, and disturbed with, on the other hand, the idea that a necessary component of living and aging is to adapt and do *bricolage* (Lévi-Strauss 1962) with the life and ingredients at hand to create a product of some kind.

The Mutuality of Grad School and Family

At the beginning of my post-master's PhD program in 1976, we had a one-year-old and I was pregnant with my second child. Following his birth, I continued course work and completed my first set of prelims and the language requirement. After more course work, I wrote my dissertation proposal and passed my second set of prelims. I developed and taught an undergraduate course on aging called "The Twilight Zone" and finished my last courses the following year. I joked about "burning the life cycle at both ends" by having kids and studying/doing aging. (I also wrote a book about having kids around this time [Shield 1983], which led to book tours and TV, radio, and print media interviews.) I began fieldwork in a nursing home that continued for fourteen months, starting when my third child was one. After fieldwork, I wrote and then defended my dissertation. My husband and kids (now eight, seven, and three years old) accompanied me to my graduation in May 1984. Being greedy, we topped off with a fourth child in 1987.

My dissertation was originally going to be about how retired workers perceived their work as well as their retirement. I planned to observe and interview employees from a local large factory who were about a year from retirement and follow them for the next year in retirement, and I had a factory lined up so I could understand retirement in relation to their work. Good plan, but the plant's human relations officer made herself the gatekeeper and effectively blocked my access to employees. (Meanwhile, Joel Savishinsky provided a masterful study several years later in *Breaking the Watch* [2000].)

Deeply disappointed by my foe's unwillingness to help or get out of the way, I changed gears and decided to try to understand what it was like to live and to work in a New England nursing home. This change of plans introduced me to a complex world! There was the world of the staff and its divisions, as Gubrium had richly elaborated in his classic ethnography of Murray Manor (Gubrium 1975). Nursing home residents were of different kinds too, I soon discovered, as were their visiting family and friends. The nursing home was embedded in its city but was its own self-contained world and separated, almost as if polluted, from the city. Non–nursing home residents consisted of administrators, trustees, physicians, social workers, activities and rehabilitation therapists, unionized and nonunionized staff, and others. I found everything about the nursing home strange. I tried to capture this sense of otherworldly strangeness in my subsequent book (Shield 1988), which benefited greatly by conversations and negotiations with the Cornell series editor, Roger Sanjek.

Staff bustled around and residents sat around, some staring disturbingly, unseeing. I felt awkward and out of place. Each time I entered the place, I was unmoored in this eerie, rather timeless setting. I had to reimagine a plan and negotiate with myself all over again about what I was going to attempt to do that day. Was I going to just let a situation unfold and see what happened, and if so, where should I go first, and did I need permission, and how would I enter this or that room? Or maybe I should approach random residents, family members, and/or staff and introduce myself and go from there, wherever that was. I yearned for a set role, as everyone else seemed to have: a family member visiting a resident, a housekeeper pushing a mop, a dietary staff member bringing up meals, a nurse aide getting a resident dressed, a physical therapist encouraging another step in a stroke patient. Each person *except me* seemed to have a place to go and a route to get there. The seeming certainty of a set role, a time card to punch in and out, a job description written down somewhere, and defined tasks to carry out looked immensely appealing. But I had chosen this separate role, the anthropologist as deliberately outside, needing to negotiate and ascertain on a continual basis and, in so doing, create and define interactions.

The Resident Care Conference: There Is No Free Lunch

As I felt my way toward accommodating to the nursing home and engaging in mutuality with one person, and sometimes one group, at a time, one regular time and place in which I could situate myself was in the Resident Care Conference, held weekly and presided over by the medical director. I listened and watched as members of departments of nursing, nutrition, physical therapy, activities, and social work convened to present their perspectives on a particular resident. The medical director created a long "problem list" on the blackboard from these presentations. Then the resident, usually accompanied by a family member and occasionally by a nurse aide, would enter the room. The medical director would lean across from the resident, knee to knee, and take the resident's hands to ask questions about the person's well-being, care, and concerns. As if doing a kinship chart or describing a musical performance, I noted where people sat in the meeting and recorded the chronology and content of the discussion as fully as possible.

One Tuesday morning early on, the medical director challenged me: "Renée," he said, "I expect you to contribute. There is no free lunch." I had somehow assumed he respected my detached anthropological stance when I had explained the fieldwork and he had allowed me to sit in, but no. Friendly though his confrontation was, I stewed about it and did not know what form a "contribution" would take. However, when, at the next meeting, I mentioned the work *Growing Old in Silence: Deaf People in Old Age* (Becker 1983) in relation to the strengths that some individuals bring to their old age, the medical director said it was a great contribution to the discussion. Then, and especially in retrospect, I am grateful to him for helping me realize that I was a part of the situation and that, in his eyes at least, I *owed* the group something in exchange for the privilege of observing their activities. I learned in this small way a lesson embedded in the list of anthropological "responsibilities" toward those we study (Sanjek 2004): mutuality is required. In traversing this little rite of passage, I had earned my right to be there as an anthropologist.

My fieldwork in the nursing home dramatized how residents were dependent on others and the institution by dint of their limits in function. It seemed that they had exchanged independence, autonomy, and adult status for care in the nursing facility (Dowd 1975), and this became an important theme in my thesis and subsequent book. My awareness of how residents tried to assert reciprocity with others, including staff and visitors—despite their enfeebled condition that, it seemed to me, was exacerbated by the institution's rules and constraints—grew with exposure to the residents and the ways of the institution.

For example, I saw that residents were prohibited from a task as simple as wheeling a neighbor's wheelchair down the hallway to the dining room. However, a resident who thought the rule silly and inapplicable to her clarified to me that this was a way she could be helpful and told me it made her feel good to do this subversive activity. Several female residents I talked with would press little candies on me, and they kept a jar of these handily nearby to offer. I started to see this as a gesture of reciprocity: you visit, I give you candy. The one-way visiting seemed to further the dependency, for which only gratitude was an appropriate response. Infantilization was also institutionalized and exacerbated; after all, only children and incapable people have things done to and for them without recourse to repaying the "favor."

Mutuality with Nursing Home Residents and Balancing Roles with Staff

Once I had established the beginning of a relationship with residents, I felt obliged to continue visits, but I also felt like a mooch. I wanted to deepen my knowledge of residents' lives and experiences, which I knew was rewarding to them, but I also felt intrusive and beholden to them for tolerating my questions and curiosity: I was taking information and insight from them. Then too, I wanted to broaden my reach to access numerous residents, but I felt it necessary to maintain the relationships I had already established. Similarly with staff members: when I started research, the administrator put me under the wing of the head social worker. Although that office became a kind of safe home base, I could not let myself get comfortable there; I had to complement my growing familiarity with the social worker team by acquainting myself with nurses—and then with other specialists, such as activity and physical therapists, dietary and housekeeping workers, union and nonunion staff. This negotiation and balancing of relationships felt delicate and fraught. The repercussions from aligning too closely with social workers would mean that nurses could consider me untrustworthy. By the same token, if I spoke too often and too comfortably with administrators and professional, nonunion staff, the unionized employees might distrust my motives and be less than candid. My effort to be neutral became especially important in the months and weeks before the strike occurred.

When it came down to it, I could never take sides or feel completely allied with any one individual or group. I found myself drawn to some people more than others as I grew to know them. The effort to engage as fully as possible with all individuals resulted in my becoming sympathetic with every point of view expressed at the same time. Listening carefully and being with people to attempt to understand their work or lives as staff or residents always affected me as I learned to see life in a new way through their eyes.

As became increasingly evident by my weekly engagement with the resident care conferences and in my daily encounters and conversations with residents and staff members, I was learning about the divisions that existed between groups of people. I saw how this more negative kind of relationship also was a cement keeping people involved, much in the way that Barbara Myerhoff described elderly Jewish senior center participants (1979). Residents in the nursing home here were, in some cases, united by a common history and affiliations formed over the years, and they and the staff seemed to be divided by personal and professional disagreements of recent as well as long duration. Residents seemed to view one another with distrust and scrutinized themselves and others for incipient slippage. They knew one another's histories: where they had lived, who family members were—school, marriage, and work pasts. In the present tense, they watched and learned and jumped to conclusions: who was showing signs of early dementia? Why had that person gone to the hospital? Would he be allowed to stay on the present floor when he returned, or would he be demoted to a unit for the less capable? Were others noticing themselves in return?

While nurses generally held to a life-at-any-cost view related to medical interventions, social workers argued for resident preferences and quality-of-life considerations in end-of-life decisions. Nurses and social workers each asserted a superior ownership and claim to the resident's proper care; by the same token, they felt misunderstood and sometimes victimized by members of the other profession. Further, union members and the administration pitted themselves against each other, nursing grievances and eyeing the contract and a possible strike.

Mutuality and Life After the Nursing Home

I must have had the implicit expectation that anthropological roles would remain somehow separate from my life roles, even as I attempted to maintain them synchronically; however, as time went on, there were times that individuals and I encountered each other in overlapping or surprising ways. Years after I audio recorded a resident's oral history and her recollections of experiencing pogroms in Russia when she was a young mother, I met her son when we were nursing home board members. He appreciated learning new things about her from the recording after she died.

I continued to visit one particular resident long after my research and dissertation were complete. Looking through my papers from that time, I see a thank-you note from my son that looks like kindergarten or first-grade writing. He thanked her for a Tootsie Roll she had given him. I would sometimes bring my kids to see her, and we occasionally made it a treat for everyone by taking her out and going to McDonald's. Someone was kind enough to give me this and other mementoes after she died.

When *Uneasy Endings* came out, it made waves in the nursing home I had studied. I had concealed the identity of the institution and the players, but I heard that some staff members objected to how they thought I had characterized them. The director of nurses said she told them, "If the shoe fits, wear it." The board of the nursing home I had studied asked me to provide a few presentations about what my book's conclusions suggested for reform and improvement. This has become an important value in my work as I describe my results to those I study and incorporate their feedback.

An eighty-seven-year-old resident of a nursing home in the Midwest wrote to me after she read my op-ed column, which had been reprinted in the local paper. I sent her my book, and this continued the correspondence. She was a nurse who had lived in a nursing home for the past five years. She said I understood how terrible her life was in the facility, and that comforted her. I was thrilled by the validation she offered. I had not just made it up!

An avid writer and correspondent, she documented the daily routines and some of her confrontations with staff members and administrators, and she also set down a great deal of her and her family's history. I asked if she would like to contribute to our nursing home newsletter and/or to correspond with one or more residents. In response, she sent a multipaged letter about memories and past incidents in her life. But her cover letter said,

> I've written as well as I can—several incidents. None may appeal to you—or your friends—so feel free to cast them out—
>
> I feel too nervous, I wander, and my writing poor—I've done most of this in early morning—when I am fresh and bright—
>
> I appreciate your interest—
>
> But my mind is not so alert anymore—I am forgetful—
>
> Most sincerely yours, [signed]

Our correspondence ended about six months later. After she died, someone from the facility mailed my book back, with a note: "Dear Ms. Shield, Mrs. H appreciated your book so much. She made a few comments in the margins. Thank you. [Signed, friend of Mrs. H.]" The book is filled with marginal notes of her comments and underlined passages. Some page corners are turned down. Her notes in the book included a few poems and some wise homilies, such as, "Humility is that strange Possession, which you lose, The Moment you find you've got it." Throughout the book, she maintained a dialog with me, noting, "True" in some places and "Is this true?" in others. When I documented what I considered the denial of death in the nursing home I studied, she wrote that in contrast to what I had written, there were memorials and funerals in her facility. In the chapter where I had detailed my sense of endless liminality in the nursing home, she wrote, "The Dr. said to me Severely—'Yes, I know you are a Nurse—You know everything.' He is Over bearing yet, at times He can be kind. I feel non existent to my Dr. here."

I found the folder about this correspondence in my basement in 2013 as I was writing this. The notated book is on my study's shelf at home. As I had not looked at it for years, it overwhelmed me that in reading through this history now, I was trying to understand how something I wrote reached an old lady in a nursing home halfway across the country and established a connection. It hurt me then and now to hear her expressions of pain, yet, I was gratified that she somehow felt comforted by what she considered my understanding. Perhaps my welter of emotions was based in the idea that although there was evidence of relationship and mutuality, it was partial and exposed the profound ways in which nursing home life diminishes individuals. I fear and know that nursing home life still continues this way for many.

The experience also clarified inexorable time for me. In 1990, I was forty-two. My children will soon be the age I was then. What frailties will be exposed in me with time? At the end of the book, she wrote in the margin, "After reading this Book—I ask a question—Will I keep my Dignity—my control—My Respect—for I have lost much—? Or Will I become lost—Never to rise to the Life ahead of me?" Me too, and you, dear reader.

My knowledge of nursing home realities was complemented by additional roles and new opportunities for mutuality in subsequent years. As the director of research and education at a nursing home, I organized noon teaching conferences on topics in long-term care, which professionals from area nursing homes and hospitals attended. Also in the 1990s I worked for a health-care reform project, Aging 2000, focused on elderly Rhode Islanders. In these roles, I learned how care was organized and provided in multiple settings in the state. I saw the same individuals at the nursing home teaching conferences, and I interviewed them for the health-care reform project. The circles of involvement sprang from and enlarged upon the original nursing home work. Hearing about daily routines of dilemmas of care in the finances of nursing homes and other health-care facilities anchors us in experiences on the ground. This knowledge must stay rooted in people and specifics.

I became a trustee, then a member, and finally the chair of a nursing home ethics committee (Shield 1995). The ethics committee work benefited from the nursing home fieldwork and was broadened by engagement with on-the-ground ethical issues, such as whether a resident should be "permitted" to move to an apartment in a part of town considered unsafe. I had seen some daily ethics played out during fieldwork; now I was helping to judge whether adult children had the right to interfere with their father's choice of a mate now that he was in the early stages of dementia. (They did not.) I had been impressed with certified nursing assistants (CNAs) I knew from fieldwork and approved of CNA representation in the Ethics Committee. In my fieldwork, I had frequently witnessed a resident's irritation that her tomato juice was always unsalted despite her repeated requests and protests: there is nothing worse than unsalted tomato juice! Now the committee was deciding whether cardiac or other medically prescribed diets could be overridden by residents for whom food was one of the only daily pleasures. We usually decided that a resident had that right, and our cases echoed those showcased in *Everyday Ethics* (Kane and Caplan 1990).

All this knowledge became newly relevant in the mid-1990s as my family and I began to suspect, then acknowledge, that my mother was showing signs of dementia. I was a so-called expert in this field, although the physicians in my family had complementary and competing knowledge of what constituted dementia and how to interpret signs in my mother as she displayed increasingly inexplicable behaviors. It was a deeply troubling time for all of us. As the years went by and we argued among ourselves about interpreting what we were witnessing, I wondered who she was, and whether the self she seemed to be as dementia became more pronounced was a self that should be understood newly in real time rather than only mourned for the self it was replacing. These thoughts and dialogs with family members were awful, especially when we were witnessing my mother's occasional with-it and characteristically sharp insight and subsequent anguish over the losses she showed us she saw too.

Investigating My Family's Present and Past: Mutuality in Time?

I had also been exploring my family's history. I started an ambitious project in the mid-1980s to learn about my mother's family's involvement in the New York diamond business (Shield 2002). Prior to World War I, my maternal grandparents had emigrated from Poland to Antwerp, Belgium, where my grandfather purchased a machine and began a business cleaving diamonds. The youngest son and his wife went to New York to expand the business in 1938, and from there, my uncle began to send ominous telegrams to Antwerp urging the family to leave because of what he saw as the obvious threat to Jews from Hitler's rise to power. Eventually, the core of the family was able to escape by different routes during the war and reunite in New York at the war's end. I wanted to understand my uncles' and my history through their work. When I phoned my uncles to pitch the project to them, they were delighted that I would pay this attention to them.

I was pregnant with child number four when I began to take monthly trips to New York for three to five days at a time. There were two offices: one office, which I considered my primary home base, was occupied by two uncles and two cousins; the other office was maintained by three other cousins. My modus operandi was to sit, watch, interject questions, and ask if I could follow one of them around when they went to either the Diamond

Dealers Club or to another diamantaire's office. Each visit included the sharing of news from my family, updates on my parents and siblings, and news of their side.

I had grown up surrounded by cousins, aunts, uncles, and grandparents in "the New York family," the European relatives who had resettled in New York postwar. In exploring the men's work, I was representing my mother as an outside observer. Her family saw her as "the American," but she never fully assimilated and felt more European the longer she was here. The diamond world was a place where my mother, the youngest and only daughter among four children, was both embedded and excluded. She told me that when she had asked questions about the business as a child, she had been hushed up, dismissively humored. Her older brothers' questions were taken seriously, because they were being groomed to join their father in his office soon after their bar mitzvahs at age thirteen.

Mutuality occurred in multiple ways: I could give my mother information about her brothers and cousins. She knew some of the stories and jokes I related, and some were new to her. She also contested various memories and information they passed on. I interviewed her about her recollections about the business, which were laced with ambivalence, affection, and resentment about her pampered and devalued status. I could relay her questions without their knowing that the source was her. I would transform conflicting or validating information I received into new questions to explore. That I was an anthropologist studying them and their work was gratifying to my mother, who saw me as her stand-in. That she, who had not been taken seriously, had a daughter who was granted access to their world and who as an anthropologist brought a professional authority they respected, provided a kind of justice to the brush-off she had experienced from them all her life.

That I could interact with cousins and uncles as an adult and as an anthropologist added a dimension to our past knowledge of one another. My interaction with one office and then the other contributed another layer of mediated contact. Their business circles were separate from each other, and my traffic between their offices provided each with new content about the other—one uncle commented that I was like a breeze bringing in news from the other office. My relatives' introduction to their colleagues allowed me access that I never would have achieved through more official routes. Rules were at times somewhat relaxed for me because my uncle was doing the asking. His introduction of me to his colleagues went something like this: "This is my niece, Renée. She is an anthropologist studying the diamond business. I want her to talk with you. She already knows the basic stuff, so tell her the real stuff."

As pregnancy and research progressed, I would stay with a cousin or uncle each evening, and fieldwork would continue as I heard from wives and daughters about their perceptions and experiences of their men. I learned about the anxiety and brooding over deals that they would bring home. Who knew? They always seemed calm and cool to me. My uncles would often ask about the people I had spoken to that day in the club, and I would deflect those questions to maintain confidentiality. Because the viscosity of links among the diamond traders was thick, they probably had all that knowledge already; plus, they were probably hearing from the traders how I was doing.

I learned how respected my uncles and cousins were. One uncle and one cousin were consistently voted by the dealer membership to be arbitrators, the highly respected individuals who hear and rule on disputes between members. My informants would tell me, "Do you have any idea how honest your uncle is?" "Your cousin is one of the very few who is beyond reproach." Or, "Your uncle is a genius with a stone, the way he can transform it into a thing of beauty—no one better." And so on.

The embedded mutuality included levels of access and their limits. An outsider as a woman and as a non–diamond trader, I was excluded from much of the men's talk in the diamond business. On the other hand, I had more instant access to the few women diamond dealers who had managed to succeed in this male-dominated business. One told me how the club had only recently added a women's bathroom to the premises; she regaled me with tales of slights she had weathered and successes she had eked out. Our bond as women and mothers gave me wonderful entrée to this world as she knew it.

Our fourth child was born in 1987, and because of family and new part-time teaching and research jobs, I did not return to the diamond fieldwork until the mid-1990s. My oldest diamond-dealer uncle died during this time. I had an adjunct teaching job at the University of Rhode Island and a clinical teaching appointment at Brown University, through which I oversaw how medical students learned about aging and approached older adults in nursing homes.

When I finally managed to restart my New York trips in 1995, I had a new vantage point on the passage of time. My surviving uncle pointed out changes in how the club's membership had declined and that fewer people were dealing in the large trading hall each day as more and more business shifted to individual offices and as increasing numbers of middleman brokers had become bankrupt.

I also felt an urgency to visit my parents in Connecticut and check in on my mother as we began to suspect dementia. On some of the visits, my father and I consulted with experts and began to arrange for part-time help in the home that would provide supervision and support to my mother while my father worked. In one visit, I accompanied my mother to a neurologist, who saw nothing whatsoever wrong with her. We knew better. Family negotiation was about whether my mother was being willful or was incapable. We had separate interpretations of her behavior. My trips to New York included my telling her big brother and my cousins, the diamond dealers, how she was doing. Discussing my mother's condition even came with me into the club, where I would, to my astonishment, meet traders who had known my grandparents and my mother from Antwerp fifty years before, and they inquired about her and asked about the sad, evolving news.

The writing of *Diamond Stories* (Shield 2002) was as difficult as the flitting between my anthropological and family roles in conducting the fieldwork. When I wrote up my notes, I wanted to convey my situatedness, because it was central to my ability to have had access to this world, but I was concerned about including myself too centrally in the work, a worry I also bring to this volume, of describing mutuality in my life and work. In *Diamond Stories*, I worked to maintain a distance and an involvement that, as much as I could manage it, would clue the reader in to my effort at understanding, given my subjective involvement.

Another challenge haunted me: fieldwork and writing seemed to last forever, as they were always intruded upon by life around home and concerns about my mother and father. In defining and describing notions about the business, the economics, the history, and the geography of this complex trade and in weaving a narrative of stories and information that readers would find stimulating, I worried about whether my uncle and cousins would find glaring errors in what I described. My uncle was by now eighty-seven; he would pester me with what I took as stinging rebukes, such as, "Haven't you learned *everything* about the business to write the book yet? I sure hope I get to read it before I die!" I took his impatience to heart, but I could go no faster.

One day, I had the insight that I could ask him directly about what to do if he died before I had a draft to show him. Until that moment, I had thought such a question was prohibited. When I considered it suddenly now, I realized, why not ask it? Indeed, mutuality requires respect of the other person and of the relationship. Assuming that the question is taboo dishonors the other person's ability to consider the question. The next day, I put it to him.

He looked momentarily startled, but then he considered my suggestion that I could ask one of the cousins to read it for accuracy if he was not available. Still, he hoped he would have first crack at it. The conversation was a game changer for me. My subsequent relief somehow freed me to tackle the writing more concertedly. Before too long, I presented him with a first draft, which he read and commented on. Although he did not live to see the published book, I was able to incorporate the substance of subsequent conversations with him about what I had written, plus his written comments on the printout, into the final text.

When I heard the terrific news that my manuscript had been accepted, my mother was living in a nursing home near me. I wondered more than ever whether she understood our conversations and whether she had insight into her condition. She rarely spoke with any lucidity that we could decipher. Now with the news of my coming book, I rushed to visit her and I told her the news. She said the best words a daughter can hear from her mother at any time: "You are wonderful." I will always believe she understood what I told her, and even if it is just my belief, I cherish the words she said.

Since publication, diamond dealers have told me that I "got it right," without the sentimentality or the muckraking typical of other accounts. I was invited to participate in a Discovery Channel episode about the diamond business and contributed an encyclopedia entry on the diamond industry (2007).

Time and Aging

Another project in mutuality that proved challenging and satisfying was my partnership with my mentor and co-author, Stanley M. Aronson, MD. We wrote a book about aging from our contrasting perspectives of gender, age, and profession (Shield and Aronson 2003). Almost thirty years apart in age, he a physician and I an anthropologist, we brought some vivid differences to our mutuality. In the book, we devised a conversation format. Alternating chapters on various topics, including the demographics of aging, institutions, aging as a problem, falls, dementia, and retirement, were taken up by each of us. As we wrote the book, we swapped chapters and commented on each other's writing and content. In trying to reconcile some of my coauthor's protests and qualifications of what I had written, I decided to keep what I wrote, add in what he had written, and then provide a response. Our talmudic-like exchange, which used alternating regular and italic print for our different voices, became the format of the book and immensely enlivened the project for us as we celebrated the irreconcilable and complementary aspects of our attempts at mutuality.

Through these years of studying nursing homes, end-of-life care, and aging, my kids have grown up. They witnessed my anguish about my mother as her dementia worsened and she entered the local nursing home, and they saw me sometimes consumed by weepy visits with her and talk about her. Over the years, I wrote about my changing perspectives of age in fieldwork and of my mother and contrasted how I evolved from a metaphorical granddaughter of residents in my original nursing home fieldwork to alignment with daughters of the current nursing home residents. Finally, I was the actual daughter of a resident in a nursing home. I described the layers of perspectives and mutuality in a paper that also critiqued the scholars of age and time (including me) who pretend to be insulated from the fact of their own aging (Shield 2003).

At the same time, I could see how my kids were worried about me and were perhaps imagining what they would do when I got old and demented and had to enter a nursing home. We talked about it some. I said something like, "Please, just be good to me. I will not make you promise not to place me in a nursing home." I do not think this talk reassured either them or me, but the things needed saying. I did not like to see their concern bald on their faces. There is no way to reconcile this, but mutuality does not guarantee resolution no matter how it maintains the conversation.

Straddling academia and other work with family has entailed continual weighing of the options, benefits, and costs of mutuality. As clinical faculty, I have been sometimes been considered staff and other times faculty. Working part-time outside academia precluded my following a more traditional academic route. (Full-time employment in the university followed the deaths of my mother and mother-in-law, who required my time.) As an anthropologist in an interdisciplinary health-care department, I love the interaction with geriatrician physicians, health economists, statisticians, and others. I collaborate with these quantitative researchers and health-care providers in mixed methods research and evaluation. Colleagues and I produced a coedited volume, *Improving Aging and Public Health Research: Qualitative and Mixed Methods* (Curry, Shield, and Wetle 2006), as we saw the potential of qualitative and mixed methods in health-care research. Increasingly, I teach physicians, medical students, and undergraduates about the value and application of qualitative methods. My focus on translating the experiences of specific people has spurred recent research. I used interviews with nursing home residents to create a curriculum for newly minted physicians about how patients experience hospitalizations and transfers in sites of care. I am now speaking to nursing homes about this research and its impact on physicians in an effort to "complete the circle" and receive their feedback.

Negotiation continues on all fronts. Paul's and my life together continues to be satisfying and pretty even so far. The kids are up and out. Periodic debates with them are sometimes about their versions of their childhoods. Astonishingly, they claim their own versions, although we insist we know what happened, after all.

Perhaps I am more accepting of the fact of aging by now or, perhaps, not at all. Aging allows me both a keener awareness of old people and a feeling that I am implicated with and connected to them. I may possibly have greater access to them, too, because of my age, as Sedgwick has nicely described in his work (2011). But in my internal negotiation, I also put a wall between them and me—I am not old. This denial is denial, no doubt, and is perpetuated by the continued survival of older relatives, who insulate us by their existence and who constitute our ceiling.

I accompanied my eighty-nine-year-old father to lunch with his big sister, ninety-three, in her assisted living facility last week. They stitched their memories together, validating the names of past piano teachers and first friends. They recalled how big sister protected little brother from his nightmares and fears that the policeman was going to take him to reform school for some imagined bad deed he had done. My father asked my aunt's advice about how to be more patient in his life, and she waxed philosophic about trying to be content and in the moment. He asked her what her life was like now, and she said, "It feels good. My life is very pleasant, not very interesting, but with no troubles either. The people here are pleasant. I have nice conversations and it's not boring. There is no one I really want to know better, but they are nice people. I like being here, I like being alive right now very much."

On leaving, they embraced and gazed at each other with extraordinary love and tenderness. They touched each other's faces. They knew it could be the last time . . . but maybe not. I am still trying to make a dent in understanding all of this. So I am taking notes.

Epilogue

My aunt died at age 94, several months after I wrote the previous paragraph. In her last weeks, she told us not to be afraid of her death, and she asked each of us to visit her. She knew, she taught, we accept, and we still hate that she's gone.

PART IV

PUBLICS

Chapter 13

Dancing in the Chair

A Collaborative Effort of Developing and Implementing Wheelchair Taijiquan

Zibin Guo

On September 5, 2008, fifty wheelchair Taijiquan practitioners dressed in white silk uniforms and moving in slow graceful harmony performed the "Thirteen Postures of Wheelchair Taijiquan" on the main stage of the Beijing 2008 Olympics/Paralympics Cultural Festival, one of the kickoff events for the opening ceremony of the Beijing 2008 Paralympics the next day. "They moved so beautifully and it was so inspirational," was how one of the reporters on the scene described them. "It was as if they were dancing in the chair."

This group wheelchair Taijiquan (also known as Tai Chi) performance was organized by the Beijing 2008 Olympics Committee and the China Disabled People's Federation (CDPF). It introduced to the world a seated form of Taijiquan that I developed in 2005 as a mind/body healing art for people with ambulatory impairments. A key feature of this innovative program is that by integrating wheelchair motion—the rolling and turning of the chair—with the dynamic, gentle, and flowing movements of Taijiquan, it transforms the wheelchair from an assistive device into a tool of empowerment.

This wheelchair Taijiquan program was first introduced to China in 2006. In the short span since its introduction it has not only thrived and become a popular fitness and recreational activity, benefiting tens of thousands of people throughout the country, but it has also been endorsed by the CDPF as part of its national program of health promotion. This chapter discusses the rationale for developing this wheelchair Taijiquan program as an intervention strategy and the author's participatory and ethnographic experience in working with various organizations in China to implement and promote wheelchair Taijiquan.

The Light Switch

After having served as a member of the teaching faculty in Taijiquan and other forms of Chinese martial arts at Nanjing University for nearly four years, in January 1986, I came to the United States and enrolled in a graduate program in therapeutic sports at the University of Connecticut. At that time, I had hopes that somehow my passion for and expertise in Taijiquan and Chinese traditional healing arts would continue to be a major part of my future professional career, but I was not at all clear on how exactly I could make this happen. While enrolled as a graduate student, I continued to teach Taijiquan, both as a way to financially support my studies and as a way to make new friends.

One day in the fall of 1986, I received a phone call from a man asking if I would be interested in offering him private Taijiquan lessons. Paul was a freelance writer, and he had read quite a few volumes of the Chinese classics, including Chinese history, philosophy, and writings on Taijiquan. "I always wanted to learn the art of Taijiquan and now the opportunity has come," he said over the phone. I was indeed quite excited to meet him and experience the opportunity of sharing Taijiquan with a person who knew so much about Chinese culture and the ideas behind Taijiquan.

After a brief conversation, we agreed to start lessons the following week in the basement office at his home. He instructed me to go directly to the basement after entering the house, and he said that he would leave both the front and basement doors open for me. When we were about to hang up, he added, "By the way, I am blind and I hope you don't mind teaching me. I am actually quite good at following verbal instructions." I was not prepared to hear this last comment, nor had I ever taught Taijiquan to anyone who was blind. But there was no time at that moment for me to think twice about it. After a pause, I replied, "Of course I do not mind."

On the day of our first scheduled lesson, I went to his home and found the open door leading to the basement. When I entered the basement, I discovered that it was pitch-black in darkness. So I shouted, "Hey Paul, I am here.

Where is the light switch?" Within a second, Paul shouted back from inside his basement office, "Light switch? Why do we need light?" A few moments later he turned the light on, and greeted me with a humorous apology. But by then, I was already enlightened.

Over the following weeks, we would spend the first part of each lesson sitting in his office discussing Chinese history, philosophy, and the ideas behind Chinese medicine. I greatly enjoyed listening to his interpretation of the rise and fall of Chinese dynasties and the strengths, as well as the ambiguities, of various Chinese philosophies. Watching the way he elegantly moved his arms and body during these discussions, I often forgot that he was a blind person.

Unfortunately, the lessons did not continue too long. After Paul fell a few times during practice, we decided it was time to call it quits. At the end of our last lesson, and to comfort me, Paul said, "Don't worry, the few moves that you have taught me are enough for me to enjoy."

Although it was a limited encounter, meeting Paul offered me a lasting gift. Our seemingly ordinary conversation about the light switch had delivered extraordinary insights. It not only challenged my own sense of normality but provoked me to ponder the ambiguous nature of the use of assistive devices in ways that could "normalize" one person but not another. I was too naïve then to take on fully this outwardly complicated and puzzling question, but I am certain now that pondering it began my journey of studying medical anthropology and the quest to develop a form of seated Taijiquan that would transform an assistive device—the wheelchair—into a tool that would "normalize" the practitioners.

Learning in the Field

In 1989, I enrolled in the medical anthropology PhD program at the University of Connecticut to study the dynamics of social and cultural forces that shape our perceptions, as well as our practices, in making sense of and dealing with health problems. Using an applied focus, I found that the medical anthropology program at the University of Connecticut provided me with both theoretical and methdological knowledge for dealing with health issues. It also further inspired my interest in applying the knowledge, principles, and methods of traditional healing arts to develop socially and culturally sound intervention programs that would meet the needs of contemporary life and social reality.

In May 1992, I moved to Flushing, New York, to begin more than a year of dissertation research. Funded by the National Center for Health Statistics, my fieldwork focused on examining the social and cultural factors affecting the practice of health-care management among the Chinese American elderly population of Flushing, a fast-growing Asian American community (Guo 2000, 24–28). To obtain firsthand understanding of the lives of elderly Chinese immigrants, I quickly immersed myself in their community life. During my research in Flushing, I served as translator for their hospital visits, assisted them in obtaining Medicaid, participated in their family and social festivities, took part in a Bible-study group, volunteered at senior centers, and sang karaoke at their birthday parties. To reach out to those who were homebound due to poor health, I became a call-in guest on a local Chinese radio station and shared information with the listeners about the American health-care system and many commonly reported issues related to health seeking in their community.

Through my engagement in these participatory research activities, I established close bonds with many Chinese elderly immigrants and learned in great depth about the challenges they were encountering in dealing with health-related issues. I was inspired by their spirit and efforts at achieving physical well-being and peace of mind, despite the abundant disadvantages and barriers they faced in obtaining access to health care, including limited financial means, language barriers, different cultural assumptions about health and illness, and the cultural stereotyping and discrimination they experienced from mainstream health-care providers (Guo 2000).

After I obtained my PhD degree in 1994, I joined a multidisciplinary research team at Harvard Medical School and participated in a National Institute of Aging–funded longitudinal study exploring social and cultural factors influencing the experience, recognition, and response to dementia-related symptoms among caregivers from several ethnic groups in the Boston area. During the three years of ethnographic research, I learned an enormous amount about the dynamics of disease labeling and its power in affecting individual and social perceptions regarding interactions relating to the "diseased" body. Although physiological and psychological discomforts, including disability, are experienced by people across all human groups, the way of interpreting and labeling these abnormalities is culturally and socially constructed. Disease labels not only can evoke different levels of stigma but can also force patients and their family members to carry the burden of societal reactions. The reluctance to accept dementia-related labels within the Chinese

American community in particular, this study revealed, did not necessarily indicate a complete repudiation of dementia-related symptoms. Rather, the disassociation of such symptoms from clinical labels—thus "normalizing" mental decline—often helped the elderly and their family members to better cope with the manifestations of the problem (Guo et al. 2000).

Shortly afterward, in 1998, I joined the University of Tennessee–Chattanooga as a faculty member, and I began to immerse myself in understanding local health culture. At the same time that I was promoting Taijiquan and other forms of traditional medical practice, I was developing a wide network within the local medical community. I collaborated with physicians, therapists, and patients at a local rehabilitation hospital and began refining a series of Taijiquan movements and modifying them according to the characteristics and health needs of people using wheelchairs.

Based on the knowledge I acquired through all these activities, I developed a wheelchair Taijiquan program that would benefit individuals with ambulatory disabilities and transform an assistive device into a tool that could "normalize" the users. Considering my familiarity with Chinese society and culture, both in the United States and in China, I decided next to work with disability organizations in China to promote and expand the wheelchair Taijiquan program there.

Background

As the most populous nation in the world, China also has the largest population of people with disabilities. According to a recent Chinese national survey on disability (China Disabled People's Federation 2007), some 83 million people with disability live in China, which represents more than 6 percent of the total population. Among them, 24 million (29 percent) have various degrees of physical disability, and the number rises significantly when the effects of chronic diseases are also considered. Currently, 75 percent of the population with disability in China live in rural areas, where social and economic development lags, and in urban areas, more than 60 percent of the population with disability are unemployed and depend on state and family support (Leonard Cheshire Disability 2009). Although the rapid economic development in China during recent years has brought significant policy changes aimed at protecting the rights and interests of people with disabilities (Kohrman 2005), the well-being of this population still falls below that of the general population in every category, particularly in the areas of employment opportunity, health care, and fitness program participation.

In an effort to promote physical fitness among people with disabilities, China has, over the years, allocated large resources and placed significant emphasis on developing Special Olympics and Paralympics sports and other forms of competitive activities at both the state and local levels. To a great extent, this approach has improved social perception and imagery about disability, has cultivated a significant number of world-class Paralympics athletes, and has provided inspiration to people with disabilities. However, it has had less impact on the improvement of physical activity participation rates for the majority of this population. Individuals with disability are expected, by and large, to rely on their own initiative to engage in physical activity.

At the local level, since the founding of the Chinese Disabled People's Federation in 1984, CDPF subsidiary organizations have been established in every province, prefecture, and major city, as well as in most counties, districts, and townships. Funded by and administered under local government, the major responsibility of these organizations, according to the policy and guidelines provided by CDPF, is to provide services meeting the basic needs of people with disabilities living in their respective regions. However, because limited resources have been allocated to promote Paralympics and Special Olympics events as a priority, most of these local organizations have few remaining resources available to develop other fitness facilities and programs that are suitable for participation by the vast majority of people with a physical disability.

For this population, spending valuable resources on fitness is likely to be seen as of lesser importance than the struggle to find ways to support the family and meet basic needs. In addition, widespread social stigma still exists in China for people with disabilities, particularly for people with a visible physical disability or ambulatory impairment, and this often further deters people with disabilities from engaging in community and fitness activities (CDPF 2008; Zhang 2007). A recent national survey on the living conditions of people with disabilities in China found that only 5 percent of the surveyed population indicated that they regularly participated in a physical fitness program or community cultural events (CDPF 2008).

Physical inactivity is not only one of the leading causes of premature death, it also tends to increase the risk of functional limitations and secondary health conditions among people with a disability (Boslaugh and Anderson 2006; Department of Health and Human Services 2000). Therefore, it has become imperative to develop and promote an effective, low-cost, accessible, culturally and socially sound model for physical fitness programs for people with disabilities in China. It is within this context that the work of introducing and promoting the Thirteen Postures of Wheelchair Taijiquan began to unfold.

The Rationale

Taijiquan is a form of traditional Chinese healing and martial art and has been embraced worldwide. It is characterized by movements that are low impact, flowing, circular, and easy to learn. Outwardly graceful, the movements require coordination and synchronization of a calm but alert mind and a relaxed body. In conjunction with deep abdominal breathing, the practice of these flowing movements can offer body/mind benefits to practitioners with virtually no negative side effects (Mayo Clinic Staff 2012).

The rationale behind developing wheelchair Taijiquan as a fitness and recreational alternative for people with ambulatory impairments was based, first of all, on the well-documented health benefits of Taijiquan practice and the assumption that a thoughtfully designed wheelchair Taijiquan form would promote health and fitness, including prevention of secondary conditions. Second, because of Taijiquan's popularity in Chinese society and its accessibility and low cost, it would be most likely to gain social acceptance and therefore could effectively attract participation.

A large volume of clinical studies has demonstrated that regularly practicing Taijiquan contributes not only to overall good health for people of all ages and levels of fitness but also has potential therapeutic benefits for individuals with various types of chronic health conditions. These include depression (Cho 2008; Fasko and Grueninger 2001), fibromyalgia (Taggart et al. 2003; Wang et al. 2010), lower limb disabilities (Cheung et al. 2007), cardiopulmonary difficulties (Hong, Li, and Robinson 2000; Klein and Adams 2004), multiple sclerosis (Husted et al. 1999), Parkinson's disease (Klein and Rivers 2006), severe rheumatoid arthritis (Kirsteins, Dietz, and Hwang 1991), stroke (Taylor-Piliae and Haskell 2007), and vestibular disorder (McGibbon et al. 2004). It has also been shown to provide positive physical and psychological effects for individuals with chronic diseases related to disabilities (Mustian et al. 2004; Taggart et al. 2003; Thornton, Sykes, and Tang 2004; Tsai et al. 2003; Wang, Collet, and Lau 2004; Wang et al. 2005). Medical teaching and research institutions throughout the world, including Harvard Medical School (2005), Johns Hopkins Medical School (Johns Hopkins Health Alerts 2007), and the Mayo Clinic (Mayo Clinic Staff 2012), have advocated the practice of Taijiquan as a way to regulate blood pressure, reduce stress, prevent falls, improve cardiovascular health, alleviate various types of musculoskeletal pain, improve sleep, and enhance the immune system.

Taijiquan is rooted in Chinese cultural traditions, including Chinese medicine, philosophy, and the martial arts. In China, the practice of Taijiquan enjoys enormous popularity and is recognized as an effective way of cultivating one's physical and mental/emotional strengths and flexibilities, with the goal of achieving harmony with nature and society (Breslow 1995). Because traditional Taijiquan practice does require ambulatory movement, all its many benefits have been considered off-limits to people with ambulatory impairments—even though a significant amount of Taijiquan movements are performed by the upper body and upper extremities.

Based on years of research and teaching related to the effects of modified Taijiquan movements on individuals with various types of physical disabilities, including those with ambulatory impairments (Brown 2009), I realized that a form of wheelchair Taijiquan designed according to the needs of people with ambulatory impairments could be implemented in a way that would offer them enormous health benefits, including addressing secondary conditions, within a practical and sustainable intervention program.

First, when in a seated position, wheelchair Taijiquan would allow the practitioner to move the lower back and hip area in a wide range of motion without being concerned about losing balance. Thus it would promote much-needed fitness for people who spend significant amounts of time in a sitting position. Second, because the practitioner is seated, less stamina would be required, thus encouraging a relaxed and peaceful state of mind. Last, while seated, the practitioner is in a comfortable position to rotate the spine without overloading the sacroiliac joints. Because all stress on body joints is minimized, the seated position would also eliminate the fear that the movements might cause pain or injury.

Since the practice of seated Taijiquan does not require additional assistive devices or equipment, it would minimize any highlighting of a participant's disability. Most important, by integrating wheelchair motion—the rolling and turning of the chair—with the dynamic, gentle, flowing movements of Taijiquan, the practice of wheelchair Taijiquan would transform the image of the wheelchair from an assistive device into a self-directed tool for creating beauty and power. Thus it would provide practitioners with an uplifting sense of normalization that would inspire not only themselves but also those who were watching.

Wheelchair Taijiquan is accessible, low cost, and safe. Like traditional Taijiquan, it can be practiced anywhere and at any time—and with even less space constraints than traditional ambulatory Taijiquan. So from the outset, I felt confident that the perceived benefits of a well-designed wheelchair Taijiquan program would provide an enormously practical, accessible, and convenient form of mind/body fitness and recreational activity for most people with ambulatory impairments.

Bridging Common Interests

Based on my understanding of the social and cultural factors contributing to physical inactivity among Chinese people with disabilities, of the popularity of Taijiquan practice, and, in particular, of the organizational structure and policy-making process in China, it became clear that developing a close collaborative relationship with the China Disabled People's Federation would be the key to a constructive and meaningful effort of promoting wheelchair Taijiquan in China. In 2005, I presented a comprehensive proposal to the CDPF, detailing the characteristics of the wheelchair Taijiquan program and its health and social implications for people with an ambulatory disability.

The CDPF recognized the popularity of Taijiquan in both medical and popular cultures in Chinese society and also the factors contributing to the high prevalence of physical inactivity among people with an ambulatory disability. They welcomed my proposal and quickly organized an expert panel to review it, along with my accompanying video illustrating wheelchair Taijiquan as I had developed it. The panel concluded that the Thirteen Postures of Wheelchair Taijiquan could potentially become an effective, low-cost, and popular method of physical activity for people with ambulatory disabilities in China.

Based on the panel's recommendation, the CDPF directed the Chinese Paralympics Sports Administrative Center to invite me to conduct the first national wheelchair Taijiquan instructors' training workshop in Beijing. As a first step to promoting the program, the workshop would serve three purposes: (1) it would seek more feedback from professionals throughout China concerning the applicability and effectiveness of wheelchair Taijiquan as a new form of basic health practice for people with an ambulatory disability, (2) it would provide workshop participants with sufficient knowledge and methods to teach the Thirteen Postures of Wheelchair Taijiquan to people with various types of disability conditions, and (3) it would develop an implementation strategy that would ensure the effectiveness of the promotion.

With sponsorship and funding from the CDPF and the China Paralympics Committee, in October 2006, the Chinese Paralympics Sports Administrative Center invited more than forty professionals, representing eighteen provincial disability organizations in China, to participate in a four-day long national wheelchair Taijiquan training workshop in Beijing. Among the participants were program directors of regional disability organizations, Taijiquan practitioners, and university professors specializing in developing physical fitness programs for people with disabilities. Quite a few of the participants had a physical disability themselves, including the vice president of the CDPF.

At the opening ceremony of the training workshop, I was invited to speak about the rationale for developing wheelchair Taijiquan and about the health and social implications of promoting it within the Chinese cultural and social context. My presentation was met with an overwhelming response from the workshop participants. They expressed their enthusiastic welcome of and support for my wheelchair Taijiquan program and concurred that it could become a practical and sustainable intervention strategy that would promote physical activity among people living with an ambulatory disability. This delightful spirit of accord at the start quickly transformed the training workshop into a mutually beneficial discussion and exchange of ideas.

During the four-day training workshop, many participants discussed, both with me and among themselves, various ways of promoting wheelchair Taijiquan in their home areas. Those who were Taijiquan experts also provided constructive suggestions on improving the fluidity of the routine. These suggestions were incorporated into the final version of the Thirteen Postures of Wheelchair Taijiquan. Before the end of the training workshop, many participants had already made plans to promote wheelchair Taijiquan when they returned to their respective regions.

The success of this training workshop encouraged the CDPF and the China Paralympics Committee to move forward to formally endorse the new wheelchair Taijiquan program at the national level. By the spring of 2007, CDPF had issued an official request to all provincial organizations responsible for providing services for people with disabilities to promote the Thirteen Postures of Wheelchair Taijiquan program in their areas.

Encouraged by the enthusiasm expressed by the returning workshop participants, many local government bodies and organizations providing services to people with disabilities throughout China began to offer their own wheelchair Taijiquan instructor training workshops and provide wheelchair Taijiquan classes for all participants free of charge. Seeing wheelchair Taijiquan as a new and welcomed phenomenon, many local news media throughout China, including newspapers, web-based organizations, and television and radio stations, began to take a special interest in reporting on wheelchair Taijiquan. As the news spread, and with the success stories related by wheelchair Taijiquan participants, demand to offer wheelchair Taijiquan throughout China grew exponentially.

Inspired by this initial success, the CDPF and the Beijing 2008 Olympics/Paralympics Committee decided to further promote the program by including a wheelchair Taijiquan demonstration at the opening ceremony of its 2007 Olympics Cultural Festival in Beijing. Funded by the Chinese Olympics Committee, in the summer of 2007, eighty individuals with ambulatory disabilities were chosen from regions across China to participate in this demonstration. By bringing wheelchair Taijiquan to a national stage, this event not only indicated that wheelchair Taijiquan had become a government-recognized program, it also played a role in normalizing and empowering it as a form of fitness activity.

To gauge the effectiveness of wheelchair Taijiquan, I returned to Beijing in the summer of 2007 to conduct interviews with disability services program directors from Shanghai, Tianjin, Hebei, and Shanxi provinces and with new wheelchair Taijiquan practitioners invited by the CDPF to participate in the 2007 Olympics Cultural Festival demonstration. All agreed that, unlike activity programs promoted in the past, wheelchair Taijiquan was encouraging people with ambulatory impairments to practice in public places and to do so on their own initiative. Indeed, in Beijing I saw wheelchair Taijiquan practitioners gather daily at city parks and town centers, at both dawn and dusk, alongside hundreds of Taijiquan lovers from the general urban population.

During my interviews, a man from Shanghai commented: "When we practice at the park every morning, people look at us with admiration, and it makes me feel so proud and confident. Now I always look forward to going out to practice wheelchair Taijiquan." A woman from Tianjin added, "That is where [able-bodied] people practice Taijiquan in the morning, and we wanted to show them that we [people with disabilities] also can perform Taijiquan and . . . perform it beautifully."

Subsequently, more and more cities throughout the country began to include wheelchair Taijiquan as either a demonstration or a competition event in their cultural festivities and sports programs. In the spring of 2008, Yongnian County, Hebei province—where the most popular style of Taijiquan in the world today, Yang Family Style, originated—staged a wheelchair Taijiquan demonstration at a province-wide cultural event in which several hundred wheelchair users participated. Later during 2008, the CDPF and the China Administration Center for Paralympics Sports sponsored the first national wheelchair Taijiquan competition in Beijing, and more than two hundred individuals with disabilities from various parts of the country took part.

The rapid acceptance and rising popularity of wheelchair Taijiquan prompted the 2008 Beijing Olympics Committee and CDPF to bring wheelchair Taijiquan to the international stage on September 5, 2008, as one of the opening ceremony kickoff events of the Beijing 2008 Paralympics Games. Seeing it as a new and welcomed phenomenon, national journals and local newspapers, television and radio stations, and websites throughout China began to report on wheelchair Taijiquan. Once again, as media coverage spread, demand for wheelchair Taijiquan throughout China grew exponentially. Today, not only has wheelchair Taijiquan been embraced by people with disabilities as a popular fitness and recreational alternative throughout China, it has become an official part of China's national program to promote health.

Conclusion

Since the global debut of wheelchair Taijiquan at the 2008 Paralympics, the enthusiasm for embracing forms of seated Taijiquan has spread far beyond China. In the United States, for example, health-care professionals from various disciplines—including physical therapy, occupational therapy, chiropractic, therapeutic recreation, and acupuncture—have begun to explore the therapeutic implications of seated Taijiquan for patients who are temporarily mobility-challenged due to disease or injury.

In 2008, a team of researchers at the University of Tennessee–Chattanooga and Siskin Physical Rehabilitation Hospital conducted a pilot study exploring the effectiveness of a short-form seated Taijiquan for patients with ambulatory difficulties resulting from spinal cord injury, stroke, fibromyalgia, and multiple sclerosis. After examining participants' self-efficacy with continuing participation in the practice of seated Taijiquan program two years later, the researchers in this study suggested that physical therapists might consider prescribing seated Taijiquan for patients as a self-care modality (Guo 2009).

Since 2011, I have been participating in a study in Chattanooga examining the effectiveness of seated Taijiquan in enhancing fitness levels in a group of individuals with severe mental illness. Positive preliminary findings suggest that a simply designed, seated Taijiquan program that combines education and activity-based approaches and that is structured and implemented according to the characteristics and needs of people with severe mental illness deserves further investigation.

During recent years, various forms of seated Taijiquan have emerged as self-care methods for office workers at their desks, residents of nursing homes and assisted-living facilities, and individuals at senior centers. Thus, a disability-engendered innovation—with thanks to Paul—has widening applications and creative implications.

Chapter 14

Fragments of a Limited Mutuality

Brett Williams

Mutuality works like a dialectic in that it is never complete, never over, and always rich with the possibilities of its opposites: alienation, estrangement, and exploitation. I cannot claim a fully satisfying, unfolding, or linear mutuality that grows deeper and more mutual over time. Rather, I want to show how I have experienced it contingently in thirty-five years of doing research in Washington, D.C., while living in abandoned neighborhoods on the cusp of new investment.

Although I have often called this condition gentrification, that tag these days seems too small and bounded. I return instead to Peter Marcuse's lasting call (1985, reprinted 1986, 2010) to see investment, disinvestment, and abandonment as mutually constituted and constituting processes always at work all over the city. Surplus capital loves and seeks out real estate, and the rent gap that Neil Smith identified looms when abandonment has lasted long enough that reinvestment is profitable (Harvey 2009; Smith 1986). State complicity in upscaling the city and the involvement of Wall Street and private equity firms in storing value and speculating in urban real estate have complicated this process. So the mutuality I discuss seems to be contingent on capital flows and capital accumulation, but it acts back on those processes as well (Harvey 2009).

I use "fragments" in my title (with thanks to David Graeber 2004) precisely because this is not a tidy story but one filled with contradictions, discontinuities, and change. I begin with my work with community ethnographers, much lauded in contemporary anthropology and, I regret to say, the mostly invisible authors of writing I call my own (Lamphere 2004a; Sanjek 2014, xi–xii).

Community Ethnographers

"He's thinking with his lunch," Jackie Brown remarked as we watched a man sitting beside the Anacostia River. We were working for the National Park Service, which had hired us to explore how local residents experienced D.C.'s national parks (Williams et al. 1997). I was searching for people fishing or gathering for family reunions or playing soccer. But Thoreau? I could not see it, but Jackie was right. Again and again we interviewed people who came to the river to be alone, to seek peace: sometimes with a new baby, sometimes to grieve.

Another day, I was riding around with Kenny Pitt to visit some more isolated parks, and Susie McFadden-Resper remarked that "people think you're the 'jump-out lady.'" Not an anthropologist but a cop. I had wondered why people were so accommodating to Kenny and me, but I had not thought of this possibility. I had recruited Kenny because, like many young men, he was HIV-positive, had served time, and had grown up during the parks' local heyday in the 1970s when funk and then go-go greats had filled "summer in the parks" with music. I had been busily documenting Kenny's memories of concerts in the parks and his ease at engaging anglers because he knew all about which fish they were trying to catch, regardless of the warning signs about eating those fish. On another occasion, when we were trying to meet people with still different perspectives on the parks, Kenny had an idea: "What about the Christmas tree lightings? Activists from all over come out for those." Who would have known that so many people gather outside to create neighborhood Christmas trees?

And on another day, I tried to defend Terik Washington, who had been riding about on the bus interviewing young mothers, from our employer, who challenged her meticulous accounting, which included the cost of a bus transfer and perhaps undervalued the somewhat off-message stories and recommendations Terik was gathering about how parks could be safer and more welcoming for women with babies. What had most eluded and surprised me was how precious the dirty little Anacostia River is to many people who are poor, who need space, and who sometimes need the peace of nature to expand or to be alone and think. I became a fan of urban nature and, along with many people I care about, I watch sadly as the shabby Anacostia waterfront blooms with development: concrete and condos that, according to the Anacostia Riverkeeper,[1] offer owners a million-dollar view of "their own raw sewage."

Later, in an interview for the *Washington City Paper*, I found myself glibly claiming that "Washingtonians like to do things outdoors." Still later, I went with my friends Joan Gero and Steven Loring, who have canoed all over North America, to visit the headwaters of the Anacostia River. "Isn't this beautiful?" I crowed. Sadly, Steven replied, "No Brett, it isn't." Community ethnographers, it seemed, had come to live in my head, or as another friend put it: "You're trapped in the local."

Because of their local knowledge and our hard work, Jackie Brown, Kenny Pitt, Susie McFadden-Resper, Terik Washington, and I completed the project with what I thought were brilliant and appropriate recommendations for the park service. Terik and Jackie had many ideas (including a stroller path and guard rail, which would have made the park usable for young mothers). Older people who remembered summers in the parks wanted more music, and those who had participated in the then-invisible struggle to integrate the pools and schools thought commemorative plaques would be inspiring. Everybody wanted technical support for community gardeners and table and trash facilities to accommodate the church, class, and family reunions that, throughout the summer, enlivened the parks. We called for a cleanup of the Anacostia Watershed, because our parks lay at the bottom of the watershed, and much of the river's fish-killing filth came from upstream.

Not a one of our recommendations was adopted, and commercial development of the waterfront proceeded without the concerns of its champions, who were displaced. So, was this mutuality? We had fun, I learned a lot, and the community ethnographers earned a little cash and perhaps some credentials. They got a voice but it was not heard.

Marianna Blagburn and I tried again when were asked to cocurate the Smithsonian's Folklife Festival program "Washington, D.C.: It's Our Home." Marianna and I brought aboard fifty community ethnographers to develop a festival celebrating what we were sure were the cultural themes and traditions of the city. Assuming that community ethnographers embody local knowledge, we felt almost like community ethnographers ourselves, and we surrounded ourselves with people we felt were the kinds of local experts who are largely unseen and unheard by the federal city (Blagburn and Williams 2000). Many came from devalued neighborhoods east of the Anacostia River; many grew and prepared southern foods; the beloved local band Rare Essence, known by every young African American in the city, brought go-go music to the National Mall for the very first time.

But as the festival approached, we lost most of what we had argued for: the people were not famous or bland enough for the National Mall. Smithsonian insiders took over. As just one example, three of the community ethnographers had documented and recruited vibrant, possibly outlandish, lesbian and gay artistic and political traditions such as the dance complex embodied in Runway, introduced to us by the intrepid Michael Twitty. The Smithsonian is always looking over its shoulder at Congress, uneasily and already worried that the Chinese government disapproved of the festival because the Dalai Lama planned to visit. Gay and lesbian performances were reduced to a single concert on an off day by the staid and respectable Gay and Lesbian Chorus. On the other hand, some of my friends from the river built a boat that they still proudly display at their club. Representing D.C. on the Mall is always fraught, but as we struggled to get the proper wood to build the boat or to enliven the offerings with what we felt was the real richness of the city, I asked again if this was mutuality: to have fun, share ideas, gain a voice, not be heard.

Nuk

I first met him when he was a lovable eight-year-old, knocking at my door with an offer to walk my dogs. He was often on hand to help out, and I sometimes spotted him in the Safeway parking lot, hustling shoppers who might need help with their bags. When his little brother was born, he spent the night with his two older brothers sleeping crosswise on my bed. We have not been neighbors for years, but he tracks me down from the various relatives and institutions he is sometimes assigned to, wherever I move. He calls himself my third son, and were it not for the objections of my family, I think he might long ago have moved in with me.

Unlucky in many ways and sometimes careless, Nuk is blessed with a staunch girlfriend with a job, whose mother occasionally allows him to live with them. From me, he gets a lot of unwanted advice, computer and laundry help, occasional work, money, food, a court appearance on his behalf. He has given me access to his ever-changing story and permission to write about it, has gathered up low-level drug sellers for me to interview, and has impressed upon me how stuck in a small place he is and how lost he feels in just the suburbs of D.C.

Nuk is now twenty and less lovable to many. Some in my family have grown to fear and distrust him. I have learned how precarious his life is, how much bad luck he has, how many mistakes he makes, how impossible it is for him to find work (even if he were truly literate), how hard it is for him to be good, and how hard it will be for him to stay out of jail. I see our relationship as brimming with mutuality (we even work on his GED, and I am his only source of income), but others insist I am not helping him, really.

The temptations, the oppression, are just too large, and cute little black boys grow up to be too feared. Nuk makes harsh, out-of-control incarceration in the punitive state (Hyatt 2011; Lancaster 2011) way too real for me, the precipice young men walk as they search for work and try not to deal. I have learned how normal and how devastating it is to think about and to do time, how stuck and vulnerable young black men feel, how close to home they stay, and how hard it is not to look at a windfall as seed money that could be invested to make a little more. Selling weed is both supplementary and complementary to other ways of making money. Nobody I know just wakes up and decides to become a drug dealer. Drugs are part of the flow of credit and debt.

Gift Economies

When I was in graduate school, Carol Stack changed my life. I had gone to the University of Illinois to study with Oscar Lewis, who passed away from a heart attack before I arrived. Carol was completing the research for *All Our Kin* (Stack 1974) and brimming with conviction about how poor people pool and share to cope with poverty. She was also full of good ideas about how to do research among the poor to discover kin relations not visible to survey researchers seeking nuclear family households. I liked the people she wrote about, and I wanted to be like them: thickly connected to a web of relatives and friends who offered more security and even satisfaction than individual upward mobility ever would. Carol's ideas shaped not only my dissertation but most of the work I have done since. Wherever I work among the poor, I see networks of cooperating kin that persist despite members' displacement from a city that each year becomes more expensive. I am unable to see pathology among the poor, and I have been unsurprised by the recent surge of interest in gift economies (Gibson-Graham 2006; Graeber 2010) and the many noncapitalist ways people actually live their lives under capitalism. What has surprised me is that these researchers (just like American politicians) rarely mention the urban poor.

Buffeted by the turbulence of Washington's real estate market and its ever-moving development targets, I have lived in ten different homes in four different neighborhoods. Because I am white but a single mother and not rich, the places I could both bear and afford have most often been neighborhoods on the cusp of gentrification. These communities were settled after restrictive covenants were struck down in 1949 and school segregation was outlawed in 1954; white flight began soon after. They were all multigenerational and deeply rooted in an older generation of government workers benefiting from newfound access to secure jobs and housing after the civil rights movement. Most often, younger kin lived with them too, struggling, trying to get past the screens of discrimination that face those who, since the civil rights movement, have enjoyed legal access to institutions within a framework of racial inequality that has only grown worse.

Being on the cusp of gentrification is a particular urban circumstance. There is a long tradition of neighborliness but a growing condition of having less to give. As the older generation dies, leaving houses that are paid for in full, their relatives often find that they cannot afford not to sell. Renters like me get pushed out by deferred maintenance and higher rents, and the life of the neighborhood teeters. Some people squat in the front yards of their former houses or double up with kin rather than leave the neighborhood. But people tend to hang on while they can, and in these precarious circumstances, exacerbated by the shredded safety net, gift economies flourish. Food stamps are like gold, arriving on the eighth day of each month but bringing to mind Bone Thugs 'n Harmony's brilliant "First of the Month," which captures the excitement of the day the money comes.

Without enough money or jobs, the informal economy and the gift economy rule and draw in newcomers who want to be part of them. My family and I shared cash, food, our computer, our telephone, our washing machine. Like others, we shared gardening tips, clippings, tools, vegetables, and flowers. We got help with everything. On my birthday, I was showered with gifts reclaimed from people's closets. We gathered to glare at the police when they swooped in to dig up a large marijuana plant being cultivated by a senior citizen. On Fridays, we bought fried fish from the family across the street. A neighbor asked if she could avoid detection by parking in our back yard and offered, in exchange, twice-weekly hauls of designer bread from the bakery where she worked. That bread travels throughout the neighborhood, as do plates of cooked food, medicines, baby clothes, and all manner of things to smoke. I treasure being allowed to live like this, more fluidly and less isolated than in a tight nuclear household, drawn there by what I believed to be common practices among people who are poor. In these neighborhoods, I am not ashamed to have a grown son in my basement. I am slightly embarrassed by working outside the informal economy, but I do help move funds there, as people walk my dogs, wash my car, do hair, shovel show, rake leaves, bootleg videos, and mow the lawn.

I do not mean to romanticize this life. Residents suffer from poor health, each day is a struggle to share food and funds, and both windfalls (an inheritance, eligibility for Supplemental Security Income [SSI], a job for a young man in booming North Dakota so desperate for laborers that it recruits them from the inner city) and crises often disrupt the flow of services and goods. As Kim Hopper (2003) argues, the struggling near-poor often have to triage problematic kin. I have not had to do that, but I have grown to understand how heartbreaking it can be. I have felt like the canary of gentrification when prospective buyers stop to call at me things like "Is it safe here?" and I realize that my very presence makes the neighborhood seem more inviting. I have fled gentrification myself, as its pincers render more and more neighborhoods unaffordable and as D.C. seems to be fulfilling the promise of Mayor Anthony Williams to fill the city with ten thousand DINCs (dual income, no children) and upscale the whole town.

I see mutuality as dialectic in theory and practice: I decided to work among the poor because I liked the poor people I read about, and I liked the anthropologist's take on them. Jonathan Kozol wrote, in *Amazing Grace* (1995), that his middle-class friends worried for his safety in the South Bronx but that he himself feared for his soul when dining with those same people at the elegant Four Seasons Hotel. I never fail to think of Kozol when I drive by suburban Washington's mighty, self-contained palatial estates. Working with poor people has strengthened and nuanced my original convictions, and those convictions have peppered my writing. When I was young, I wrote condescendingly about why old people liked to garden, to immerse themselves in cycles of life, growth, and death. Why did I think I knew that, and why do I like to garden so much now? Is it because I read my own writing or because I have lived the last thirty-five years among devout urban gardeners? Richard Dienst's book *The Bonds of Debt* (2011) rang true to me when he argued that we can think of those bonds as a good thing, because they connect us all in cross-cutting ways. And Marcel Mauss (1990 [1925]) would be happy, I think, to see how exchanges cement neighborhood life: no deal is ever fully closed, ever complete, ever all paid up. With everyone off-balance in some way with others, neighborhood life goes on until it does not.

Consumption and Climate Change

Lasting stereotypes hold that poor people consume excessively. They buy big TVs and cars, kill for jackets and shoes. Working, riding the bus, and living near poor people quickly puts these clichés to rest. I just do not see the waste, excess, and overconsumption that make me fear for my soul in the SUV-littered wealthy Washington suburbs. There may be piles of stuff everywhere, but it is old, recycled, reclaimed, and reused. Poor people rent or live in a small part of the family home or sleep under the kitchen table of a friend. They often speak of where they stay rather than where they live. They ride the bus, shop at thrift stores, recycle and reuse everything; they fish, hunt, forage, and garden to supplement their groceries. They live annoyed but patient without water, sleep on the roof or in the yard when it is too hot, suffer hot and cold weather without utilities. They carry used plastic bags rather than expensive briefcases or backpacks; they walk, lift, and lug rather than patronize for-profit gyms for individual workouts; they operate in an informal economy with no permanent infrastructure; and they make full use of our waning public facilities: water fountains, public schools, public pools, public libraries. They do not fly.

Yet, like all the world's poor urban residents, living modestly, they experience climate change earlier and differently: through new bugs and pests; mosquitos and ticks with, now, two reproductive cycles; changing gardens; and harsh exposure to the new normal of extreme temperatures. When I feel unsophisticated because I have not traveled all over the world, I think of Nuk, who has never been anywhere and felt hopelessly lost when his family was displaced to an inner suburb. He began sleeping on the floor of a friend so as not to leave D.C. I wonder if I think this way and see things this way because overconsumption disgusts and worries me, if I have adopted anticonsumerism because poor people seem to live more sustainably and I want to be like them, although I know in my heart that every once in a while I should buy a new dress for a conference. My wilted, used clothing shames my family. That the wealthy hog so much and the poor have so little angers me every day.

Poverty as a Kind of Robbery (Edsall 2012)

In college, I read *The Poor Pay More* (Caplovitz 1967), and about ten years ago, I stumbled onto the extraordinary journalism of Mike Hudson, who astonished me by documenting the rise of subprime and predatory lenders in poor neighborhoods. Rather than invest in jobs-producing enterprises, they sold debt. Hudson (2002) also argued that these shops were linked to Wall Street, and minimal online research confirmed that he was right. Rugh and Massey (2010) historicized this view of poverty as robbery in the old redlining strategies that confined poor people to neighborhoods where they would not invest in mortgages. They drew red lines around them on their development maps to signal no investment and thus set up a scene for reverse redlining, places where people are a captive market for sucking up the little surplus poor people have access to.

This can mean grabbing the Earned Income Tax Credit at tax time, when many observers notice that evictions slow down and electronic refunds boom. Mostly, this has meant selling debt (Williams 2004, 2008, 2009), but lenders have become more and more resourceful in conjunction with the privatization of public facilities. Two examples are cell or smart phones and auto loans. I will illustrate them with two stories and then turn at last to the way the foreclosure crisis in Washington mimicked this robbery of the poor.

My friend Tanisha graduated from high school, got certified at the University of the District of Columbia as a child-care worker, makes minimum wage, and supports her mother and long-time boyfriend. Bright and brazen, she tried to manage a better-paying job in the suburbs, but traveling there on several buses was arduous and frightening. She did not know the way, there were no public telephones, and she was far away from everyone and everything she knew. She returned to the child-care center in her neighborhood and eventually leased a cell phone, her only way to connect to her dispersed family and friends and to listen to music. Like many young people, her cell phone is essential at the same time that it tethers her to high-interest debt. It goes on and off, alerting her constantly to the amount she owes. The smart phones that so delight university students would be invaluable for Tanisha, but as things stand, she has not bought a phone but a debt.

One day, I went with my young friend April to buy a car. She works the overnight shift at Checkers, which serves fast food to people coming home from work or from a night out. She walks there and back, often in the middle of the night, and it was becoming too scary and hard for her. April also reasoned that with a car, she could escape the boundaries of the neighborhood and find a better job. This seemed logical to me, and the car dealers were happy to sell her a debt with 23 percent interest disguised as a car. Meticulously assessing her income through biweekly checks, the salesman calculated that she could use one of those checks for the more than four hundred dollar car note and live off the other one. He encouraged her to find a credit union to refinance at a lower rate after a few months of proving she was a good risk and could make her payments. He made it sound like it would work, but she has no margin for error. When her car was totaled two months later, the insurance company reimbursed the loan company for the cost of the car, but the loan company is still pursuing her for the interest she would have paid if she had driven the car and made monthly payments over the whole five years.

I find it impossible to work with poor people and not rage against the banks. If April had been someone like me, she could have bought this used car with cash and spent thousands less. Her neighborhood places her in a captive market besieged by lenders, and her credit score (tainted by a long-ago repo) consigns her to usury (Rugh and Massey 2010).

The foreclosure crisis is like April's car writ large. The national story featuring strapped buyers choosing homes they could not afford misses what actually happened in D.C. The national story holds true for some, mostly young immigrant families in the inner suburbs. Other foreclosures stemmed from refinancing. The civil rights generation, which had integrated D.C.'s rowhouse neighborhoods, refinanced their homes to pay medical or college bills for struggling kin. These teaser loans, which often reverted to high interest rates in three years, were more than many could manage on fixed incomes.

Finally, many foreclosures in undervalued neighborhoods in D.C. came from the antics of young speculators, flush with cash from the dot.com bubble or sometimes from drugs, anticipating development that would drive up the value of the house, walking away when development did not materialize quickly, ruining neighborhoods in the process with boarded-up, abandoned homes. When investment did follow, speculators backed by private equity bought old houses for cash; rehabbed them using day laborers lined up near Home Depot and the mass-produced stainless steel, crown molding, and granite counters Home Depot sells; and thus redesigned the city with a new speculator aesthetic of tan, vinyl-sided houses and generic gardens. Thus, in D.C.'s poorest neighborhoods, a shocking number of homes are now owned by institutions such as Germany's Deutsche Bank, or consortiums of investors, or people in prison.

Shortly after we moved in to our latest house, a tall man knocked at the door, presenting himself as a graduate student making a film on gentrification, in which he planned for me to be the star. My neighbor Michelle (who is both admired and castigated by locals because, in the words of one neighbor, she "lives freely") saved me from public humiliation by messing with his storyline and insisting that his film should really be about "how Brett came home." (She remembered that I had lived in the neighborhood for some years during the 1980s). This felt like mutuality to me.

Politics

Strike debt. End the war on drugs. Green the city. Make college free. Tax the rich. Stop invading other countries. My political beliefs, stemming from the conviction that government must restrain capital because inequality is too harsh, were nurtured by my liberal Texas mother and first articulated as an undergraduate at Tufts University, but they have grown deeper and stronger through my working and living with poor people in D.C. They feel inarguable. But can I really speak of mutuality? My friend Iley Brown, who first appeared in my life as a community ethnographer/D.C. music expert, insists that to do big things, you have to leave this city. We settle, says Iley. Perhaps it is the overbearing presence of the state or that our schools do not teach us to demand justice. I worry he may be right and that, ironically, one can do anthropology among some of the world's most progressive people, learn to understand fully what needs to happen, and then settle for much less. Perhaps all I can do is to continue to write about what I know to be true and to support activists as much as I can.

Chapter 15

On "Making Good" in a Study of African American Children with Acquired and Traumatic Brain Injuries

Lanita Jacobs

Ethnography entails calls to mutuality; that is, invitations to partake in the vulnerable exercise of seeing and being seen and of feeling and being felt. Fieldwork calls us to deep empathy in this way; it requires us to negotiate various positionalities and power differentials and, ultimately, to reckon with (or wrestle with) a story born of inductive research and a soulful commitment to bearing nuanced witness. Recently I have been thinking a lot about making good in relation to ethnographic thought and practice. If ethnography's inherent intersubjectivity is itself a call to mutuality, then making good is, arguably, one right response to that call.

I employ the term *making good* to reference several implicit calls to mutuality beckoned by a longitudinal ethnographic study of African American children diagnosed with acquired and traumatic brain injuries (ABI, TBI).[1] Broadly, *making good* connotes a complex ideological, if not moral, stance concerning how to do fieldwork and, later, tell a good story. It is, admittedly, a highly interpretive and intersubjective exercise mediated by our complex engagements in the field, our emotions, our investments in particular forms of theorizing and storytelling, and the sheer time needed to figure out what we even have to say. In regard to my fieldwork, *making good* also manages to capture the tremendous emotional, linguistic, affective, and political work African American children and their caregivers do when negotiating ways of seeing and being seen anew in the face of acute illness, trauma, and disability. Additionally, *making good* functions as a necessary mantra for me, prodding me to tell a story that might one day resonate with the children, families, teachers, and clinicians who shared parts of their lives with me.

When and Where I Enter

It has taken some time to wrest hold of making good as both a thesis and a mantra. In 2011, in anticipation of the American Anthropological Association panel that inspired this volume, I revisited a videotaped conversation between myself and "Desmond," one of three children whose lives I observed over a span of eight years.[2] I had asked Desmond if he remembered how he got to the hospital, and he returned to me an answer as candid as it was poignant.

"I disappeared here," he said. When I asked him how he had done that, he replied, "Easy. When I went to sleep and I woke back up, I was *here*." Then, after a long pause, he shrugged and ate a French fry. Desmond's reply felled me then, as did his death two years later from a malignant brain tumor. I could not write about Desmond for a long time without grief clouding my vision. Yet, when I revisited our conversation, I discerned this mantra and thesis concerning the imperative of making good. Desmond's words were all the more poignant in his absence. His juxtaposition of disappearing and reappearing jolted me to see and remember him and, most importantly, contend with his and other children and caregivers' attempts to broker empathy in life and death situations. This chapter is an initial pursuit; Desmond is its catalyst.

Rightly so. Desmond was the first of the three children I followed after accepting the invitation of my colleagues, Mary Lawlor and Cheryl Mattingly, to join the Boundary Crossing Research Team, first as a consultant-researcher in 2002 and later as a co-principal investigator in 2005.[3] I was compelled to participate for several reasons. My twin sister had suffered a traumatic brain injury in 1994 during a car accident. I had intellectual questions, not to mention unresolved grief, to contend with, and I imagined this project could help me with that. Apart from Desmond, I have observed two African American girls (one of whom is biracial); like my twin, both sustained traumatic brain injuries after car crashes. In this chapter, I focus primarily on Desmond because his life and death at age seven as a result of an initially misdiagnosed and malignant brain tumor provided one of my most intimate glimpses into the experiences of African American children with ABI and TBI and into the work these children do with caregivers, clinicians, teachers, and others to make good in the wake of trauma, disability, and even imminent death.

Making Good: Love and Empathy

I should concede outright that I fell in love with Desmond rather quickly because of his intelligence, humor, and generosity. As I sought to see him in and beyond the recovery ward, he, in turn, attempted to see me and consider the merits of my questions. For example, when I told him matter-of-factly why I was doing this work (because of my twin's car accident), he paused for a long while and then offered this consolation: "Man. She shouldn't have even been in there [the car] like that." Desmond's gracious empathy made me love him all the more.

Love beget empathy, an affective way of seeing and observing that privileged caretaking over scholarly curiosity. It was the only way to proceed. Observing Desmond (and the two girls I followed) encompassed serving as a coconspirator in hope (Mattingly 2010) throughout the various stages of his illness, remission, and death. To love him entailed feeling some of the pain, alienation, fear, and worry that beset him and his family as they struggled to traverse cross-cultural, class-marked, and discursive boundaries. It also meant nurturing optimism when his tumor resurfaced and harnessing faith when his death seemed inevitable. This project was, thus, both an investigation of and engagement in empathy.

Empathy is a gift that is often generated and reciprocated in fieldwork. It is also something earned and actively negotiated for. The promise of empathy was the primary condition under which many, if not all, of the families recruited to Boundary Crossing agreed to enlist. Desmond's mother, "Sinead," was grief stricken when I and two of my colleagues approached her at Desmond's bedside about our study. She listened to our brief spiel and enrolled after recognizing one of my colleagues, Jeanne Adams, to be her trusted and former high school classmate. She expected all of us, especially me, to enter into her and Desmond's lives with a mind to return something tangible and of value to them, whether through our observations at the hospital and conversations with doctors, nurses, and therapists, or through our scholarly writing and teaching. Desmond and his family conveyed these expectations in explicit and implicit ways.

Desmond's grandmother, "Garnet," described me several times as "Desmond's resource person" in the presence of Desmond and his mother. In doing so, she was providing a conceptual frame that situated me within the context of her family and a model for me to pursue as Desmond's principle observer. I also acted in maternal ways during my triweekly visits to the hospital. I moisturized Desmond's face and legs; transported him to his various therapy sessions when his family could not be there to do it; and gently reproved him when he grew angry, lest he be deemed "resistant" and "uncooperative." I also gazed at him with love; angst; hope; fear; regret; pain; and, on some occasions, disappointment during critical stages of his hospitalization, reintegration to school, return to the hospital, and final days. In all of these affective brokerings, love and empathy emerged as two of the unstated but widely shared imperatives of this emotionally laden research project, and they delimited the ways in which I saw and observed in the field (see also Lawlor and Mattingly 2001).

Reconciling Multiple Perspectives

My research has also required me to see and reconcile multiple perspectives (Lawlor 2004; Lawlor and Mattingly 2009), including those of caregivers, clinicians, doctors, principals, teachers, and Desmond himself. Desmond had a tenacious spirit that his family wanted clinicians and doctors to appreciate—not change or pathologize. "His name is Bubba," they chidingly informed hospital staff in an attempt to get them to see him beyond his diagnosis and patient status. "All this you are seeing from Bubba is what he was like before," they would add. Yet nurses and therapists who had to contend with Desmond's obstinacy were not always appreciative of this presenting disposition. Nor, I admit, was I, because I worried that it would deem him "noncompliant" or, worse, unempathetic. For example, during one of my hospital visits, Desmond repeatedly kicked a nurse who was ever so patiently trying to change his diaper. Despite the "Assistant Professor" ID on my jacket, I found myself apologizing to her as if he were my own child.

I was elated, then, when Desmond began to smile. Several times as I accompanied Desmond around the rehab ward, therapists and doctors stopped us to compliment him on both his new grey sweater and demeanor. "Bubba, you're so good. I like it when you're like this!" some said. Although several doctors attributed Desmond's fussiness to the trauma he experienced after suddenly waking up in a hospital, they were nonetheless happy that Desmond was no longer as agitated as he had been earlier.

I also took steps to make him smile and laugh whenever possible via impromptu raps, jokes, and games. Desmond's innate gifts made him unwittingly complicit in this venture: he was not just smart, he was also funny. When he acclimated to the hospital after several weeks and began to exercise his humor, I could not help but think that perhaps his humor might save him from stigmatizing categories such as "resistant" and "hostile" (Jacobs-Huey, Lawlor, and Mattingly 2011; Rouse 2004).

Desmond had a hand in this. His laments about the hospital, his declarations of what he would and would not do, and his increasing tolerance of me were also attempts to shape his own seeing and reception. This was true during his transition back to elementary school, where he donned a protective helmet to protect his head and rather skillfully rebuffed the well-meaning caretaking attempts of his female classmates. This was true even during his final days, when he observed, "Wow. I've never been as sick as this before. . . . Somebody needs to get me some Fruit Loops." Desmond, who constantly defied expectations pre- and post-op by excelling in both mainstream and special-education classes, technically challenging videogames, and humor, insisted that we see him beyond (and in spite of) his status as a child and his diagnosis.

There were other perspectives warranting reconciliation in Desmond's life after his tumor diagnosis. Clinicians had to align with each other around the implication of a foot brace in order to best abet Desmond's motor skills. Desmond's primary doctor had to overcome institutional constraints, budget restrictions, and a staff that had been abruptly restructured without so much as a foreshadowing memo. Desmond's teacher (a lupus survivor and support-group leader) and Desmond's principal (himself father to a child with special needs) worked tirelessly to accommodate Desmond despite limited district resources and funding. Each of these engagements offers insights into delicate and nuanced work of "partnering up" and "boundary crossing" among key players in Desmond's life.[4] I remain struck, too, by the work of empathy in these engagements; that is, *how, when*, and, to the extent discernible, *why* folks manage affective alignments that enable them to see and be seen and feel and feel felt. I want to closely examine these moments of mutuality so I can distill their productive outcomes and potentialities (Frank 2004); might there be times and strategies that enable people to succeed and/or fail (for better or worse, sometimes)? Further, might alternative endings be actualized or even imagined that might inform future attempts at partnering up involving children, caregivers, clinicians, and others?

As an ethnographer, I find that appreciating these various perspectives and possibilities has required diligent observance of the everyday contingencies affecting peoples' behaviors, moods, and capacities for empathy. Sometimes a therapist's seeming apathy during a session with a child may, instead, reflect listlessness brought on by a minor illness. Other times, a child's obstinacy has less to do with their being ornery and more to do with their desire to be held. In my own shifting positionalities as a Boundary Crossing researcher and Desmond's "helpmate," I (along with my Boundary Crossing colleagues) have had to continually establish a rapport of mutual trust and vulnerability with the children we followed and the therapists and doctors who permitted us to observe them on their (and their patient's) best and worst days. For me, this meant sometimes wielding a notepad and, other times, putting it ceremoniously, if not figuratively, away.

I have also sought, sometimes in hindsight, to police my own ways of asking, particularly in regard to Desmond's illness. Desmond's tumor was detected late, and the reasons for this are complicated and fraught. Desmond's family did not recognize his early symptoms (such as dizziness, headaches, trouble concentrating, slurred speech, poor balance). On several occasions, they felt that Desmond, a gifted and occasionally cunning child, was just kidding around to avoid school. When Desmond began throwing up, they rushed him to the hospital, where he received a faulty diagnosis and was sent home. By the time Desmond's tumor was accurately diagnosed and operated upon (at another hospital), members of his family were relieved but beset with regret and disappointment. Desmond's grandmother did not want to discuss Desmond's tumor with him, because she wanted him to focus on his present and future, not on his past. Additionally, and not unlike other caregivers we have observed (Jacobs-Huey et al. 2011; Lawlor and Mattingly 2009; Mattingly 2010; Rouse 2004) and parents of children with ABI/TBI (Morningstar and Dorszynski 1997; Swanson 1999), neither she nor Sinead wanted Desmond to see himself merely through the lens of his diagnosis. My early conversations with Desmond about his illness, then, risked breaching his family's preferences at the same time that I was colluding with clinicians who thought it best for Desmond to understand his illness.

There were additional limitations to mutuality (im)posed by my very positionality as a researcher, however emotionally invested I sought to be. For although I stood ready and willing to bear witness and even "help," my incessant witnessing also documented Desmond's losses and his ultimate death in a very literal sense. I videotaped Desmond's funeral at Sinead's request and later viewed the footage with her and Desmond's dad, "Damion." Doing so provided Sinead with some comfort and a chance to see her child one more time, but I could see and feel that it compounded Damion's sense of loss. Mine too.

Later, in the weeks and months following Desmond's funeral, Sinead and I had trouble finding our way to each other for promised coffee dates and conversations. I think we both struggled with what to say to each other after Desmond's passing. When we did finally talk, Sinead tearfully asked me, "If I'm not Desmond's mother, then who am I?" She and Damion's dreams of themselves and for Desmond shifted in the aftermath of his diagnosis and radically after his death; as parents who had lost a child, they felt as though they were missing a core part of their identity (Rouse 2004; Simons 1987; Singer, Glang, and Williams 1996).

Interrogating Race and Disability

Another imperative of this work and, indeed, of Boundary Crossing more broadly, involves wrestling with issues of race and disability in nuanced and complicated ways. As I noted before, my own positionality as scholar/lover of this child fueled my worries about Desmond's early tantrums. These concerns had a lot to do with race and gender; specifically, I worried that some hospital staff would be unable to empathize with this Black boy's rage, particularly because Desmond's tantrums had become so notorious as to be labeled "the Desmond tantrum." Some nurses and secretaries were so disturbed by the vehemence and shrillness of his cries that they began to wonder if his home life could have made him somehow resistant to being tied down in safety restraints. One nurse, who happened to be African American, celebrated when Desmond temporarily left her floor for another and said, within earshot of his family, "Good. The noise is gone."

Race was implicated in these speculations and laments and in other confided grievances as well. Several African American staff spoke to me privately about their discomfort with seeing Black children like Desmond being occasionally tied down (presumably for their safety) or "parked" in their wheelchairs (presumably for monitoring) in front of the rehab reception desk. They wondered (as did I) if race was a potential factor in the witting/unwitting withholding of empathy and culturally sensitive care and, alternatively, acute sensitivity in the handling of Desmond and other Black children.

Desmond's mother also relayed a bad experience she had had with a hospital social worker, which, while never explicitly framed through the lens of race, evidenced traces of it. She had confided in the social worker about her challenges in marriage and work and her own sadness and depression. When she missed a few doctor's appointments because of miscommunication and transportation difficulties, she received a visit from Child Protective Services. Sinead felt betrayed and in danger of being seen as a "bad Black mother," a stigmatizing category made all the more injurious by the embedded racial stereotype. This instance of boundary crossing gone awry was sadder still because it diminished her faith in seeking help from hospital social workers.

There were other instances in which race and class colluded in Sinead's failed attempts to broker empathy as a "good mother" who cared for her child despite her inability to be "bedside." During Desmond's initial weeks at the hospital, Sinead brought his best clothes (expensive, brand-name urban gear such as FUBU, Adidas, and others) to signal that he was a well-cared-for and well-appointed child. But Desmond's attire troubled an African American nurse who routinely took it upon herself to care for the Black children in the rehab ward by combing their hair and soothing and chiding them when their parents could not be "bedside." She worried that Desmond's clothing made him resemble a thug or gangbanger. When Desmond's high-end clothing ended up missing (Sinead feared they were stolen by the families of other patients), Desmond spent most of his time in hospital gowns. This introduced yet another set of worries concerning Desmond's familial engagement in his care.

Tell a "Thick" Story

One of the most significant imperatives emerging from this work is a need to make good via my own scholarly work. For me, this means rendering a story that is rich in complexity, honors the love I had for Desmond, and details the implications of this love for the ways I positioned myself and was positioned by others, as well as the ways in which I observed; appreciates multiple perspectives and scenes in the lives of Desmond and the other children I have followed; and diligently attends to matters of race and disability that emerged in subtle and explicit ways in this work.

In my attempts to make good, I have been homing in lately on the advice of scholars and writers whose commitment to "thick" stories (Crapanzano 2004; Fadiman 1997; Geertz 1973, 3–30; Keyes 1995; Sacks 1984; Zimmerman 2002; Zinsser 1988) has, together with Desmond's prompt, served to shake me out of a merely silent and grieving place. I have also drawn inspiration from other ethnographers who have successfully contended with grief, trauma, and loss in fieldwork, their own lives, and, finally, on the page (Bluebond-Langner 1978; Frank 2000; Mattingly 2010; Rosaldo 1989b; Rouse 2004, 2009; Scheper-Hughes 1993). Best, I can better see and hence delineate shared concerns among the three children and families I observed.

In this longitudinal ethnographic study of African American families raising children with acquired or traumatic brain injury, I have witnessed African American children and caregivers, together with clinicians and teachers, asking, "Can you see me? Can you empathize with me?" More poignantly, they asked each other, "How can I be empathetic to you?" Attending to Desmond's life and death pushes my questions even further, to include: How do intersubjective matters such as likeability, popularity, "normalness," and their many intersections augment and/or complicate children's bids to empathy? What tropes (such as able-bodied, disabled), master narratives, or even counter narratives do kids, parents, family members, clinicians, and others struggle to be seen within or outside of in the service of rehabilitation and the often contingent creation of an empathetic self? And what are the limits and constraints of mutuality? What happens when the ethnographer's presence compounds the grief and sense of loss experienced by parents who have lost a child?

Deciphering and contending with these queries compels and, at times, fells me. Such are the intersubjective demands of ethnographic fieldwork. Ethnographers and research subjects alike yearn to see and be seen, and all of us must struggle for mutual intelligibility. As a "native" scholar (Jacobs-Huey 2002), I feel this call to mutuality palpably, especially when race, gender, class, sexuality, and so on intercede and color the quest to see and be seen.

Although it seems naïve to me now, I never counted on figurative and literal loss being such a significant part of this research experience. In my mind, I envisioned telling stories of an initial loss. Traumatic brain injuries entail tremendous loss for children and their families in terms of their visions of the future. But these losses, I reasoned, were often mitigated as parents and children struggled to rebuild their lives and new or alternative versions of self and social networks. So, even though I was compelled to write about the tremendous work that families do on a daily basis to "recover," there was considerable room in my imagined story for optimism. In fact, the very mantra I had worked with for so long—*the work of recovery*—bespoke my early commitment to an optimistic ending.

Desmond's swift death after his brain tumor reappeared and ravaged his body disrupted this narrative inclination. The cumulative losses emerged as an overriding theme. I have since struggled—too long, I fear—to come to terms with what this kind of loss has meant and how to write about how loss changes a working narrative and gives it new meaning.

Now, when I review some of my early conversations with Desmond, I find them didactic, formulaic—doomed, in some ways, to simplify the complexity of his experience and the weight of his day-to-day and moment-by-moment experiences in and beyond the hospital. In hindsight, I see the luxuries I indulged in by asking questions I certainly might not have asked had I known Desmond's tumor would prove malignant, irremovable, and fatal.

Only recently has Desmond's answer to my question, "I disappeared here," opened up new analytical and narrative possibilities for me. In this response, Desmond was inviting me to see and know him where he was. He was also announcing, "I have reappeared and I am living fitfully with this new reality." Desmond, by sheer virtue of his intelligence and humor, made me see him and see myself and others in his attendance within that moment. For that, I must endeavor, as best I can, to "make good" on this work—in the telling of this and other stories.

Chapter 16

On Ethnographic Love

Catherine Besteman

A number of years ago, I presented a paper at the University of Cape Town that offered a critique of Robert Kaplan's infamously dystopic depiction of Africa in the *The Atlantic* called "The Coming Anarchy" (Kaplan 1994). My paper, titled "Why Robert Kaplan Should Have Studied Anthropology," reviewed Kaplan's characterizations of Africa in order to refute them, claim by claim, using anthropological evidence (Besteman 2000). Although my ostensible argument was to use ethnographic data to correct Kaplan's account, my primary goal was one of disciplinary patriotism: to argue that, had Kaplan studied anthropology, he would have produced a description of Africa far different than the shallow, cartoon-like, nightmarish representation of Africa as a doomed continent of violence, disease, and deteriorating culture.

A political scientist in my audience that day challenged my assertion that if Kaplan had studied anthropology he would have produced a different portrayal of contemporary Africa or one that conformed more closely to what I suggested he should have written. On the contrary, my critic suggested that anthropologists are as prone as anyone else to finding what they wish to find, no matter their training—that if anthropologists want to find violence and disease and cultural degradation, they will, disputing my claim that no anthropologist would have produced a portrait like Kaplan's and that anthropological training would have saved him from his egregious errors in representation (at least as I saw them).

Although this event occurred more than a decade ago, I have returned time and time again to my critic's two-part question: "How do you know that

Kaplan would have produced a different portrait if he had studied anthropology? How can you predict how anthropological training would have altered Kaplan's perspective on Africa?" Over the past decade, these questions have resonated for me far beyond the specific concern with Robert Kaplan and his trashy travel writing. The questions provoke, even demand, an assessment of "the anthropological perspective" and, in particular, the assumptions I hold about what is particular and unique to the experience of ethnographic practice that distinguishes it from other forms of reporting. Are there particularities about ethnographic practice that would mitigate against the kind of portrait produced by Kaplan?

In my session at Cape Town, I stumbled through an answer about anthropology's holistic perspective; about our attention to context, most especially regional and global political economies; about accounting for history; about our abhorrence of essentializing culture. But I remained unsatisfied by my answer, which did not adequately capture what I consider to be unique about the anthropological perspective. I have finally realized that what I failed to acknowledge in my response is anthropology's signature embrace of mutuality, a fundamental experience of the ethnographic encounter.

There is an obvious danger in suggesting that all (cultural) anthropologists find mutuality as a dimension of their work. In this chapter, I probe the ways in which some anthropologists have expressed their experience of mutuality as a central dimension of ethnographic practice and have experienced ethnography as a practice of mutuality. In what follows, I will build an argument about the importance of ethnographic love in the anthropological endeavor, a form of love defined by the experience of mutuality, solidarity, collaboration, and self-transformation that I believe shapes the ethnographic encounter for many anthropologists. As will become clear, my argument about mutuality and ethnographic love is shaped particularly by contexts in which anthropologists are engaged in discussions and understandings of social values, struggle, and change, an orientation that characterizes my own history of ethnographic engagement. I believe, however, that ethnographic love is often just as present in encounters that are not necessarily tied to projects of social change.

Who Are We to Our Interlocutors?

Postcolonialism and postmodernism required anthropologists to take account of our subject positions with regard to our interlocutors (by which I mean our research subjects), quite rightly exposing the ways in which, among other things, anthropologists constructed heroic selves by constructing research subjects as "others" through a process that offered both personal and professional validation (see Moore 1995, 107–128). Anthropologists have been talking ever since about how to define and imagine our professional identity, if not that of heroic anthropologists. Several alternative models that acknowledge, resist, and deconstruct the power relations and hierarchies often intrinsic to anthropological research are currently ascendant in the discipline. Luke Eric Lassiter (and the journal he edits, *Collaborative Anthropologies*) promotes a model in which anthropologists work with interlocutors as collaborators to produce ethnographies attuned to and defined by the interests of the collaborators (rather than just those of the anthropologist) (Lassiter 2005, 2006). Others promote anthropology as activism, in which anthropologists embrace as their own the concerns of those whose lives they are writing about and orient their research toward promoting those concerns in politically meaningful ways. Anthropologist as activist means, for many, subverting academic goals and products of anthropology and using the privileged position of anthropology to advocate for specific objectives defined and desired by the anthropologist's coactivists (see, for example, Checker 2005; Sanford 2006).

The turn to envisioning anthropology as a collaborative form of activism troubles some, however, who warn that activist engagement defined by the goals of our collaborators might displace theory. In a provocative interview, George Marcus (2008) wonders if theory has been replaced by (reduced to?) activism in anthropology, producing a discipline in which "the center is fragmented and, while not empty literally, is indeed empty of coherent ideas about what anthropological research is, does, and means in the contemporary world." He opines, in what is perhaps an additional jab at activism, that "in place of ideas, anthropological discourse has become overly moralistic" (4). He and his collaborators suggest that anthropology might be redirected toward a sort of ethnographic camaraderie, with opportunities for cotheorizing with curious intellectual collaborators who are "paraethnographers," engaged in reflexive, critical analysis of their work (Holmes and Marcus 2008; Westbrook 2008). For Holmes and Marcus (2008), interlocutors are not subjects in the classic sense, because through their intellectual curiosity they are already engaged in paraethnography; the anthropologist joins them in this endeavor. David Westbrook, a paraethnographer-interlocutor of Holmes and Marcus, envisions ethnographers as navigators who learn things of interest through a series of conversations in which they position themselves as collaborators rather than as critics, with the goal of experience and education rather than critique. Although all parties to the conversation are engaged in collaborative paraethnography for epistemological purposes, professional ethnographers document the discussion with attention to context and history, provide the audience beyond the subject, and speak truths that are often difficult for others to articulate (Westbrook 2008).

The experience of mutuality sought in these models thus varies, from collaborating on a commonly defined documentary or activist project to engaging in stimulating intellectual exchanges about particular topics of mutual interest. All of these models position the anthropologist and his or her interlocutors as subjective equals engaged in a common project, whether of documentation, social transformation, or epistemology.[1] Marcus and Holmes's model of paraethnography attempts to recapture the possibility for theoretical innovation that Marcus suggests may be absent from activist collaborations, but anthropologists engaged in the latter argue that a collaborative approach to activist engagement can enable cotheorizing about topics of mutual interest that are useful to the pursuit of activist goals *and* theoretical progress. In a reflective article about her application of activist feminist praxis to her interpersonal engagements during fieldwork in her husband's family's Nepalese community, Elizabeth Enslin observes, "we need to create a space for praxis, where both theory and practice are constantly clarified through critical engagement in social struggles" (1994, 540). Bruce Knauft (2006), in his configuration of "anthropology in the middle," similarly claims that anthropology's engagement with activism and advocacy emerges from and produces a much more nuanced theoretical landscape, because practical engagements provoke specific theoretical interventions for anthropologists based in the academy, and critical reflection brings a sustained counterbalance to shifting agendas of policy and activism. "Viewed positively, the respective trade-offs between these alternatives [academic and activist/engaged/policy anthropology] can provide an important check and balance on their respective excesses—ivory tower detachment, on the one hand, handmaiden service to the organizations and ideologies of others, on the other" (416). Knauft suggests that activist engagement and theory building as mutually enriching processes have been particularly evident in the work of environmental and medical anthropologists and, increasingly, with anthropologists of human rights issues (and, I would argue, with feminist anthropologists).

David Graeber's (2004) innovative project of theorizing an anarchist anthropology offers another example. Graeber, most recently of Occupy Wall

Street fame, describes ethnography as a gift given in reciprocity by anthropologists to those who are its subjects, a gift that emerges from intentionally engaged conversations with a reciprocal and reflective component and potentially transformative power. Graeber's conception of an anarchist anthropology assumes, among other things, an interactive cotheorizing of models of social transformation and alternative forms of sociality and politics, drawing on diverse ethnographically documented forms of social organization, social and political theory, and the imagination. Maximilian Forte echoes Graeber's understanding of the anthropologist as cotheorizer in the collective project of understanding in order to transform when he writes:

> This type of engagement, for me, is among the better forms of anthropology that I can envision for now. . . . If anthropology is not about seeking peaceful coexistence between diverse peoples, about dialogue across the boundaries of cultural difference, about a world big enough to permit the self-determination of multiple and divergent societies, about respecting the autonomy and self-determination of others, about questions of the contemporary human condition in a specific context of war and capitalism, and *about participating with others in building an understanding of these problem*—then what is anthropology about, and why should anyone care about it? (Forte 2011, 15, emphasis mine)

Collaboration between anthropologists and activists in pursuit of anarchist transformation and/or understandings of human social problems is not unlike Marcus's paraethnography; the primary difference is the importance of an explicit desire to change society through collaboratively envisioned interventions.

Yet, there is still something important about mutuality missing from these outlines, which capture the pragmatic, strategic, intentional, goal-oriented interests of anthropologists as well as those of our interlocutors/collaborators. Anthropologists' interlocutors certainly expect assistance in achieving their goals; documentation of their beliefs, practices, and/or life-worlds; and, possibly, interesting conversation (see Edelman 2009). But this sort of description gives anthropological collaboration the veneer of a business partnership, in which each participant invests intellectual energy and time in the process and expects certain outcomes desirable to all parties. Left unremarked and unacknowledged is the emotional interpersonal dimension of anthropological engagement, an affective component of ethnography often inadequately acknowledged by even the most passionate writers in the discipline. For example, in his recent collection of powerful and moving essays, Paul Farmer advocates and models an ethnography of solidarity, which he calls "perhaps the noblest of human sentiments" (2010, 431), yet on the next page, he admits that "one thing that scarcely appears in this book is the deep emotion that accompanies the work of solidarity" (432). Some ethnographers do reveal glimpses of the close emotional bonds they form with research subjects, which transcend the research altogether, such as in this passage in which anthropologist Alisse Waterston quotes one of her research subjects, a woman living in a homeless shelter: "Nora took my hands in hers. 'The book, the book, the book, you'll write the book,' she admonished, 'but the really important thing is—you've come into my life and I've come into yours'" (1999, 24).

I imagine that many anthropologists have developed, over the course of long-term research, a similar understanding that perhaps the most profound and significant outcome of their research is their personal relationships with research subjects rather than their published results. The sort of love that characterizes such long-term relationships is often fraught, marked by tensions, ambivalences, ambiguities, disappointments, and ruptures, all of which inflect and stumble the experience of mutuality. Ethnographic love is also persistent, however, demanding effort and the belief that the relationships are worth it, even when, or especially when, the ethnographic commitment transforms those involved. Is it important, for our discipline, to address how the participants in the ethnographic encounter are personally changed by their involvement and how this change is significant for ethnography?

A Focus on Process

The focus on the *research process* in the work reviewed above insists on the centrality to disciplinary self-understanding of anthropological praxis. Anthropology is distinguished from other social sciences and from journalism because of our methodology of social embeddedness: forming relationships, developing trust, building networks of care, and working with collaborators who have a role and a stake in the shape and focus of anthropological research and in whose goals and dreams anthropologists invest. The praxis of anthropology is an effort in building social relationships, so turning the spotlight on what that interpersonal engagement means and feels like ethically, politically, personally, and professionally is part of the quest to understand the anthropological experience of mutuality (see Pina-Cabral 2013; Enslin 1994; Jackson 2010). Anthropologists are seldom just intellectual collaborators—we are often also friends, kin, neighbors. Theorizing the multiple forms of engagement that anthropologists construct and experience with research subjects and collaborators can be a productive and critical dimension of our work, because the process of doing anthropology is the process of creating our own humanity—not as heroic selves, but as human beings centered in networks of social relations and communities.[2]

This process is a creative, imaginative process of becoming.[3] Discussing their own work with a woman consigned to a zone of abandonment in Brazil and in a country defined as collectively suffering from PTSD, Biehl and Locke (2010) write about how the ethnographer supports the visions of people struggling against social structures that oppress or constrain them by listening with great personal investment to their stories, striving to grasp and write about subjectivity-in-the-making. Suggesting that Foucauldian and Marxist theories of oppression are useful but confining, Biehl and Locke advocate an ethnographic praxis of listening, with a literary sensibility, respect, and empathy, to what our research subjects have to say about their lives and dreams. "Listening as readers and writers, rather than clinicians, our own sensibility and openness become instrumental in spurring social recognition of the ways ordinary people think through their conditions" (335). They make a strong case for the vital and fundamental importance of ethnography and argue that because of its embrace of the everyday messiness of life, the ethnographic encounter breaks through the constraints imposed by theoretical models to bring a perspective on the emergent: "Simply engaging with the complexity of people's lives and desires—their constraints, subjectivities, projects—in ever-changing social worlds constantly necessitates the rethinking of our theoretical apparatuses" (320). Wanting to write in a way that "unleashes something of this vitality rather than containing it" through theoretical edifices or doctrines, they explain that they "are more interested in writing for a certain vision of anthropology and the anthropologist's relationship to people than against a set of simplified foils" (ibid.). Thus, for Biehl and Locke, mutuality as praxis nurtures both theory and the intimate involvement of the ethnographer in the emergent.

The ethnographer is not immune to personal transformation through such intimate engagements. When ethnographers join with those who are pushing against socially and materially defined boundaries to transform society as well as their own subjectivities, ethnographers participate not only in writing new realities into possibility but also in creating a new self. My six years of fieldwork in Cape Town on social transformation initiatives, in which all who participated in these initiatives did so specifically in order to change themselves, as well as in the hope that they could contribute to creating a better society, could not but transform me as well (Besteman 2008). Many of these initiatives were characterized by enormous tension and conflict, in which the daily excitement of activist work was focused less on the imagined outcome (or theoretical model of a possible outcome) and more on the day-to-day struggle to confront and overcome deep divisions (based on race, class, historical experience) among participants in order to hold open a discursive space in which they could talk to each other about how to envision and work toward a better society. As an anthropologist-participant in some of these initiatives, I was as subject to personal transformation as the other participants, and thus the lessons I learned about the rage of poverty, the guilt of white privilege, the fear of violent crime, the mistrust of forgiveness, and the enormous challenges of learning to trust those with profoundly different life experiences were as personal as they were anthropological. My point here is that participatory engagement in which my own subjectivity was as available to challenge and redefinition as the subjectivities of my research subjects enabled me to write about postapartheid transformation in a way that is distinctly anthropological specifically because of the embrace of ethnographic mutuality.

The initiatives I wrote about were organizations with concrete and material goals, but the participants were actively involved in the process of becoming, envisioning a new kind of society and new possibilities for personal subjectivities. Many participants drew inspiration from the South African concept of *ubuntu* (despite its arguably overused application in South African reconciliation initiatives and moral discourses). Its popular definition, as captured in South African President Thabo Mbeki's memorialization of Steven Biko, sounds affirmingly close to the anthropological ethic: "Ubuntu places a premium on the values of human solidarity, compassion and human dignity. It is a lived philosophy which enables members of the community to achieve higher results through collective efforts. It is firmly based on recognising the humanity in everyone. It emphasises the importance of knowing oneself and accepting the uniqueness in all of us so as to render meaningless the complexes of inferiority and superiority. Indeed, Ubuntu connects all of humanity irrespective of ethnicity or racial origins" (Mbeki 2007).

The concept of ubuntu contains a philosophical claim that people are constituted through their engagements with other people (an understanding of personhood shared by a wide range of non-Western societies; see, for example, Sahlins 2011a, 2011b), not in order to produce a uniform whole but rather to create a collective of singularities, to borrow an image from Hardt and Negri (2009). To the extent that anthropologists purposefully and meaningfully seek out transformative engagements with other human beings, conscious attention to how we are shaped as human beings through these engagements means focusing on the experience of mutuality. Anthropologists construct themselves as individuals through anthropological engagements; we reshape our understandings of ourselves, our place in the world, our personal relationships, and the kinds of society we desire through our close attention to and involvement in the lives of those we study, as well as through their involvement in our lives. Paul Stoller (2007) recounts how his mentor "of things Songhay" (178) used to tell him, "You may write a good deal about us, but to understand us, your life must become entwined in ours. To understand us you must grow old with us" (181). In his love letter to anthropology for Valentine's Day in 2011, Rex (Alex Golub) at Savage Minds blog wrote:

> I love anthropology because it is the discipline that takes seriously the idea that our common humanity with those we study is a boon and a strength, not an impediment that distorts objective judgment. It works with and works through the fact that we can be powerfully changed by our research, and that this change is a strength. . . . Above all I love how anthropology, a science of the human, articulates with our lives: we study kinship, and raise children. We read about enculturation, and we teach students. We analyze power and we try to create a democratic, just world. Our discipline is connected, intimately and irrevocably, to our whole persons—and that's what I love about it most of all. (Golub 2011)

Similarly, Maple Razsa recounts how his anarchist informants in Croatia engaged in politically motivated activities as much to change themselves personally as to provoke political change, noting that anthropologists who study direct action as a form of paraethnography, like himself, are also engaged "in a process of becoming-other-than-we-now-are as ethnographers" through fieldwork (Razsa and Kurnik 2012, 240).

My Cape Town book is only a footnote to the enduring friendships I maintain with some of those whose stories are captured within its pages, some of whom have never read the book because they do not consider it a particularly important part of our friendship or work together. The relationships I developed through my Cape Town research changed the quality of the friendships I have at home in Maine specifically because of what I learned about racism, trust, and reciprocity—qualities I attempted to describe in book chapters that alternate with chapters on ethnographic material. In writing *Transforming Cape Town* (2008), the best way I could imagine to demonstrate the most vital, important, and disturbing currents of postapartheid city life was by articulating as clearly and intimately as I could how I came to understand and feel the impact of those currents through my personal relationships with city residents. Readers tell me that the most compelling dimension of the book is the emotional commitment to my research subjects, which they perceive through my writing. This emotional commitment is love.

Where Is the Love?

As noted above, an anthropologist's interlocutors might collaborate with anthropological research as a strategic move toward achieving a goal. Less certain is whether an anthropologist's interlocutors expect friendship, personal commitments, trust, or love, and yet, as I have noted for Farmer, Waterston, and Stoller, those sentiments are often (if ever so subtly) apparent in ethnographic accounts. In her biography of Bourdieu, Reed-Danahay explains that, for his 1999 book *The Weight of the World*, he chose to interview only people known to members of his research team "in order to minimize the social distance between" interviewer and interviewee and to ensure that "there was no omniscient narrator who adopted the 'lofty' gaze" that, in Bourdieu's opinion, so often characterized the position of the researcher (Reed-Danahay 2005, 145). Bourdieu promotes the researcher's involvement in a sociological interview as "a sort of intellectual love," "a welcoming disposition, which leads one to make the respondent's problems one's own, the capacity to take that person and understand them just as they are in their distinctive necessity" (Bourdieu 1999, 614), perhaps a reflection of Bourdieu's interest, at the end of his career, in directing his research toward political interventions sympathetic to the concerns of his research subjects. A reviewer remarks that, for Bourdieu, "the concept of 'love' represents a relationship of mutuality that, however momentarily, rises above or steps out of the agonistic relationships characteristic of most human life. This relationship provides the ground for true understanding" (Barnard 2008). Still, one is left wondering if this kind of "intellectual love," which produces "true understanding," is possible only between a researcher and research subject who share an identity.

In an essay on love in anthropological fieldwork, Virginia Dominguez argues that love, rather than identity politics, is the most important sentiment enveloping ethnographic research and representation. She argues that, whereas minoritized scholars are usually expected to undertake research with their "own people" out of a commitment we might identify as intellectual love, other scholars are not, even though she is certain that many scholars experience—and are motivated by—a love they feel for their research subjects yet are hesitant to betray: "Let us not make the mistake of assuming that only longtime 'insiders' are ever driven by love—or even that they are always driven by love. . . . Love, yes, love—the thing most of us are not open about in our scholarly writing, the kind most of us have been professionally socialized into excising from our scholarly writing" (Dominguez 2000, 365). She challenges her disciplinary colleagues to acknowledge and describe the love they feel for their research subjects as a powerful dimension of anthropology that gives it validity and value: "It is important that we all pay attention to the presence or absence of love and affection in our scholarship—at all stages of the production of our scholarship. If it is not there, it is important to ask ourselves why and what we should do about it. If it is there, we owe it to our readers to show it, to enable them to evaluate its role in the nature of our work. To maintain a bifurcated view of who should and who should not is to diminish us all and to make everyone's work suspect" (388).

Dominguez's argument is that anthropologists should be able to defend their scholarly interests not through a politics of identity but rather through an acknowledgment of love, a defense that could claim: "I study these people because I love them (rather than because they are 'my people'). 'My people' are those I love, regardless of the identity constructions that define categories of political belonging (on the basis of race, religion, citizenship, and so forth)." This understanding of love is closer to the form of "love as a material, political act" advocated by Hardt and Negri (2009, 184), for whom alterity, not similarity, is the basis of love that produces new subjectivities, "new forms of the common" (186). Love of the same and love that insists on unification, Hardt and Negri clarify, are corrupt forms of love that champion nationalism, racism, patriotism, and other sentiments of exclusion, as opposed to the form of love they commend, "love that composes singularities . . . not in unity but as a network of social relations" (184).

Among those anthropologists who do acknowledge how and why their love for their subjects motivates their writing, Dominguez finds particularly compelling evidence in the photographs some anthropologists choose to accompany their texts, such as those of Sidney Mintz's cherished friend Don Taso Zayas in his classic *Worker in the Cane* (Mintz 1960), which Dominguez calls "a testimonial of love" (2000, 368). A more recent example is Ruth Behar's (2007) book, *An Island Called Home: Returning to Jewish Cuba*, which is a visual love letter to Cuba in which her text responds to the photographs taken by Humberto Mayol, and her loving longing for the present-absent community depicted in the photographs is a central story of the book. Not all loving photographic depictions are images of beauty; consider the extremely disturbing photographs that accompany *Righteous Dopefiend*, the collaborative photoethnography of homeless heroin addicts by Philippe Bourgois and Jeffrey Schonberg (2009). About this project, Bourgois writes, "Anthropologists cannot escape seeing, feeling, and empathizing with the people they study" (2011, 11), a sentiment that Bourgois says he intentionally displays in the choice of photographs and their strategic placement throughout the book, with no captions and surrounded by running text.

While Dominguez suggests that anthropologists' love for their research subjects may be most evident in their choice of photographs, it is worth remembering Roland Barthes's (1972) critique of *The Family of Man* photography exhibition, which warns of photography's failure to offer a representation of a common humanity when the photograph is devoid of context. Remarking on the exhibition, he says, "To reproduce birth or death tells us, literally, nothing. For these natural facts to gain access to a true language, they must be inserted into a category of knowledge which means postulating that one can transform them, and precisely subject their naturalness to our human criticism" (100). The context in which photographs are taken and exhibited makes all the difference, and for anthropologists, that context is often shaped by ethnographic love.

Exhibiting Mutuality

Photographs, then, can be testimonials and representations of ethnographic love, and, as such, they can be strategically utilized in ethnographic projects in an attempt to render visually, and perhaps produce in viewers, an experience of mutuality. Incorporating photographs into ethnographic museum exhibitions, websites, and films can offer a powerful intervention to a viewer's consciousness. I had a remarkable opportunity to use my collection of ethnographic photographs from fieldwork in Somalia (taken by myself and Jorge Acero) for a project specifically designed to evoke sentiment and empathy in viewers. In 2006, refugees from the small village in Somalia where I had conducted my dissertation fieldwork in 1987–1988 began moving to Maine, where we rediscovered each other after almost twenty years. The upheaval caused by Somalia's civil war and the flight of many villagers to Kenyan refugee camps, as well as the challenges of illiteracy, meant that I had lost touch with everyone I knew until our surprise encounter in 2006. After the joy of our reunion and the delight of sharing our collection of hundreds of photographs of their younger selves and family members (many now deceased), the refugees in Lewiston were eager to use the photographs to collaborate on a variety of projects that would educate the broader Maine public about their background and experiences and combat the predominantly negative popular perception of Somali refugees as criminals, poor parents, immoral foreigners, and undeserving welfare dependents. Drawing on the photographic collection (see figure 10), a collaborative (formed by members of the refugee community, my college students, and myself) created a website[4] and a museum exhibition that traveled to three different museums in Maine. Our desire in crafting these exhibitions was to use the photographs to provide a visible representation of Somali community life, faith, love, strength, and happiness—to humanize refugees as people (see figure 11) who actually do have a meaningful history in ways that might provoke respect, admiration, greater understanding, and even feelings of mutuality in viewers. Some of the photographs included here were among those on exhibition (see figure 12).

The exhibition at Museum L/A in Lewiston, which included text and audio authored by those represented in the photographs and a program of educational events intended to introduce the people in the photographs to Lewiston's citizens, was viewed by thousands of Mainers. At the conclusion of the year-long exhibition, the museum's director, Rachel Desgrosseilliers, remarked that despite continuing to "hear the same old garbage" about the Somalis from her local acquaintances, she believed the exhibit had shifted the thinking of some in Lewiston's predominantly Franco-American community. Visitors to the exhibition commented on their new understanding of how much the refugees lost in the war, how much they had to sacrifice to come to the United States, and how much Lewiston's Franco-American community and the Somalis shared as people with personal experiences of immigration

Figure 10. Amina Abdulle with her baby, Bilow Ali, in Banta, 1987. Amina died in the war. Bilow now lives in Texas. Photograph by Jorge Acero.

Figure 11. Macallin Caddow studying his Quran, in Tey Tey, Somalia, 1988. His son lives in Lewiston, Maine. Photograph by Jorge Acero.

Figure 12. Ali Deerow with his children, Aboy and Isha, in Banta, Somalia, 1988. Photograph by Jorge Acero.

(see figures 13, 14, 15). Rachel also reflected on how the exhibit changed her own attitude toward her new neighbors, making her "curious to learn more. Now I'm not afraid to walk down the street and to walk through a bunch of them." She noted her particular realization that "family is very important to them. It reminds me of my childhood, how every Sunday we had to spend with our family. It was very, very important."

Much more can be said about why some of Lewiston's residents might be more comfortable viewing photographs of Somalis than meeting or interacting with them (or walking through a bunch of them) face to face, but the important point here is that a museum with deep roots in the local Franco-American community could collaborate with a local anthropologist and a group of refugee newcomers to the city to use photographs taken and displayed in a context of trust, empathy, and love to chip away at the potential hostility of viewers about those depicted in the photographs. The photographs of Somalis laughing, playing, and working offer to viewers a glimpse of the potential for mutuality, a way to possibly insert themselves into the frame.

Does Anthropology Have a Common Set of Values and Morals?

Because a fundamental perspective guiding anthropological research is the desire to understand how and what others think, anthropologists engage in interpersonal relationships in order to grasp what the world looks like to our interlocutors. For those anthropologists who enter into collaborative projects with interlocutors motivated by a desire for social change, ethnography is often about imagination, hope, and the desire for beneficial transformation. The presence of the ethnographer, according to Biehl and Locke, Razsa and Kurnik, Graeber, Knauft, and others cited here, catalyzes a description or a reflection of the emergent, a vision of future possibilities collaboratively imagined by the ethnographer and his or her interlocutors. But projects of social change are always values driven. Although anthropology has a code of ethics, to what extent are ethnographers also guided by a commonly understood set of values? Should we be?

In his call for a radical anthropology, George Henriksen hopes for an anthropology that explicitly contests "urgent issues of domination, conflict and structural violence" that continue to structure relations between indigenous peoples and the state. But, he cautions, "To engage in this kind of anthropol-

Figure 13. Ali Osman, a poet, musician, carpenter, and farmer, in Banta, 1988. He died in the war. His wife and youngest children live in Lewiston. Photograph by Jorge Acero.

Figure 14. Kaltuma and her friends, in Banta, Somalia, 1987. Photograph by Jorge Acero.

ogy . . . necessitates that one has an idea of what a good society is" (Henriksen 2003, 122). For anthropologists, where does that idea come from? Do anthropologists have a shared idea of what it takes to make a good society? Henrikson insists that such ideas must come from those with whom we work, whose visions are then adopted and advocated by the anthropologist-as-collaborator.

But should anthropologists who seek to explicitly contest domination, conflict, and structural violence always do so from a relativist position in which we accept and work within only that definition of a good society constructed by the communities in which we work? Jeffrey Deal (2010) explores this challenge in an example from his work as a physician and anthropologist in South Sudan, where torture and excessive beatings are used by authorities as a way of reducing violence. Because everyone with whom he spoke affirmed the necessity of these sorts of beatings, even when used against the innocent, Deal reasoned that in the immediate context he must also accept these beatings as legitimate forms of social structure and governance, even as he sought (sometimes unsuccessfully) to offer treatment to the victims. But he also argues that in the broader context, anthropologists must begin to acknowledge the possibility of a universal code of human rights that does not subordinate

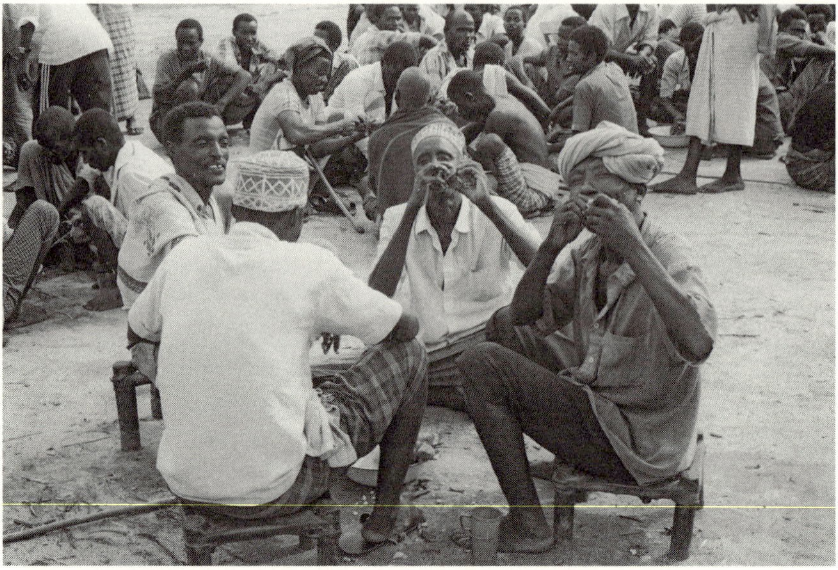

Figure 15. Brothers mugging for the camera at a village feast, Banta, Somalia, 1988. These men died in the war. Their relatives live in Lewiston. Photograph by Jorge Acero.

the interests of the individual to the social group, such as when innocent people are tortured in a socially sanctioned practice. Deal argues that anthropologists have, to date, mostly avoided any real engagement with the Universal Declaration of Human Rights because of our disciplinary insistence on relativism and social construction, an insistence that contradicts the discipline's simultaneous commitment to resisting violence and torture—even when all participants seem to agree about their appropriateness. For Deal, the choice is to advocate for the interests of the individual and to resist the idea that a "good society" might be one in which innocent people might be subject to torture in the name of the public good.

We have many examples of anthropologists who reject the relativist position on violence and choose, instead, to intervene on behalf of those being harmed even when the social context defines violence as moral, laudable, and necessary. For example, Philippe Bourgois, who works within the United States with homeless drug addicts, rejects his society's definition of a good society, in which there is widespread agreement that those who break the law, including those who use illegal drugs, are criminals who should be held ac-

Figure 16. The anthropologist and her neighbor, Abdulle Abdi, Banta, Somalia, 1987. Abdulle died in 1990. His son lives in Lewiston, Maine. Photograph by Jorge Acero

countable for their actions according to the law. Bourgois discredits the application of a strictly legal/criminal assessment of the actions of homeless drug addicts, arguing instead that the cultural mores are wrong and that repeated incarceration of homeless drug addicts contributes to a form of violence he calls "lumpen abuse" (Bourgois and Schonberg 2009).

Thus, although anthropologists may indeed share a desire to use anthropology to make the world a better place and to fight violence, torture, and social structures that cause suffering, exactly how to do that is, of course, subject to considerable debate. Anthropologists do not subscribe to a single vision, nor are we in agreement about whether to promote a relativist or a liberal or a personal understanding of what constitutes a good society (see Rapport 2011). Didier Fassin worries that the desire to use anthropology for the benefit of humanity may cause moral confusion if anthropologists conflate or mix up moral indignation with critical analysis (2008, 338). Thus, he urges anthropologists to consider "moral reflexivity" in our analyses and question the values and judgments that underlie our work.

If we understand that anthropological values rest on a disciplinary orientation to an ethic of social justice that emerges from mutuality (rather than paternalism or charity), then perhaps what is called for is a reflexive acknowledgment of mutuality. In his book of essays about the impact of neoliberalism in Africa, James Ferguson (2006) writes about how Africans assume that inequality must be explained; their queries are the same as those of their anthropologist. Anthropologists *are* in agreement about the value of listening to and engaging with interlocutors who are asking questions similar to those we have about how to envision and work toward a better society, and, as I have argued, anthropologists who acknowledge mutuality recognize that their personal and theoretical understandings of social formations are continually evolving with their research as a result. Perhaps a shared anthropological value is the desire to be open to alternative and new visions of society and to seriously engage with these visions in a collaborative process of imagining societies to come; to simultaneously document the emergent and the imagined; and to place our personal values alongside those held by our research communities, thereby stretching, challenging, and transforming the values of all who participate in the ethnographic encounter. In his book on ethnographic sorcery, Harry West (2007) suggests that anthropologists conjure worlds alongside and in dialogue with our research subjects; ideas about what makes a good society are also collaborative imaginings conjured by anthropologists together with those with whom we work. As Biehl and Locke (2010) suggest, "Grasping subjectivity as becoming—rather than structural dependence—may be the key to anticipating, and thereby making available for assessment and transformation, the futures and forms of life of emerging communities. . . . This project includes the active participation of readers. Thus also at stake is our capacity to generate a "we," an engaged audience and political community, that has not previously existed—our craft's potential to become a mobilizing force in this world" (337).

One of the most exciting things about anthropology is how the understandings that emerge from relationships of mutuality reverberate along networks of engagement. This is why it is so important for anthropologists to be able to recognize how their values are shaped in dialogue both with their interlocutors within the profession and with their interlocutors in their sites of research and engagement and to continually reflect on and infect each arena with insights from the other. An anthropology conceived in mutuality is about what it means to be a human being engaged in discussions about what makes a good society and what sorts of actions are provoked by such imaginings.

Interlude

And yet, we cannot be hasty in assuming a universal "anthropological perspective" defined by an ethic of mutuality as the basis for collaborative visions of a good society. In Somalia's ongoing agony, the political scene in 2012, prior to the September 2012 presidential election included a variety of militia leaders claiming control over swaths of territory and the populations who live there. One of these militia leaders, Mohamed Abdi Mohamed—a man who calls himself Professor Gandhi and who used to be the defense minister in the ineffective, impotent, foreign-aid–supported Somali government—declared himself president of Azania, a breakaway new republic comprising the southern quarter of Somalia. As president of a country largely of his own creation, he headed an armed militia that was allegedly supported by Kenya and China (Gettelman 2011). According to a New York Times article, he claimed that his status as president and militia head would allow him to destroy al Shabaab (a group identified by the United States as a terrorist organization with ties to al Qaeda), but he had no democratic mandate, most of those who live within the borders of so-called Azania played no part in its designation and did not support his presidency, and he himself did not even live there. But what makes his behavior relevant to my dilemma about the shared values of an "anthropological perspective" is that he is a trained anthropologist with a PhD, many publications on Somali political and cultural life, and a long record of work in peace and demobilization efforts in Somalia. Can we reconcile a belief in a shared anthropological perspective, with its insistence on mutuality, with the reality of an anthropologist who takes up arms and claims political and military leadership of a territory whose population may not support him? That the anthropologist-turned-warlord is such an anomaly may be a meaningful indication of the discipline's orientation toward seeking a model of a good society through collaborative, nonviolent means.

When Mutuality Is Antagonistic

Showcasing mutuality—or at least acknowledging it—offers a counternarrative to popular images of anthropology that portray disciplinary practitioners as cold, detached, unempathetic observers/critics of others (Hannerz 2010). Dominguez argues that writing with an ethic of love imbues our work with clarity and power. But writing with an ethic of love and understanding oneself to be engaged in a mutual project of imagining a new and better society is challenged when the anthropologist's vision of a good society directly contradicts those of his or her research subjects. In her review of ethnographies of the far right, for example, Kathleen Blee (2007) reveals just how rare it is for anthropologists to study social movements whose aims they do not share, a lacuna she attributes to the limitations of anthropologists' personal and professional networks and political allegiances, problems of access, and a profound mistrust of outsider academics by the leadership in far-right movements.

Yet, powerful and empathetic portrayals have been penned by those who loathe the values or actions of those they study—for example, Pumla Gobodo-Madikizela's (2003) portrait of South Africa's heinously murderous former security official Eugene de Kok and Antonius Robben's reflection on his interview with an Argentine Dirty War general (1995)—or reject the politics or practices of those they portray—such as in Susan Harding's (2001) ethnography of Jerry Falwell's potent evangelical Christian movement and Hugh Gusterson's (1998) portrait of nuclear bomb makers. Each of these ethnographies succeeds precisely because the subject is humanized through an account shaped by ethnographic mutuality rather than by political or moral reproach. By drawing the reader into an imagined association with the subject, the ethnographer locates the reader in a moral universe that requires critical reflection through engagement rather than disengagement or alienation. Writing with love, respect, and/or empathy rather than with moral indignation about the immoral, harmful, or unpalatable actions or beliefs of research subjects offers readers an experience of mutuality that might prompt productive self-reflection and potential enlistment in a collaborative project of envisioning alternatives.

Nevertheless, ethnographic engagements with those whose values or practices the anthropologist loathes may require such a dramatic reformulation of the concept of mutuality that we would be better served by using terms such as *respect* or *sincerity* instead. Ethnographies of the odious, such as those of torturers like Eugene de Kok, may compel the anthropologist to probe the limits of ethnographic mutuality. Yet, to the extent that anthropology is about creating a shared understanding—even about something like torture—that is translated to readers by the ethnographer, the ethnographic experience of mutuality inflects the text in a way that few other perspectives are able to do.

Conclusion

I suggest that the relationships forged through ethnographic praxis are a variant of Sahlins's (2011a, 2011b) definition of kinship as "mutuality in being," an ontology that distinguishes kin relations from other sorts of social relations because "kinsmen are persons who belong to one another, who are members of one another, who are co-present in each other, whose lives are joined and interdependent" (2011a, 11). As analyzed by Sahlins, kinship involves the incorporation of others into the constitution of the person, a quality of being found in ethnographic reports of kin relations from throughout the world and elucidated most beautifully by Marilyn Strathern in her description of the Melanesian understanding of the person as "the plural and composite site of the relationships that produced them" (Strathern 1988, cited in Sahlins 2011a, 12).

Although he argues that the *incorporation* of others into the person distinguishes kin relations from other sorts of relations, I wonder about the fungibility of Sahlins's kinship model for ethnographic relationships, which often assume qualities of kin relations.[5] The mutuality of ethnographic relations may lack certain characteristics of the "mutuality in being" of kinship, such as "transpersonal praxis" (where the actions of one are attributed to the many; the group is held responsible for the actions of one; and the experiences of one may be shared, mystically or magically, by others by virtue of their kin connections; Sahlins 2011b, 230), but there is an essence here, sometimes experienced through the presence or formation of kin relations in ethnographic fieldwork, that is important and distinct to anthropology.

The "mutuality-in-being" that Sahlins describes as the basis of what kinship is thus might be extended to ethnography as well, to the extent that people become anthropologists, in part, through the social relationships created during fieldwork that, quite actually, make them. Sahlins argues that to understand kinship, we should privilege "intersubjective being over the singular person as the composite site of multiple others" (2011a, 14), because the former better captures the special and specific qualities of kin relations, qualities that I argue exist in ethnographic relationships as well.

To return to my interlocutor in Cape Town, an ethnographer writing about Africa would not produce a portrait like Kaplan's because ethnographic praxis is so often an experience of mutuality. Mutuality emerges from a commitment to collaborative solidarity, the creative process of imagining new forms of sociality and society, and ethnographic love. Often engendered through the exploration of difference, the ethic of mutuality is an openness to self-transformation and to the changes in intersubjectivity that happen over time. It insists on moral reflexivity, a critical moral awareness that shapes and defines the ethnographic encounter. Rejecting the self-love of the heroic anthropologist—the sort of self-love evident in Kaplan's work—ethnographic love combines moral reflexivity, affection, solidarity, and an embrace of the ethnographic process as an experience of becoming someone other than who we are now.

Conclusion

Mutuality and Anthropology

Terms and Modes of Engagement

Roger Sanjek

In 1965, I conducted my first fieldwork in Sitio, a fishing village in Bahia, Brazil. Settled in a wattle-and-daub house on a sandy lane leading to the beach, I began my interviews on racial categories (Sanjek 1971, 2000) with Mãezinha Dos Santos, an expressive and engaging middle-aged woman who lived in the house facing ours. I quickly expanded my interview pool to other parts of the village and also included other neighbors, among them Mãezinha's fisherman husband, two sons, and daughter Olga, pregnant with her third child. She soon gave birth, but tragically the baby died within days, and I joined family members in mourning.

A couple of days later, I asked Olga's husband Aessu, also a fisherman, if I could interview him. He told me yes, but asked to wait until the family's distress over the infant's passing subsided. I felt like a jerk, realizing that my desire for anthropological data, the reason I was there, had clouded my sense of how to treat a fellow human being, one who had just lost a child. Some weeks later, Aessu, thirty-five, and more a gentleman than I, then twenty, agreed we meet as earlier requested.

This episode dispirited me, and my response was to give up plans to become an anthropologist. I felt I had taken what I wanted—information—but given nothing in return. I took a detour to journalism school, thinking I might apply the knowledge and perspective from my anthropology classes, which I continued to enjoy, to a career in that field. Hoping to find in journalism more of the "socially relevant" spirit of the 1960s, I spent an unhappy semester disappointed by a faculty reluctant to question the "objectivity" justifying decisions, which I disagreed with, about what was newsworthy and what was not. Still unsettled, in 1967, I began graduate school in anthropology with a vague commitment to eventual fieldwork concerning social and political issues in my own society (see Sanjek 1969).

Extractive Research or Mutuality?

My Brazil experience had been one of "extractive" fieldwork, as Sylvia Rodríguez labels it in Chapter 3. Mutuality was not of concern in determining research goals and conduct; what mattered was a fledgling anthropologist's progress up the professional career ladder. In fact, the summer field-training program in which I participated was designed for that purpose, as were similar programs at the time (Kottak 2004; Vogt 1994). I discussed my misgivings with my advisor, Marvin Harris. His commitment to social and political issues deeply impressed me (Sanjek 1995), and in his view, our studies of racial categorization in Brazil were important to larger intellectual struggles about the meaning of "race" (Harris 1964). Yet, his candid reply concerning the fieldwork situation—that "at best," anthropologists are like "parasites" that coexist with, but "do no harm" to, their host (compare Salzman 1994, 31)—was not what I was looking for.

In a prescient essay, "Anthropology and Colonialism," in *Current Anthropology* in 1973, Diane Lewis linked the interpersonal distancing of extractive fieldwork with the dominant academic-career complex values of outsider "objectivity" and detachment, "professional advancement," "unlimited right of access to data of any kind," the "interests of the discipline," and primary concern with "refinement of theory." She stressed that this value set arose in the "era now fading . . . of Western colonization and white supremacy" and asked: "Is anthropology a truly universal discipline? Can it be utilized for explicit self-study and self-knowledge by all peoples?" (582, 584, 588–590).

Lewis counterposed "extraction" of information from fieldwork subjects[1] with "a sense of commitment to them and their needs" and a willingness to engage in "activism stemming from explicit involvement," which was then still "considered inappropriate for the anthropologist in his professional role." In this regard, she distinguished the current and potential future situations of white American and European anthropologists, on one hand, and their Native

American, African American, Asian, African, and Latin American colleagues, on the other. She called for more "insider" fieldwork among one's own group, which was then also professionally discouraged, by both sets of anthropologists, but for different reasons. Lewis wanted anthropologists from historically oppressed populations to voice "common interests . . . which members of the group share" and to redefine and broaden "the positive contributions of anthropology." The historically privileged white anthropologist, she said, needed to help rehumanize the discipline and "consider, as both social scientist and citizen, that his own world seems to be falling apart around him" (581, 584, 589). Anticipating later arguments that all fieldwork involves positionality and partial truths (Clifford 1986; Rosaldo 1989), Lewis (1973) concluded, "The notion of a single, valid, objective knowledge must be replaced with that of . . . knowledge which is partial and which views reality from the particular existential position occupied by the observer" (586).

By the mid-1980s, Clifford Geertz detected increased awareness among anthropologists that "treating people as objects" and assuming that their profession "exist[s] less for the world than the world exists for them" was no longer defensible or sustainable. "One of the major assumptions upon which anthropological writing rested until only yesterday, that its subjects and its audience were not only separable but morally disconnected, . . . has fairly well dissolved" (Geertz 1988, 10, 48, 132). Yet, two decades later, in her moving book *Acequia: Water Sharing, Sanctity, and Place* (2006), Rodríguez referred to anthropological fieldwork as still marked by "the sin of ethnographic objectification" (100). She admitted that she was able to minimize this through local community sponsorship affording "the least invasive circumstances possible" but that she could not fully extinguish the tension between anthropology's two value systems (xxii-xxv, 100).

Fieldwork and Mutuality: Own and Other Cultures[2]

My second fieldwork episode brought me and my wife, Lani Sanjek, to Accra, Ghana, in 1969–1971 and 1974. We studied eleven apartment buildings in the multiethnic, multilingual neighborhood of Adabraka, a population of landlords, business owners, market traders, clerks, teachers, seamstresses, taxi drivers, and food sellers we came to know in nearly Malinowskian intimacy. We enjoyed a welcomed "rapport" with many Adabraka people and reciprocated with our resources, time, and responsiveness in ways we believed mattered to them. Our sojourn was "successful" according to academic-career complex criteria—my PhD dissertation, a job, and publications followed (Sanjek 1972, 1977a, 1978a, 1982b, 1983a, 1990c; Sanjek and Sanjek 1976)—and the experience consolidated Lani's decision to pursue a career in health care. Still, our fieldwork had addressed issues of ethnicity, social organization, and gender arising in academic anthropology, not concerns voiced within Adabraka or Ghanaian society more broadly.

After I began teaching at Queens College, City University of New York, in 1972, I was undecided what direction my career should take—further engagement with Ghana, or fieldwork in my own city? One model for the Africanist area scholar path was anthropologist Simon Ottenberg, whom we met in Ghana. He had conducted lengthy fieldwork in Nigeria twice in the 1950s but was unable to return because of the 1967–1970 Nigerian civil war. I had enjoyed his first book about the Afikpo Igbo, and in 1970 he was at work on the third (Ottenberg 1968, 1975). I admired his continuing ties with Igbo scholars and support of Nigerian students pursuing degrees in the United States. Following fieldwork in Sierra Leone during the 1970s, Ottenberg returned to Nigeria in the 1980s and 1990s, where he traced the social history of the Nsukka group of contemporary artists. He later organized an exhibition of their work at the Smithsonian National Museum of African Art in Washington, D.C., and produced a symposium volume that included essays by five Nsukka artists, as well as several Nigerian and American scholars (Ottenberg 1997, 2002).[3]

My interests and values, molded by the 1960s civil rights and antiwar movements (Sanjek 1995), oriented me toward ongoing urban social and political change. Although Ghana had turned from military to limited civilian rule in 1969, there were no political campaigns during our stay to study along "Manchester School" lines (Bailey 1963; Deshen 1970; Mayer 1966), although there was plenty of political opinion. Issues of environmental and economic disruption and of human rights concerns were not evident in Ghana then. We did have searching conversations with David Beckmann, a socially committed Yale student who produced an insightful study of a spiritual church in Accra (Beckmann 1975). He later became a Lutheran minister, studied economics, worked on development issues for the World Bank, and since 1991 has headed Bread for the World, a nongovernmental advocacy organization focused on global hunger and poverty. Other anthropologists who did fieldwork in Africa in the 1960s and later decades undertook NGO work on human needs and rights (Abusharaf 2006; de Waal 1989; Hart 1982; Hoben 1982; Malkki 1995), but that was not a direction I considered at the time.

My position at Queens College during the early 1970s was split between anthropology and urban studies departments, and my courses covered African and U.S. cities. I continued to read, and now teach, the work of anthropologists who conducted fieldwork in their own societies, work I aspired in some way to emulate: Srinvas (1966) in India; Deshen and Shokeid in Israel (Deshen 1970; Deshen and Shokeid 1974); Bott (1957), Dennis, Henriques, and Slaughter (1956), Frankenberg (1966), and Young and Wilmott (1957) in Britain; Barth and colleagues in Norway (Barth 1963); Nakane (1967) in Japan; and Keil (1966), Mitchell-Kernan (1971), Warner (1962), and Whyte (1955) in the United States.

As a native New Yorker who lived part of my childhood in Queens, I felt privileged to teach first-generation-to-attend-college students like me in a public institution, then with free tuition. When New York City's fiscal crisis arrived in 1975, I hoped to avoid the possible loss of my Queens job due to budget cuts by being officially on leave, and, fortunately, I obtained a postdoctoral fellowship at the University of California, Berkeley. Within a few months of our arrival, I was recruited by Lani Sanjek as an applied anthropologist at the Gray Panthers–sponsored Over 60 Health Clinic, where she had volunteered as a nurse practitioner and had been asked to become director. I joined the Berkeley Gray Panthers, a group of old and young activists, and participated in actions and advocacy campaigns on health care, housing, and peace issues in Berkeley during 1977–1978, and worked with other Gray Panther groups in New York in the 1980s and 2000s (Sanjek 1977b, 1982b, 1984a, 1987, 2009a).

In Berkeley, I never thought of myself as a "native anthropologist." Gray Panthers became members by choice, not birth, and I was not there to do academic fieldwork. But I was an anthropologist by occupation, and, like other Gray Panther members, I contributed what useable professional skills and knowledge I could—in my case, analyzing data; recording meeting minutes; and producing reports, funding proposals, and newsletters. When, later, I decided to write a book about the national movement and its Berkeley and New York chapters (Sanjek 2009a, 2009b), I did so self-consciously, as an "insider," and I introduced the book as "part history, part ethnography, part memoir" (Sanjek 2009a, xviii).[4]

Unlike my experiences in Brazil and Ghana, in those with the Gray Panthers, I became politically involved as a "citizen" in my own society (Barnes 1977; compare Besteman 2010; Okely 1996, 22–26; Pace 1998, 1–12). At the same time, I saw and interpreted the political arenas in which I participated from the perspective of anthropology. Here mutuality, in its interpersonal and wider social dimensions, eclipsed the values of anthropology's academic-career complex: when a choice between academic research goals or participation and advocacy confronted me following passage of California's Proposition 13 in 1978, research was shelved (Sanjek 1987).

I did not confront this dichotomy in the next of my anthropological deep grooves: team fieldwork during 1983–1996 on the impact of racial change and immigration in Elmhurst-Corona, Queens, and subsequent public engagement following my book about this work (Sanjek 1998, 2004). In Queens, I was not doing applied or advocacy anthropology, although my team members and I did respond to a variety of requests from community groups and leaders. We agreed to undertake an "applied research" survey of the local business sector, as well as speak at meetings, write newsletter and newspaper articles, and participate in a neighborhood reconciliation "task force" following an incident of black-Korean conflict at a local supermarket (Sanjek 2004). Moreover, the issues I was studying had "relevance" to me as a New Yorker, a public employee, and a teacher of students from Queens neighborhoods, including those we studied.

As an anthropologist working in my own society, I was, as John Barnes puts it, "no more, and no less, a citizen than the people" I worked among. I understood that what I did had "significance for them as well as for [me], even though this significance may not be identical." And I realized that I needed "to communicate to [them] a deep and constructive appreciation of what [my] research [was] really aimed at. . . . [For] if [an anthropologist] wants information, they cannot get it simply on demand; there must be . . . negotiation" (Barnes 1977, 4, 38–39, 58).

Even more than in Brazil and Ghana, my fieldwork in Queens and assistance from fellow Gray Panthers while writing my book involved continuing negotiation. Welcomed by some anthropologists and resisted by others (these contending stances in relation to NAGPRA and the Kennewick Man controversy are well portrayed in Burke et al. 2008), negotiation is essential to mutuality. This is true for all anthropologists—whether they are viewed by those they study, or themselves, as insiders or as outsiders; and whether they are newly arrived or have long-established reservoirs of trust (see Narayan 1993; Jacobs-Huey 2002; and, for examples, Flores-Meiser 1980; McClaurin 2001a; Shokeid 1989; Zavella 1996; Zentella 1997, 1–16).

Together, the coauthors of *Mutuality* illustrate "a sliding sense of insiderness"[5] (compare Lewis 1973, 599). Some have worked solely or mainly within groups they are affiliated with by birth, in some instances beginning with family and natal community roots. And some have worked among populations with which, more broadly, they share mutually acknowledged social or national identities. Others turned to such research (as I did) after previous fieldwork in cultures wherein they were unambiguously outsiders. Still others have constructed deep grooves among people and communities they encountered first as outsiders and with whom they developed mutualities of trust and collaboration (Narayan 1993, 677–678), as must also those who begin as insiders (Jacobs-Huey 2002, 793).

Mutuality crosscuts an insider/outsider dichotomy. Although "each perspective has its advantages and disadvantages, both intellectual and practical," Diane Lewis noted, "there is nothing intrinsic to the role of insider that assures commitment to one's own people" (1973, 587, 600). Strict adherence to academic-career complex values by anyone (see Narayan 1993, 677, on "hit-and-run" ethnography) not only can undermine mutuality but may expose a would-be insider to being labeled "an educated fool" (Jacobs-Huey 2002, 795).

Anthropologists Write. . . .

"'What does the ethnographer do?'—he writes," wrote Clifford Geertz, famously, in his "Thick Description" essay in 1973 (Geertz 1973, 19). Repercussions to this observation include the influential "textualist" focus on ethnographic writing (Clifford 1983; Clifford and Marcus 1986; Geertz 1988; Marcus and Cushman 1982; Marcus and Fischer 1986), as well as attention to "inscription" as part of the fieldwork process (Clifford 1990; Geertz 1973, 19n; Ottenberg 1990; Sanjek 1990b). The textualists took theoretically driven ethnography in book and journal article formats to be the "what" of anthropological production, although Geertz observed that anthropologists also produce other "modes of representation," including "films, [long-playing audio] records, museum displays, . . . and so on" (1973, 19n). We return to these (and other) modes and their audiences later, but first we consider how and why theoretically driven ethnographic writing has occupied center stage in social-cultural anthropology debates since Geertz and the textualist turn—to the detriment of greater mutuality—and why this may be changing.

In 1973, the year "Thick Description" appeared, there were, for the first time in two decades, more new PhD applicants seeking academic jobs than there were openings. I remember. With one peer-reviewed article already published, unusual at a time when a PhD sufficed, I was hired at Queens College in 1972, the last of anthropology's fat years. The next year, things were different, and the applicants-to-job ratio has worsened since.

Since 1973, the expectation of publications from "top rank" academic journals in job applicant dossiers has grown. As Diane Lewis observed in 1973, "theory" was the capstone of the academic-career value set, and, in subsequent years, its centrality within a tightening job market and an overcrowded publication arena—as a sorting mechanism if nothing else—continued to escalate. Increasingly, "not theoretical enough" became a handy criterion for winnowing out excess job application packets. In regard to this, Jeremy Sabloff (2011, 411) has pointed to the growing reliance on peer-reviewed publication counts and citation indexes in making personnel decisions. As Brazilian anthropologist Roberto DaMatta observed of the United States, "the more established a university system is—the more individualistic the intellectual career, the more compartmentalized and autonomous and market-oriented the system of promotions and raises—the more debate tends to be viewed as 'theoretical,' 'technical,' and frankly, 'academic'" (1994, 127).

New theoretical schools, paradigms, vocabulary, and gurus proliferated, and "keeping up" theoretically became either passion or burden. Anthropology as a discipline grew more self-focused and self-referential and less publically accessible and attentive. These shifts were noted by participant observers. Kirin Narayan pointed to "refereed journal articles, dense with theoretical analyses [that] tend to be exclusively of interest to academics initiated into the fellowship of professional discourse" (1993, 680–681). Fredrik Barth worried that "a highly intellectual and internal critique has set priorities and focused interests so that we have lost much of our engagement with the real world and urgent issues. . . . There is much pressure toward a stereotyped originality in American academia which easily produces individual narrowness and local dogmatism, schools, and sects" (1994, 350). Ulf Hannerz observed that "the American academic job market, in its upper regions at least, has indeed seemed more like a marketplace, with its particular logic of competing offers and geographical mobility, and of creating stars and fashion" (2010, 132; see also Sabloff 2011, 411). Moshe Shokeid spotlighted the prominence of "Keynote Speakers at . . . conferences and AAA sessions organized by a strong network of [academic] entrepreneurs" (2007, 316).

In this competitive climate, "theory" became a "commodity," whatever else it might be, and professional gatherings were high-profile sites of what Arjun

Appadurai (without intending this to apply to anthropology) calls "tournaments of value":

> Participation in them is likely to be both a privilege of those in power and an instrument of status contests between them. The currency of such tournaments is also likely to be set apart through well understood cultural diacritics. . . . [W]hat is at issue in such tournaments is not just status, rank, fame, or reputation of actors, but the disposition of the central tokens of value in the society in question. . . . [T]hough such tournaments . . . occur in special times and places, their forms and outcomes are always consequential for the more mundane realities of power and value in ordinary life. (Appadurai 1986, 21)

A major consequence of these post-1973 developments was increasing polarization between those employed at elite institutions, where theory is cultivated (see Harrison 2012), and the actually existing work worlds inhabited by more and more anthropologists.

> Prestigious departments occupy the symbolic center of the academic universe, and their centrality . . . grants them a high degree of control over the resources necessary to do the kind of anthropology that confers professional credibility. Hierarchies of practice and place ensure that aspiring anthropologists who "don't make the grade" are shipped off to the colonies ("the margins"), where long hours, temporary status, lack of leave time, too many committees, too many classes, high student-teacher ratios, and research conducted on the fly make a ticket to the center more improbable with each passing megawork day. (Weston 1997, 177; see also Dereisiewicz 2011; Narayan 1995)

If the anthropological pendulum in recent decades has swung forcefully toward the academic-career complex pole, movement back toward greater mutuality in relation to readerships, publics, and even non–academically employed colleagues has also been set in gear.

In a widely read 1993 article, Narayan called for ethnographic writing to be "accessible . . . laden with stories. It seems more urgent than ever that anthropologists acknowledge that it is *people* and not theoretical puppets who populate our texts, and that we allow these people to speak out from our writings [thus] enacting theory" (1993, 680–681). Jeremy MacClancy exhorted anthropologists "to engage with contemporary realities, in ways meaningful to subjects and readers" (1996, 46). As editor of a book series, Cornell University Press's *Anthropology of Contemporary Issues*, during 1982–2003, as well as a teacher on the lookout for readable ethnographies, I searched for such manuscripts and found them. Indeed, I met four of this volume's coauthors as Cornell series editor (Abusharaf 2002; Guo 2000; Shield 1988; Williams 1988) and was introduced to others through their engaging and readable ethnographic work (Bhachu 1985; Fienup-Reardon 1990; Lobo 1982; Rodríguez 1996).

Also propelling anthropologists in a reader-friendly direction was the inescapable fact, encapsulated by Caroline Brettell in a pithy book title, that today the subjects of ethnographies "read what we write" (Bretell 1993; compare Ames 1986, 74; Okely 1996, 26; Rosaldo 1989, 45). This signaled not simply professional alarm or expanding reader numbers and book sales but, more important, opportunities for greater mutuality between anthropologists and the people and communities they write about. Such mutualities have been major concerns among feminist, lesbian and gay, and African American anthropologists, who expect and welcome nonanthropologist readers who share their perspectives, identities, and backgrounds. This registered strongly in three important essay volumes that, in part, were responses to postmodern theoretical ascendance: Behar and Gordon's *Women Writing Culture* (1995), Lewin and Leap's *Out in the Field* (1996), and McClaurin's *Black Feminist Anthropology* (2001a).

Finally, by the mid-1990s, half of new anthropology PhDs were finding jobs in "applied" rather than in academic arenas (Stocking 2001, 327); moreover, by 2004, the number of anthropology master's degrees conferred was triple the number of doctorates, and two-thirds of master's recipients were members of national anthropological organizations (Fiske et al. 2010). Articles about applied, practicing, collaborative, and public anthropologists working in government, NGO, private sector, and community-based settings, as well as in universities, have become frequent in AAA's *Anthropology News* and *American Anthropologist* and in the Royal Anthropological Institute's *Anthropology Today*. With a majority of academic anthropologists themselves employed outside elite institutions or PhD programs, demand is growing for greater attention to mutuality in teaching and student fieldwork training. Even in elite programs, according to George Marcus, blowback has arrived:

> The priorities of the best [PhD] candidates have shifted. . . . The excitement of theory and academic debate . . . has receded among students in favor of activism, driven by a healthy combination of pragmatics

> and idealism. The "typical" highly motivated candidate today comes with experience from work in the world of NGOs and activist organizations. One can no longer count on a background in the knowledge of, or at least the desire for, the theories and debates that brought students into anthropology previously. (Marcus 2009, 16–17, quoted in Hannerz 2010, 180n; see also Besteman, this volume, Chapter 16)

In this emerging twenty-first century order, ethnography oriented toward mutuality will likely become more acceptable, perhaps even mainstream (Lamphere 2004a). Increasingly, it may incorporate what Liisa Maalki, drawing on human rights work, calls "witnessing" and "testimony" by the ethnographer. She envisions this as "a form of a caring vigilance" (1997, 94–95; compare Lawlor and Mattingly 2001) and proposes it as something to be added to the traditional elements of ethnographic inscription/description and incorporation of "the native's points of view" (see, for example, Abusharaf 2009b, 2011; Besteman 2009; Fienup-Riordan and Rearden 2012; Mullings and Wali 2001; Rodríguez 2006; Sanjek 2009a).

. . . But What Do They Write, and for Whom?

Anthropologists, in fact, do write in a variety of formats, and in their bodies of work, they address many diverse readerships beyond fellow anthropologists. Lewis Henry Morgan, whose foundational ethnography *The League of the Ho-de-no-sau-nee, or Iroquois* (1851) was critical of U.S. Indian policy, in 1876 authored an opinion piece in the national magazine *The Nation* excoriating his government for its recent attack on the Sioux at Little Big Horn (Sanjek 2004). In 1904, Columbia University anthropologist Franz Boas contributed a short piece on West African civilizations, "What the Negro Has Done in Africa," to *The Ethical Record*, a quarterly magazine of the Philadelphia Society for Ethical Culture. This led to an invitation from scholar-activist W. E. B. Du Bois to deliver the 1906 commencement address at Atlanta University, a black institution, which issued Boas's presentation as a pamphlet. Both pieces were reprinted in Boas's posthumous *Race and Democratic Society* (1945), along with other of his writings between 1909 and 1941 "directed at lay audiences" in such venues as *Everybody's Magazine*, *The Dial*, *The New York Evening News*, *The Nation*, *The Christian Register*, and *The American Teacher* (see, however, Sanjek 1994, 2004).

Margaret Mead and Ruth Benedict, both mentored by Boas, wrote for large "lay audiences." Mead's writings included commercially published books with commentary on U.S. sexual and child-rearing patterns—*Coming of Age in Samoa* (1928) and *Growing Up in New Guinea* (1930a)—which preceded her museum series monographs for anthropological colleagues (Mead 1930b, 1934). Mead's other writings aimed at popular audiences included opinion columns during the 1960s and 1970s in *Redbook*, a mass-market woman's magazine. Benedict's *Patterns of Culture* (1934), a comparative study of four cultures including her own, became anthropology's all-time best seller. Her subsequent *Race: Science and Politics* (1940) brought Boasian views of the social and cultural roots of racial thinking to wider audiences (Caffrey 1989, 291–300). A pamphlet version, *The Races of Mankind*, by Benedict and her Columbia University colleague Gene Weltfish (1943), ignited a firestorm when a Kentucky member of the U.S. House of Representatives objected to its distribution to wartime service members as "communist propaganda." Other public figures defended it, and by 1945, more than three quarters of a million copies were in circulation. A children's version, *In Henry's Backyard: The Races of Mankind* (Benedict and Weltfish 1948), followed, and by 1986, Benedict and Weltfish's pamphlet was in its thirty-sixth printing.

Boas also edited and cowrote the discipline's first twentieth century four-field (physical anthropology, linguistics, archaeology, cultural anthropology) textbook, *General Anthropology* (Boas 1938; also see Kottak 1998). During World War II, the United States Armed Forces Institute, part of the War Department, issued a paperback edition "for use . . . in certain educational activities of the armed forces," through which service members "may . . . qualify for a certificate . . . . to use in meeting school or college requirements or in qualifying for a job" after the war (Boas 1944). As anthropology departments and undergraduate enrollments expanded through the 1950s and 1960s, the market for introductory textbooks, often the only exposure to anthropology for millions of students, grew enormously, and more "intro texts" followed.

In addition to ethnographies and journal articles, *Mutuality*'s coauthors, like many of our colleagues, have written for undergraduate anthropology students, general readers, ethnic studies audiences, members of the groups and communities we study, museum goers, schoolteachers, health-care professionals, and policy- and public-opinion audiences. Bailey coauthored a widely used textbook, *Humanity: An Introduction to Cultural Anthropology*, first published in 1988 and now in its tenth edition (Peoples and Bailey 2014). And in 2005, following the death of Vine Deloria, Jr., he took over editorship of the final volume—*Indians in Contemporary Society*—of the Smithsonian Institution's fifteen-volume *Handbook of North American Indians* reference work for library users, general readers, and scholars. The authors in other *Handbook* volumes were mainly anthropologists (from all four fields) who specialized in specific groups and time periods, as did Bailey himself, a scholar of the Osage (Bailey 1973, 1978, 1995, 2001, 2004, 2010; Bailey and Swan 2004). For this volume, however, his forty-nine contributors, half of indigenous backgrounds, came from diverse academic disciplines, including law and Native American studies, and from government agencies and Native-directed institutions. Addressing such topics as activism, land claims and sovereignty, powwows, language programs, theater and literature, tribal colleges, and repatriation, *Indians in Contemporary Society* (Bailey 2008) is held by more than three thousand libraries worldwide.

Many anthropologists teach in ethnic studies programs or departments, and their writings engage the historical, political, and humanistic perspectives of these multidisciplinary fields (see Drake 1980; Hirabayashi 2002b; Johnson 2012; Rosaldo 1985, 1986, 1989; Smedley 2012). Hirabayashi has edited or coedited a half dozen essay collections in Asian American and ethnic studies (Hirabayashi 1998, 2011; Hirabayashi and Hu-DeHart 2002; Hirabayashi, Kikumura-Yano, and Hirabayashi 2002; Kikumura-Yano, Hirabayashi, and Hirabayashi 2005; Xing and Hirabayashi 2003); moreover, following his ethnography of Zapotec migrants in Mexico City (Hirabayashi 1993), his major focus has been the incarceration of Japanese Americans during World War II and its aftermath (Hirabayashi 1995, 1999; Hirabayashi with Shimada 2009; G. Hirabayashi, Hirabayashi, and Hirabayashi 2013). His books are written to be read by those who experienced these events, their family and community members, and their friends, as well as by academics. Lobo also first conducted research among urban migrants, in Lima, Peru (Lobo 1982). Her focus on American Indian issues began soon thereafter and led to a book about the San Francisco Bay Area Native American community (Lobo and Editorial Committee 2002). Meanwhile, she taught Native American studies and coedited two textbooks for this field (Lobo and Peters 2001; Lobo, Talbot, and Morris 2010).

My ethnic studies experiences occurred after New York State funded Queens College to create its Asian/American Center in 1987, and I became acting director for three years. I hired researchers working on PhD dissertations (later published—H. Chen 1990; Khandelwal 2002; Park 1997; Tchen 1999) and initiated a working papers series to make center work and conference papers available without charge to Asian American and Queens community groups, the press, the public, scholars, and students. The papers were staff rather than peer reviewed, edited by me as director, and included papers by center personnel (Chen and Tchen 1989; Leon 1990; Sanjek 1989, 1990a; Sanjek et al. 1991), a Queens College foreign student who later published a novel in English (X. Chen 1990, 2000), and a Westinghouse Science Talent Search national finalist from a Queens high school (Choi 1989). And, like Bailey with Osage readers of his work (see Shaw Duty 2013), Hirabayashi, and Lobo, my Queens colleagues (including Gregory 1998; Ricourt and Danta 2003) and I found there were nonacademic readers of our work in the groups and societies we live among (Sanjek 1998, 2004).[6]

Fienup-Riordan is well-known in Alaska through her many books about the Yup'ik people. Four of her volumes are of "art book" size and production quality and include numerous illustrations and historical or contemporary photographs (Barker, Fienup-Riordan, and John 2010; Fienup-Riordan 1996, 2005b, 2007). Two, *The Living Tradition of Yup'ik Masks* (1996) and *Yuungaqpiallerput/The Way We Genuinely Live: Masterworks of Yup'ik Science and Survival* (2007), accompanied museum exhibitions at Alaskan venues as well as in Washington, D.C., and New York. These works exemplify still another mode of anthropological writing, the museum exhibit catalog (Sabloff 2011), and like the best of this genre, they combine deep scholarship, accessible writing, audience-friendly contextualization of objects and images, and the native's point of view.[7] Increasingly, Fienup-Riordan's books have Yup'ik coauthors and contain precise attribution of each collaborator's words (see Barker, Fienup-Riordan, and John 2010). The evolution of her work might be described as from "when they read what we write" to "when they cowrite what we write."

Moses's efforts as part of the AAA's *RACE: Are We So Different?* Project included the coauthored volume *How Real Is Race?: A Sourcebook on Race, Culture, and Biology* (Mukhopadhyay, Henze, and Moses 2007), written for middle and high school teachers and school of education faculty and intended to improve teaching and encourage class discussion. Moses and *RACE* Project staff also prepared downloadable teacher guides posted on the project's website (Jones et al. 2007a, 2007b). In 2012, the project's companion book, *RACE: Are We So Different?* (Goodman, Moses, and Jones 2012), became available at the museums and science centers where the traveling exhibit appeared through 2014; it is also a stand-alone resource for general readers, students, and scholars.

Anthropologists who focus on aging, disability, illness, injury, and public health use the journals, technical language, and research conventions of health-care professions to communicate with practitioners and policy makers. Shield, who teaches in a medical school, writes for anthropologists (1988, 2002, 2003) but also collaborates with gerontologists and physicians in research, evaluation, and medical school curriculum projects, as well as publishing in their peer-reviewed journals (see Shield et al. 2010a, 2010b, 2011, 2012; Tyler et al. 2011). Her coedited volume, *Improving Aging and Public Health Research: Qualitative and Mixed Methods* (Curry, Shield, and Wetle 2006), has been adopted in health professions courses nationwide. Guo, an applied medical anthropologist, also works and publishes with health professionals (see Guo et al. 2000). Abusharaf's edited book, *Female Circumcision: Multicultural Perspectives* (2006), brought human rights advocates, lawyers, a doctor, NGO program officers, and African and Western anthropologists into dialogue regarding the culturally valued or devalued practices of genital cutting, or mutilation, undergone by more than one hundred million living women and girls, and her contributors assessed cultural, legal, practical, and human rights impediments and strategies to ending these practices in several African countries. Abusharaf has written about this operation in ethnographies of Sudanese migrant women in North America and Khartoum (where it is increasing) (2002, 2009b), but her edited volume moves directly to policy issues and discussion of implementation.

The Gray Zone

Although books, including ethnographies, may influence public and organizational policy debate, direct "hands on" involvement by anthropologists often occurs via "gray literature": commissioned reports with recommendations written for organizations, including NGOs and government agencies (see Kottak 1998). Some reports involve lengthy ethnographic research, but many utilize "rapid assessment" methods that depend on an anthropologist's prior familiarity with a site or similar sites or with a particular problem. A gray literature report might also synthesize available information or use existing organizational records and files. When an analysis is largely quantitative, anthropologists typically draw on prior or current knowledge of underlying cultural and social parameters.

Some reports remain internal documents; others are circulated, sometimes without acknowledgment of individual authorship, to public officials, the press, or various publics, freely or for a price. Much gray literature in the past existed in typescript; other examples were issued as bound reports or pamphlets. Today, gray literature is often posted on organization websites. Agreements or contracts between an anthropologist and organization specify whether or not the content of a report may be used in other writings, including books or peer-reviewed journal articles.

Most contributors to *Mutuality* have authored policy-relevant gray literature resulting from employment or consultancies that, in some cases, provided major or supplemental funding for ongoing research. Writing gray literature is an important part of what many, perhaps most, anthropologists actually do, occasionally or often, and some reports might be read more widely, and by key readerships, than the anthropologist's "theoretical" writings, even on the same topic, in monograph or journal article format (compare Khanna et al. 2008:8).

For example, with funding from the U.S. Agency for International Development, Besteman authored a report on the impact of land title registration in the Somalia village she studied in 1987–1988 (Besteman 1990, 1994, 2010). In 1989, after Bhachu submitted her report *Parental Perspectives on Schooling: An Exploratory Case Study* to the Economic and Social Science Research Council in the United Kingdom, she distributed a second version in accessible language to staff and British and immigrant parents of the school she studied. Expanding on fieldwork about the impact of a dam project on Kuna and other rural communities in Panama (Wali 1989), Wali and Shelton Davis coauthored reports in the early 1990s for the World Bank that reviewed research (including gray literature) on indigenous peoples and tropical forest development in South and Central America (Davis and Wali 1993; Wali 2012). And building on long-term research and residence in the nation's capital (Williams 1988, 1994, 2001; Williams with Pitt 2002), Williams's report to the National Park Service on how Washingtonians use two city parks recommended that the facilities be more responsive to African Americans by commemorating local historical experiences of nineteenth-century freedmen and the twentieth-century civil rights movement (Williams et al. 1997; see also Lamphere 2004a, 434).

My gray literature experience began in 1977, when Lani Sanjek drafted me to analyze the Over 60 Health Clinic's 639 patient records. My report was utilized in funding applications, and its recommendations concerning outreach, record keeping, and the formation of a community board were largely implemented (Sanjek 1977b, 1987, 2009a, 61–73). My second 1977 report, *Employment and Hiring of Women in American Departments of Anthropology: The Five-Year Record, 1972–1977* (Sanjek, Forman, and McDaniel 1979), was written at the request of the Executive Board of the AAA and followed my 1974–1975 service on the association's Committee on the Status of Women in Anthropology (see Sanjek 1978b). After sitting in limbo with an AAA committee for more than a year, the report appeared in the *Anthropology Newsletter* (sent to all AAA members) without prior notification to me, an indication of the tide beginning to turn in the decade-long struggle to implement the 1972 AAA Resolution on "Fair Practices in Employment of Women" (Sanjek 1982a). Both my 1977 reports were primarily quantitative, but they reflected "on the ground" familiarity with the clinic, where I was also an intake and health-screening volunteer, and my anthropology colleagues' attitudes and behavior concerning gender equity in hiring and promotion.

In 1983, after serving on the board of the New York City Coalition for the Homeless for more than a year and chairing its committee on the elderly, I drafted *Crowded Out: Homelessness and the Elderly Poor in New York City*, a report based on government, academic, and advocacy group publications, press accounts, and interviews with shelter and service providers and a near-homeless woman who contacted the New York Gray Panthers office. Shortly after it was published, a staff member of the U.S. House of Representatives Select Committee on Aging requested permission to reprint it in the official record of subcommittee hearings on homeless older Americans (Sanjek 1984a, 2009a, 121–123; see also Sanjek 1982b). In all three of my reports, I worked "in collaboration with activists and communities rather than policy-makers" and operated "as a committed participant and not just an observer" (Besteman 2010, 409, 413; compare Price 2008, 270–271).

Much gray literature is aimed at influencing and changing policy outcomes. Indeed, it is emphasized in professional ethics codes that "among our goals are the dissemination of anthropological knowledge and its use to solve human problems" (American Anthropological Association Statement on Ethics 2012), and that "We should communicate our understanding of human life to the society at large" (Society for Applied Anthropology n.d.). Beyond reports, an additional next step toward shaping public outlooks is writing for nonanthropological readers in magazines, pamphlets, children's publications, and newspaper op-ed columns (as Morgan, Boas, Mead, and Benedict and Weltfish have done; see also Harris 1958, 1967, 1968, and Besteman and Gusterson 2005). I followed my report on homelessness with op-eds in the

Gray Panther national newspaper *Network* (fifty thousand circulation) and in *Newsday* and *West Side Tenants Advance*, a housing newspaper, in New York City (Sanjek 1983b, 1984b, 1985); I later published a piece on the Gray Panthers in the American Museum of Natural History children's magazine *Faces* (Sanjek 1986).

It may come as a surprise to anthropology students to hear that most forms of writing just mentioned—textbooks, reference works, community-oriented writings, museum exhibit catalogs, materials for teachers, gray literature reports, popular magazine and opinion writing, children's materials—count little or not at all in academic hiring, tenure, and promotion decisions, although dissatisfaction with this situation is increasing (American Anthropological Association 2011; Bennett and Khanna 2010; Besteman 2010; Khanna et al. 2008; Sabloff 2011). Although some leading anthropologists, such as Fredrik Barth, assert, "I think it is important to speak out in contexts that are not made up only of anthropologists" (Borofsky 2001), in the academic marketplace, it is ethnographic monographs "that make some kind of contribution to 'theory'" (Kottak 1998, 742) and peer-reviewed journal articles that remain the sole or most significant coin. And here, academic-career complex values continue to outweigh mutuality.

Mutuality in Old and New Media

One of the earliest anthropologist radio guests was Bronislaw Malinowski. His provocative British Broadcasting Corporation (BBC) talk *Science and Religion* in 1930 led to a six-part BBC face-off with Robert Briffault on the topic of marriage in 1931, with the installments also published in the BBC magazine *The Listener* (Malinowski 1962, 256–265; Montagu 1956). In 1950, E. E. Evans-Pritchard presented six BBC talks later published as *Social Anthropology* (Evans-Pritchard 1951), and in 1955, Max Gluckman presented a six-lecture BBC series titled *Custom and Conflict in Africa* (Gluckman 1956). In 1967, Edmund Leach was invited to present the BBC's prestigious Reith Lectures, and the volume *A Runaway World?* followed (Leach 1968).

Meanwhile, in the United States, Margaret Mead made her first radio talk show appearance in 1941 and her television debut on the CBS science series *Adventure* in 1951. She remained a media figure into the 1970s, with appearances that included spots on the late-night *Tonight* show hosted by Johnny Carson (Lutkehaus 2008, 18, 64–65, 171–176, 181–186, 202–204, 210, 254).

During 1951–1953, Walter Goldschmidt supervised production for the National Association of Educational Broadcasters of *Ways of Mankind*, a series of twenty-six half-hour radio programs dramatizing anthropological concepts and findings that was aired on more than eighty educational stations and issued on long-playing records (Social Forces Notice 1953). In 1962, Marvin Harris joined an interdisciplinary Columbia University faculty lecture series that was broadcast in New York on WNEW-TV and nationwide on Metropolitan Broadcasting stations, and his talk was expanded into a short book, *Patterns of Race in the Americas* (Harris 1964). He soon turned to popular writing, beginning with a column in the American Museum of Natural History's magazine *Natural History*, and his book *Cows, Pigs, Wars, and Witches* (Harris 1967, 1974). With this, Harris, too, became a *Tonight* guest of Johnny Carson.

If not as "modern-day Margaret Meads" (Sabloff 2011), numerous anthropologists continued to appear on radio and television. In the 1980s, Alvarez collaborated with Paul Espinosa, a graduate school colleague who became an award-winning documentary film maker. Their coproduction *The Trail North* (1983), shown nationally on PBS, featured Alvarez and focused on his family's history of migration within Baja California and to the United States (see Alvarez 1995a). *The Lemon Grove Incident* (1985), produced and written by Espinosa, dramatized the successful 1931 school desegregation court case in which Alvarez's father was plaintiff and for which the Mexican American community of Lemon Grove, California, near San Diego, organized in support (Alvarez 1986). It was also shown nationally on PBS and received a certificate of merit from the American Bar Association, among other awards.

Mutuality contributor Bhachu has been interviewed about her work and books on BBC radio several times since the 1980s; Lobo was a producer and on-air host of *Living on Indian Time*, a radio show on KPFA in Berkeley, California, between 1984 and 1994; Shield has, over the years, spoken on radio and television about her book on parenting and her research on health-care issues; and during the 2000s, Abusharaf has addressed human rights in Sudan on NPR, Voice of America, and Ontario Public Television. In Chapter 3, Rodríguez recalls her recent exchange with a Taos radio talk show listener; earlier, she was consultant for a 1995 KUNM public radio series, *Farmers of New Mexico*, and in 1999, she wrote and produced *This Town Is Not for Sale: The 1994 Santa Fe Mayoral Election*, a documentary televised on New Mexico PBS station KNME.

In the 1980s, I did several New York City radio talk show programs on housing issues and appeared on two local television news broadcasts the day *Crowded Out* was released by the Coalition for the Homeless. In the late 1990s, I appeared on three half-hour Queens Public Television programs. The first featured twenty paintings of Corona stores and people by "informal artist" (Wali et al. 2002) and block association leader Carmela George. Before the videotaping, we met in her basement studio and agreed upon the order in which we would present and discuss the paintings she had selected. The other programs were an interview of me about my book *The Future of Us All* (1998), by *Flushing Times* reporter Jyoti Thottam (who in 2008 became *Time* magazine's South Asia Bureau chief), and my interview of Carmela and two neighbors following a *Daily News* feature about their block titled "Melting Pot Avenue." These productions were directed by Richard George, Carmela's son, using public access studio equipment and facilities. In the following years, I heard from several Queens residents and Queens College students that they had seen one or more of the programs, which re-aired several times.

My fieldwork and book on neighborhood change in Queens also led to appearances in New York City on WNYC's *On the Line* with Brian Lehrer and nationwide on NPR programs *Talk of the Nation* with Ray Suarez, *The World* with Marco Werman, and *All Things Considered* with Noah Adams (Sanjek 2004). In 2009, I was interviewed about my book *Gray Panthers* (Sanjek 2009a) on television book programs hosted by the distinguished journalists Brian Lockman—*PA Books* on Pennsylvania Cable Network—and John Seigenthaler—*A Word on Words* on Nashville Public Television.

With the rise of digital formats, Melissa Checker forecasts an expanded mediascape: "We are on the brink of a new anthropology that makes the most of novel forms of communication to disseminate knowledge widely and freely" (2009, 167). Anthropology in the twenty-first century now inhabits websites—such as those of the AAA *RACE* Project, the Calista Elders Council and the *Masterworks of Yup'ik Science and Survival* museum exhibit, and "The Somali Bantu Experience: From East Africa to Maine." "The Shift of Land," a website originating in a KRZA radio series about environmental issues, features online podcasts with Rodríguez on water, *acequias*, culture, and ritual, as do KSFR-FM's *Santa Fe Radio Café* and Cultural Energy Independent Radio and Television's *Radio Rio*. Many anthropologists also appear in productions accessible via YouTube videos, including "Parminder, A Cosmopolitan" and "Film Director Mira Nair and Professor Parminder Bhachu: A Conversation," Zibin Guo's "Seated Tai Ji: Strengthening Mind & Body," and "Digging Deep: An Interview with Brett Williams," a discussion of Williams's fieldwork and projects in Washington, D.C.

Mutuality in Museums and Public Programs

A continuing process of "democratization" marks the history of museums over the past two centuries. From the 1960s onward, the definition of "the public" has expanded to include all classes, racial and ethnic groups, indigenous peoples, ages, and impairments or disabilities. This has affected how exhibits and events are conceived and presented; how museum programs and holdings are made accessible or are externally located or repatriated; and how public voices are welcomed and incorporated. Democratization has not been completed—clashes between academic-career values and mutuality persist in museum worlds—and anthropology is deeply involved in its past, present, and future (Ames 1986).

In the 1920s, my mother, then a child, lived a block away from the American Museum of Natural History (AMNH), founded in 1869, and played there on Saturdays, even climbing into the Northwest Coast Haida canoe. In the 1950s, my parents brought me there often, and, like Yolanda Moses's childhood trips to the Los Angeles County Museum of Natural History, these visits propelled me toward anthropology (see Jacknis 2004). I was deeply pleased when, in 1999, I was invited to speak about "The Future of Us All in Multicultural Queens" to four weekend visitor audiences at the AMNH as part of the Education Department's Asian Pacific American Heritage Celebration, and I greatly enjoyed the questions and discussion. In 2002, I moderated an AMNH panel on Sikh, Afghan, and Arab communities in Brooklyn and Queens, again organized by the Education Department; as the panel occurred just four months after the September 11, 2001, World Trade Center jet plane attacks, discussion focused on that day's impact on the lives of South Asian and Middle Eastern New Yorkers (see Checker 2011). In 2008, I returned to speak about museums and publics at a colloquium, this time organized by AMNH anthropology curators, on "New Directions in Collaborative and Engaged Anthropology," joining copresenters Yolanda Moses, Alaka Wali, and Leith Mullings, among others.

At another such major institution, the Field Museum of Natural History, Wali has worked from the inside out, building alliances with neighborhood-based community programs, cultural organizations, and city agencies, and creating collaborative research projects in Chicago neighborhoods. She has also worked from the margins to the center, starting in a grant-funded research and outreach unit and later moving to curating exhibitions, adding to existing collections, and defining new areas for acquisition (del Campo and

Wali 2007; Wali 2006a, 2006b, 2012; Wali et al. 2003; Wali, Severson, and Longoni 2002; Westphal et al. 2005).

In 1999, I spoke about the history and current situation of Chinese in Queens at a much smaller venue, the Museum of Chinese in the Americas (MoCA, now Museum of Chinese in America), founded in 1980 in New York City as the Chinatown History Project. MoCA is one of many community-based museums, or cultural or heritage centers, created since the 1960s by groups, including indigenous peoples, who wish to represent themselves (Ames 1986; Clifford 1997a, 107–145; Jacknis 2002). Hirabayashi's coedited volume *Common Ground: The Japanese American National Museum and the Culture of Collaborations* (Kikumura-Yano, Hirabayashi, and Hirabayashi 2005) provides a valuable case study of another such institution, which opened in Los Angeles, California, in 1992. The book's contributors—curators, designers, a board member, activists, scholars—describe a wide range of outreach activities to Japanese American and other publics, including traveling exhibits, oral history and home movie collections, and dialogue with Jewish and Arab Americans and with Nikkei in Japan and Brazil.

Anthropologists not affiliated with museums also participate in activities that bring their professional perspectives to general audiences. Columbia faculty member Gene Weltfish created her own public program to follow publication of the pamphlet *The Races of Mankind* (Benedict and Weltfish 1943). In 1943,

> Her . . . determination was to give major attention to "The Race Problem" as a public service beyond university teaching. She established a Community Council [that] focus[ed] on racial conflict between Morningside Avenue [in Harlem] and Morningside Heights (the [adjacent] locale of [Columbia] University). . . . G.W. made an extensive tour of the country lecturing on race and racial conflict at the request of churches, clubs, museums, schools—from Texas to Toronto. She presented as many as three hundred public lectures of one kind or another in a single year. (Diamond 1980, 354; see also Price 2004, 109–135; 2008, 27–30, 35–36, 40, 46–47, 49, 54, 64, 164, 201, 265–283)

In 1960, Columbia anthropologist Marvin Harris participated in a two-day "Emergency Action Conference on South Africa" at the Carnegie Endowment International Center near the United Nations in New York City. Organized by the American Committee on Africa (see Harris 1958) and co-sponsored by the NAACP, Americans for Democratic Action, and three labor unions, Oliver Tambo of the African National Congress gave the opening address, Jackie Robinson spoke on "American Action Against Apartheid," and other Africans and black and white Americans, including Harris, conducted workshops on U.S. investment, an import boycott, U.S. Africa policy, and people-to-people contacts. It was unlikely that such a public program could take place in a major museum at the time; yet, a few decades later, programs addressing racial inequality and human rights, such as the AAA *RACE* exhibit, are museum fare.

Like Weltfish in her day and Harris in his, and like many colleagues past and present, Besteman sees mutuality between anthropologists and the people and communities we study and write about as central to our professional being. In addition to her writings and the Somali Bantu website she cocreated, her advocacy in Maine involves newspaper op-eds; speaking at hospitals, schools, and libraries; meetings with public officials; service on government committees; a traveling museum exhibit; and producing and distributing a free English language–learning book in Somalia's two official languages (Besteman 2010).

Mutuality in Health-Care Settings

My experience as an applied and advocacy anthropologist at the Over 60 Health Clinic in 1977–1978 included memorable encounters with clinic service users as a volunteer (Sanjek 2009a, 64–66), but my major tasks involved data analysis, a report, drafting funding proposals, recording clinic board meeting minutes, and advocacy in public policy and political arenas (Sanjek 1977b, 1987, 2009a), activities similar to those of Stephen and Jean Schensul (Schensul 1973, 1974; Schensul and Schensul 1978) and Sue-Ellen Jacobs (1974a, 1974b, 1979) in other community-based health-care settings.

Shield writes vividly of her personal relationships with residents, family members, and care providers in nursing homes (Shield 1988, 2003; see also Miller and Shield 2007; Wetle et al. 2004), an arena where she also undertook direct advocacy as an ethics committee member. At the policy level, while director of education and research at the Jewish Home in Providence, Rhode Island, during 1986–1989, she led workshops and conferences on topics including bioethics, restraints, bereavement, sexuality, and physical design for nursing home staff, residents, community members, and Providence-area health facility administrators. During 1989–1994, Shield was director of research and education for "Aging 2000: Directions for Elder Care in Rhode Island," a statewide initiative led by policy guru Ira Magaziner, for which she developed a research plan, organized numerous public meetings, and wrote reports. Later, at Brown University, she served as project director of a four-year (2006–2010), grant-funded program aimed at integrating geriatric training into the medical school curriculum (Besdine et al. 2011; Shield et al. 2010a; Shield et al. 2012). Guo's "Thirteen Postures of Wheelchair Taijiquan," first introduced in China, continues to find new learners and applications in the United States where his current research involves collaboration with University of Tennessee–Chattanooga nursing school faculty on health improvement strategies for low-income elderly and chronic mentally ill populations.

Like his Taijiquan student Paul for Guo, her correspondent Mrs. H for Shield (and Aessu for me, and fieldwork acquaintances of other *Mutuality* coauthors), for Jacobs, her interaction with a particular person, "Desmond," was a wellspring of mutuality that shaped how she saw the world and inspired her to "make good." She encountered him through participation in a long-term study of "thirty African American children with illnesses, disabilities, or special health care needs, their families, and the practitioners who serve them" initiated by University of Southern California colleagues in the Department of Occupational Science and Occupational Therapy (Lawlor and Mattingly 2001). Through Jacobs' account, she and Desmond shape and inspire us too.

Anthropology in the Balance

In Chapter 1, Bailey recalls that "as a young faculty member, after returning from Washington, D.C., where I had testified before the U.S. House of Representatives Subcommittee on Indian Affairs, I was told by a university administrator to 'stop wasting my time,' and that I needed to work on publishing 'professional' articles." Many anthropologists, contributors to this volume and others, could relate similar experiences of such institutional assertions of academic-career complex values over personal inclinations to mutuality. In Chapter 9, Alvarez sees this as a "fault line of the discipline" that he has crossed and recrossed throughout his career. Yet he stresses that "the tensions and conflicts" between mutuality and anthropology's "canon of professional goals and methods" can be a "productive force" and "[reveal] the creative possibilities and potential of our field." In Chapter 7, Hirabayashi writes, with gratitude, about his father, anthropologist and activist James Hirabayashi, who taught him to balance mutuality and scholarship at an early stage of his career.

My Brazil and Ghana fieldwork experiences—as an outsider whom no one invited—left lasting satisfactions in terms of academic-career values but also a belief that this was not all there was to anthropology. Values I absorbed during the 1960s continued to animate me, as did a wish that my anthropological commitments "at home" might somehow expand beyond teaching in my city's public university. Both my Gray Panther and Elmhurst-Corona, Queens, experiences—deep grooves professionally, personally, temporally—confirmed for me that disciplinary values and mutuality could be compatible. The positive responses to my books *The Future of Us All* and *Gray Panthers* from Queens neighborhood activists and residents, Gray Panther members and allies, and journalists and public office holders have meant as much to me as those from my anthropological peers. Both matter.

This sense of balance did not arrive early or easily, and many times over the years I felt I was living parallel lives, one inside anthropology and one outside it. But what was I if not an anthropologist? As Rodríguez concludes in Chapter 3, anthropology departments are designed to propagate "extractive" fieldwork, not collaboration and participatory research, yet she is not ready to abandon anthropology either: "The full mutual approach may become a kind of guerilla anthropology in that the first master is the research community/team itself. . . . The second, inner master remains the theory building intrinsic to sociocultural anthropology. . . . I do not mean to imply that any of this is easy, but I do consider it possible and worth attempting."

Perhaps one resolution of this clash of value systems is to acknowledge that anthropology departments not only teach Anthropology in its overt, canonical sense but also, tacitly, create opportunities for each student to fashion their own "my anthropology." My analogy is to the concept "my music" presented in the revealing book *My Music: Explorations of Music in Daily Life*, by ethnomusicologist Charles Keil and colleagues (Crafts, Cavicchi, and Keil 1993). They report on how the people they interviewed actually enjoy, experience, and use music—what they listen to, search out, may perform with others, keep returning to in their heads. "My anthropology" is similar—it is the anthropology we each create as we read, hear speakers, discuss, remember, synthesize, conduct fieldwork, write, cite, and use our anthropology to understand the world. Alvarez points at this when he observes that "each of us brings a nuanced interpretation of the canon" and that "as individuals, we bring varied . . . versions of mutuality to" canonical Anthropology. "Anthropology's World" (Hannerz 2010) houses both Anthropology and a multiplicity of "my anthropologies."

My "my anthropology," yours, and everyone's begins in "the wider social worlds in which we have grown up and in which we live as persons, actors, and citizens" (see the introduction to this book). For many anthropologists, and increasingly among students, academic-career complex values are unsuccessful in eliminating these deeper roots of "my anthropology." It is true that each "anthropologist has a unique genealogy . . . tracing her or his relationships to the ideas, institutions, and social networks of the profession" (Darnell 2001, 24), true that canonical Anthropology is a component of every "my anthropology." But anthropology's world (Hannerz 2010) is enriched by allowing, and even welcoming, everyone's "my anthropology" to include the values "we place upon mutually positive relations with the people we study, work with, write about and for, and communicate with . . . as anthropologists" (Introduction).

None of this is easy, as Rodríguez cautions. We need to reconsider how hiring, promotion, and tenure are evaluated (American Anthropological Association 2011; Bennett and Khanna 2010; Besteman 2010; Khanna et al. 2008; Sabloff 2011), and not be naïve about forces in the academy that support or resist such reconsideration. And maybe we need to broaden anthropology curricula, including "writing culture" courses, to expose students early to the many "modes of representation" anthropologists past and present have used to engage with diverse publics.

If more mutuality is likely to be part of anthropology's future, we have stories to tell, like those in this book, about how and why it matters. And we take our lead with Lobo in Chapter 11 that "we answer this question together, through collaborative thought and action."

Notes

Introduction

In addition to the inspiration and cooperation of the coauthors of this book, I wish to acknowledge the expert editing of Catherine Chilton and Erica Ginsburg of the University of Pennsylvania Press, and the support and assistance of Peter Agree, George C. Bond, Damon Dozier, Paul Espinosa, Ira Jacknis, Barbara Rylko-Bauer, Lani Sanjek, and Rachel Taube.

1. This chapter's title and my thinking about my own and my coauthors' careers in terms of "deep grooves" derive from Charles Keil and Steven Feld's *Music Grooves* (1994; Sanjek 2002). Only later did I realize it might be construed as a variation on Clifford Geertz's well-known essay "Deep Play" (1973, 412–452), which is not my intention.

Chapter 2

1. This chapter draws upon Moses 2004, 2007, 2010a, 2010b, 2011; Moses and Jones 2011; Overbey and Moses 2006; and "The Making of *RACE: Are We So Different?*," a talk presented at the Smithsonian Institution National Museum of Natural History, June 17, 2011.

2. Here is the itinerary—2007: Wright Museum of African American History, Detroit, Michigan; Exploration Place, Inc., Wichita, Kansas. 2008: Liberty Science Center, Jersey City, New Jersey; Mashantucket Pequot Museum and Research Center, Mashantucket, Connecticut; Cleveland Museum of Natural History, Cleveland, Ohio. 2009: Cincinnati Museum Center, Cincinnati, Ohio; Franklin Institute, Philadelphia, Pennsylvania; California Science Center, Los Angeles, California. 2010: Missouri Historical Society History Museum, St. Louis, Missouri; Institute of Texan Cultures, San Antonio, Texas; Lawrence Hall of Science, Berkeley, California; Science Center of Iowa, Des Moines, Iowa; Mayo Clinic, Rochester, Minnesota; Riverside Metropolitan Museum, Riverside, California; Arizona Science Center, Phoenix, Arizona; Kalamazoo Valley Museum, Kalamazoo, Michigan. 2011: Museum of Science, Boston, Massachusetts; Discovery Place,

Charlotte, North Carolina; Santa Barbara Museum of Natural History, Santa Barbara, California; Louisiana State Museum, New Orleans, Louisiana; Smithsonian National Museum of Natural History, Washington, D.C.; The Health Museum, Houston, Texas; Museum of Life and Science, Durham, North Carolina. 2012: Science Museum of Virginia, Richmond, Virginia; Center of Science and Industry, Columbus, Ohio; University of Northern Iowa Museums, Cedar Falls, Iowa; Oregon Museum of Science and Industry, Portland, Oregon; Maryland Science Center, Baltimore, Maryland; ECHO Lake Aquarium and Science Center, Burlington, Vermont. 2013: Rochester Museum and Science Center, Rochester, New York; Museum of Science and History, Jacksonville, Florida; University of Michigan, Ann Arbor, Michigan; Pacific Science Center, Seattle, Washington; The Breman Museum, Atlanta, Georgia; Miami Museum of Science, Miami, Florida. 2014: The Pink Palace, Memphis, Tennessee; Carnegie Natural History Museum, Pittsburgh, Pennsylvania; The North Museum, Lancaster, Pennsylvania; History Colorado, Denver, Colorado; Illinois Holocaust Museum, Skokie, Illinois. 2015: The Muhammad Ali Center, Louisville, Kentucky.

In 2015, one of the two larger versions of the *Race* exhibit will return to the Science Museum of Minnesota for long-term installation, and the smaller version will begin long-term display at the San Diego Museum of Man. The second large version will continue to tour through 2018.

3. The board members were Michael Blakey (College of William and Mary), Louis Casagrande (Children's Museum of Boston), Alan Goodman (Hampshire College), Robert Hahn (Centers for Disease Control and Prevention), Faye Harrison (University of Florida), Thomas Holt (University of Chicago), Janis Hutchinson (University of Houston), Marvin Krislov (Oberlin College), Richard Lewontin (Harvard University), Jeffrey Long (University of New Mexico), Shirley Malcom (American Association for the Advancement of Science), Carol Mukhopadhyay (San Jose State University), Michael Omi (University of California, Berkeley), Kyeyoung Park (University of California, Los Angeles), Kenneth Prewitt (Columbia University), Enid Schildkrout (Museum for African Art), Theodore Shaw (NAACP Legal Defense and Educational Fund), Marcelo Suarez-Orozco (New York University), David Hurst Thomas (American Museum of Natural History), Russell Thornton (University of California, Los Angeles), and Arlene Torres (City University of New York).

4. The organizations included the American Association of Museums, the American Academy of Forensic Sciences, the American Association for the Advancement of Science, the American Association of Physical Anthropologists, the American Historical Association, the American Political Science Association, the American Psychological Association, the American Society of Human Genetics, the American Sociological Association, the American Statistical Association, the Association of American Law Schools, the Human Biology Association, the Linguistic Society of America, the National Coalition for Health Professional Education in Genetics, and the Society for the Psychological Study of Social Issues. The institutions were the California Science Center Foun-

dation, the Field Museum of Natural History, the Franklin Institute, the Louisville Science Center, the New Mexico Museum of Natural History and Science, the Pacific Science Center, and the Smithsonian National Museum of Natural History.

5. Kamari Clark, Ian Haney López, Faye Harrison, Nina Jablonski, Kenneth Kidd, Carol Mukhopadhyay, Michael Omi, Nell Irvin Painter, Mica Pollock, Susan Reverby, Audrey Smedley, Deborah Thomas, Arlene Torres, Bonnie Urciuoli, and Joseph Watkins.

6. On the diverse and intergenerational speaker roster were Dawn Baum (Native American Rights Fund), David Bositis (Joint Center for Political and Economic Studies), Toby Chaudhuri (Campaign for America's Future), Farai Chideya (journalist and author), George Curry (*Philadelphia Inquirer* columnist), Joseph Gaskins (Human Rights Campaign), Brenda Girton-Mitchell (National Council of Churches), Jehmu Greene (Women's Media Center), Eric Jolly (Science Museum of Minnesota), Mark Jurkowitz (Pew Research Project for Excellence in Journalism), Shelby Knox (reproductive rights activist), Melissa Lazarin (Center for American Progress), Marc Mauer (Sentencing Project), Heather McGhee (Demos), Latoya Peterson (Racialicious), Sayyid Sayeed (Islamic Society of North America), Rinku Sen (Colorlines.com), Hilary Shelton (NAACP), Doua Thor (Southeast Asia Resource Action Center), and Ronald Walters (University of Maryland).

Chapter 4

I am indebted to the many men and women throughout southwest Alaska who have so generously shared their knowledge. I am also grateful to the Calista Elders Council, especially Alice Rearden, Mark John, and the CEC's board of elders, who guide our work. Much of what I say is drawn from our most recent book, *Ellavut/Our Yup'ik World and Weather* (Rearden and Fienup-Riordan 2011), which Alice and I authored together. I have also drawn from the introduction I wrote for *Words of the Real People: Alaska Native Literature in Translation* (Fienup-Riordan and Kaplan 2007) as well as a paper I presented in a session honoring Julie Cruikshank at the 2011 AAA annual meeting in Montreal and published as "Linking Local and Global" in *Polar Geography* 37 (1): 5–23 (2014); this chapter is a revised and expanded version of that article. We are deeply grateful to the National Science Foundation, both to Polar Programs and the Bering Ecosystem Study Program (BEST), for funding our work. Special thanks to Roger Sanjek for including me in the original session on mutuality in anthropology hosted at the 2011 AAA annual meeting.

1. Each elder's contribution cited is identified by name, Calista Elders Council gathering date, transcript page number, and place of residence. Transcripts are housed at CEC's Anchorage office.

2. Many have written about the relationship between human communities and the environment. Although the concept of environmental adaptation has a long history in

anthropology, newer approaches are beginning to emerge that emphasize the cultural significance of weather and climate. See especially Basso 1996; Ingold 2000; Strauss and Orlove 2003.

3. To date, CEC has produced four sets of "paired" books: *Wise Words of the Yup'ik People: We Talk to You Because We Love You* (Fienup-Riordan 2005a) and *Yupiit Qanruyutait/Yup'ik Words of Wisdom* (Rearden et al. 2005); *Yup'ik Elders at the Ethnologisches Museum Berlin: Fieldwork Turned on Its Head* (Fienup-Riordan 2005b) and *Ciuliamta Akluit/Things of Our Ancestors* (Meade and Fienup-Riordan 2005); *Yuungnaqpiallerput/The Way We Genuinely Live: Masterworks of Yup'ik Science and Survival* (Fienup-Riordan 2007) and *Paitarkiutenka/My Legacy to You* (Andrew 2008); *Ellavut/Our Yup'ik World and Weather: Continuity and Change on the Bering Sea Coast* (Fienup-Riordan and Rearden 2012) and *Qaluyaarmiuni Nunamtenek Qanemciput/Our Nelson Island Stories: Meanings of Place on the Bering Sea Coast* (Rearden and Fienup-Riordan 2011).

Chapter 6

1. The following information comes from an undated U.S. Veterans Administration file on Richard Schneidewind. Many thanks to Keith Eirinberg for his help with this research.

2. *Jusis* and *piñas* were identified by Patricia Afable in an e-mail message, August 31, 2007.

3. Several anthropologists have conducted research among "Igorot" groups from the 1930s onward: see the many publications of Roy F. Barton, Felix M. Keesing, Fred Eggan, Harold C. Conklin, Edward P. Dozier, Albert S. Bacdayan, and Deirdre McKay.

Chapter 7

I dedicate this chapter to my late father, James Akira Hirabayashi (1926–2012), who was also my teacher, colleague, and friend. Many thanks to colleagues Jeffrey H. Cohen, Akemi Kikumura-Yano, and Tritia Toyota, who read the manuscript and gave me comments, and to Erica Ginsburg and Catherine Chilton at the University of Pennsylvania Press for their editorial suggestions. To Roger Sanjek I owe gratitude for suggesting that I write a chapter on mutuality, and for his encouragement and support as I grappled with this critically important theme.

1. Sylvia Rodríguez (Chapter 3) offers an instructive overview of the two approaches in her thoughtful autoethnography of research in her home town.

2. An example of the point of view that objectivity is the supreme virtue in ethnographic research can be found in Emerson and Pollner 2001.

3. In what I consider a mainstream fashion, "mutuality" has been discussed in terms of the close relationship that field researchers can develop with their research subjects and has been seen as a special kind of relationship that evolves after an informant, so to speak, becomes a friend. Here, information, along with feelings of identification and

support, flow back and forth in reciprocal fashion between researcher and previously distanciated subject. For this and allied mainstream approaches to mutuality, see Pina-Cabral 2013. A similar kind of account is presented by Pitts and Day (2007), who discuss a "stage model of participant-researcher relationships in fieldwork"; the stage they term "partnership" (189, 194), is similar to mainstream anthropologists' portrayal of mutuality. Other recent references to mutuality are multiple and varied, and anthropological discussions of the term are not limited to researcher/subject relationships. Gudeman (2009) uses the concept of mutuality to characterize noncapitalist economic formations, and Dominguez (2012) deploys the concept to address dilemmas of "anthropology in the world." I cite these references only to signal that my own chapter will explore mutuality from an autobiographical angle, unlike these discussions, which consider mutuality from the standpoint of the conduct of social research or considerably more broadly. It is also worth noting that although I view mutuality in a basically positive light, others (Andrews 2010; Warren 1984) take it to be inherently problematic.

4. The essays in Gronseth and Davis's edited collection (2010) approach mutuality in terms of a phenomenology centered on feelings that develop between anthropological fieldworkers and informants. For similar treatments, see Davies and Spencer 2010. In this context, it is worth noting that early on, anthropologist Carol A. B. Warren (1984) warned against the naïveté of assuming that mutuality between researcher and informants was a solution to ethical and political dilemmas raised in fieldwork. Andrews (2010) makes a similar point in her examination of a Mexican protorevolutionary social movement that self-consciously tried to establish terms of mutuality with its allies.

5. I have published one piece (Hirabayashi 2002a) that details how mutuality evolved between myself as researcher and a Japanese American community-based organization in Los Angeles that was dedicated to winning redress and reparations from the federal government for mass removal and incarceration during the 1940s. In that case, two years of meetings and educational forums with this group sharpened my understanding of the collective losses entailed, specifically in terms of the destruction of prewar community institutions and critical mass. As I suggest therein, the relationships I developed with Japanese American redress and reparations organizations in the early 1980s were predicated on previous research experiences I had with my father during the 1970s.

6. I drew from these interview materials for an early publication (Hirabayashi 1986b).

7. My father and I later edited a book based on my uncle Gordon Hirabayashi's letters and diaries that contains a chapter detailing my grandfather and grandmother's backgrounds and the family's prewar life in a small farming enclave south of Seattle, Washington (Hirabayashi, Hirabayashi, and Hirabayashi 2013).

8. I published an extended version of my half of our joint testimony (Hirabayashi 1986a). For a record of the hearing, which cites both the written and transcribed testimony Jim and I jointly presented in 1981, see Herzig-Yoshinaga and Lee 2012.

9. The main point of my book *Cultural Capital* (Hirabayashi 1993) was that Zapotec

cultural notions of *paisanazgo*, rooted in practices long held in their Oaxacan mountain communities, were reenergized and refashioned for new purposes in the context of their nation's capital.

10. Jerome Bruner was one of my father's favorite writers about the psychology of learning; see Bruner 1996. Bruner, as far as I can remember, was the source of Jim's interest in the idea of "tacit" knowledge transmission.

11. For a brief online account of my involvement in Bay Area bands, see http://www.bay-area-bands.com/bab00026.htm.

12. Kendis used the phrase "a matter of comfort" to title her study of the Japanese American community in Gardena, California (Kendis 1989). Rodríguez (Chapter 3) discusses "home" as the site of her fieldwork.

13. In my doctoral dissertation (Hirabayashi 1981), I described my contribution to developing a newsletter for the Zapotec migrant community in Mexico City. I included a long discussion of why it was important to give something back to one's respondents. It is now revealing that this "applied" dimension of my first sustained anthropological fieldwork was deleted from the formal publication of my research findings in the book that was derived from the dissertation (Hirabayashi 1993).

14. To a certain extent, the role of friendship in ethnographic fieldwork is relevant to mutuality as Jim and I practiced it. For an intriguing discussion, see Tillman-Healy 2003.

15. I am aware of extended discussion about the merits of "insider" research but am reluctant to assume that what I am discussing here is exactly that. I have never considered myself a full "insider" in any of but one or two of the Japanese American local community organizations I have belonged to during the past forty years. And I have never considered carrying out fieldwork "on" any of these organizations, only with them or on their behalf. For a detailed analysis of interests at stake in terms of an "insider" research paradigm, from a Chicano/a studies viewpoint, see Chavez 2008. From the standpoint of American Indian Studies scholars, who often participate in this debate, readers may consult a thoughtful essay by Innes (2009). And for a pertinent discussion relevant to mutuality as both method and epistemology in relation to collaborative fieldwork strategies, see Rappaport 2008.

Chapter 8

I dedicate this chapter to the memory of the late Bernard Magubane, to Ambassador Mohamed Abdel Majid Ahmed for his high expectations, and to James C. Faris for his keen interest in both my trajectory and that of Sudanese anthropology at large.

Chapter 9

1. In 1972, I began Stanford University's International Development Education Center (SIDEC), a doctoral program in international educational development, but a year later I was accepted into Stanford's anthropology PhD program.

2. My cohort included Juan Garcia, Martha Ramirez, Steve Arvizu, Willie Baber, Carole Lavale, Bill Demarest, Robin Wright, and Karen Sacks. Cohorts that followed included Ted Gordon, Faye Harrison, Ruth Wilson, Tony Vaska, Leo Chavez, Paul Espinosa, Juan Felipe Herrera, and others.

3. I had entered Stanford with a strong interest in anthropology and education, and in fact, it was George Spindler who initially supported my application to the anthropology department. My MA thesis at Stanford focused on the ethnography of an alternative high school. Educational ethnography would carry me into a variety of anthropology and education venues throughout my career. At Teachers College, I was a postdoctoral fellow in the Institute for Urban and Minority Education (IUME), under the direction of Edmond Gordon. I moved from New York and TC to work in bilingual education at the Cross Cultural Resource Center. At Arizona State University, my first tenured academic position, I worked closely with the Project for the Improvement for Minority Education and the Office of Youth Preparation. These experiences centered on minority and disenfranchised school youth, high school success, and college entrance. I have participated in school evaluations using ethnography in New York City, Washington, D.C., Seattle, and throughout the state of Arizona, and I did teacher training in Micronesia, the Northern Mariana Islands, and Belau.

Chapter 10

1. I was working with the Environment and Conservation Program (ECP), begun in 1994. Its staff was dedicated to using rapid assessment methods for biodiversity identification, from the results of which they would make recommendations for the conservation of large landscapes in the Amazon-Andes interface in South America. The ECP was very successful in raising funds, and in 2004, ECP and the Center for Cultural Understanding and Change, which I headed, joined together to form the Environment, Culture, and Conservation Division.

2. The film is available from Alexander Street Press through their Ethnographic Video Online series and can be accessed at the following URL: https://www.academicvideostore.com/subjects/anthropology?page=31.

3. The study was done under the auspices of the Chicago Center for Arts Policy at Columbia College. The center was dedicated to "democratizing" arts practices and advocating for arts policies that broadened arts participation. The center's directors commissioned the study of the "informal arts" to demonstrate that arts have a broader base than is conventionally acknowledged. Although other arts policy researchers had alluded to the broader participation of people in art making, our study was the first to examine the phenomena qualitatively and in such depth (Wali, Severson, and Longoni 2002).

4. Social asset mapping is a methodology pioneered by urban planners Jody Kretzmann and John McKnight (1993) to counteract culture-of-poverty paradigms. We modified their methods to include an environmental component.

Chapter 11

1. For more information about TOCA, go to www.tocaonline.org.

Chapter 14

1. For more information about the Anacostia Riverkeeper organization, go to its website, www.anacostiariverkeeper.org.

Chapter 15

1. This work is supported by grants from the National Institutes of Health (nos. 1R01HD38878 and 1R01HD38878-01A1S2). Singer, Glang, and Williams (1996) report that annually, more than one hundred thousand children and youth (from birth to age twenty-one) are hospitalized with ABI; roughly one third of these injuries are so severe that the children experience long-term disabilities (May Institute 1993; Rivara and Mueller 1986). The umbrella term *ABI* often includes internal brain injury that has occurred since birth, including from stroke, brain hemorrhage, and tumor. TBIs often result after birth from such external traumas as motor vehicle accidents, acts of violence, sports and recreational injuries, electric shocks, falls, and blows to the head. Children with moderate to severe ABI and TBI, such as the three children I followed, sometimes share symptoms, including initial (or enduring) loss of coordination and balance, changes in personality and behavior, increased agitation and aggression, dizziness, memory loss, disinhibition (difficulty not acting on inappropriate thoughts or actions), depression, or fatigue, among other social and physical impairments (Gronwall, Wrightson, and Waddel 2002; Schoenbrodt 2001; Singer et al. 1996).

2. All names used to describe research participants are pseudonyms.

3. The Boundary Crossing Research Team's projects included *Boundary Crossing: Re-situating Cultural Competence* (#2 RO1 HD 38878, 2005–2009), funded by the National Institute of Child Health and Human Development; *Boundary Crossing: A Longitudinal and Ethnographic Study* (#R01 HD 38878, 2000–2004), funded by the National Center for Medical Rehabilitation Research, National Institute of Child Health and Human Development, National Institutes of Health; and *Crossing Cultural Boundaries: An Ethnographic Study* (#MCJ 060745, 1996–1999), funded by the Maternal and Child Health Bureau.

4. "Partnering up" and "boundary crossing" are key analytical distillations of the Boundary Crossing Study.

Chapter 16

Thanks to Roger Sanjek, Maple Razsa, Mary Beth Mills, William Hope, Britt Halvorson, and Karin Friederic for their comments on early drafts, to audiences at the University of Washington and University of California, Berkeley, and to Janelle Taylor and Bill Hanks.

1. I wish to be clear that in defining collaborators as "subjective equals" I do not mean to imply that power dynamics are absent. Obviously this is never the case. Anthropologists are "disciplined" by their interlocutors even as their class and citizenship status may afford them other kinds of power. I am trying to get at the ways in which ethnographic love works through these power gradients to produce mutuality, as a form of engagement, not of equalizing.

2. Although my discussion is oriented toward the interpersonal dimension of ethnographic praxis, mutuality and ethnographic love may not depend on face-to-face encounters but may also emerge from sustained engagement in collaborative projects with large groups and networks, including those mediated through technology. See, for example, Boellstorff 2008.

3. Pina-Cabral (2013) writes, "The ethnographer and the informant are not only exchanging information, they are jointly attentive to the world. Being jointly attentive, however, is a gesture that goes beyond communication, as it is formative of the worldview of those involved. The desire to help mutual understanding is part and parcel of the ethnographic process. The ethnographer affects his informants in their future life choices quite as much as their concerns and fascinations affect his work, his personality, and the worldviews of his future students" (261).

4. *The Somali Bantu Experience: From East Africa to Maine*: http://wiki.colby.edu/display/AY298B/Home;jsessionid=11AFB233AC87FA9EA2E0415087F8F226.

5. João de Pina-Cabral (2013) argues that Sahlins is incorrect in asserting that kinship is "a separate realm of sociality" (269).

Conclusion

1. In a critique of fieldwork by Western social scientists in Third World nations, Norwegian sociologist Johan Galtung, whom Lewis cited, referred to the "extracted data, to be processed at home" produced by social anthropologists (1967, 305).

2. With thanks to Judith Okely (1996).

3. In 2005, Ottenberg completed a rich historical account of Abakaliki, the Igbo region and its emerging urban center, which he had studied in the late 1950s (Ottenberg 2005). A year later, Africa World Press published two retrospective volumes of Ottenberg's essays, with appreciative introductions by Nigerian Igbo scholars (Ottenberg 2006a, 2006b).

4. *Native anthropologist* is a more problematic label than *insider*, as Kumar (1992), Narayan (1993), and Jacobs-Huey (2002) make clear. Its colonial-era connotation—of anthropology's origins in "the days in which natives were genuine natives (whether they liked it or not)" (Narayan 1993:672)—give it a political weight quite different from that of *insider*, a point excellently developed by McClaurin (2001b, 74). Adoption of this label by a white anthropologist studying other white people (see Narayan 1993, 677) would be historically insensitive and presumptuous. I am, to anyone, unquestionably a "native New Yorker," but I am not a "native anthropologist" because I have done fieldwork in

New York City or because I have focused my research on white Elmhurst-Corona residents or on the mainly white Gray Panthers. As Zavella (1996), notes, "we are insiders and outsiders within several constituencies, each with its own norms and responsibilities" (153); see also Rappaport 2008.

5. Apologies to Elinor Keenan Ochs (Keenan 1975).

6. Other *Mutuality* contributors have also anticipated and discovered such audiences for their ethnography—Abusharaf (2002, 2009b); Alvarez (1995a, 2005); Besteman (2008); Bhachu (1985, 1991, 2004); Bhachu and Battacharyya (2009); Guo (2000); Jacobs-Huey (2006a, 2006b); Mullings and Wali (2001); Rodríguez (1996, 2006); Shield (1988, 2002); Wali, Severson, and Longoni (2002); and Williams (1988, 2004).

7. Bailey coauthored a similar museum exhibit catalog (Bailey and Swan 2004) and contributed a chapter to another (Bailey 2004; Townsend 2004).

Bibliography

Abdel Ghaffar, M. Ahmed, and Leif Manger. 2007. *Understanding the Crisis in Darfur.* Bergen, Norway: Nordic Institute.

Abdul-Jalil, Musa Adam. 1988. Some Political Aspects of Zaghawa Migration and Resettlement. In *Rural Migration and Identity Change: Case Studies from the Sudan.* Edited by Fouad Ibrahim and Helmut Ruppert, 13–36. Bayreuth, Bavaria: Druckhaus Beyreuth Verlagasgsellschaft.

Abu-Lughod, Lila. 1991. Writing Against Culture. In *Recapturing Anthropology: Working in the Present.* Edited by Richard Fox, 137–162. Santa Fe, N.M.: School of American Research Press.

Abusharaf, Rogaia Mustafa. 1998. Structural Adaptations in an Immigrant Muslim Congregation in New York. In *Gatherings in Diaspora: Religious Communities and the New Immigration.* Edited by R. Stephen Warner and Judith Wittner, 235–261. Philadelphia: Temple University Press.

———. 2002. *Wanderings: Sudanese Migrants and Exiles in North America.* Ithaca, N.Y.: Cornell University Press.

———, ed. 2006. *Female Circumcision: Multicultural Perspectives.* Philadelphia: University of Pennsylvania Press.

———. 2009a. Marx in the Vernacular: Abdel Khaliq Mahgoub and the Riddles of Localizing Leftist Politics in Sudanese Philosophies of Liberation. *South Atlantic Quarterly* 108 (3): 483–500.

———. 2009b. *Transforming Displaced Women in Sudan: Politics and the Body in a Squatter Settlement.* Chicago: University of Chicago Press.

———. 2010a. Debating Darfur in the World. *Annals of the American Academy of Political and Social Science* 632: 67–85.

———. 2010b. Introduction: Writing the Dialectic. In "What's Left of the Left? The View from Sudan." *South Atlantic Quarterly* 109 (1): 1–7. Special issue edited by Rogaia Mustafa Abusharaf.

———, ed. 2010c. What's Left of the Left? The View from Sudan. Special issue of *South Atlantic Quarterly* 109 (1).

———. 2011. A Doha-Darfur Encounter: A Sufi Mystic's Whirling Trance for Peace. *Black Renaissance/Renaissance Noire* 11 (1): 146–158.

Achenbach, Joel. 2004. Taking off the Color Blinders: Geneticists and Historians Grapple with the Gray Areas of Race. *Washington Post*, September 15, C1.

Afable, Patricia. 2004. Journeys from Bontoc to the Western Fairs, 1904–1915: The "Nikimalika" and Their Interpreters. *Philippine Studies* 52: 445–473.

———, and Deana L. Weibel. 2012. "The Igorrote Village" at the Alaska-Yukon-Pacific Exposition, 1909: Bontoc Performers and Their American Showman. In *Igorot by Heart*. Edited by John D. Dyte et al., 215–229. Philippine Islands: Igorot Global Organization.

Aiyar, S. A. 2010. Jugaad Is Our Most Precious Resource. *The Economic Times*, August 15. Accessed March 10, 2013. http://articles.economictimes.indiatimes.com/2010-08-15/news/27567823_1_jugaad-frugal-engineering-innovation.

Aiyyapan, A. 1944. Iravas and Culture Change. *Bulletin of the Madras Government Museum* 5 (1): i–204.

———. 1965. *Social Revolution in a Kerala Village: A Study of Culture Change*. New York: Asia Publishing House.

Alexander, Hartley. 1933. Francis La Flesche. *American Anthropologist* 35: 328–331.

Alvarez, Robert R. 1972. A Kuna Indian Cooperative: A Voluntary Association as a Vehicle for Change. Master's thesis, Department of Anthropology, San Diego State University.

———. 1986. The Lemon Grove Incident: The Nation's First Successful Desegregation Court Case. *Journal of San Diego History* 32 (2): 116–136.

———. 1987. The Foundations and Genesis of a Mexican-American Community: A Sociohistorical Perspective. In *Cities of the United States: Studies in Urban Anthropology*. Edited by Leith Mullings, 176–197. New York: Columbia University Press.

———. 1994. Un Chilero in la Academia: Sifting, Shifting, and the Recruitment of Minorities in Anthropology. In *Race*. Edited by Steven Gregory and Roger Sanjek, 257–269. New Brunswick, N.J.: Rutgers University Press.

———. 1995a. *Familia: Migration and Adaptation in Alta and Baja California*. Berkeley: University of California Press.

———. 1995b. The Mexico-U.S. Border: The Making of an Anthropology of Borderlands. *Annual Review of Anthropology* 24: 447–470.

———. 1997. How Close Can We Get? *Parientes* and *Camaradas* in the Anthropological Paradigm. Paper presented at the meeting of the American Anthropological Association, Washington, D.C., November 19–23.

———. 2005. *Mangos, Chiles, and Truckers: The Business of Transnationalism*. Minneapolis: University of Minnesota Press.

———. 2007. The March of Empire: Mangos, Avocados, and the Politics of Transfer. *Gastronomica* 28: 28–34.

———. 2012a. Neoliberalism and the Transnational Activity of the State: Offshore Control in the U.S.-Mexican Mango and Persian Lime Industry. In *Neoliberalism and Commodity Production in Mexico*. Edited by Thomas Weaver, James Greenberg, W. Alexander, and Anne Browning Aiken, 51–74. Boulder: University Press of Colorado.

———. 2012b. Reconceptualizng the Space of the Mexico-U.S. Border. In *A Companion to Border Studies*. Edited by Thomas M. Wilson and Hastings Donnan, 538–556. Oxford: Wiley-Blackwell.

American Anthropological Association. 1969. *Guide to Departments of Anthropology 1969–70*. Washington, D.C.: American Anthropological Association.

———. 2008. *AnthroGuide 2008–2009*. Arlington, Va.: American Anthropological Association.

———. 2011. *Guidelines for Evaluating Scholarship in the Realm of Practicing, Applied, and Public Interest Anthropology for Academic Promotion and Tenure*. Arlington, Va.: American Anthropological Association. http://www.aaanet.org/cmtes/copapia/upload/Final-T-P-Document-2011.pdf.

———. 2012. *Statement on Ethics: Principles of Professional Responsibility*. Arlington, Va.: American Anthropological Association. http://www.aaanet.org/profdev/ethics/upload/Statement-on-Ethics-Principles-of-Professional-Responsibility.pdf.

Ames, Michael. 1986. *Museums, the Public, and Anthropology: A Study in the Anthropology of Anthropology*. New Delhi: Concept Publishing Company.

Anchorage Museum and Calista Elders Council. 2008. *Yuungnaqpiallerput/The Way We Genuinely Live: Masterworks of Yup'ik Science and Survival*. Accessed April 3, 2013. http://www.yupikscience.org.

Andrew, Frank, Sr. 2008. *Paitarkiutenka/My Legacy to You*. Seattle: University of Washington Press.

Andrews, Abigail. 2010. Constructing Mutuality: The Zapatistas' Transformation of Transnational Activist Power Dynamics. *Latin American Politics and Society* 52: 89–120.

Appadurai, Arjun. 1986. Introduction: Commodities and the Politics of Value. In *The Social Life of Things: Commodities in Cultural Perspective*. Edited by Arjun Appadurai, 3–63. Cambridge: Cambridge University Press.

Asad, Talal, ed. 1973. *Anthropology and the Colonial Encounter*. London: Ithaca Press.

Asch, Timothy, and Napoleon Chagnon. 1974. *A Man Called Bee: Studying the Yanamamo* (film). Watertown, Mass.: Documentary Educational Resources.

Asian American Studies Department. 2009. *At 40: Asian American Studies @ San Francisco State: Self-Determination, Community, Student Service*. San Francisco: Asian American Studies Department, San Francisco State University.

Ata-Ullah, Naazish. 1998. Stylistic Hybridity and Colonial Art and Design Education: A Wooden Carved Screen by Ram Singh. In *Colonialism and the Object: Empire, Material Culture and the Museum*. Edited by Tim Barringer and Tom Flynn, 68–81. London: Routledge.

Bacdayan, Albert S. 2012. Igorot Bridge to Success in North America. In *Igorot by Heart*. Edited by John D. Dyte et al., 25–46. Philippine Islands: Igorot Global Organization.

Baden-Powell, Baden Henry. 1872. *Hand-Book of the Manufactures and Arts of the Punjab*. Lahore: Punjab Printing Company.

Bailey, F. G. 1963. *Politics and Social Change: Orissa in 1959*. Berkeley: University of California Press.

Bailey, Garrick. 1973. *Changes in Osage Social Organization 1673–1906*. University of Oregon Anthropological Papers 5. Eugene: University of Oregon Press.

———. 1978. John Joseph Mathews, Osage, 1894–. In *American Indian Intellectuals*. Edited by Margot Liberty, 205–214. St. Paul, Minn.: West.

———, ed. 1995. *The Osage and the Invisible World: From the Works of Francis La Flesche*. Norman: University of Oklahoma Press.

———. 2001. Osage. In *Plains*. Vol. 13 of *Handbook of North American Indians*. Edited by Raymond DeMallie, 476–496. Washington, D.C.: Smithsonian Institution.

———. 2004. Continuity and Change in Mississippian Civilization. In *Hero, Hawk, and Open Hand: American Indian Art of the Ancient Midwest and South*. Edited by Richard Townsend, 83–91. New Haven, Conn.: Yale University Press.

———, ed. 2008. *Indians in Contemporary Society*. Vol. 2 of *Handbook of North American Indians*. Washington, D.C.: Smithsonian Institution.

———, ed. 2010. *Traditions of the Osage: Stories Collected and Translated by Francis La Flesche*. Albuquerque: University of New Mexico Press.

———, and Roberta Glenn Bailey. 1986. *A History of the Navajos: The Reservation Years*. Santa Fe, N.M.: School of American Research Press.

———, and Daniel Swan. 2004. *Art of the Osage*. Seattle: University of Washington Press.

Barenboim, Daniel, and Edward Said. 2004. *Parallels and Paradoxes: Explorations in Music and Society*. New York: Vintage.

Barker, James, and Ann Fienup-Riordan, with Theresa Arevgaq John. 2010. *Yupiit Yuraryarait: Yup'ik Ways of Dancing*. Fairbanks: University of Alaska Press.

Barnard, Henry. 2008. Review of *Locating Bourdieu*, by Deborah Reed-Danahay. *American Ethnologist* 33 (3): 3031–3032. Accessed April 4, 2013. http://onlinelibrary.wiley.com/doi/10.1525/ae.2006.33.3.3031/abstract.

Barnes, J. A. 1977. *The Ethics of Inquiry in Social Science*. Delhi: Oxford University Press.

Barth, Fredrik, ed. 1963. *The Role of the Entrepreneur in Social Change in Northern Norway*. Bergen: Universitetsforlaget.

———. 1994. A Personal View of Present Tasks and Priorities in Cultural and Social Anthropology. In *Assessing Cultural Anthropology*. Edited by Robert Borofsky, 349–360. New York: McGraw-Hill.

Barthes, Roland. 1972. *Mythologies*. Selected and translated by Annette Lavers. New York: Hill and Wang.

Basso, Keith. 1996. *Wisdom Sits in Places: Landscape and Language Among the Western Apache*. Albuquerque: University of New Mexico Press.

Bateson, Mary Catherine. 1989. *Composing a Life*. New York: Grove Press.

BBC World Service. 2012. Discovery: Tejinder Virdee, CERN Physicist. June 4. Accessed March 10, 2013. http://www.bbc.co.uk/programmes/p00s5p5b.

Bebb, Bruce. 1988. Improv: Where Did You Come from and What Are You Doing in My Living Room? *Hollywood Reporter Comedy Special Report*, January 26. Accessed April 20, 2013. http://www.spolin.us/where-did-hollywood-rep/.

Becker, A. L. 2000. *Beyond Translation: Essays Toward a Modern Philology*. Ann Arbor: University of Michigan Press.

Becker, Gay. 1983. *Growing Old in Silence: Deaf People in Old Age*. San Francisco: University of California Press.

Beckmann, David. 1975. *Eden Revival: Spiritual Churches in Ghana*. St. Louis, Mo.: Concordia.

Behar, Ruth. 2007. *An Island Called Home: Returning to Jewish Cuba*. New Brunswick, N.J.: Rutgers University Press.

———, and Deborah Gordon, eds. 1995. *Women Writing Culture*. Berkeley: University of California Press.

Belaunde, Lusia. 2009. *Kené, Arte, Ciencia y Tradición en Diseño*. Lima: Instituto Nacional de Cultura.

Belen, Yvonne. 2009. Brief Profile of the Cordillera Region. In *Cordillera Rituals as a Way of Life*. Edited by Yvonne Belen, 7–8. N.p.: Igorot Cordillera BIMAAK Europe (ICBE).

Ben-Amos, Dan. 1972. Toward a Definition of Folklore in Context. In *Toward New Perspectives in Folklore*. Edited by Americo Paredes and Richard Bauman, 3–15. Austin: University of Texas Press.

Benedict, Ruth. 1934. *Patterns of Culture*. New York: Houghton Mifflin.

———. 1940. *Race: Science and Politics*. New York: Viking.

———, and Gene Weltfish. 1943. *The Races of Mankind*. Public Affairs Pamphlet No. 85. New York: Public Affairs Committee.

———, and Gene Weltfish. 1948. *In Henry's Backyard: The Races of Mankind*. New York: Henry Schuman.

Bennett, Linda, and Sunil Khanna. 2010. A Review of Tenure and Promotion Guidelines in Higher Education: Optimistic Signs for Applied, Practicing, and Public Interest Anthropology. *American Anthropologist* 112: 648–650.

Bennett, Linda, and Linda Whiteford, ed. 2013. Anthropology and the Engaged University: New Vision for the Discipline Within Higher Education. Special issue of *Annals of Anthropological Practice* 37 (1).

Bernard, H. Russell, ed. 2000. *Handbook of Methods in Cultural Anthropology*. Lanham, Md.: Altamira Press.

Besdine Richard, Renée Shield, Lynn McNicoll, Susan Campbell, and Terrie Wetle. 2011. Integrating and Evaluating Geriatrics in Medical School: A Novel Approach for the Challenge. *Journal of Gerontology and Geriatrics Education* 32 (4): 295–308.

Besteman, Catherine. 1990. *Land Tenure in the Middle Jubba Valley, Somalia: Customary*

Tenure and the Effect of Land Registration. Madison: University of Wisconsin–Madison Land Tenure Center.

———. 1994. Individualisation and the Assault on Customary Tenure in Africa: Title Registration Programmes and the Case of Somalia. *Africa* 64: 484–515.

———. 1999. *Unraveling Somalia: Race, Violence, and the Legacy of Slavery*. Philadelphia: University of Pennsylvania Press.

———. 2000. Political Economy and Robert Kaplan in Africa. *PoLAR: Political and Legal Anthropology Review* 23 (1): 25–32.

———. 2008. *Transforming Cape Town*. Berkeley: University of California Press.

———. 2009. The Somali Bantu Experience: Using Multimedia Ethnography for Community Building, Public Education and Advocacy. *Anthropology News* 50 (4): 23.

———. 2010. In and out of the Academy: Policy and the Case for a Strategic Anthropology. *Human Organization* 69: 407–417.

———, and Hugh Gusterson, eds. 2005. *Why America's Top Pundits Are Wrong: Anthropologists Talk Back*. Berkeley: University of California Press.

Bhachu, Parminder. 1985. *Twice Migrants: East African Sikh Settlers in Britain*. London: Tavistock.

———. 1991. The Re-socialisation of an Anthropologist: Fieldwork Within One's Own Community. In *From the Female Eye: Accounts of Women Fieldworkers Studying Their Own Communities*. Edited by M. N. Panini, 66–73. Delhi: Hindustan Publishing Corporation.

———. 2003. Film Director Gurinder Chadha: Image Maker of the Diaspora. *International Journal of Punjab Studies* 9 (2): 253–273.

———. 2004. *Dangerous Designs: Asian Women Fashion the Diaspora Economies*. New York: Routledge.

———, and Gargi Battacharyya. 2009. Diaspora Conversations: Ethics, Ethicality, Work and Life. In *Ethnicities and Values in a Changing World*. Edited by Gargi Bhattacharyya, 45–64. Burlington, Vt.: Ashgate.

Biehl, João, and Peter Locke 2010. Deleuze and the Anthropology of Becoming. *Current Anthropology* 51 (3): 317–351.

Blakey, Michael L. 1998. The New York African Burial Ground Project: An Examination of Enslaved Lives, a Construction of Ancestral Ties. *Transforming Anthropology* 7 (1): 53–58.

Blagburn, Marianna, and Brett Williams. 2000. Research Practices: How We Learned About the Traditions of D.C. Folk. In *34th Annual Smithsonian Folklife Festival*. Edited by Carla M. Borden, 16–18. Washington, D.C.: Smithsonian Institution Center for Folklife and Cultural Heritage.

Blee, Kathleen M. 2007. Ethnographies of the Far Right. *Journal of Contemporary Ethnography* 36 (2): 119–128.

Bluebond-Langner, Myra. 1978. *The Private Worlds of Dying Children*. Princeton, N.J.: Princeton University Press.

Boas, Franz. 1904. What the Negro Has Done in Africa. *The Ethical Record* 5 (2): 106–109.

———. 1945. *Race and Democratic Society*. New York: J. J. Augustin.

———, ed. 1938. *General Anthropology*. New York: D. C. Heath.

———, ed. 1944. *General Anthropology*. War Department Education Manual EM 226. New York: D. C. Heath for the United States Armed Forces Institute.

Boellstorff, Tom. 2008. *Coming of Age in Second Life: An Anthropologist Explores the Virtually Human*. Princeton, N.J.: Princeton University Press.

Bond, George C. 1988. A Social Portrait of John Gibbs St. Clair Drake: An American Anthropologist. *American Ethnologist* 15: 762–781.

———. 1990. Fieldnotes: Research in Past Occurrences. In *Fieldnotes: The Makings of Anthropology*. Edited by Roger Sanjek, 273–289. Ithaca, N.Y.: Cornell University Press.

Borofsky, Robert. 2001. Envisioning a More Public Anthropology: An Interview with Fredrik Barth. Accessed June 10, 2013. http://www.publicanthropology.org/interview-with-fredrik-barth/.

Boslaugh, Sarah, and Elena M. Andersen. 2006. Correlates of Physical Activity for Adults with Disability. *Preventing Chronic Disease* 3 (3): 1–14.

Bott, Elizabeth. 1957. *Family and Social Network*. London: Tavistock.

Bourdieu, Pierre. 1984. *Distinction: A Social Critique of the Judgment of Taste*. Translated by Richard Nice. Cambridge, Mass.: Harvard University Press.

———. 1990. *The Logic of Practice*. Stanford, Calif.: Stanford University Press.

———. 1999 (1993). *The Weight of the World: Social Suffering in Contemporary Society*. Translated by Priscilla Parkhurst Ferguson, Susan Emanuel, Joe Johnson, and Shoggy T. Waryn. Stanford, Calif.: Stanford University Press.

Bourgois, Philippe. 2011. Lumpen Abuse: The Human Cost of Righteous Neoliberalism. *City and Society* 23 (1): 2–12.

———, and Jeffrey Schonberg. 2009. *Righteous Dopefiend*. Berkeley: University of California Press.

Bourriaud, Nicolas. 2009. *Relational Aesthetics*. Dijon: Presses du Réel.

Breslow, A. L. 1995. *Beyond the Closed Door: Chinese Culture and the Creation of T'ai Chi Ch'uan*. Jerusalem: Almond Blossom Press.

Brettell, Caroline, ed. 1993. *When They Read What We Write: The Politics of Ethnography*. Westport, Conn.: Bergin & Garvey.

Brown, S. Dale. 2009. Wheelchair Taiji Featured at Beijing Paralympics. *T'ai Chi: The International Magazine of T'ai Chi Ch'uan* 33 (1): 6–11.

Bruner, Jerome. 1996. *The Culture of Education*. Cambridge, Mass.: Harvard University Press.

Burke, Heather, Claire Smith, Dorothy Lippert, Joe Watkins, and Larry Zimmerman, eds. 2008. *Kennewick Man: Perspectives on the Ancient One*. Walnut Creek, Calif.: Left Coast Press.

Button, Gregory. 2010. *Disaster Culture: Knowledge and Uncertainty in the Wake of Human and Environmental Catastrophe*. Walnut Creek, Calif.: Left Coast Press.

Caffrey, Margaret. 1989. *Ruth Benedict: Stranger in This Land*. Austin: University of Texas Press.

Calista Elders Council. 2009. *Yup'ik Traditional Narratives: Stories for Future Generations*. http://www.surrealstudios.com/cec/.

Capiteyn, André. 1913. Een plaatsnaam voor Timicheg (1885–1913), overleden in het Filippijns Dorp van de Wereldtentoonstelling 1913 in Gent. *Stadsarchief Gent*. Accessed July 8, 2012. http://www.gent.be/docs/Departement%20Cultuur/Stadsarchief%20-%20De%20Zwarte%20Doos/Timicheg.wereldexpo.1913.pdf.

Caplovitz, David. 1967. *The Poor Pay More: Consumer Practices of Low-Income Families*. New York: Free Press.

Cartmill, Matt. 1998. The Status of the Race Concept in Physical Anthropology. *American Anthropologist* 100: 651–660.

Caulfield, Mina Davis. 1972. Culture and Imperialism: Proposing a New Dialectic. In *Reinventing Anthropology*. Edited by Dell Hymes, 182–212. New York: Vintage Books.

Chagnon, Napoleon. 1968. *Yanomamo: The Fierce People*. New York: Holt, Rinehart and Winston.

Chana, Leonard, Susan Lobo, and Barbara Chana. 2009. *The Sweet Smell of Home: The Life and Art of Leonard F. Chana*. Tucson: University of Arizona Press.

Chavez, Christina. 2008. Conceptualizing from the Inside: Advantages, Complications, and Demands on Insider Positionality. *Qualitative Report* 13: 474–494.

Chavez, Leo. 1992. *Shadowed Lives: Undocumented Immigrants in American Society*. Fort Worth, Tex.: Harcourt Brace Jovanovich.

Checker, Melissa. 2005. *Polluted Promises: Environmental Racism and the Search for Justice in a Southern Town*. New York: New York University Press.

———. 2009. Anthropology in the Public Sphere, 2008: Emerging Trends and Significant Impacts. *American Anthropologist* 111: 162–169.

———, ed. 2011. "Year That Trembled and Reel'd": Reflections on Public Anthropology a Decade After 9/11. *American Anthropologist* 113: 491–497.

Chen, Hsiang-shui. 1990. *Chinatown No More: Taiwan Immigrants in Contemporary New York*. Ithaca, N.Y.: Cornell University Press.

———, and John Kuo Wei Tchen. 1989. *Towards a History of Chinese in Queens*. Flushing, N.Y.: Asian/American Center, Queens College, CUNY.

Chen, Xuya [Chia]. 1990. *Studying in the United States: The Experience of Chinese Students at Queens College*. Flushing, N.Y.: Asian/American Center, Queens College, CUNY.

———. 2000. *Among the 36 Strategies, Running Away Is the Top One*. Victoria, BC: Trafford.

Cheung, Siu Yin, Eva Tsai, Lena Fung, and Judy Ng. 2007. Physical Benefits of Tai Chi Chuan for Individuals with Lower-Limb Disabilities. *Occupational Therapy International* 14 (1): 1–10.

China Disabled People's Federation. 2007. *Reports on the Second National Survey on Disability*. Beijing: China Disabled People's Federation.

———. 2008. *National Survey on the Living Conditions of People with Disability*. Beijing: China Disabled People's Federation.

Cho, Kee-Lee. 2008. Effect of Tai Chi on Depressive Symptoms Amongst Chinese Older Patients with Major Depression: The Role of Social Support. *Medicine and Sport Science* 52: 146–154.

Choi, Mina. 1989. *Race, Gender and Eyeglasses: Teacher Perceptions of Asian, Black and White Students*. Flushing, N.Y.: Asian/American Center, Queens College, CUNY.

Clifford, James. 1983. On Ethnographic Authority. *Representations* 1 (2): 118–146.

———. 1986. Introduction: Partial Truths. In *Writing Culture: The Poetics and Politics of Ethnography*. Edited by James Clifford and George Marcus, 1–26. Berkeley: University of California Press.

———. 1990. Notes on (Field)notes. In *Fieldnotes: The Makings of Anthropology*. Edited by Roger Sanjek, 47–70. Ithaca, N.Y.: Cornell University Press.

———. 1997a. *Routes: Travel and Translation in the Late Twentieth Century*. Cambridge, Mass.: Harvard University Press.

———. 1997b. Spatial Practices: Fieldwork, Travel, and the Disciplining of Anthropology. In *Anthropological Locations: Boundaries and Grounds of a Field Science*. Edited by Akhil Gupta and James Ferguson, 185–222. Berkeley: University of California Press.

———, and George Marcus, eds. 1986. *Writing Culture: The Poetics and Politics of Ethnography*. Berkeley: University of California Press.

Cohen, Anthony, and Nigel Rapport, eds. 1995. *Questions of Consciousness*. London: Routledge.

Cohen, Fay G. 1976. The American Indian Movement and the Anthropologist: Issues and Implications of Consent. In *Ethics and Anthropology: Dilemmas in Fieldwork*. Edited by Michael Rynkiewich and James Spradley, 81–94. New York: John Wiley.

Cole, Johnnetta Betsch. 2011. Personal Reflections on Race, Racism and Anthropology. *AnthroNotes* 32 (1): 1–3.

Collins, Patricia Hill. 1990. *Black Feminist Thought: Knowledge, Consciousness, and the Politics of Empowerment*. New York: Routledge.

Crafts, Susan, Daniel Cavicchi, and Charles Keil. 1993. *My Music: Explorations of Music in Daily Life*. Hanover, N.H.: University Press of New England.

Crapanzano, Vincent. 2004. *Imaginative Horizons: An Essay in Literary-Philosophical Anthropology*. Chicago: University of Chicago Press.

Cruikshank, Julie. 2005. *Do Glaciers Listen? Local Knowledge, Colonial Encounters, and Social Imagination*. Vancouver: University of British Columbia Press.

Curry, Leslie, Renée Rose Shield, and Terrie Wetle, eds. 2006. *Improving Aging and Public Health Research: Qualitative and Mixed Methods*. Washington, D.C.: American Public Health Association/Gerontological Society of America.

Damasio, Antonio R. 2001. Some Notes on Brain, Imagination, and Creativity. In *The*

Origins of Creativity. Edited by Karl H. Pfenninger and Valerie R. Shubik, 59–68. New York: Oxford University Press.

DaMatta, Roberto. 1994. Some Biased Remarks on Interpretivism: A View from Brazil. In *Assessing Cultural Anthropology*. Edited by Robert Borofsky, 119–131. New York: McGraw-Hill.

Darnell, Regna. 2001. *Invisible Genealogies: A History of Americanist Anthropology*. Lincoln: University of Nebraska Press.

———. 2002. Editor's Introduction. In *American Anthropology, 1971–1995: Papers from the* American Anthropologist. Edited by Regna Darnell, 1–36. Lincoln: University of Nebraska Press.

Dauenhauer, Nora M., and Richard Dauenhauer. 1999. The Paradox of Talking on the Page: Some Aspects of the Tlingit and Haida Experience. In *Talking on the Page: Editing Aboriginal Oral Texts*. Edited by Laura Murray and Keren Rice, 3–42. Toronto: University of Toronto Press.

Davies, James, and Dimitrina Spencer, eds. 2010. *Emotions in the Field: The Psychology and Anthropology of Field Experience*. Stanford, Calif.: Stanford University Press.

Davis, Shelton, and Alaka Wali. 1993. *Indigenous Territories and Tropical Forest Management in Latin America*. Policy Research Working Paper 1100, Environment Department. Washington, D.C.: World Bank.

Deal, Jeffrey. 2010. Torture by *Cieng*: Ethical Theory Meets Social Practice Among the Kina Agaar of South Sudan. *American Anthropologist* 112 (4): 563–575.

De Beauvoir, Simone. 1970. *The Coming of Age*. New York: Warner.

De Laguna, Frederica, ed. 1960. *Selected Papers from the American Anthropologist: 1888–1920*. Evanston, Ill.: Row, Peterson and Company.

del Campo, Hilary, and Alaka Wali. 2007. Applying Asset Mapping to Protected Area Planning and Management in the Cordillera Azul National Park, Peru. *Ethnobotany Research and Applications* 5: 25–36.

Deloria, Ella. 1944. *Speaking of Indians*. Lincoln: University of Nebraska Press.

Deloria, Vine. 1969a. Anthropologists and Other Friends. *Playboy Magazine* 16 (8): 131–132, 172–175.

———. 1969b. *Custer Died for Your Sins: An Indian Manifesto*. New York: Macmillian.

DeMallie, J. Raymond. 2007. Vine Deloria, Jr. (1933–2005). *American Anthropologist* 108: 931–933.

Dennis, Norman, Fernando Henriques, and Clifford Slaughter. 1956. *Coal Is Our Life: An Analysis of a Yorkshire Mining Community*. London: Tavistock.

Department of Health and Human Services. 2000. Disability and Secondary Conditions. In *Healthy People 2010*. Vol. 1, 6-1-6-28. Washington, D.C.: U.S. Government Printing Office.

Dereisiewicz, William. 2011. Faulty Towers: The Crisis in Higher Education. *The Nation*, May 23. Accessed July 1, 2013. http://www.thenation.com/article/160410/faulty-towers-crisis-higher-education#axzz2XpkfNSvp.

Deshen, Shlomo. 1970. *Immigrant Voters in Israel: Parties and Congregations in a Local Election Campaign*. Manchester: Manchester University Press.

———, and Moshe Shokeid. 1974. *The Predicament of Homecoming: Cultural and Social Life of North African Immigrants in Israel*. Ithaca, N.Y.: Cornell University Press.

de Waal, Alexander. 1989. *Famine That Kills: Darfur, Sudan, 1984–1985*. Oxford: Oxford University Press.

———, ed. 2007. *War in Darfur and the Search for Peace*. Cambridge, Mass.: Harvard University Press.

Dewey, John. 1934. *Art as Experience*. New York: Perigee Books.

Diamond, Stanley. 1980. Some Salient Events in the Professional Life of Gene Weltfish. In *Theory and Practice: Essays Presented to Gene Weltfish*. Edited by Stanley Diamond, 351–356. The Hague: Mouton.

Dienst, Richard. 2011. *The Bonds of Debt*. London: Verso.

di Leonardo, Micaela. 2004. Human Cultural Diversity. Accessed February 14, 2014. http://www.understandingrace.org/resources/pdf/myth_reality/di_leonardo.pdf..

Dinesen, Isak [Karen Blixen]. 1937. *Out of Africa*. New York: Modern Library.

Dominguez, Virginia. 2000. For a Politics of Love and Rescue. *Cultural Anthropology* 15 (3): 361–393.

———. 2012. Mutuality, Responsibility, and Reciprocity in Situations of Market Inequality: Dilemmas of, and Concerning, U.S. Anthropology in the World. *Focaal* 63: 51–61.

Dowd, J. P. 1975. Aging as Exchange. *Journal of Gerontology* 30 (5): 584–594.

Dozier, Damon. 2010. AAA Brings RACE Project to Capitol Hill. *Anthropology News* 51 (3): 14.

Drake, St. Clair. 1980. Anthropology and the Black Experience. *The Black Scholar: Journal of Black Studies and Research* 11 (7): 2–31.

Drewal, Margaret Thompson. 1991. Whatever Happened to Primitive Art? *Anthropology and Humanism Quarterly* 16 (3): 102–107.

Dunford, Christine Mary. 2009. Deploying Nature: A Performance Ethnography of Community Gardens, Gardeners, and Urban Change in a Chicago Neighborhood. PhD diss., Northwestern University.

Dyte, John D., Yvonne K. Belen, Carolyn W. Hildebrand, Dalisay A. Leones, Jocelyn Noe, Gloria O. Simon, and Philian Louise Weygan-Allan. 2012. Preface to *Igorot by Heart*. Edited by Dyte et al., xv–xvii. Philippine Islands: Igorot Global Organization.

———, eds. 2012. *Igorot by Heart*. Philippine Islands: Igorot Global Organization.

Earley, Gerald. 1998. Adventures in the Colored Museum: Afrocentrism, Memory, and the Construction of Race. *American Anthropologist* 100: 703–711.

Edelman, Marc. 2009. Synergies and Tensions Between Rural Social Movements and Professional Researchers. *Journal of Peasant Studies* 36 (1): 245–265.

Edsall, Thomas. 2012. Is Poverty a Kind of Robbery? *New York Times*, September 16. Accessed April 15, 2013. http://campaignstops.blogs.nytimes.com/2012/09/16/is-poverty-a-kind-of-robbery/.

Emerson, Robert, and Melvin Pollner. 2001. Constructing Participant Observation Relations. In *Contemporary Field Research: Perspectives and Formulations.* Edited by Robert Emerson, 239–259. Long Grove, Ill.: Waveland Press.

Enslin, Elizabeth. 1994. Beyond Writing: Feminist Practice and the Limitations of Ethnography. *Cultural Anthropology* 9 (4): 537–568.

Ethnic Studies Department. 2012. Ethnic Studies Department: Our Vision. *UC San Diego.* http://www.ethnicstudies.ucsd.edu.

Evans-Pritchard, E. E. 1951. *Social Anthropology.* New York: Free Press.

Fadiman, Anne. 1997. *The Spirit Catches You and You Fall Down.* New York: Farrar, Straus, and Giroux.

Faris, James C. 1996. *Navajo Photography: A Critical History of the Representation of an American People.* Albuquerque: University of New Mexico Press.

Farmer, Paul. 2010. *Partner to the Poor: A Paul Farmer Reader.* Edited by Haun Saussy. Berkeley: University of California Press.

Fasko, Daniel J., and R. W. Grueninger. 2001. T'ai Chi Ch'uan and Physical and Psychological Health: A Review. *Clinical Kinesiology: Journal of the American Kinesiotherapy Association* 55 (1): 4–12.

Fassin, Didier. 2008. Beyond Good and Evil? Questioning Anthropological Discomfort with Morals. *Anthropological Theory* 8 (4): 333–344.

Feld, Steven, and Aaron A. Fox. 1994. Music and Language. *Annual Review of Anthropology* 23: 25–53.

Ferguson, James. 2006. *Global Shadows: Africa in the Neoliberal World Order.* Durham, N.C.: Duke University Press.

Fienup-Riordan, Ann. 1983. *The Nelson Island Eskimo: Social Structure and Ritual Distribution.* Anchorage: Alaska Pacific University Press.

———. 1990. *Eskimo Essays: Yup'ik Lives and How We See Them.* New Brunswick, N.J.: Rutgers University Press.

———. 1994. Collaboration on Display: A Yup'ik Exhibit at Three National Museums. *American Anthropologist* 101: 339–388.

———. 1995. *Freeze Frame: Alaska Eskimos in the Movies.* Seattle: University of Washington Press.

———. 1996. *The Living Tradition of Yup'ik Masks: Agayuliyararput (Our Way of Making Prayer).* Seattle: University of Washington Press.

———. 2000. *Hunting Tradition in a Changing World: Yup'ik Lives in Alaska Today.* New Brunswick, N.J.: Rutgers University Press.

———. 2005a. *Wise Words of the Yup'ik People: We Talk to You Because We Love You.* Lincoln: University of Nebraska Press.

———. 2005b. *Yup'ik Elders at the Ethnologisches Museum Berlin: Fieldwork Turned on Its Head.* Seattle: University of Washington Press.

———. 2007. *Yuungnaqpiallerput/The Way We Genuinely Live: Masterworks of Yup'ik Science and Survival.* Seattle: University of Washington Press.

———. 2014. Linking Local and Global. *Polar Geography* 37(1): 5–23.

———, and Lawrence D. Kaplan, eds. 2007. *Words of the Real People: Alaska Native Literature in Translation.* Fairbanks: University of Alaska Press.

———, and Alice Rearden. 2012. *Ellavut/Our Yup'ik World and Weather: Continuity and Change on the Bering Sea Coast.* Seattle: University of Washington Press.

Fiske, Shirley J. 2011. Anthropology's Voice in the Public Policy Process. *Anthropology News* 54 (4): 17.

———. 2012. Global Climate Change from the Bottom Up. In *Applying Anthropology in the Global Village.* Edited by Christina Wasson, Mary Odell Butler, and Jacqueline Copeland-Carson, 143–172. Walnut Creek, Calif.: Left Coast Press.

———, Linda Bennett, Patricia Ensworth, Terry Redding, and Keri Brondo. 2010. *The Changing Face of Anthropology: Anthropology Masters Reflect on Education, Careers, and Professional Organizations.* Arlington, Va.: American Anthropological Association.

Fletcher, Alice, and Francis La Flesche. 1911. The Omaha Tribe. *Twenty-seventh Annual Report of the Bureau of American Ethnology (1905–1906)*, 15–660. Washington, D.C.: U.S. Government Printing Office.

Flores-Meiser, Enya. 1980. Doing Fieldwork in One's Own Community. *Association of Third World Anthropologists Research Bulletin* 1: 24–29.

Forte, Maximilian C. 2011. Beyond Public Anthropology: Approaching Zero. Keynote address delivered by video to the Eighth Annual Public Anthropology Conference, American University, Washington, D.C., October 14–16. Accessed April 4, 2013. http://openanthropology.org/pacfortekeynote2.pdf.

Frank, Arthur W. 2004. *The Renewal of Generosity: Illness, Medicine, and How to Live.* Chicago: University of Chicago Press.

Frank, Geyla. 2000. *Venus on Wheels: Two Decades of Dialogue on Disability, Biography, and Being Female in America.* Los Angeles: University of California Press.

Frankenberg, Ronald. 1966. *Communities in Britain: Social Life in Town and Country.* Baltimore, Md.: Penguin.

The Free Dictionary. N.d. Mutuality. Accessed January 29, 2012. http://www.thefreedictionary.com/mutuality.

Galtung, Johan. 1967. After Camelot. In *The Rise and Fall of Project Camelot: Studies in the Relationship between Social Science and Practical Politics.* Edited by Irving Louis Horowitz, 281–312. Cambridge, Mass.: MIT Press.

Geertz, Clifford. 1973. *The Interpretation of Cultures.* New York: Basic.

———. 1983a. "From the Native's Point of View": On the Nature of Anthropological Understanding. In *Local Knowledge: Further Essays in Interpretive Anthropology.* By Clifford Geertz, 55–70. New York: Basic Books.

———. 1983b. *Local Knowledge: Further Essays in Interpretive Anthropology.* New York: Basic Books.

———. 1988. *Works and Lives: The Anthropologist as Author.* Stanford, Calif.: Stanford University Press.

———. 2002. An Inconstant Profession: The Anthropological Life in Interesting Times. *Annual Review of Anthropology* 31: 1–19.

Gell, Alfred. 1998. *Art and Agency: An Anthropological Theory*. New York: Oxford University Press.

Gettelman, Jeffrey. 2011. As an Enemy Retreats, Clans Carve up Somalia. *New York Times*, September 9. Accessed April 6, 2013. http://www.nytimes.com/2011/09/10/world/africa/10somalia.html?pagewanted=all&_r=00.

Gibson-Graham J. K. 2006. *A Post-Capitalist Politics*. Minneapolis: University of Minnesota Press.

Gluckman, Max. 1956. *Custom and Conflict in Africa*. New York: Barnes and Noble.

Gobodo-Madikizela, Pumla. 2003. *A Human Being Died That Night: A South African Woman Confronts the Legacy of Apartheid*. New York: Houghton Mifflin.

Goffman, Erving. 1959. *The Presentation of Self in Everyday Life*. New York: Anchor Books.

Golub, Alex (aka Rex). 2011. Section in Anthropology Love Letters by daniel.lende. *Neuranthropology: Understanding the Encultured Brain and Body*. Accessed April 15, 2012. http://blogs.plos.org/neuroanthropology/2011/03/06/anthropology-love-letters/.

Gomez, Felicia, Mary Margaret Overbey, Joseph Jones, and Amy Beckrich. 2007. *A Family Guide to Talking About Race*. Washington, D.C.: American Anthropological Association.

Goodman, Alan, Yolanda Moses, and Joseph Jones. 2012. *RACE: Are We So Different?* Malden, Mass.: Wiley-Blackwell.

Graeber, David. 2002. The New Anarchists. *New Left Review* 13: 61–73. http://newleftreview.org/II/13/david-graeber-the-new-anarchists.

———. 2004. *Fragments of an Anarchist Anthropology*. Chicago: Prickly Paradigm Press.

———. 2010. *Debt: The First 5000 Years*. Brooklyn: Melville House.

Gregory, Steven. 1998. *Black Corona: Race and the Politics of Place in an Urban Community*. Princeton, N.J.: Princeton University Press.

———, and Roger Sanjek, eds. 1994. *Race*. New Brunswick, N.J.: Rutgers University Press.

Gronseth, Anna Sigfried, and Dona Lee Davis, eds. 2010. *Mutuality and Empathy: Self and Other in the Ethnographic Encounter*. Canon Pyon, Herefordshire: Sean Kingston Publishing.

Gronwall, Dorothy, Philip Wrightson, and Peter Waddel. 2002. *Head Injury: The Facts*. 2nd ed. Oxford: Oxford University Press.

Gubrium, Jaber. 1975. *Living and Dying at Murray Manor*. New York: St. Martin's Press.

Gudeman, Stephen. 2009. Necessity or Contingency: Mutuality and Market. In *Market and Society: The Great Transformation Today*. Edited by Chris Hann and Keith Hart, 17–37. Cambridge: Cambridge University Press.

Guo, Zibin. 2000. *Ginseng and Aspirin: Health Care Alternatives for Aging Chinese in New York*. Ithaca, N.Y.: Cornell University Press.

———. 2009. Seated Tai Chi Chuan for Ambulatory Difficulty. *Acupuncture Today* 10 (10): 1, 37.

———, Becca Levy, Ladson Hinton, and Sue Ellen Levkoff. 2000. The Power of Labels: Recruiting Chinese American Caregivers of Dementia. *Journal of Aging and Mental Health* 6 (1): 103–112.

Gupta, Akhil, and James Ferguson, eds. 1997a. *Anthropological Locations: Boundaries and Grounds of a Field Science*. Berkeley: University of California Press.

———. 1997b. Discipline and Practice: "The Field" as Site, Method, and Location in Anthropology. In *Anthropological Locations: Boundaries and Grounds of a Field Science*. Edited by Akhil Gupta and James Ferguson, 1–46. Berkeley: University of California Press.

Gusterson, Hugh. 1998. *Nuclear Rites: A Weapons Laboratory at the End of the Cold War*. Berkeley: University of California Press.

———, and Catherine Besteman, eds. 2009. *The Insecure American: How We Got Here and What We Should Do About It*. Berkeley: University of California Press.

Hall, Robert. 1997. *An Archaeology of the Soul*. Urbana: University of Illinois Press.

Halliday, M. A. K. 1976. Anti-languages. *American Anthropologist* 78 (3): 570–584.

Haney López, Ian. 2004. Race and Colorblindness after *Hernandez* and *Brown*. Accessed February 14, 2014. http://www.understandingrace.org/resources/pdf/myth_reality/haneylopez.pdf.

Hangen, Susan. 2006. The Emergence of a Mongol Race in Nepal. *Anthropology News* 47 (2): 12.

Hannerz, Ulf. 2010. *Anthropology's World: Life in a Twenty-First-Century Discipline*. New York: Pluto Press.

Harding, Susan. 2001. *The Book of Falwell: Fundamentalist Language and Politics*. Princeton, N.J.: Princeton University Press.

Hardt, Michael, and Antonio Negri. 2009. *Commonwealth*. Cambridge, Mass.: Harvard University Press.

Harir, Sharif. 1983. *Old-Timers and New-Comers: Politics and Ethnicity in a Sudanese Community*. Bergen, Norway: Department of Social Anthropology, University of Bergen.

Harmon, Amy. 2010. Indian Tribe Wins Fight to Limit Research of Its DNA. *New York Times*, April 21. Accessed April 10, 2013. http://www.nytimes.com/2010/04/22/us/22dna.html?pagewanted=all&_r=0.

Harris, Marvin. 1958. *Portugal's African "Wards": A First-Hand Report on Labor and Education in Mocambique*. New York: American Committee on Africa.

———. 1964. *Patterns of Race in the Americas*. New York: Norton.

———. 1967. The Myth of the Sacred Cow. *Natural History*, March, 6–12.

———. 1968. Big Bust on Morningside Heights. *The Nation*, June 10, 757–763.

———. 1974. *Cows, Pigs, Wars, and Witches: The Riddles of Culture*. New York: Random House.

Harrison, Faye V., ed. 1997. *Decolonizing Anthropology: Moving Further Toward an Anthropology for Liberation*. Arlington, Va.: American Anthropological Association.

———. 1998. Introduction: Expanding the Discourse on "Race." *American Anthropologist* 100: 609–631.

———. 2012. Dismantling Anthropology's Domestic and International Peripheries. *World Anthropology Network e-Journal* 6: 87–110. Accessed May 30, 2013. http://www.ram-wan.net/documents/05_e_Journal/journal-6/5-harrison.pdf.

Hart, Donna, and Pamela Ashmore. 2006. Changing Students' Understanding of Race. *Anthropology News* 47 (3): 10–11.

Hart, Keith. 1982. *The Political Economy of West African Agriculture*. Cambridge: Cambridge University Press.

Hartigan, John, Jr. 2006. Saying "Socially Constructed" Is Not Enough. *Anthropology News* 47 (2): 8.

Harvard Medical School. 2005. Tai Chi: An Ancient Art That Helps the Heart? The Easy Exercises and Deep Breathing of the Chinese Martial Art Could Offer Excellent Self-Defense for the Damaged or Failing Heart. *Harvard Heart Letter* 15 (6): 3.

Harvey, David. 2009. *The Enigma of Capital: And the Crises of Capitalism*. New York: Oxford University Press.

Henriksen, George. 2003. Consultancy and Advocacy as Radical Anthropology. *Social Analysis* 47 (1): 116–123.

Herzig-Yoshinaga, Aiko, and Marjorie Lee, eds. 2012. *Speaking Out for Personal Justice: Site Summaries of Testimonies and Witness Registry from the U.S. Commission on Wartime Relocation and Internment of Civilians Hearings*. Los Angeles: University of California, Los Angeles Asian American Studies Center.

Hill, Jane. 1998. Language, Race, and White Public Space. *American Anthropologist* 100: 680–689.

Hirabayashi, Gordon K., James A. Hirabayashi, and Lane Ryo Hirabayashi. 2013. *A Principled Stand: The Story of Hirabayashi v. United States*. Seattle: University of Washington Press.

Hirabayashi, Lane Ryo. 1974. An Analysis of Conflict in a Private Social Service Agency in a Japanese American Community. Paper for the fulfillment of the Senior Project Requirement for the Hutchins School of Liberal Studies, California State College, Sonoma.

———. 1981. Migration, Association, and Mutual Aid. PhD diss., University of California, Berkeley.

———. 1986a. The Impact of Incarceration on Nisei Schoolchildren. In *Japanese Americans: From Relocation to Redress*. Edited by Roger Daniels, Sandra C. Taylor, Harry H. L. Kitano, and Leonard J. Arrington, 44–51. Salt Lake City: University of Utah Press.

———. 1986b. The Marriage of a *Yobiyose* Woman. *A Thousand Voices*, no. 2, 12.

———. 1993. *Cultural Capital: Mountain Zapotec Migrant Associations in Mexico City*. Tucson: University of Arizona Press.

———, ed. 1995. *Inside an American Concentration Camp: Japanese American Resistance at Poston*. By Richard Nishimoto. Tucson: University of Arizona Press.

———, ed. 1998. *Teaching Asian America: Diversity and the Problem of Community*. Lanham, Md.: Rowan and Littlefield.

———. 1999. *The Politics of Fieldwork: Research in an American Concentration Camp*. Tucson: University of Arizona Press.

———. 2002a. Community Destroyed? Assessing the Impact of the Loss of Community on Japanese Americans During World War II. In *Re/Collecting Early Asian America: Essays in Cultural History*. Edited by Josephine Lee, Imogene L. Lim, and Yuko Matsukawa, 94–107. Philadelphia: Temple University Press.

———. 2002b. Culture, Power, and Truth: A Virtual Interview with Renaldo Rosaldo. In "Asians in the Americas: Transculturations and Power." *Amerasia Journal* 28 (2): 108–127. Special issue edited by Lane Ryo Hirabayashi and Evelyn Hu-DeHart.

———, ed. 2011. Neglected Legacies: Japanese American Women and the Redress/Reparations Movement. Special issue of *Pan Japan: The International Journal of the Japanese Diaspora* 7 (1–2).

———, with Kenichiro Shimada. 2009. *Japanese American Resettlement Through the Lens: Hikaru Carl Iwasaki and the WRA's Photographic Section, 1943–1945*. Boulder: University Press of Colorado.

———, and Evelyn Hu-DeHart, eds. 2002. Asians in the Americas: Transculturations and Power. Special issue of *Amerasia Journal* 28 (2).

———, Akemi Kikumura-Yano, and James A. Hirabayashi, eds. 2002. *New Worlds, New Lives: Globalization and People of Japanese Descent in the Americas and from Latin America in Japan*. Stanford: Stanford University Press.

Hirsch, Jennifer, and Suzanne Malec-McKenna. 2011. *Engaging Chicago's Diverse Communities in the Chicago Climate Action Plan. Community #6: Roseland's African-American Community*. Chicago: Field Museum, Environment, Culture, and Conservation Division.

Hoben, Allen. 1982. Anthropologists and Development. *Annual Review of Anthropology* 11: 349–375.

Hoffman, Susanna M., and Anthony Oliver-Smith. 2002. *Catastrophe and Culture: The Anthropology of Disaster*. Santa Fe, N.M.: School of American Research.

Holmes, Douglas R., and George E. Marcus. 2008. Collaboration Today and the Re-imagination of the Classic Scene of Fieldwork Encounter. *Collaborative Anthropologies* 1: 81–101.

Holt, Thomas. 2004. Understanding the Problematic of Race Through the Problem of Race-Mixture. Accessed Feburary 14, 2014. http://www.understandingrace.org/resources/pdf/myth_reality/holt.pdf.

Hong, Youlian, Jing Xian Li, and P. D. Robinson. 2000. Balance Control, Flexibility, and Cardiorespiratory Fitness Among Older Tai Chi Practitioners. *British Journal of Sports Medicine* 34: 29–34.

Hopi Cultural Preservation Office. N.d. *Protocol for Research, Publication and Recording: Motion, Visual, Sound, Multimedia and Other Mechanical Devices*. Kykotsmovi, Ariz.: Hopi Cultural Preservation Office.

Hopper, Kim. 2003. *Reckoning with Homelessness*. Ithaca, N.Y.: Cornell University Press.

Howe, James. 2002. *The Kuna Gathering: Contemporary Village Politics in Panama*. Tucson: Fenestra Books.

Howell, Signe. 2010. Norwegian Academic Anthropologists in Public Spaces. *Current Anthropology* 51 (Supplement 2): S269–S277.

Hudson, Mike. 2002. *Merchants of Misery: How Corporate America Profits from Poverty*. Monroe, Me.: Common Courage Press.

Husted, C., L. Pham, A. Hekking, and R. Niederman. 1999. Improving Quality of Life for People with Chronic Conditions: The Example of T'ai Chi and Multiple Sclerosis. *Alternative Therapies in Health and Medicine* 5 (5): 70–74.

Hyatt, Susan. 2011. What Was Neo-liberalism and What Comes Next? The Transformation of Citizenship in the Law-and-Order State. In *Policy Worlds: Anthropology and the Analysis of Contemporary Power*. Edited by Cris Shore, Susan Wright, and Davide Pero, 205–223. New York: Berghahn Books.

Hymes, Dell, ed. 1972. *Reinventing Anthropology*. New York: Vintage Books.

Igorot Global Organization. N.d. About IGO. http://igorot.com/cms/index.php?option=com_content&view=article&id=46&Itemid=28.

Ingold, Tim, ed. 1996. *Key Debates in Anthropology*. New York: Routledge.

———. 2000. *The Perception of the Environment: Essays in Livelihood, Dwelling and Skill*. New York: Routledge.

Innes, Robert Alexander. 2009. "Wait a Second, Who Are You Anyways?": The Insider/Outsider Debate and American Indian Studies. *American Indian Quarterly* 33 (4): 440–461.

Jablonski, Nina. 2011. Why Human Skin Comes in Colors. *AnthroNotes* 32 (1): 7–10.

Jacknis, Ira. 2002. *The Storage Box of Tradition: Kwakiutl Art, Anthropologists, and Museums, 1881–1981*. Washington, D.C.: Smithsonian Institution Press.

———. 2004. "A Magic Place": The Northwest Coast Indian Hall at the American Museum of Natural History. In *Coming to Shore: Northwest Coast Ethnology, Traditions, and Visions*. Edited by Marie Mauze, Michael Harkin, and Sergei Kan, 221–250. Lincoln: University of Nebraska Press.

Jackson, John L., Jr. 2010. On Ethnographic Sincerity. *Current Anthropology* 51 (Supplement 2): S279–S287.

———. 2011. Race and the Media. *AnthroNotes* 32 (1): 11–14.

Jacobs, Sue-Ellen. 1974a. Action and Advocacy Anthropology. *Human Organization* 33: 209–215.

———. 1974b. Doing It Our Way and Mostly for Our Own. *Human Organization* 33: 380–382.

———. 1979. "Our Babies Shall Not Die": A Community's Response to Medical Neglect. *Human Organization* 38: 120–133.

Jacobs-Huey, Lanita. 2002. The Natives Are Gazing and Talking Back: Reviewing the

Problematics of Positionality, Voice, and Accountability Among "Native" Anthropologists. *American Anthropologist* 104: 791–804.
———. 2006a. *From the Kitchen to the Parlor: Language and Becoming in African American Women's Hair Care*. New York: Oxford University Press.
———. 2006b. "The Arab Is the New Nigger": African American Comics Confront the Irony and Tragedy of September 11. *Transforming Anthropology* 14 (1): 60–64.
———, Mary Lawlor, and Cheryl Mattingly. 2011. I/We Narratives Among African American Families Raising Children with Disabilities. *Culture, Medicine and Psychiatry* 35 (1): 3–25.
Jacobson, Steven A. 1984. *Yup'ik Eskimo Dictionary*. Fairbanks: Alaska Native Language Center.
Jantz, Richard. 2003. The Meaning and Consequences of Morphological Variation. Accessed February 14, 2014. http://www.understandingrace.org/resources/pdf/myth_reality/jantz.pdf.
Jenks, Albert Ernest. 1905. *The Bontoc Igorot*. Department of the Interior Ethnological Survey, pub. 1. Manila: Bureau of Printing.
Johns Hopkins Health Alerts. 2007. Try Tai Chi for Your Health. *Healthy Living Special Report*, October 3.
Johnson, Walton. 2012. Dismantling Africana Studies at Rutgers University. In *Racism in the Academy: The New Millennium*. Edited by Audrey Smedley and Janis Faye Hutchinson, 79–89. Arlington, Va.: American Anthropological Association.
Johnston, Francis. 2004. Race and Biology: Changing Currents in Muddy Waters. Accessed February 14, 2014. http://www.understandingrace.org/resources/pdf/myth_reality/johnston.pdf.
Jones, Delmos J. 1970. Towards a Native Anthropology. *Human Organization* 29 (4): 251–259.
Jones, Joseph. 2008. RACE Project Summer Update. *Anthropology News* 49 (7): 17.
———. 2009. Exhibition and Outreach Update. *Anthropology News* 50 (5): 21.
———, and Amy Beckrich. 2006. Understanding Race, Human Variation and Health. *Anthropology News* 47 (2): 25–26.
———, Yolanda Moses, and Alan Goodman. 2009. Next Steps for a Public Anthropology of Race. *Anthropology News* 50 (3): 19.
———, Mary Margaret Overbey, Alan Goodman, Carol Mukhopadhyay, Yolanda Moses, and Amy Beckrich. 2007a. *RACE: A Teacher's Guide for High School*. Arlington, Va.: American Anthropological Association.
———, Mary Margaret Overbey, Alan Goodman, Carol Mukhopadhyay, Yolanda Moses, and Amy Beckrich. 2007b. *RACE: A Teacher's Guide for Middle School*. Arlington, Va.: American Anthropological Association.
———, Mary Margaret Overbey, Stacey Lathrop, and Yolanda Moses. 2005. Rethinking Race and Human Variation. *Anthropology News* 46 (6): 19.

Judd, Neil. 1967. *The Bureau of American Ethnology: A Partial History*. Norman: University of Oklahoma Press.

Kane, Rosalie, and Arthur Caplan, eds. 1990. *Everyday Ethics: Resolving Dilemmas in Nursing Home Life*. New York: Springer Publishing Company.

Kaplan, Robert. 1994. The Coming Anarchy. *Atlantic Magazine*, February. Accessed April 4, 2013. http://www.theatlantic.com/magazine/archive/1994/02/the-coming-anarchy/4670/.

Keenan, Elinor. 1975. A Sliding Sense of Obligatoriness: The Polystructure of Malagasy Oratory. In *Political Language and Oratory in Traditional Society*. Edited by Maurice Bloch, 93–112. London: Academic Press.

Keil, Charles. 1966. *Urban Blues*. Chicago: University of Chicago Press.

———, and Steven Feld. 1994. *Music Grooves: Essays and Dialogues*. Chicago: University of Chicago Press.

Kendis, Kaoru Oguri. 1989. *A Matter of Comfort: Ethnic Maintenance and Ethnic Style Among Third Generation Japanese Americans*. New York: AMS Press.

Keyes, Ralph. 1995. *The Courage to Write: How Writers Transcend Fear*. New York: Henry Holt and Company.

Khandelwal, Madhulika. 2002. *Becoming American, Being Indian: An Immigrant Community in New York City*. Ithaca, N.Y.: Cornell University Press.

Khanna, Sunil, Nancy Romero-Daza, Sherylyn Briller, and Linda A. Bennett. 2008. *Promoting Applied Scholarship for Tenure and Promotion*. Consortium of Applied and Practicing Anthropology Programs. http://www.copaa.info/resources_for_programs/Tenure%20and%20Promotion%20for%20Applied%20Anthropologists.pdf.

Kikumura-Yano, Akemi, Lane Ryo Hirabayashi, and James Hirabayashi, eds. 2005. *Common Ground: The Japanese American National Museum and the Culture of Collaborations*. Boulder: University Press of Colorado.

Killion, Thomas, ed. 2007. *Opening Archaeology: Repatriation's Impact on Contemporary Research and Practice*. Santa Fe, N.M.: School for Advanced Research Press.

Kirsteins, Andrew, Frederick Dietz, and Shie-Ming Hwang.1991. Evaluating the Safety and Potential Use of a Weight-Bearing Exercise, Tai-Chi Chuan, for Rheumatoid Arthritis Patients. *American Journal of Physical Medicine and Rehabilitation* 70: 136–141.

Kiste, Robert. 1976. The People of Enewetak Atoll Versus the U.S. Department of Defense. In *Ethics and Anthropology: Dilemmas in Fieldwork*. Edited by Michael Rynkiewich and James Spradley, 61–80. New York: John Wiley.

Klein, Penelope, and William Adams. 2004. Comprehensive Therapeutic Benefits of Taiji: A Critical Review. *American Journal of Physical Medicine and Rehabilitation* 83: 735–745.

Klein, Penelope, and Lynn Rivers. 2006. Taiji for Individuals with Parkinson Disease and Their Support Partners: Program Evaluation. *Journal of Neurological Physical Therapy* 30: 22–27.

Knauft, Bruce M. 2006. Anthropology in the Middle. *Anthropological Theory* 6 (4): 407–430.

Koff, Clea. 2004. *The Bone Woman: A Forensic Anthropologist's Search for Truth in the Mass Graves of Rwanda, Bosnia, Croatia, and Kosovo.* New York: Random House.

Kohrman, Matthew. 2005. *Bodies of Difference: Experiences of Disability and Institutional Advocacy in the Making of Modern China.* Berkeley: University of California Press.

Kottak, Conrad. 1998. Presenting Anthropology to Diverse Audiences. In *Handbook of Methods in Cultural Anthropology.* Edited by H. Russell Bernard, 737–761. Walnut Creek, Calif.: Altamira.

———. 2004. Columbia University's Bahian Legacy. Paper presented at "O Projeto UNESCO no Brasil: Uma Volta Critica ao Campo 50 Anos Despois," Faculdade de Medicina da Bahia, Universidade Federal da Bahia, Salvador, Bahia, Brazil, January 12–14.

Kozol, Jonathan. 1995. *Amazing Grace: The Lives of Children and the Conscience of a Nation.* New York: Random House.

Kretzmann, John P., and John L. McKnight. 1993. *Building Communities from the Inside Out: A Path Toward Finding and Mobilizing a Community's Assets.* Chicago: ACTA Publications.

Kroeber, A. L. 1906. Measurements of Igorotes. *American Anthropologist* 8: 194–195.

———. 1939. *Cultural and Natural Areas of Native North America.* University of California Publications in American Archaeology and Ethnology 38. Berkeley: University of California Press.

Kumar, Nita. 1992. *Friends, Brothers, and Informants: Fieldwork Memoirs of Benares.* Berkeley: University of California Press.

La Flesche, Francis. 1900. *The Middle Five: Indian Boys at School.* Boston: Small, Maynard & Co.

———. 1905. *Who Was the Medicine Man?* Hampton, Va.: Hampton Institute Press.

———. 1921. The Osage Tribe: Rite of Chiefs. In *Bureau of American Ethnology Thirty-sixth Annual Report*, 37–597. Washington, D.C.: Smithsonian Institution.

———. 1925. The Osage Tribe: Rite of Vigil. In *Bureau of American Ethnology Thirty-ninth Annual Report*, 31–630. Washington, D.C.: Smithsonian Institution.

———. 1928. The Osage Tribe: Two Versions of the Child-Naming Rite. In *Bureau of American Ethnology Forty-Third Annual Report*, 23–164. Washington, D.C.: Smithsonian Institution.

———. 1930. The Osage Tribe: Rite of the Waxo'be. In *Bureau of American Ethnology Forty-fifth Annual Report*, 523–833. Washington, D.C.: Smithsonian Institution.

Lamphere, Louise. 2004a. The Convergence of Applied, Practicing, and Public Anthropology in the 21st Century. *Human Organization* 63: 431–443.

———. 2004b. Unofficial Histories: A Vision of Anthropology from the Margins. *American Anthropologist* 106: 126–139

Lancaster, Roger. 2011. *Sex Panic and the Punitive State.* Berkeley: University of California Press.

Lassiter, Luke Eric. 2005. Collaborative Ethnography and Public Anthropology. *Current Anthropology* 46 (1): 83–106.

———. 2006. Collaborative Ethnography Matters. *Anthropology News* 47 (5): 20–21.

Lawlor, Mary. 2004. Mothering Work: Negotiating Health Care, Illness, and Disability and Development. In *Mothering Occupations: Challenge, Agency, and Participation.* Edited by Susan Esdaile and Judith Olsen, 306–323. Philadelphia: F. A. Davis.

———, and Cheryl Mattingly. 2001. Beyond the Unobtrusive Observer: Reflections on Researcher-Informant Relationships in Urban Ethnography. *American Journal of Occupational Therapy* 55: 147–154.

———. 2009. Understanding Family Perspectives on Illness and Disability Experience. In *Willard and Spackman's Occupational Therapy.* 11th ed. Edited by Elizabeth Blesedale Crepeau, Ellen S. Cohn, and Barbara A. Boyt Schell, 33–44. Philadelphia: Lippincott Williams and Wilkins.

Leach, Edmund. 1968. *A Runaway World? The B.B.C. Reith Lectures.* New York: Oxford University Press.

Leacock, Eleanor. 1969. *Teaching and Learning in City Schools: A Comparative Study.* New York: Basic.

Lee, S. Agnes, and Michelle Farrell. 2006. Is Cultural Competency a Backdoor to Racism? *Anthropology News* 47 (3): 9–10.

Lee, Simon Craddock. 2006. Rethinking Race and Ethnicity in Health Disparities. *Anthropology News* 47 (3): 7–8.

Leon, Lamgen. 1990. *Asians in Latin America and the Caribbean: A Bibliography.* Flushing, N.Y.: Asian/American Center, Queens College, City University of New York.

Leonard Cheshire Disability. 2009. *China Country Profile.* London: Leonard Cheshire Disability. Accessed February 27, 2014. http://www.lcint.webbler.co.uk/?lid=3438&tmpl=mainprint

Leone, Mark, Jocelyn Knauf, and Amanda Tang. 2011. Frederick Douglass and the Archaeology of Wye House. *AnthroNotes* 32 (1): 15–18.

Lévi-Strauss, Claude. 1962. *The Savage Mind.* Chicago: University of Chicago Press.

Lewin, Ellen, and William Leap, eds. 1996. *Out in the Field: Lesbian and Gay Reflections.* Urbana: University of Illinois Press.

Lewis, Diane. 1973. Anthropology and Colonialism. *Current Anthropology* 14: 581–602.

Liberty, Margot, ed. 1978a. *American Indian Intellectuals.* St. Paul, Minn.: West Publishing.

———. 1978b. Francis La Flesche, Omaha, 1857–1932. In *American Indian Intellectuals.* Edited by Margot Liberty, 45–59. St. Paul, Minn.: West Publishing.

———. 1978c. Introduction to *American Indian Intellectuals.* Edited by Margo Liberty, 1–13. St. Paul, Minn.: West Publishing.

Lippert, Dorothy. 2007. The Rise of Indigenous Archaeology: How Repatriation Has Transformed Archaeological Ethics and Practice. In *Opening Archaeology: Repatri-*

ation's Impact on Contemporary Research and Practice. Edited by Thomas Killion, 151–160. Santa Fe, N.M.: School for Advanced Research Press.

Lipsitz, George. 1998. *The Possessive Investment of Whiteness*. Philadelphia: Temple University Press.

Lobo, Susan. 1977. *Kin Relationships and the Process of Urbanization in the Squatter Settlements of Lima, Peru*. PhD diss., Department of Anthropology, University of Arizona.

———. 1982. *A House of My Own: Social Organization in the Squatter Settlements of Lima, Peru*. Tucson: University of Arizona Press.

———. 1984. *Tengo Casa Propia*. Mexico City: Instituto Indigenista Interamericano.

———. 1998. Is Urban a Person or a Place? Characteristics of Urban Indian Country. *American Indian Culture and Research Journal* 22: 89–102.

———. 2001. Is Urban a Person or a Place? Characteristics of Urban Indian Country. In *American Indians and the Urban Experience*. Edited by Susan Lobo and Kurt Peters, 73–84. Walnut Creek, Calif.: Altamira Press.

———. 2009. Urban Clan Mothers: Native Women Activists. In *Keeping the Campfires Going: Native Women's Activism in Urban Communities*. Edited by Susan Applegate Krouse and Heather A. Howard, 1–21. Omaha: University of Nebraska Press.

———, and Editorial Committee, Community History Project, Intertribal Friendship House, eds. 2002. *Urban Voices: The Bay Area American Indian Community*. Tucson: University of Arizona Press.

———, and Kurt Peters, eds. 2001. *American Indians and the Urban Experience*. Walnut Creek, Calif.: Altamira Press.

———, and Steve Talbot, eds. 1998. *Native American Voices: A Reader*. New York: Addison Wesley Longman.

———, and Steve Talbot, eds. 2001. *Native American Voices: A Reader*. 2nd ed. Upper Saddle River, N.J.: Prentice Hall.

———, Steve Talbot, and Traci L. Morris, eds. 2010. *Native American Voices: A Reader*. 3rd ed. Upper Saddle River, N.J.: Prentice Hall.

Long, Jeffrey. 2003. Human Genetic Variation: The Mechanisms and Results of Microevolution. Accessed February 14, 2014. http://www.understandingrace.org/resources/pdf/myth_reality/long.pdf.

Longboan, Liezel. 2011. E-gorots: Exploring Indigenous Identity in Translocal Spaces. *South East Asia Research* 19: 319–341.

Lowie, Robert. 1917. Oral Tradition and History. *Journal of American Folklore* 30 (116): 161–167.

———. 1935. *The Crow Indians*. New York: Farrar and Rinehart.

Lutkehaus, Nancy. 2008. *Margaret Mead: The Making of an American Icon*. Princeton, N.J.: Princeton University Press.

MacClancy, Jeremy. 1996. Popularizing Anthropology. In *Popularizing Anthropology*. Edited by Jeremy MacClancy and Chris McDonaugh, 1–57. London: Routledge.

Mafeje, Archie. 1971. The Ideology of "Tribalism." *Journal of Modern African Studies* 9: 253–261.

———. 1975. Religion, Class and Ideology in South Africa. In *Religion and Social Change in Southern Africa: Anthropological Essays in Honour of Monica Wilson.* Edited by Michael Whisson and Martin West, 164–184. London: Rex Collings.

———. 1978. Soweto and Its Aftermath. *Review of African Political Economy* 5: 17–30.

Magubane, Bernard, and James C. Faris. 1985. On the Political Relevance of Anthropology. *Dialectical Anthropology* 9: 91–104.

Malinowski, Bronislaw. 1962. *Sex, Culture, and Myth.* New York: Harcourt Brace.

Malkki, Liisa. 1995. Refugees and Exiles: From "Refugee Studies" to the National Order of Things. *Annual Review of Anthropology* 24: 495–523.

———. 1997. News and Culture: Transitory Phenomena and the Fieldwork Tradition. In *Anthropological Locations: Boundaries and Grounds of a Field Science.* Edited by Akhil Gupta and James Ferguson, 86–101. Berkeley: University of California Press.

Marcus, George E. 1998. *Ethnography Through Thick and Thin.* Princeton: Princeton University Press.

———. 2008. The End(s) of Ethnography: Social/Cultural Anthropology's Signature Form of Producing Knowledge in Transition. *Cultural Anthropology* 23 (1): 1–14.

———. 2009. Notes Toward an Ethnographic Memoir of Supervising Graduate Research Through Anthropology's Decades of Transformation. In *Fieldwork Is Not What It Used to Be.* Edited by James Faubion and George Marcus, 1–32. Ithaca, N.Y.: Cornell University Press.

———, and Dick Cushman. 1982. Ethnographies as Texts. *Annual Review of Anthropology* 11: 25–69.

———, and Michael Fischer. 1986. *Anthropology as Cultural Critique: An Experimental Moment in the Human Sciences.* Chicago: University of Chicago Press.

Marcuse, Peter. 1985. Gentrification, Abandonment, and Displacement: Connections, Causes, and Policy Responses in New York City. *Washington University Journal of Urban and Contemporary Law* 28: 195–240. (Reprinted in revised form in 1986 as Abandonment, Gentrification and Displacement: The Linkages in New York City in *Gentrification of the City*, edited by Neil Smith and Peter Williams, 153–177, Boston: Allen and Unwin. Also reprinted in 2010 in *The Gentrification Reader*, edited by Loretta Lees, Tom Slater, and Elvin Wyly, 333–348, London: Routledge.)

Marino, Elizabeth. 2012. Review of *Qaluyaarmiuni Nunamtenek Qanemciput/Our Nelson Island Stories: Meanings of Place on the Bering Sea Coast*, transcribed and translated by Alice Rearden; edited by Ann Fienup-Riordan. *Arctic* 65: 239–240.

Mark, Joan. 1988. *A Stranger in Her Native Land: Alice Fletcher and the American Indians.* Lincoln: University of Nebraska Press.

Mattingly, Cheryl. 2010. *The Paradox of Hope: Journeys Through a Clinical Borderland.* Los Angeles: University of California Press.

Mattingly, Cheryl, Mary Lawlor, and Lanita Jacobs-Huey. 2002. Narrating September 11:

Race, Gender, and the Play of Cultural Identities. *American Anthropologist* 104: 743–753.

Mauss, Marcel. 1990 [1925]. *The Gift: Forms and Functions of Exchange in Archaic Societies*. London: Routledge.

May Institute. 1993. *Information on Brain Injury in Children*. Boston: Tufts New England Medical Center.

Mayer, Adrian. 1966. The Significance of Quasi-Groups in the Study of Complex Societies. In *The Social Anthropology of Complex Societies*. Edited by Michael Banton, 97–122. New York: Praeger.

Mayo Clinic Staff. 2012. *Tai Chi: A Gentle Way to Fight Stress*. Rochester, Minn.: Mayo Foundation for Medical Education and Research. Accessed April 3, 2013. http://www.mayoclinic.com/health/tai-chi/SA00087.

Mbeki, Thabo. 2007. Steve Biko Memorial Lecture Delivered by the President of South Africa, Thabo Mbeki, on the Occasion of the 30th Anniversary of the Death of Stephen Bantu Biko, Cape Town. Accessed April 4, 2013. http://us-cdn.creamermedia.co.za/assets/articles/attachments/07218_bikomemoriallecture.pdf.

McClaurin, Irma, ed. 2001a. *Black Feminist Anthropology: Theory, Politics, Praxis, and Poetics*. New Brunswick, N.J.: Rutgers University Press.

———. 2001b. Theorizing a Black Feminist Self in Anthropology: Toward an Autoethnographic Approach. In *Black Feminist Anthropology: Theory, Politics, Praxis, and Poetics*. Edited by Irma McClaurin, 49–76. New Brunswick, N.J.: Rutgers University Press.

McCurdy, David. 2007. A Tour of the AAA-Sponsored Race Exhibit. *General Anthropology* 14 (1): 3–6.

McGaghie, William. 2007. Medical Education for Cultural Competence: Policies, Initiatives, and Student Selection. Accessed February 14, 2014. http://www.understandingrace.org/resources/pdf/disease/mcgaghie.pdf.

McGibbon, Chris, David Krebs, Steven Wolf, Peter Wayne, Donna Moxley Scarborough, and Stephen Parker. 2004. Tai Chi and Vestibular Rehabilitation Effects on Gaze and Whole-Body Stability. *Journal of Vestibular Research* 14: 467–478.

McKay, J. K. 1907. *Memo*. Washington, D.C.: U.S. Government Printing Office.

McLeod, W. H. 1974. Ahluwalias and Ramgarhias: Two Sikh Castes. *South Asia* 4: 78–90.

McNickle, D'arcy. 1970. American Indians Who Never Were. *The Indian Historian* 3: 4–7.

Mead, Margaret. 1928. *Coming of Age in Samoa*. New York: William Morrow.

———. 1930a. *Growing Up in New Guinea*. New York: William Morrow.

———. 1930b. *Social Organization of Manu'a*. Honolulu: Bernice P. Bishop Museum.

———. 1934. *Kinship in the Admiralty Islands*. New York: American Museum of Natural History.

Meade, Marie, and Ann Fienup-Riordan. 2005. *Ciuliamta Akluit/Things of Our Ancestors: Yup'ik Elders Explore the Jacobsen Collection at the Ethnologisches Museum Berlin*. Seattle: University of Washington Press.

Medicine, Beatrice. 2001. *Learning to Be an Anthropologist and Remaining "Native": Selected Writings*. Urbana: University of Illinois Press.

Miller, Susan, and Renée Shield. 2007. *Palliative Care/Hospice for Persons with Terminal and/or Chronic Progressive Illness*. Providence, R.I.: Center for Gerontology and Health Care Research, Warren Albert Medical School, Brown University.

Mills, Catherine. 2008. Playing with Law: Agamben and Derrida on Postcolonial Justice. *South Atlantic Quarterly* 107 (1): 15–37.

Mills, C. Wright. 1959. *The Sociological Imagination*. New York: Oxford University Press.

Mintz, Sidney. 1960. *Worker in the Cane: A Puerto Rican Life History*. New Haven, Conn.: Yale University Press.

Mitchell Kernan, Claudia. 1971. *Language Behavior in a Black Urban Community*. Berkeley: University of California Language-Behavior Research Laboratory.

Montagu, M. F. Ashley, ed. 1956. *Marriage: Past and Present—A Debate Between Robert Briffault and Bronislaw Malinowski*. Boston: Porter Sargent.

Moore, Henrietta. 1995. *A Passion for Difference: Essays in Anthropology and Gender*. Bloomington: Indiana University Press.

Morgan, Lewis Henry. 1851. *The League of the Ho-de-no-sau-nee, or Iroquois*. New York: Corinth.

Morningstar, Louise Ray, with Alexia Dorszynski. 1997. *Journey Through Brain Trauma: A Mother's Story of Her Daughter's Recovery*. Dallas, Tex.: Taylor Press.

Moses, Yolanda. 2004. The Continuing Power of the Concept of "Race." *Anthropology & Education Quarterly* 35 (1): 146–148.

———. 2007. The Public Education Project of the AAA: "Race: Are We So Different?" *General Anthropology* 14 (1): 1–3.

———. 2010a. California Museum Welcomes RACE Exhibit. *Anthropology News* 51 (6): 25.

———. 2010b. Public Policy Implications of the RACE: Are We So Different? Project. *Anthropology News* 51 (9): 24.

———. 2011. Funding of RACE: Are We So Different? *Anthropology News* 52 (8): 11.

———, and Joseph Jones. 2011. Anthropology and the Race Project. *AnthroNotes* 32 (1): 4–6.

Mukhopadhyay, Carol, Rosemary Henze, and Yolanda Moses. 2007. *How Real Is Race?: A Sourcebook on Race, Culture, and Biology*. Lanham, Md.: Rowman & Littlefield.

Mukhopadhyay, Carol, and Yolanda Moses. 1997. Reestablishing "Race" in Anthropological Discourse. *American Anthropologist* 99: 517–533.

Mullings, Leith. 1997. *On Our Terms: Race, Class, and Gender in the Lives of African American Women*. New York: Routledge.

———. 2005. Resistance and Resilience: The Sojourner Syndrome and the Social Context of Reproduction in Central Harlem. *Transforming Anthropology* 13 (2): 79–91.

———. 2013. From the President: Communication, Engagement and Outreach. *Anthropology News* 54 (9–10): 3.

———, and Alaka Wali. 2001. *Stress and Resilience: The Social Context of Reproduction in Central Harlem*. New York: Kluwer Academic/Plenum Publishers.

Mullings, Leith, Alaka Wali, Diane McLean, Janet Mitchell, Sabiyha Prince, Deborah Thomas, and Patricia Tovar. 2001. Qualitative Methodologies and Community Participation in Examining Reproductive Experiences: The Harlem Birth Right Project. *Maternal and Child Health* 5 (2): 85–93.

Murphy, Robert, ed. 1976. *Selected Papers from the American Anthropologist 1946–1970*. Washington, D.C.: American Anthropological Association.

Mustian, Karen, Jeffrey Katula, Diane Gill, Joseph Roscoe, David Lang, and Karen Murphy. 2004. Tai Chi Chuan, Health-Related Quality of Life and Self-Esteem: A Randomized Trial with Breast Cancer Survivors. *Supportive Care in Cancer: Official Journal of the Multinational Association of Supportive Care in Cancer* 12: 871–876.

Myerhoff, Barbara. 1979. *Number Our Days*. New York: E. P. Dutton.

Myrdal, Gunnar. 1969. *Objectivity in Social Research*. New York: Pantheon.

Nader, Laura. 1976. Professional Standards and What We Study. In *Ethics and Anthropology: Dilemmas in Fieldwork*. Edited by Michael Rynkiewich and James Spradley, 167–182. New York: John Wiley.

Nakatsu, Penny. 2013. Jim Hirabayashi. *Amerasia Journal* 39 (1): 133–134.

Nakane, Chie. 1967. *Kinship and Economic Organization in Rural Japan*. London: Athlone Press.

Narayan, Kirin. 1993. How Native Is a "Native" Anthropologist? *American Anthropologist* 95: 671–686.

———. 1995. Participant Observation. In *Women Writing Culture*. Edited by Ruth Behar and Deborah Gordon, 33–48. Berkeley: University of California Press.

Nasr, Jamil M. 2007. *Muslim Communities of Grace: The Sufi Brotherhoods in Islamic Religious Life*. New York: Columbia University Press.

Nasr, Seyyed Hossein. 1989. *Knowledge and the Sacred*. Albany: State University of New York Press.

———. 2008. *The Garden of Truth: The Vision and Promise of Sufism, Islam's Mystical Tradition*. New York: Harper One.

National Writers Union. 1995. *National Writers Union Guide to Freelance Rates and Standard Practice*. New York: National Writers Union.

Norcini, Marilyn. 2007. *Edward P. Dozier: The Paradox of the American Indian Anthropologist*. Tucson: University of Arizona Press.

Nowell, April. 2010. Defining Behavioral Modernity in the Context of Neanderthal and Anatomically Modern Human Populations. *Annual Review of Anthropology* 39: 437–452.

Obbo, Christine. 1980. *African Women: Their Struggle for Economic Independence*. London: Zed.

Okely, Judith. 1996. *Own or Other Culture*. London: Routledge.

Orser, Charles E., Jr. 1998. The Challenge of Race to American Historical Archaeology. *American Anthropologist* 100: 661–668.

Ottenberg, Simon. 1968. *Double Descent in an African Society: The Afikpo Village-Group*. Seattle: University of Washington Press

———. 1975. *Masked Rituals of Afikpo: The Context of an African Art*. Seattle: University of Washington Press.

———. 1990. Thirty Years of Fieldnotes: Changing Relationships to the Text. In *Fieldnotes: The Makings of Anthropology*. Edited by Roger Sanjek, 139–160. Ithaca, N.Y.: Cornell University Press.

———. 1997. *New Traditions from Nigeria: Seven Artists of the Nsukka Group*. Washington, D.C.: Smithsonian Institution Press.

———, ed. 2002. *The Nsukka Artists and Nigerian Contemporary Art*. Seattle: University of Washington Press.

———. 2005. *Farmers and Townspeople in a Changing Nigeria: Abakaliki During Colonial Times (1905–1960)*. Ibadan, Nigeria: Spectrum Books.

———. 2006a. *Igbo Art and Culture and Other Essays*. Trenton, N.J.: Africa World Press.

———. 2006b. *Igbo Religion, Social Life, and Other Essays*. Trenton, N.J.: Africa World Press.

Overbey, Mary Margaret. 2007. AAA RACE Project Wins Awards. *Anthropology News* 48 (7): 20.

———. 2008. RACE Project Receives Second Ford Grant, Award and More. *Anthropology News* 49 (5): 25.

———, and Yolanda Moses. 2004. Interdisciplinary Conference on Race Held. *Anthropology News* 45 (8): 25.

———. 2006. Engaging Departments in Outreach on Race. *Anthropology News* 47 (2): 25.

Pace, Richard. 1998. *The Struggle for Amazon Town: Gurupa Revisited*. Boulder: Lynne Reinner.

Parezo, Nancy J., and Don D. Fowler. 2007. *Anthropology Goes to the Fair*. Lincoln: University of Nebraska Press,

Park, Kyeyoung. 1997. *The Korean American Dream: Immigrants and Small Business in New York City*. Ithaca, N.Y.: Cornell University Press.

Peoples, James, and Garrick Bailey. 2014. *Humanity: An Introduction to Cultural Anthropology*. 10th ed. Belmont, Calif.: Wadsworth.

Pina-Cabral, João de. 2013. The Two Faces of Mutuality: Contemporary Themes in Anthropology. *Anthropological Quarterly* 86 (1): 257–276.

Pitts, Margaret Jane, and Michelle Miller Day. 2007. Upward Turning Points and Positive Rapport-Development Across Time in Researcher-Participant Relationships. *Qualitative Research* 7: 177–201.

Pollock, Mica. 2006. Everyday Antiracism in Education. *Anthropology News* 47 (2): 9–10.

Price, David. 2004. *Threatening Anthropology: McCarthyism and the FBI's Surveillance of Activist Anthropologists*. Durham, N.C.: Duke University Press.

———. 2008. *Anthropological Intelligence: The Deployment and Neglect of American Anthropology in the Second World War*. Durham, N.C.: Duke University Press.

Radjou, Navi, Jaideep Prabhu, and Simone Ahuja. 2012. *Jugaad Innovation: Think Frugal, Be Flexible, Generate Breakthrough Growth*. San Francisco: Jossey-Bass.

Rappaport, Joanne. 2008. Beyond Participant Observation: Collaborative Ethnography as Theoretical Innovation. *Collaborative Anthropology* 1: 1–31.

Rapport, Nigel. 2011. The Liberal Treatment of Difference: An Untimely Meditation on Culture and Civilization. *Current Anthropology* 52 (5): 687–710.

Razsa, Maple, and Andrej Kurnik. 2012. The Occupy Movement in Žižek's Hometown: Direct Democracy and a Politics of Becoming. *American Ethnologist* 39 (2): 238–258.

Rearden, Alice, and Ann Fienup-Riordan. 2011. *Qaluyaarmiuni Nunamtenek Qanemciput/Our Nelson Island Stories: Meanings of Place on the Bering Sea Coast*. Seattle: University of Washington Press.

Rearden, Alice, Marie Meade, and Ann Fienup-Riordan. 2005. *Yupiit Qanruyutait/Yup'ik Words of Wisdom*. Lincoln: University of Nebraska Press.

Reed-Danahay, Deborah. 2005. *Locating Bourdieu*. Bloomington: Indiana University Press.

Ricourt, Milagros, and Ruby Danta. 2003. *Hispanas de Queens: Latino Panethnicity in a New York City Neighborhood*. Ithaca, N.Y.: Cornell University Press.

Ridington, Robin. 1992. Introduction to *The Omaha Indians*. By Alice Fletcher and Francis La Flesche, 1–8. Lincoln: University of Nebraska Press.

Rietsma, Jef. 2010. Speaker Impressed by Response to "RACE: Are We So Different?" in Kalamazoo, Smallest City to Host the Exhibit. *Kalamazoo Gazette*, October 3. Accessed April 3, 2013. http://www.mlive.com/news/kalamazoo/index.ssf/2010/10/speaker_impressed_by_response.html.

Rivara, Frederick P., and Beth A. Mueller. 1986. The Epidemiology and Prevention of Pediatric Head Injury. *Journal of Head Trauma Rehabilitation* 1 (4): 7–15.

Robben, Antonius. 1995. The Politics of Truth Among Perpetrators and Victims of Violence. In *Fieldwork Under Fire: Contemporary Studies of Violence and Survival*. Edited by Carolyn Nordstrom and Antonius Robben, 81–104. Berkeley: University of California Press.

———, and Jeffrey Sluka, eds. 2006. *Ethnographic Fieldwork: An Anthropological Reader*. Oxford: Wiley-Blackwell.

Rodríguez, Sylvia. 1987. Land, Water, and Ethnic Identity in Taos. In *Land, Water and Culture*. Edited by Charles Briggs and John Van Ness, 313–403. Albuquerque: University of New Mexico Press.

———. 1989. Art, Tourism, and Race Relations in Taos: Toward a Sociology of the Art Colony. *Journal of Anthropological Research* 45: 77–99.

———. 1990. Applied Research on Land and Water in New Mexico: A Critique. *Journal of the Southwest* 32: 298–315.

———. 1990. Ethnic Reconstruction in Contemporary Taos. *Journal of the Southwest* 32: 541–555.

———. 1992. The Hispano Homeland Debate Revisited. *Perspectives in Mexican American Studies* 3: 95–114.

———. 1994. The Tourist Gaze, Gentrification, and the Commodification of Subjectivity in Taos. In *Essays on the Changing Images of the Southwest*. Edited by Richard Francaviglia and David Narrett, 105–126. College Station, Tex.: Texas A&M University Press.

———. 1996. *The Matachines Dance: Ritual Symbolism and Interethnic Relations in the Rio Grande Valley*. Albuquerque, N.M.: University of New Mexico Press.

———. 1997. The Taos Fiesta: Invented Tradition and the Infrapolitics of Symbolic Reclamation. *Journal of the Southwest* 39: 33–57.

———. 1998. Fiesta Time and Plaza Space: Resistance and Accommodation in a Tourist Town. *Journal of American Folklore* 111 (493): 39–56.

———. 2001. Tourism, Whiteness, and the Vanishing Anglo. In *Seeing and Being Seen: Tourism in the American West*. Edited by David M. Wrobel and Patrick T. Long, 194–210. Lawrence: University Press of Kansas.

———. 2002. Procession and Sacred Landscape in New Mexico. *New Mexico Historical Review* 77 (1): 1–26.

———. 2003. Tourism, Difference, and Power in the Borderlands. In *The Culture of Tourism, the Tourism of Culture*. Edited by Hal Rothman, 185–205. Albuquerque: University of New Mexico Press.

———. 2006. *Acequia: Water Sharing, Sanctity, and Place*. Santa Fe, N.M.: School for Advanced Research Press.

———. 2007. Honor, Aridity, and Place. In *Expressing New Mexico*. Edited by Philip B. González, 25–41. Tucson: University of Arizona Press,

———. 2011. What Tunnels Under Taos Plaza? In *The Plazas of New Mexico*. Edited by Chris Wlson and Stephanos Polyzoides, 77–87. San Antonio, Tex.: Trinity University Press.

Rosaldo, Renato. 1985. Chicano Studies, 1970–1984. *Annual Review of Anthropology* 14: 405–427.

———. 1986. When Natives Talk Back: Chicano Anthropology since the Late Sixties. *Renato Rosaldo Lecture Monograph Series* 2: 3–20.

———. 1989a. *Culture and Truth: The Remaking of Social Analysis*. Boston: Beacon.

———. 1989b. Grief and a Headhunter's Rage. In *Culture and Truth: The Remaking of Social Analysis*. By Renato Rosaldo, 1–21. Boston: Beacon.

Rothstein, Edward. 2004. Who Should Tell History: The Tribe or the Museums? *New York Times*, December 21. Accessed April 10, 2013. http://www.nytimes.com/2004/12/21/arts/design/21muse.html.

Roy, Kaushik. 2011. *War, Culture and Society: Early Modern South Asia, 1740–1849*. London: Routledge.

Rouse, Carolyn M. 2004. "If She's a Vegetable, We'll Be Her Garden": Embodiment, Transcendence, and Citations of Competing Cultural Metaphors in the Case of a Dying Child. *American Ethnologist* 31: 514–529.

———. 2009. *Uncertain Suffering: Racial Health Care Disparities and Sickle Cell Disease.* Los Angeles: University of California Press.

Rugh, Jacob S., and Douglas S. Massey. 2010. Racial Segregation and the American Foreclosure Crisis. *American Sociological Review* 75: 629–651.

Rydell, Robert. 1984. *All the World's a Fair: Visions of Empire at American International Expositions, 1876–1916.* Chicago: University of Chicago Press.

———. 2008. New Directions for Scholarship About World Expos. In *Seize the Day: Exhibitions, Australia and the World.* Edited by Kate Darian-Smith, Richard Gillespie, Caroline Jordan, and Elizabeth Willis, 21.1–21.13. Melbourne: Monash University ePress.

Rylko-Bauer, Barbara, Merrill Singer, and John van Willigen. 2006. Reclaiming Applied Anthropology: Its Past, Present, and Future. *American Anthropologist* 108: 178–190.

Saberwal, Satish. 1990. *Mobile Men: Limits to Social Change in Urban India.* New Delhi: Manohar.

Sabloff, Jeremy. 1998. Distinguished Lecture in Archeology: Communication and the Future of American Archeology. *American Anthropologist* 100: 869–875.

———. 2011. Where Have You Gone, Margaret Mead? Anthropology and Public Intellectuals. *American Anthropologist* 113: 408–416.

Sacks, Karen Brodkin. 1988. *Caring by the Hour: Women, Work, and Organizing at Duke Medical Center.* Urbana: University of Illinois Press.

Sacks, Oliver. 1984. *A Leg to Stand on.* New York: Simon & Schuster.

Sahlins, Marshall. 2011a. What Kinship Is (Part One). *Journal of the Royal Anthropological Institute* 17: 2–19.

———. 2011b. What Kinship Is (Part Two). *Journal of the Royal Anthropological Institute* 17: 227–242.

Said, Edward. 1979. *Orientalism.* New York: Vintage.

Salih, Tayeb. 2009. *Season of Migration to the North.* New York: NYRB Classics.

Salvador, Mari Lynn. 1997. *The Art of Being Kuna.* Seattle: University of Washington Press.

Salzman, Philip. 1994. The Lone Stranger in the Heart of Darkness. In *Assessing Cultural Anthropology.* Edited by Robert Borofsky, 29–38. New York: McGraw-Hill.

Sanford, Victoria. 2006. Introduction. In *The Engaged Observer: Anthropology, Advocacy, and Activism.* Edited by Victoria Sanford and Asale Angel-Ajani, 1–18. New Brunswick, N.J.: Rutgers University Press.

Sanjek, Roger. 1969. Radical Anthropology: Values, Theory and Content. *Anthropology U.C.L.A.* 1: 21–32.

———. 1971. Brazilian Racial Terms: Some Aspects of Meaning and Learning. *American*

Anthropologist 73: 1126–1143. (Reprinted 2002 in *American Anthropology, 1971–1995: Papers from the American Anthropologist*, edited by Regna Darnell, 65–92, Lincoln: University of Nebraska Press.)

———. 1972. *Ghanaian Networks: An Analysis of Interethnic Relations in Urban Situations*. PhD diss., Department of Anthropology, Columbia University.

———. 1977a. Cognitive Maps of the Ethnic Domain in Urban Ghana: Reflections on Variability and Change. *American Ethnologist* 4: 603–622.

———. 1977b. *A Profile of Over 60 Health Services Users: A Report and Recommendations*. Berkeley, Calif.: Over 60 Health Clinic Geriatric Health Services Program.

———. 1978a. A Network Method and Its Uses in Urban Ethnography. *Human Organization* 37: 257–268.

———. 1978b. The Position of Women in the Major Departments of Anthropology, 1967–1976. *American Anthropologist* 80: 894–904.

———. 1982a. The American Anthropological Association Resolution on the Employment of Women: Genesis, Implementation, Disavowal and Resurrection. *Signs* 7: 845–868.

———. 1982b. *Federal Housing Programs and Their Impact on Homelessness*. New York: Coalition for the Homeless. (Reprinted 1986 in *Housing the Homeless*, edited by John Erickson and Charles Wilhelm, 315–321, New Brunswick, N.J.: Center for Urban Policy Research.)

———. 1982c. The Organization of Households in Adabraka: Toward a Wider Comparative Perspective. *Comparative Studies in Society and History* 23: 57–103.

———. 1983a. Female and Male Domestic Cycles in Urban Africa: The Adabraka Case. In *Female and Male in West Africa*. Edited by Christine Oppong, 330–343. London: George Allen & Unwin.

———. 1983b. Mean Streets: Two Million Call the Sidewalks Home. *Gray Panther Network*, November/December, 12. (Reprinted 1984 in *The Alternative Press Annual, 1983*, edited by Patricia Case, 183–186, Philadelphia: Temple University Press.)

———. 1984a. *Crowded Out: Homelessness and the Elderly Poor in New York City*. New York: Coalition for the Homeless & Gray Panthers of New York City. (Reprinted 1984 in *Homeless Older Americans: Hearing Before the Subcommittee on Housing and Consumer Interests of the Select Committee on Aging, House of Representatives, 98th Congress*, Comm. Pub. No. 98-461, 119–184, Washington, D.C.: U.S. Government Printing Office.)

———. 1984b. Crowded Out: Homelessness. . . . *West Side Tenant Advance*, summer.

———. 1985. Viewpoints: Don't Blame the Homeless. *Newsday*, February 8, 82–83.

———. 1986. The Gray Panthers. *Faces* 2 (7): 14–17.

———. 1987. Anthropological Work at a Gray Panther Health Clinic: Academic, Applied, and Advocacy Goals. In *Cities of the United States: Studies in Urban Anthropology*. Edited by Leith Mullings, 148–175. New York: Columbia University Press.

———, ed. 1989. *Worship and Community: Christianity and Hinduism in Contemporary Queens*. Flushing, N.Y.: Asian/American Center, Queens College, CUNY.

———, ed. 1990a. *Caribbean Asians: Chinese, Indian and Japanese Experiences in Trinidad and the Dominican Republic*. Flushing, N.Y.: Asian/American Center, Queens College, CUNY.

———, ed. 1990b. *Fieldnotes: The Makings of Anthropology*. Ithaca, N.Y.: Cornell University Press.

———. 1990c. Maid Servants and Market Women's Apprentices in Adabraka. In *At Work in Homes: Household Workers in World Perspective*. Edited by Roger Sanjek and Shellee Colen, 35–62. Washington, D.C.: American Anthropological Association.

———. 1993. Anthropology's Hidden Colonialism: Assistants and Their Ethnographers. *Anthropology Today* 9 (2): 13–18. (Revised version printed 2014 in *Ethnography in Today's World: Color Full Before Color Blind*, by Roger Sanjek, Philadelphia: University of Pennsylvania Press.)

———. 1994. Intermarriage and the Future of Races in the United States. In *Race*. Edited by Steven Gregory and Roger Sanjek, 103–130. New Brunswick, N.J.: Rutgers University Press. (Revised version printed 2014 in *Ethnography in Today's World: Color Full Before Color Blind*, by Roger Sanjek, Philadelphia: University of Pennsylvania Press.)

———. 1995. Politics, Theory, and the Nature of Cultural Things. In *Science, Materialism, and the Study of Culture*. Edited by Martin Murphy and Maxine Margolis, 39–61. Gainesville: University Press of Florida. (Revised version printed 2014 in *Ethnography in Today's World: Color Full Before Color Blind*, by Roger Sanjek, Philadelphia: University of Pennsylvania Press.)

———. 1998. *The Future of Us All: Race and Neighborhood Politics in New York City*. Ithaca, N.Y.: Cornell University Press.

———. 2000. Keeping Ethnography Alive in an Urbanizing World. *Human Organization* 59: 280–288. (Revised version printed 2014 in *Ethnography in Today's World: Color Full Before Color Blind*, by Roger Sanjek, Philadelphia: University of Pennsylvania Press.)

———. 2002. Worth Holding Onto: The Participatory Discrepancies of Political Activism. *City & Society* 14 (1): 103–117. (Revised version printed 2014 in *Ethnography in Today's World: Color Full Before Color Blind*, by Roger Sanjek, Philadelphia: University of Pennsylvania Press.)

———. 2004. Going Public: Responsibilities and Strategies in the Aftermath of Ethnography. *Human Organization* 63: 444–456. (Revised version printed 2014 in *Ethnography in Today's World: Color Full Before Color Blind*, by Roger Sanjek, Philadelphia: University of Pennsylvania Press.)

———. 2009a. *Gray Panthers*. Philadelphia: University of Pennsylvania Press.

———. 2009b. The Book That Wrote Me. In *Anthropology Off the Shelf: Anthropologists on Writing*. Edited by Alisse Waterston and Maria Vesperi, 172–181. Malden, Mass.: Blackwell.

———. 2014. *Ethnography in Today's World: Color Full Before Color Blind*. Philadelphia: University of Pennsylvania Press.

———, Hsiang-shui Chen, Madhulika Khandelwal, and Kyeyoung Park. 1991. *Chinese, Indian and Korean Elderly in Queens: Backgrounds and Issues for the Future*. Flushing, N.Y.: Asian/American Center, Queens College, CUNY.

———, Sylvia H. Forman, and Chad McDaniel. 1979. Employment and Hiring of Women in American Departments of Anthropology: The Five-Year Record, 1972–1977. *Anthropology Newsletter* 20 (1): 6–19.

———, and Lani Sanjek. 1976. Notes on Women and Work in Adabraka. *African Urban Notes* 2 (2): 1–25.

Savishinsky, Joel. 2000. *Breaking the Watch: The Meanings of Retirement in America*. Ithaca, N.Y.: Cornell University Press.

Schensul, Stephen. 1973. Action Research: The Applied Anthropologist in a Community Mental Health Program. In *Anthropology Beyond the University*. Edited by Alden Redfield, 106–119. Athens: University of Georgia Press.

———. 1974. Skills Needed in Action Anthropology: Lessons from El Centro de la Causa. *Human Organization* 33: 203–209.

———, and Jean Schensul. 1978. Advocacy and Applied Anthropology. In *Social Scientists as Advocates: Views from the Applied Disciplines*. Edited by George Weber and George McCall, 121–165. Beverly Hills, Calif.: Sage.

Scheper-Hughes, Nancy. 1993. *Death Without Weeping: The Violence of Everyday Life in Brazil*. Berkeley: University of California Press.

Schoenbrodt, Lisa, ed. 2001. *Children with Traumatic Brain Injury: A Parents' Guide*. Bethesda, Md.: Woodbine House.

Sedgwick, Mitchell W. 2011. At a Tangent to Belonging: "Career Progression" and Networks of Knowing Japanese Multinational Corporations. *Anthropology and Humanism*, 36 (1): 55–65.

Sennett, Richard. 2008. *The Craftsman*. New Haven, Conn.: Yale University Press.

Sered, Susan. 2000. *What Makes Women Sick? Maternity, Modesty, and Militarism in Israeli Society*. Hanover, N.H.: Brandeis University Press.

Shanklin, Eugenia. 1998. The Profession of the Color Blind: Sociocultural Anthropology and Racism in the 21st Century. *American Anthropologist* 100: 669–679.

Sharma, Harish.1996. *Artisans of the Punjab: A Study of Social Change and Historical Perspective 1849–1947*. New Delhi: Manohar.

Shaw Duty, Shannon. 2013. Works of Francis La Flesche Discussed at Osage Tribal Museum. *Osage News*, February 19. Accessed May 1, 2013. http://osagenews.org/article/works-francis-la-flesche-discussed-osage-tribal-museum.

Sherzer, Joel. 2001. *Kuna Ways of Speaking*. 2nd ed. Tucson, Ariz.: Hats Off Books.

Shield, Renée Rose. 1983. *Making Babies in the '80s: Common Sense for New Parents*. Boston: Harvard Common Press.

———. 1988. *Uneasy Endings: Daily Life in an American Nursing Home*. Ithaca, N.Y.: Cornell University Press.

———. 1995. Ethics in the Nursing Home: Dynamics of Decision-making in a Nursing

Home Ethics Committee. In *The Culture of Long Term Care: Nursing Home Ethnography*. Edited by J. Neil Henderson and Maria D. Vesperi, 111–126. Westport, Conn.: Greenwood Press.

———. 2002. *Diamond Stories: Enduring Change on 47th Street*. Ithaca, N.Y.: Cornell University Press.

———. 2003. Wary Partners: Family-CNA Relationships in Nursing Homes. In *Gray Areas: Ethnographic Encounters with Nursing Home Culture*. Edited by Philip Stafford, 203–233. Santa Fe, N.M.: School of American Research Press.

———. 2007. American Jews and the Diamond Business. In *Encyclopedia of American Jewish History*. Edited by Stephen Norwood and Eunice Pollack, 404–406. Santa Barbara, Calif.: ABC-CLIO.

———. 2012. Thinking Ourselves Old. Editorial. *Journal of Gerontology and Geriatrics Research* 1: 1.

———, and Stanley Aronson. 2003. *Aging in Today's World: Conversations Between an Anthropologist and a Physician*. New York: Berghahn.

———, Timothy W. Farrell, Aman Nanda, Susan Campbell, and Terrie Wetle. 2012. Integrating Geriatrics into Medical School: Student Journaling as an Innovative Strategy for Evaluating Curriculum. *The Gerontologist* 52 (1): 98–110.

———, Roberta E. Goldman, David A. Anthony, Nina Wang, Richard J. Doyle, and Jeffrey Borkan. 2010a. Gradual Electronic Health Record Implementation: New Insights on Physician and Patient Adaptation. *Annals of Family Medicine* 8 (4): 316–326.

———, Iris Tong, Maria Tomas, and Richard Besdine. 2011. Teaching Communication and Compassionate Care Skills: An Innovative Curriculum for Pre-Clerkship Medical Students. *Medical Teacher* 33 (8): e408–e416.

———, Terrie Wetle, Joan Teno, Susan C. Miller, and Lisa C. Welch. 2010b. Vigilant at the End of Life: Family Advocacy in the Nursing Home. *Journal of Palliative Medicine* 13 (5): 573–579.

Shokeid, Moshe. 1989. From the Anthropologist's Point of View: Studying One's Own Tribe. *Anthropology and Humanism Quarterly* 4 (1): 23–28.

———. 2007. From the Tikopia to Polymorphous Engagements: Ethnographic Writing Under Changing Fieldwork Circumstances. *Social Anthropology* 15: 305–319.

Shor, Ira, and Paulo Freire. 1987. *A Pedagogy for Liberation*. Westport, Conn.: Bergin & Garvey.

Simmons, Kimberly Eison. 2006. Racial Enculturation and Lived Experience: Reflections on Race at Home and Abroad. *Anthropology News* 47 (2): 10–11.

Simons, Robin. 1987. *After the Tears: Parents Talk About Raising a Child with a Disability*. San Diego, Calif.: Harvest.

Singer, George, Ann Glang, and Janet Williams. 1996. *Children with Acquired Brain Injury: Educating and Supporting Families*. London: Paul H. Brookes.

Smedley, Audrey. 1998. "Race" and the Construction of Human Identity. *American Anthropologist* 100: 690–702.

———. 2007. The History of the Idea of Race . . . And Why It Matters. Accessed February 15, 2014. http://www.understandingrace.org/resources/pdf/disease/smedley.pdf.

———. 2012. A Black Woman's Ordeal in White Universities. In *Racism in the Academy: The New Millennium*. Edited by Audrey Smedley and Janis Faye Hutchinson, 50–61. Arlington, Va.: American Anthropological Association.

Smith, Neil. 1986. Gentrification, the Frontier, and the Restructuring of Urban Space. In *Gentrification of the City*. Edited by Neil Smith and Peter Williams, 15–34. London and Boston: Allen and Unwin.

Social Forces Notice. 1953. Ways of Mankind Radio Series. *Social Forces* 31: 362.

Society for Applied Anthropology. n.d. *Ethical and Professional Responsibilities: About SfAA*. Accessed February 15, 2014. http://www.sfaa.net/sfaaethic.html.

Spradley, James. 1976. Trouble in the Tank. In *Ethics and Anthropology: Dilemmas in Fieldwork*. Edited by Michael Rynkiewich and James Spradly, 17–31. New York: John Wiley.

Srinivas, M. N. 1966. *Social Change in Modern India*. Berkeley: University of California Press.

Stack, Carol. 1974. *All Our Kin: Strategies for Survival in a Black Community*. New York: Harper & Row.

Stein, Alan, Paula Becker, and Historylink Staff. 2009. *Washington's First World's Fair: Alaska-Yukon-Pacific Exposition: A Timeline History*. Seattle: History Ink/History Link in association with University of Washington Press.

Steiner, Stan. 1970. *La Raza: The Mexican Americans*. New York: Harper & Row.

Stern, Mark, and Susan Seifert. 1997. *Community Revitalization, Diversity and the Arts in Philadelphia*. Social Impact of the Arts Project. University of Pennsylvania, School of Social Work.

Stocking, George W., Jr., ed. 1976. *Selected Papers from the American Anthropologist 1921–1945*. Washington, D.C.: American Anthropological Association.

———. 1992. *The Ethnographer's Magic and Other Essays in the History of Anthropology*. Madison: University of Wisconsin Press.

———. 2001. *Delimiting Anthropology: Occasional Inquiries and Reflections*. Madison: University of Wisconsin Press.

Stoller, Paul. 2007. Ethnography/Memoir/Imagination/Story. *Anthropology and Humanism* 32 (2): 178–191.

Strathern, Marilyn. 1987. Out of Context: The Persuasive Fictions of Anthropology. *Current Anthropology* 28: 251–281.

———. 1988. *The Gender of the Gift: Problems with Women and Problems with Society in Melanesia*. Berkeley: University of California Press.

Strauss, Sarah, and Benjamin S. Orlove. 2003. *Weather, Climate, Culture*. New York: Berg.

Strickland, Rennard. 1979. The Absurd Ballet of American Indian Policy or American Indian Struggling with Ape on Tropical Landscape: An Afterword. *Maine Law Review* 31: 213–221.

Stull, Donald, and Michael Broadway. 2004. *Slaughterhouse Blues: The Meat and Poultry Industry in North America*. Belmont, Calif.: Wadsworth.

Sussman, Robert. 1998. Preface: Contemporary Issues Forum: Race and Racism. *American Anthropologist* 100: 607–608.

Swanson, Kara L. 1999. *I'll Carry the Fork: Recovering a Life After Brain Injury*. Los Altos, Calif.: Rising Star Press.

Taggart, Helen, Christine Arslanian, Sejong Bae, and Karanet Singh. 2003. Effects of T'ai Chi Exercise on Fibromyalgia Symptoms and Health-Related Quality of Life. *Orthopaedic Nursing* 22 (5): 353–360.

Takezawa, Yasuko. 2006. Race Should Be Discussed and Understood Across the Globe. *Anthropology News* 47 (3): 6–7.

Taylor-Piliae, Ruth, and William Haskell. 2007. Tai Chi Exercise and Stroke Rehabilitation. *Topics in Stroke Rehabilitation* 14 (4): 9–22.

Tchen, John Guo Wei. 1999. *New York Before Chinatown: Orientalism and the Shaping of American Culture, 1776–1882*. Baltimore, Md.: Johns Hopkins University Press.

Teckney-Callagan, Rosalynda. 2012. In *Igorot by Heart*. Edited by John D. Dyte et al., 5–24. Philippine Islands: Igorot Global Organization.

Templeton, Alan. 1998. Human Races: A Genetic and Evolutionary Perspective. *American Anthropologist* 100: 632–650.

Thomas, David Hurst. 2000. *Skull Wars: Kennewick Man, Archaeology, and the Battle for Native American Identity*. New York: Basic Books.

Thompson, Eric. 2006. The Problem of "Race as a Social Construct." *Anthropology News* 47 (2): 6–7.

Thornton, Everard, Kevin Sykes, and Wai K. Tang. 2004. Health Benefits of Tai Chi Exercise: Improved Balance and Blood Pressure in Middle-Aged Women. *Health Promotion International* 19: 33–38.

Tice, Karen. 1995. *Kuna Crafts, Gender, and the Global Economy*. Austin: University of Texas Press.

Tillmann-Healy, Lisa M. 2003. Friendship as Method. *Qualitative Inquiry* 9: 729–749.

Touma, Habib. 1996. *La Musique Arabe*. Paris: Institut International d'Etudes Comparatives.

Townsend, Richard, ed. 2004. *Hero, Hawk, and Open Hand: American Indian Art of the Ancient Midwest and South*. New Haven, Conn.: Yale University Press.

Tsai, Jen-Chen, Wei-Hsin Wang, Paul Chan, Li-Jung Lin, Chia-Huei Wang, Brian Tomlinson, Ming-Hsiung Hsieh, Hung-Yu Yang, and Ju-Chi Liu. 2003. The Beneficial Effects of Tai Chi Chuan on Blood Pressure and Lipid Profile and Anxiety Status in a Randomized Controlled Trial. *Journal of Alternative and Complementary Medicine* 9: 747–754.

Tyler, Denise A., Renée R. Shield, Marsha Rosenthal, Susan C. Miller, Terrie Wetle, and Melissa Clark. 2011. How Valid are the Responses to Nursing Home Survey Questions? Some Issues and Concerns. *Gerontologist* 51 (2): 201–211.

Visweswaran, Kamala. 1994. *Fictions of Feminist Ethnography*. Minneapolis: University of Minnesota Press.

Vogt, Evon. 1994. *Fieldwork Among the Maya: Reflections on the Harvard Chiapas Project*. Albuquerque: University of New Mexico Press.

Wali, Alaka. 1989. *Kilowatts and Crisis: Hydroelectric Power and Social Dislocation in Eastern Panama*. Boulder, Colo.: Westview Press.

———. 2006a. Beyond the Colonnades: Changing Museum Practice and Public Anthropology in Chicago. *Sociological Imagination* 42: 99–113.

———. 2006b. The Spiral Path: Toward an Integrated Life. *NAPA Bulletin* 26: 209–222.

———. 2011. After Welfare: Work, Creativity and Resilience in a Mixed Income Housing Development. Paper presented at the annual meeting of the Society for Applied Anthropology, Seattle, Washington, March 29–April 2.

———. 2012. The Arc of Justice: Indigenous Activism and Anthropological Intersections. *Tipití: Journal of the Society for the Anthropology of Lowland South America* 9 (2): article 2. Accessed June 1, 2013. http://digitalcommons.trinity.edu/tipiti/vol9/iss2/2/.

———, Gillian Darlow, Carol Fialkowski, Madeleine Tudor, Hilary del Campo, and Douglas Stotz. 2003. New Methodologies for Interdisciplinary Research and Action in an Urban Ecosystem in Chicago. *Ecology and Society* 7 (3): article 2. Accessed June 1, 2013. http://www.ecologyandsociety.org/vol7/iss3/art2/main.html.

———, Rebecca Severson, and Mario Longoni. 2002. *Informal Arts: Finding Cohesion, Capacity and Other Cultural Benefits in Unexpected Places*. Chicago: Chicago Center for Arts Policy at Columbia College.

———, and Madeleine Tudor. 2010. Creating a Chaotic Civic Aesthetic: The Circulation of Art in Chicago's Public Spaces. Paper presented at the annual meeting of the American Anthropological Association, New Orleans, Louisiana, November 17–21.

Walker, Brian, and David Salt, eds. 2006. *Resilience Thinking: Sustaining Ecosystems and People in a Changing World*. Washington, D.C.: Island Press.

Wang, Chenchen, Jean Paul Collet, and Joseph Lau. 2004. The Effect of Tai Chi on Health Outcomes in Patients with Chronic Conditions: A Systematic Review. *Archives of Internal Medicine* 164: 493–501.

Wang, Chenchen, Ronenn Roubenoff, Joseph Lau, Robert Kalish, Christopher Schmid, Houcine Tighiouart, Ramel Rones, and Patricia Hibberd. 2005. Effect of Tai Chi in Adults with Rheumatoid Arthritis. *Rheumatology* 44: 685–687.

Wang, Chenchen, Christopher Schmid, Ramel Rones, Robert Kalish, Janeth Yinh, Don Goldenberg, Yoojin Lee, and Timothy McAlindon. 2010. A Randomized Trial of Tai Chi for Fibromyalgia. *New England Journal of Medicine* 363: 743–754.

Ward, Gregory. 1997. Battle over Anaphoric "Island": Syntax vs. Pragmatics. In *Directions in Functional Linguistics*. Edited by Akio Kamio, 199–219. Amsterdam: John Benjamins.

Warner, W. Lloyd. 1962. *American Life: Dream and Reality.* Chicago: University of Chicago Press.

Warren, Carol A. B. 1984. Toward a Cooptive Model of Qualitative Research. *Communication Quarterly* 32 (2): 104–112.

Waterston, Alisse. 1999. *Love, Sorrow, and Rage: Destitute Women in a Manhattan Residence.* Philadelphia: Temple University Press.

West, Harry. 2007. *Ethnographic Sorcery.* Chicago: University of Chicago Press.

Westbrook, David A. 2008. *Navigators of the Contemporary: Why Ethnography Matters.* Chicago: University of Chicago Press.

Weston, Kath. 1997. The Virtual Anthropologist. In *Anthropological Locations: Boundaries and Grounds of a Field Science.* Edited by Akhil Gupta and James Ferguson, 163–184. Berkeley: University of California Press.

Westphal, Lynne, Jeffrey Levengood, Alaka Wali, David Soucek, and Douglas Stotz. 2005. Brownfield Development: A Hidden Opportunity for Conservation Biology. In *Policies for Managing Urban Growth and Landscape Change: A Key to Conservation in the 21st Century.* Edited by David Bengston, 21–26. St. Paul, Minn.: U.S. Department of Agriculture, Forest Service, North Central Research Station.

Wetle, Terrie, Joan Teno, Renée Shield, Lisa Welch, and Susan C. Miller. 2004. *End of Life in Nursing Homes: Experiences and Policy Recommendations.* Washington, D.C.: AARP.

White, Leslie. 1962. *The Pueblo of Sia, New Mexico.* Bureau of American Ethnology Bulletin 184. Washington, D.C.: U.S. Government Printing Office.

Whyte, William Foote. 1955. *Street Corner Society: The Social Structure of an Italian Slum.* Chicago: University of Chicago Press.

Williams, Brackette. 1995. The Public I/Eye: Conducting Fieldwork to Do Homework on Homelessness and Begging in Two U.S. Cities. *Current Anthropology* 36: 25–51.

Williams, Brett. 1988. *Upscaling Downtown: Stalled Gentrification in Washington D.C.* Ithaca, N.Y.: Cornell University Press.

———. 1994. Babies and Banks: The "Reproductive Underclass" and the Raced, Gendered Masking of Debt. In *Race.* Edited by Steven Gregory and Roger Sanjek, 348–365. New Brunswick, N.J.: Rutgers University Press.

———. 2001. A River Runs Through Us. *American Anthropologist* 103: 409–431.

———. 2004. *Debt for Sale: A Social History of the Credit Trap.* Philadelphia: University of Pennsylvania Press.

———. 2008. The Precipice of Debt. *In New Landscapes of Inequality: Neoliberalism and the Erosion of Democracy in America.* Edited by Jane Collins, Micaela di Leonardo, and Brett Williams, 65–90. Santa Fe, N.M.: School of Advanced Research Press.

———. 2009. Deadly Inequalities: Race, Illness, and Poverty in Washington, D.C., Since 1945. In *African American Urban History Since World War II.* Edited by Kenneth Kusmer and Joe W. Trotter, 142–159. Chicago: University of Chicago Press.

———, with John Henry Pitt. 2002. "Without Go-Go This Shit Ain't the Same Dog." *City & Society* 14 (1): 87–102.

———, with Tanya Ramos, Jacqueline Brown, Ray Chesterfield, Melinda Crowley, Benjamin Daugherty, Robin Dean, Lisa Kinney, Sherri Lawson, Susie McFadden, Patrick Pierce, Kenneth Pitt, and Terik Washington. 1997. *Rapid Ethnographic Assessment: Park Users and Neighbors, Civil War Defenses of Washington and Anacostia Park, District of Columbia, for Park Management Plans.* Washington, D.C.: Jualrez and Associates.

Xing, Jun, and Lane Ryo Hirabayashi, eds. 2003. *Reversing the Lens: Ethnicity, Race, Gender, and Sexuality Through Film.* Boulder: University Press of Colorado.

Young, Michael, and Peter Wilmott. 1957. *Family and Kinship in East London.* Baltimore, Md.: Penguin.

Zavella, Patricia. 1996. Feminist Insider Dilemmas: Constructing Ethnic Identity with Chicana Informants. In *Feminist Dilemmas in Fieldwork.* Edited by Diane Wolf, 138–159. Boulder, Co.: Westview.

———. 2011. *I'm Neither Here nor There: Mexicans' Quotidian Struggles with Migration and Poverty.* Durham, N.C.: Duke University Press.

Zentella, Ana Celia. 1997. *Growing up Bilingual: Puerto Rican Children in New York.* Malden, Mass.: Blackwell.

Zhang, Jinming. 2007. A Survey of the Needs of and Service for Persons with Physical Disability in China. *Asia Pacific Disability Rehabilitation Journal* 18 (2): 49–85.

Zimmerman, Susan. 2002. *Writing to Heal the Soul: Transforming Grief and Loss Through Writing.* New York: Three Rivers Press.

Zinsser, William. 1988. *Writing to Learn.* New York: Harper.

Index

Contributors

Rogaia Mustafa Abusharaf (PhD University of Connecticut) is associate professor of anthropology at the Georgetown University School of Foreign Service, Qatar. She has held fellowships at Brown, Durham, and Harvard Universities and has written widely on human rights issues and the Darfur conflict. Her books include *Wanderings: Sudanese Migrants and Exiles in North America* (2002) and *Transforming Displaced Women in Sudan: Politics and the Body in a Squatter Settlement* (2009). She has edited *Female Circumcision: Multicultural Perspectives* (2006) and "What's Left of the Left? The View from Sudan" (2010), a special issue of *South Atlantic Quarterly* placing resistance to military rule in her homeland in historical perspective.

Robert R. Alvarez (PhD Stanford University) is president of the Society for Applied Anthropology (2013–2015) and emeritus professor of ethnic studies, University of California, San Diego; he previously taught in the Arizona State University anthropology department, where he founded the Program in Applied Anthropology. His books *Familia: Migration and Adaptation in Baja and Alta California, 1800–1975* (1987) and *Mangos, Chiles, and Truckers: The Business of Transnationalism* (2005) are rooted in his personal history growing up along the United States–Mexico border and working in the family produce trade. His research interests include the application of anthropology to practical problem solving, especially regarding minority communities and high school students.

Garrick Bailey (PhD University of Oregon) was born in Hartshorne, Oklahoma, of Choctaw and Cherokee descent, and since 1968, he has been a professor of anthropology at the University of Tulsa. He has been consultant to many Indian tribes and organizations and served on the Osage Tribal Museum Board of Directors and the Native American Graves Protection and Repatriation Act (NAGPRA) Review Committee. In addition to publications on the Osage, he is coauthor with Roberta Bailey of *A History of the Navajos: The Reservation Years* (1986); editor of *Indians in Contemporary Society*, volume 2 of the *Smithsonian Institution Handbook of North American Indians* (2008); and coauthor with James Peoples of *Humanity: An Introduction to Cultural Anthropology* (2014, 10th edition).

Catherine Besteman (PhD University of Arizona) is the Francis F. Bartlett and Ruth K. Bartlett Professor of Anthropology at Colby College in Maine. She is author of *Unraveling Somalia: Race, Violence, and the Legacy of Slavery* (1999) and *Transforming Cape Town* (2008) and coeditor with Hugh Gusterson of *Why America's Top Pundits Are Wrong: Anthropologists Talk Back* (2005) and *The Insecure American: How We Got Here and What We Should Do About It* (2009). A museum exhibition she codeveloped, "Rivers of Immigration: From the Jubba to the Androscoggin," received awards from the American Association for State and Local History and the New England Museum Association.

Parminder Bhachu (PhD London University), a thrice migrant, was born in Tanzania and lived in Uganda and Kenya before moving to Britain and then to the United States. Since 1991, she has been the Henry R. Luce Professor of Cultural Identities and Global Processes and professor of sociology at Clark University in Massachusetts. She is author of *Twice Migrants: East African Sikh Settlers in Britain* (1985) and *Dangerous Designs: Asian Women Fashion the Diaspora Economies* (2004), as well as coeditor of *Enterprising Women: Ethnicity, Economy and Gender Relations* (1988) and *Immigration and Entrepreneurship: Culture, Capital, and Ethnic Networks* (1993). Multilingual, she speaks English, Punjabi, Hindi-Urdu, Gujarati, and Swahili. Her current work concerns contemporary diasporic creativity and innovation.

Ann Fienup-Riordan (PhD University of Chicago), an independent scholar, has participated in collaborative research projects with Alaska Native organizations over four decades, including working with the Calista Elders Council since 1999. She has authored and collaborated on more than twenty books, among them *Eskimo Essays: Yup'ik Lives and How We See Them* (1990), *Freeze Frame: Alaska Eskimos in the Movies* (1995), and *Hunting Tradition in a Changing World: Yup'ik Lives in Alaska Today* (2000). In 2000, she received the Alaska

Federation of Natives President's Denali Award; in 2001, the Alaska Governor's Award for Distinguished Humanist Educator; and in 2012, with coauthor Alice Rearden, a Before Columbus Foundation American Book Award.

Zibin Guo (PhD University of Connecticut) is UC Foundation Professor of Anthropology at the University of Tennessee–Chattanooga and previously was a lecturer in social medicine at Harvard Medical School and director of clinical studies at the New England School of Acupuncture. A medical anthropologist specializing in Chinese health traditions, aging, and disability, he is author of *Ginseng and Aspirin: Health Care Alternatives for Aging Chinese in New York* (2002). In 2003, he received a certificate in Chinese medicine from the Academy of Chinese Traditional Medicine in Beijing, and his work on wheelchair taijiquan has received grant support in both China and the United States.

Lane Ryo Hirabayashi (PhD University of California, Berkeley) is the George and Sakaye Aratani Professor of Japanese American Incarceration, Redress, and Community in the Department of Asian American Studies, University of California, Los Angeles. He is author of *Cultural Capital: Mountain Zapotec Migrant Associations in Mexico City* (1993); *The Politics of Fieldwork: Research in an American Concentration Camp* (1999), concerning anthropologist Tamie Tsuchiyama; and *A Principled Stand: The Story of Hirabayashi v. United States* (with Gordon and James Hirabayashi, 2013); as well as several edited volumes in Asian American studies. He has been consultant to many Japanese American community organizations over more than three decades.

Lanita Jacobs (PhD University of California, Los Angeles) is associate professor of anthropology and American studies at the University of Southern California. A linguistic anthropologist, her work focuses on language as a mediator of African American culture and identity, and she employs ethnography as a dynamic way of seeing and being in the world. She conducted multisited fieldwork and utilized discourse analysis in research for her book *From the Kitchen to the Parlor: Language and Becoming in African American Women's Hair Care* (2006) and also in her longitudinal studies of African American children coping with acquired or traumatic brain injury and of African American stand-up comedy.

Susan Lobo (PhD University of Arizona) has been an independent practicing anthropologist since 1984. Currently a distinguished visiting scholar in American Indian studies at the University of Arizona, she has authored *A House of My Own: Social Organization in the Squatter Settlements of Lima, Peru* (1982); coauthored *The Sweet Smell of Home: The Life and Art of Leonard F. Chana* (2009); and coedited *Urban Voices: The Bay Area American Indian Community* (2002) and *Native American Voices: A Reader* (2010). In her consultation, evaluation, and advocacy projects, she has worked with and for many North, Central, and South American indigenous peoples. Lobo is an active member of the National Writers Union.

Yolanda T. Moses (PhD University of California, Riverside) is associate vice chancellor for diversity, equity, and excellence and professor of anthropology at the University of California, Riverside. She has been president of the American Anthropological Association (AAA) (1995–1997), president of City College, City University of New York (1993–1999), and president of the American Association for Higher Education (2000–2003). She continues to serve on national organizations, boards, and commissions concerned with higher education and social justice issues. The leading organizer of the AAA *RACE* project, she is coauthor of *How Real Is Race? A Sourcebook on Race, Culture, and Biology* (2007) and *RACE: Are We So Different?* (2012).

Sylvia Rodríguez (PhD Stanford University) is emeritus professor of anthropology at the University of New Mexico, where she was director of the Alfonso Ortiz Center for Intercultural Studies. She is author of *The Matachines Dance: Ritual Symbolism and Interethnic Relations in the Rio Grande Valley* (1996), winner of the Chicago Folklore Prize, and *Acequia: Water Sharing, Sanctity and Place* (2006), which received the Association of Latina and Latino Anthropologists 2007 Book Award. She lives in Santa Fe, New Mexico, and has been a researcher, expert witness, and consultant for several organizations, projects, and media productions in northern New Mexico and elsewhere.

Roger Sanjek (PhD Columbia University) was a professor of anthropology at Queens College, City University of New York, from 1972 to 2009. He is editor of *Fieldnotes: The Makings of Anthropology* (1990); coeditor of *Race* (1994); and author of *The Future of Us All: Race and Neighborhood Politics in New York City* (1998), *Gray Panthers* (2009), and *Ethnography in Today's World: Color Full Before Color Blind* (2014). Sanjek is a recipient of the Squeaky Wheel Award of the AAA Committee on the Status of Women in Anthropology

(2000) and the J. I. Staley Prize of the School of American Research (2002). He lives in New York City, where he is an active member of New York State-Wide Senior Action Council.

Renée R. Shield (PhD Brown University) is clinical professor of health services, policy, and practice at the Center for Health Care Research, Alpert Medical School of Brown University, where she taught part-time from 1987 to 2008 and full-time since then. Her books include *Uneasy Endings: Daily Life in an American Nursing Home* (1988); *Diamond Stories: Enduring Change on 47th Street* (2002); and as coauthor, *Aging in Today's World: Conversations Between an Anthropologist and a Physician* (2003) and *Improving Aging and Public Health Research: Qualitative and Mixed Methods* (2006). She has authored and coauthored many reports and medical and gerontology journal articles on health-care planning, end-of-life issues, the nursing home "culture change" movement, and implementation of electronic health records.

Alaka Wali (PhD Columbia University) joined the Field Museum of Natural History in 1994 as curator in anthropology and founding director of the Center for Cultural Understanding and Change, focusing on applied urban research in Chicago. In 2001, she began a collaboration with the museum's conservation ecologists, and in 2004, she became applied cultural research director of the Environment, Culture, and Conservation Division; in 2010, she assumed curatorial duties for the North American Anthropology Collection. Wali conducts collaborative and participatory action research in Chicago neighborhoods and in indigenous communities adjoining Peru's Cordillera Azul National Park. Her earlier work resulted in *Kilowatts and Crisis: Hydroelectric Power and Social Dislocation in Eastern Panama* (1989) and, with Leith Mullings, *Stress and Resilience: The Social Context of Reproduction in Central Harlem* (2001).

Deana L. Weibel (PhD University of California, San Diego) is associate professor and chair of anthropology at Grand Valley State University in Michigan. Her publications focus primarily on religion, especially on the topics of pilgrimage and sacred space. Her fieldwork takes place in France at such Marian pilgrimage sites as Rocamadour, Lourdes, and Saintes-Maries-de-la-Mer, and she has also conducted research at the pilgrimage center of Chimayó, New Mexico. Her interests include religious cognition, sacred objects, religion and space travel, and the role of anthropology and her own family in the "ethnological" displays of Philippine tribal peoples at fairs and carnivals in the 1900s.

Brett Williams (PhD University of Illinois) is professor of anthropology at American University. Since coming to Washington, D.C., in 1976, she has published *John Henry: A Bio-bibliography* (1983) concerning this African American folk hero, *Upscaling Downtown: Stalled Gentrification in Washington, D.C.* (1988), *Debt for Sale: A Social History of the Credit Trap* (2004), and many articles and book chapters about displacement, homelessness, public housing, race, poverty, go-go music, and environmental justice in the Anacostia River watershed. Working with community ethnographers and students, she has consulted for the National Park Service, the Department of Housing and Urban Development, and the Smithsonian Institution Festival of American Folklife.